Muslim Studies

Ignaz Goldziher

Muslim Studies

Edited by

S.M. Stern

Translated by C.R. Barber and S.M. Stern

With a major new introduction by

Hamid Dabashi

ALDINETRANSACTION
A Division of Transaction Publishers
New Brunswick (U.S.A.) and London (U.K.)

Second printing 2008

This book is printed on acid-free paper that meets the American National Standard for Permanence of Paper for Printed Library Materials.

Library of Congress Catalog Number: 2006042714
ISBN: 978-0-202-30778-7
Printed in the United States of America

Library of Congress Cataloging-in-Publication Data

Goldziher, Ignac, 1850-1921.
[Muhammedanische Studien. English]
Muslim studies / Ignaz Goldziher ; edited by S.M. Stem ; translated by C.R. Barber and S.M. Stem; with a new introduction by Hamid Dabashi.
p.cm.
Includes bibliographical references and index.
Contents: Introductory chapter: Muruwwa and Din—The Arabic tribes and Islam—'Arab and 'ajam—The Shu'ubiyya—The Shu'ubiyya and its manifestataion in shcolarship: (a) genealogy (b) philology—Excursuses and annotations—What is meant by 'al-Jahiliyy'a — On the veneration of the dead in paganism and Islam—Pagan and Muslim linguistic usage—The use of of the kunya as a means of paying respect—Black and white people—Traditions about the Turks—Arabicised Persians as Arabic poets.
ISBN 0-202-30778-6 (alk. paper)
1. Islam. 2. Islam—Miscellanea. I. Stem, S. M. (Samuel Miklos), 1920-1969. II. Title.

BP25.G6143 2006
297—dc22 2006042714

I dedicate these pages
to my dear Friend
C. SNOUCK HURGRONJE

CONTENTS

Introduction to the AldineTransaction Edition

Ignaz Goldziher and the Question Concerning Orientalism

Hamid Dabashi

For Philip Rieff and in memory of George Makdisi—
With love, admiration, and gratitude.

"Ich lebte mich denn auch während dieser Wochen so sehr in den mohammedanischen Geist ein, dass ich zuletzt innerlich überzeugt wurde, ich sei selbst Mohammedaner und klug herausfand, dass dies die einzige Religion sei, welche selbst in ihrer doktrinär-offiziellen Gestaltung und Formulirung philosophische Köpfe befriedigen könne. Mein Ideal war es, das Judenthum zu ähnlicher rationeller Stufe zu erheben. Der Islam, so lehrte mich meine Erfahrung, sei die einzige Religion, in welcher Aberglaube und heidnische Rudimente nicht durch den Rationalismus, sondern durch die orthodoxe Lehre verpönt werden."

[I truly entered in those weeks into the spirit of Islam to such an extent that ultimately I became inwardly convinced that I myself was a Muslim and judiciously discovered that this was the only religion which, even in its doctrinal and official formulation, can satisfy philosophical minds. My ideal was to elevate Judaism to a similar rational level. Islam, my experience taught me, was the only religion in which superstition and pagan elements were proscribed, not by rationalism but by the Orthodox doctrine.]

—*Ignaz Goldziher,* Tagebuch[1]

Publication of a new edition of Ignaz Goldziher's *Muslim Studies*, long out of print, some 116 years after its original appearance in German in 1889, close to forty years after its English translation was released in 1966, and above all more than a quarter of a century after the publication of Edward W. Said's *Orientalism* (1978) has the necessary signs of an extended reflection. Neither Goldziher nor Said can be neglected, and yet the implicit celebration of one seems to contradict the other. That apparent contradiction, and an attempt to address (if not to resolve) it, will inform much of this introductory essay.

How is one to read an Orientalist—in fact, one of the most learned Orientalists there ever was—today? Isn't Orientalism over? Did Edward Said not deliver a *coup de grace* to the aging temple of Orientalism? Is Orientalist scholarship today of only antiquarian interest? Does a scholar like Ignaz Goldziher still have anything to teach students of Islamic studies? Is there in fact any disciplinary validity left to the practice of "Islamic studies"? Has Goldziher's scholarship not been superseded even by scholars who continue to study Islam in the context of a variety of disciplines (from anthropology to political science), let alone in the aftermath of a fundamental challenge to the epistemic foregrounding of his scholarship? Much of what I have to say in this introduction surrounds not just the particular scholarship that Goldziher best represents but also the more fundamental problem of reading any Orientalist at all, in the aftermath of Edward Said's *Orientalism* and the mighty intellectual tradition that it best exemplifies.

In 1984, I received a dual Ph.D. in sociology of culture and in Islamic Studies at the University of Pennsylvania. The seeming paradox stretched between Ignaz Goldziher and Edward Said, to both of whom I was first introduced as a graduate student, has been definitive to my own work on the borderlines of those two disciplines. Between Philip Rieff and the late George Makdisi, with whom I studied sociology of culture and Islamic studies, respectively, Edward Said and Ignaz Goldziher are not mere bibliographical references in the itinerary of an intellectual paradox. They are the presiding figures of an intellectual pedigree that locates and defines me. It is from a confident corner of that space that I wish to share these reflections on two monumental scholars and intellectuals in the making of my own mind.

* * *

Goldziher represents Orientalism at its highest and most productive stage, a moment in its emerging history, when Orientalists thought themselves sitting on top of a heap of untapped knowledge about a universe of which they and the European world they represented knew nothing—and yet they must. Before anything else, it is imperative to have an understanding of Goldziher's range and depth of knowledge about Islam, for at the heart of that sweeping knowledge also dwelled its Achilles' Heel.

In May 1906, Ignaz Goldziher (1850-1921) received an invitation to deliver a series of six lectures at various universities in the United States—"Honorarium," he noted in his *Tagebuch*, "$2,500."[2] It is something more than an indication of the rate of inflation to take that figure today as an index of the esteem he was held in at the height of his scholarly reputation. A combination of his declining health, however, and his frustration with the inadequacy of the English translation of his lectures combined to prevent him from coming to the United States and delivering those lectures. Goldziher subsequently published the original German of his lectures, *Vorlesungen über den Islam*, in 1910. Translations of these lectures soon appeared in many languages—including the notorious English translation (1917) that had helped prevent Goldziher from coming to the U.S.[3] Despite that inauspicious beginning, the prominent Hungarian Orientalist finally made it into the English speaking world when his most ambitious scholarly work, *Muhammedanische Studien* (1889-1890) was competently translated into English as *Muslim Studies* and published in 1966 (volume I) and 1971 (volume II). It is that first volume that is here being reissued.

If in 1906, a group of American scholars went to the trouble of raising a rather handsome honorarium to invite and listen to one of the most distinguished Islamists alive, a century later, the world at large, now perhaps globally far more in jeopardy than it was a century ago, remains even more in need of accurate knowledge about the subject of Goldziher's scholarship. If the honorarium offered Goldziher is the index of his significance as a scholar at the time, the essays you are about to read are the solid indices of a sweep of scholarship rarely matched in the field of Islamic Studies either in Europe or the United States.

It is not just Orientalists who (discredited and dispirited) seem to have forever lost their legendary competence in doing what they were doing best. Ironically, while the world at large is more than ever in need of accurate and reliable knowledge about Islam, a field of studies that Goldziher and a handful of other prominent Orientalists like him effectively created, Orientalism itself, as a mode of knowledge production has lost its ability to produce scholars of Goldziher's stature and competence—with the catholicity of his learning, the consistency of his critical mind, and above all his *feeling intellect*.[4] Reading Goldziher today is like a walk through a museum of antiquities—full of fine and delicate objects, but now mostly of antiquarian interest. One reads Goldziher as one watches a master craftsman perform his art with competence and delicacy. But the objects themselves, the essays so finely sculpted, are mere museum pieces—full of outdated elegance. Ever since Goldziher wrote these essays in the late nineteenth century, the field of Islamic studies has developed far beyond the specifics of the scholarship these essays contain. Every one of these essays is now the subject of practically an entire field of inquiry, covered by an army of scholars. But no one seems to be capable of producing an essay, as Goldziher did one after another, with such a vast topography of learning, ease and grace of diction, historical vision, or with a gestalt view of an entire civilization so competently fine-tuned in the minutiae of discussing its sacred doctrines and enduring institutions, political histories and intellectual movements. Ignaz Goldziher was a master craftsman, the very elegance of his scholarly prose and the sinuous grace of his probing intellect are now among the rarest and most forgotten virtues of an entirely different world. "Specialists without spirit," one cannot help remembering the prophetic words of Max Weber at the end of *The Protestant Ethics and the Spirit of Capitalism*, when comparing what is written today on Islam with Goldziher's essays, "sensualists without heart; this nullity imagines that it has attained a level of civilization never before achieved."[5]

More than anything else, it is the range of these essays—for Ignaz Goldziher's *Muslim Studies* and most of his other writings are essentially collections of interrelated essays—that today strikes us as quite rare and extraordinary. Ours is the age of professedly competent but publicly irrelevant specialists, on one side, and dangerously incompetent public experts, on the other. As the systematic and perhaps inevitable fragmentation of various disciplines—ranging from social sciences to the humanities—have fragmented the academic world into the domains and fiefdoms of specialists, the public at large is at the mercy of overnight experts opining on matters of vital global significance without so much as an elementary knowledge of a language necessary to venture an opinion about a matter. "Islam" in particular, as a floating signifier, has today (more than ever) emerged as the perilous field of terrifying frivolity, with the U.S. and European airwaves, print media, and the Internet inundated with dangerous disinformation. Between academic specialists knowing more and more about less and less relevant issues and public experts shooting from the hip, stands a bewildered public that today could have, but alas is not, much benefited from a gifted and erudite essayist like Ignaz Goldziher. What is most remarkable about these essays is the ease of their diction, the fluidity of their scholarly competence communicated with an almost deceptive simplicity. Goldziher's essays on the moral and intellectual institutions of Islam could very well be published in a newspaper or a magazine today—a world religion much politically maligned (by its own adherents and its detractors alike) and rarely explained to the world at large.

Like most gifted essayists, Goldziher is well informed in his scholarship, highly competent in his delivery, and unabashedly opinionated. In the six essays collected in the first volume of *Muslims Studies* Goldziher begins with a general treatment of Islam and its rise from the pre-Islamic Arab context through two critical concepts of *Muruwwa* and *Din*, trying to articulate what is at the heart of a religion with so many manifestations of which he was deeply familiar. In this essay, Goldziher wishes to introduce the moral and normative revolution that Muhammad and his teachings had introduced in Arabia. The essay is written on the most abstract level of ethical speculation about the nature of Islam as a world religion, facing stiff resistances from pre-Islamic Arab paganism. The result is an attempt to get at the ethical and normative roots of a world religion, later expanded into so many moral and intellectual directions. In the second essay, "The Arab Tribes and Islam," Goldziher tries to do the same but this time with the social revolution that Islam had launched from within pagan Arab tribalism. Here, too, Goldziher's objective is to see how a world religion in effect changed not just the worldview but also the enduring social institutions of a global community. In the third chapter, "'Arab and 'Ajam," Goldziher picks up this issue and this time runs it through the major historical challenges of Islam, namely its open and democratic spirit welcoming people of all races and ethnicities to a global brotherhood/sisterhood of humanity, while the tribal elitism of the early Arab patrimonialism institutionally resisted that Islamic promise. The last two chapters of the volume are Goldziher's groundbreaking studies of Shu'ubiyya, at times characterized as a literary-humanist movement launched to assert the moral foregrounding of a universal equality among all people (Muslim or otherwise), irrespective of their faith, race, or ethnicity.[6] The cumulative result of these collected essays is effectively an attempt to get at the heart of Islam as a world religion, the specific resistances it has historically faced, the inner dialectics of its enduring struggles, and what ultimately constitutes its *weltanschauung*—all through a close and detailed attention to Arabic primary resources.

The second volume of *Muslim Studies* consists mainly of Ignaz Goldziher's seminal study of *Hadith* (Prophetic traditions), again in eight consecutive and interrelated essays. These essays progress methodically, from the most basic to the most advanced, from introducing the elementary terminology of Hadith scholarship to a highly controversial attempt at historicizing the origin and political function of Hadith literature throughout Islamic history. At the heart of Goldziher's Hadith scholarship is his contention that opposing schools of jurisprudence, changing social formations, and vacillating political expediencies more often than not necessitated the fabrication of Hadith, of sayings and doings attributed to the Prophet of Islam, in order to justify a politically necessary course of action. The practice was not something unknown to Muslim scholars themselves long before Ignaz Goldziher. The production of the sixth canonical collection of Hadith—the *Sihah Sitta*—is itself an indication of Muslim scholars' attempt to separate the authentic from the fabricated words and deeds of their Prophet. The two famous *Sahihs—Sahih Muslim*, compiled by Muslim ibn al-Hajjaj al-Nisaburi (circa 817-875) and *Sahih Bukhari*, compiled by Abdullah Muhammad al-Bukhari (810-870)—are the two most trustworthy canonical texts of the Hadith painstakingly put together by pious and meticulous Muslims scholars whose scrupulous attention to details of authenticity was for them a mater of religious observance and pious anxiety. To be sure, the intervening ten centuries between the time of

Muslim and Bukhari and that of Goldziher allows the Hungarian scholar the space of reflecting critically on the pros and cons of his Muslim peers' achievements—but he does so fully conscious of their rigorous scholarship.[7] Goldziher's scholarship on Hadith literature is marked by an ease and fluency with which he engages with his Muslim peers, as if they were his contemporaries, or he theirs. With very few and sporadic references to European Orientalists, Goldziher's essays are filled with references to Muslim primary sources (most of which were, in fact, not even critically edited and published at this time but were still in scattered manuscripts), not just corroborating his argument but also engaging in a trans-historical debate with them—as if he was sitting in a college in Baghdad at the time of Muslim and Bukhari and debating with them.[8] This particular aspect of Goldziher's essays is now almost entirely lost in contemporary scholarship. It seems that more than *Islam* being Goldziher's object of scholarly investigations, it is *Muslim scholars* who were his actual (at al-Azhar, where he studied) and imaginative (transhistorical) peers, with whom he most immediately identified, and into their debates he brought along a comparatist perspective (particularly with his insights into the Talmudic—both Halakha and Haggada—influences on both Islamic law and Qur'anic exegesis). Goldziher, in a very peculiar way, saw himself as a "Muslim scholar," though to his dying day (and against extraordinary odds in the horrid days of European anti-Semitism) he remained a proud, pious, and observant Jew.[9]

The second volume of *Muslim Studies* includes a pioneering study of "Veneration of Saints in Islam" in a volume otherwise exclusively devoted to the study of the legalistic and formal aspects of the faith. Here, Goldziher demonstrates the process by which the Prophet of Islam was gradually endowed with miraculous attributes despite doctrinal and his own personal testimonies to the contrary. Goldziher characterizes this as the necessity of filling "the gap between the divine and the human."[10] The dialectical disposition of Goldziher's scholarship had always necessitated a multifaceted conception of Islam, never allowing his particular attention to one crucial dimension of the faith (particularly its jurisprudence, with which Goldziher was primarily concerned) totally to color his general conception of it. Here, Goldziher's attention to the development of the figure of *wali* is a pioneering reflection on the doctrinal development of the more mystical dimension of Islam, with specific attention to the role of women saints in Sufism. The detail with which Goldziher examined the more popular dimensions of Islam would not be repeated until much later with the rise of the interest of anthropologists in Islamic fields.

The six essays that Goldziher wrote when he was invited to travel to the United States demonstrate a similar range of interest and complexity. What he had intended to teach his American audience shows the particular penchant of Goldziher for the multifaceted realities of a civilization to which he had devoted his scholarly life. First he wanted to talk about "Muhammad and Islam." In this essay, Goldziher gives a rather detailed account of the prophetic career of Muhammad, the composition of the Qur'an, and the rise of Islam against the background of pre-Islamic Arabia. After this introductory essay, it is to Islamic law (both a primary point of his own scholarship and the most enduring social institution of Islam) that Goldziher turns his attention. Here one can see his preferred methodology of juxtaposing historical developments with doctrinal articulations in Islamic jurisprudence in full operation. His objective is to demonstrate how "Hadith formed the framework for the earliest development of religious and ethical thought in Islam."[11] Goldziher's third essay, "The Growth and Development of Dogmatic Theology" is a testimony to the natural outgrowth of Muslim scholars' initial preoccupation with law. Goldziher's historical awareness leads him to demonstrate how the formation of a new class of speculative theologians was chiefly responsible for carrying the theological implications of the Qur'anic revelation to a new level of abstraction. Goldziher is quite particular in linking the nascent political developments that gradually led to the establishment of the Umayyad dynasty (661-750) and to the rise of major theological issues that subsequently became questions *sui generis* and followed their own abstract course of articulation.[12]

After his two lectures on Islamic law and Islamic theology, Goldziher turns his attention to "Asceticism and Sufism" in the fourth lecture. Although the field of Islamic mysticism has advanced by leaps and bounds since Goldziher's time and extraordinary works of scholarship have been produced—particularly in Arabic and Persian—covering the most detailed minutiae of the subject, Goldziher's essay remains exemplary in its persistent attempt to link the rise of Islamic mysticism to the initial material expansionism of Muslim conquests. Once he thus locates Islamic mysticism historically, he goes through a sweeping panorama of both Arabic and Persian sources, linking Ibn Arabi and Rumi, while remaining equally attentive to prose narratives and polemical sources. His account of Sufism is at once comprehensive and sympathetic, comparative and investigative—from a solid intellectual history perspective that never loses sight of Sufism as one among a number of contending discursive and institutional forces in the general contour of Islam as a cultural universe.

Goldziher's next move is to make sure that he communicates no monolithic conception of Islam to his audience. His sixth lecture on "The Sects" is a comprehensive account of the social conditions and political circumstances dictating the rise of various Muslim sects, after a critical evaluation of what does in fact constitute a "sect" as distinct from mainline orthodoxy (*sunna*). The guiding principle of Goldziher's discussion of sectarian movements in early Islam is, again, a careful attention to the historical developments, beginning with the question of succession to the Prophet, which had politically occasioned them. Goldziher's observations, characterizing the formation of Islamic sects as "the infusion of religious ideas into political strife,"[13] is typical of the way he sought to understand a plethora of sectarian movements otherwise lost in a sea of doctrinal and revolutionary convictions. Goldziher's study of Islamic sects is a good example of his habitual attention to historical circumstances, while taking their varied and multifaceted doctrinal and dogmatic positions seriously, examining them closely for their diverse political consequences. Goldziher is not an altogether disinterested or impartial observer of sectarian movements in Islam, and does not hesitate to make such polemical observations as Shi'ism being "a particularly fecund soil for absurdities suited to undermine and wholly disintegrate the Islamic doctrine of God."[14] Obviously a Shi'i reader of Goldziher would not agree with such a harsh pronouncement. But evident in Goldziher's discussion is the supposition that his command of primary sources, critical intimacy with issues and doctrines and movements, and detailed hermeneutic conversation with what animated Islamic moral and intellectual history in general seem to have effectively entitled him to such (however controversial) observations. He had, as it is quite obvious in his writings, an intimate knowledge of Islamic intellectual history, and that knowledge, ipso facto, entitled him, and he felt himself entitled, to make creative and critical observations on a matter to which he had devoted his entire scholarly life. Disagreement in this respect with Goldziher, as a result, cannot be on the grounds of his having offended certain Muslim (Shi'i in this case) sensibilities. Muslims themselves, of varied theological convictions and sectarian persuasions, have always taken serious issues with each other on a variety of doctrinal matters, and thus gravely offended (and in fact waged war against) each other. Goldziher seems to have been convinced that he had in fact earned the privilege of entering into the domain of such theological and sectarian disputations—for in many significant ways he considered himself a "Muslim scholar." There is a relentlessness about Goldziher's manner of mobilizing an army of evidence to make a point that is entirely medieval, scholastic, and classical in its resemblance to Islamic (or Jewish or Christian for that matter) scholarly method of *jadal* (disputation). When reading Goldziher one has the uncanny sense of reading a medieval Arabic text on law or theology—except it is written in German (or translated into English). If aspects of his scholarship on Muslim sects have now been superceded, it is not because of the substance or range of his knowledge, which remain exemplary, but because of his epistemic limitations, such as not being able to break through the unexamined assumption that there was an "Orthodoxy" from which then certain "heterodoxies" seceded—rather than seeing the formation of various theological and juridical movements on historically equal terms.[15]

Among the six lectures that Goldziher intended to deliver in the United States his last one is on "later developments," in which he gives an account of the most recent events in Islamic history—theological issues and political movements contemporary to his own time. It is in this particular essay that one can learn much from Goldziher for our own time—what he would have said and how he would have written were he present in the anxiety-provoking environment of the post-9/11 world. There are two major social movements in the Islamic world to which Goldziher turns in this last lecture—the Wahhabi movement in Arabia and the Babi movement in Iran.[16] What is remarkable about Goldziher's account of these two movements is first, his detailed knowledge of their doctrines and beliefs, second, his analytical facility with conversing with a range of political and doctrinal issues, and third, his simultaneously critical and intimate exchanges with their pros and cons—neither condoning the puritanical proclivities of the Wahhabis and the revolutionary zeal of the Babis, nor indeed dismissing them altogether. If he takes issue with Wahhabism, which he does, he does so on the basis of a doctrinal disagreement with them, that "to abandon *ijma'*, to cast aside what the consensus of the community of believers—as it has historically evolved—acknowledges as sound and true, is to forsake orthodox belief."[17] If he has a healthy dose of skepticism about the mutation of the Babi movement into Baha'ism (particularly of their propaganda missions in Europe and the United States),[18] which he does, he does so without once casting doubt on the sincerity of the Baha'is. His discussion of both Wahabism and Babism leaves no doubt that Goldziher most immediately identified with what he considered mainline Sunni Orthodoxy.

Throughout his work as a scholar, perhaps Goldziher's most important contribution was his sweeping knowledge of various (and conflicting) Islamic discourses. Because he had no institutional or dogmatic connection to any particular Islamic discourse (neither a jurist, nor a philosopher, nor a mystic, nor even a Muslim), he could see them all at the same time. There is no question, that Goldziher identified most with Muslim (Sunni) jurists. But unlike Muslim jurists, he had a deeply sympathetic understanding of Islamic mysticism, but then, unlike Muslim mystics, he had an equally broad understanding of Islamic philosophy; and then unlike all of them he had no aversion to the most recent social and intellectual developments in the Islamic world—the revolutionary movements that Muslim jurists, mystics, and philosophers alike would have dismissed as whimsical and unworthy of their critical and scholarly attention. That catholicity of learning, granted Goldziher by virtue of being an outsider insider, was perhaps the most significant dimension of his scholarship. To be sure, such Muslim scholars as al-Baghdadi (d. 1037) in his *al-Farq bayn al-Firaq* or al-Shahrastani (d. 1153) in his *al-Milal wa al-Nihal* were Goldziher's predecessors in comparative analysis of various Muslim sects and their doctrines. But none of them had the historical and spatial distance from varied Islamic intellectual discourses that Goldziher enjoyed. At once *universal* in his command of Islamic material, *dialectical* in his analytical reading of them, and fully aware of the multifaceted expressions of Islam throughout its intellectual history, Goldziher had an unfailingly *historical* conception of Islam, a *comparative* vision of its various discursive and institutional formations, and he attended to all of these with a critical intimacy otherwise exclusive to Muslim scholars themselves—a self-understanding that Goldziher consciously cultivated in himself throughout a long and productive scholarly career.

* * *

Today, we mostly remember Goldziher for his *Muslim Studies*. But Goldziher produced far more than these two volumes of essays, or the six lectures that he intended to deliver in the United States. He wrote extensively and authoritatively on a variety of subjects, including Arabic grammar, Arabic literature, Qur'anic hermeneutics, even a book on Hebrew mythology.[19] The scholarly legacy of Goldziher bespeaks the range and depth of his intellectual preoccupation with Islam. Because of his historical and spatial distance from Islamic intellectual history, he was able to bring a unique perspective to his scholarship, at once intimate and critical, comparative and global—though at a deep emotive level (and directly under the influence of his own religious convictions and practices) he identified with the Sunni Orthodoxy. The power of Goldziher's scholarship, the fact of his universal command of a variety of discourses that collectively and dialectically constitute the Islamic intellectual history, is squarely rooted in a pioneering point in the history of Orientalism when Orientalists thought themselves at the commanding center of producing a global knowledge about a world religion scarcely known to non-Muslims—particularly to Europeans at the zenith of their colonial interests in Muslim lands. The result is an all but inevitable and evident paradox, that the knowledge that was thus produced *about* Islam *became* Islam—meaning, the pioneering generation of European Orientalists that included Goldziher manufactured a kind of global perspective that was radically different from an entire history of Muslim scholarship about their own religion, culture, and civilization. The principle insights of Orientalists (and, as such, covering their blind spot) into Islam was fundamentally rooted in the fact that at their best they were not invested in it, while the worst of them were heavily invested in producing a particular knowledge of Islam and Muslims compatible with European colonial interests. At their best, such European Orientalists as Goldziher had nothing at stake in the historical outcome of Islamic history, nor did they in any shape or form share the fate of Muslims. The reason that Goldziher could place a discussion of Islamic law next to one of Islamic mysticism and then compare the result to Islamic philosophy, followed by a discussion of Islamic sects, and thus come up with quite crucial insights about all of them, is that he was neither a Muslim jurist, nor a mystic, nor a philosopher, nor did he (except for an emotive affinity with the Sunni Orthodoxy) have anything but a scholarly interest in varied sectarian divisions within Islam. The knowledge that he thus produced was in its very epistemic foundations different from the one produced by Muslims themselves—jurists, mystics, theologians, philosophers, historians of ideas, etc., scholars who would put their neck on the line for what they wrote. Goldziher had no such stake in the matter—and thus his ability to have a surgeon's point of view over what amounts to the unconscious body of a patient, and thus, in turn, both the insights and the blindness of Orientalism that Goldziher best represented and practiced.

Many of these basic issues at the epistemic roots of Orientalism as a system of knowledge production have today become overshadowed by a succession of entirely *ad hominem* assumptions and accusations about Orientalists and Orientalism—one specifically targeted against Goldziher, and the other extended to Orientalism in general. It is imperative to depersonalize any discussion of Goldziher and Orientalism and take the argument back to its discursive and institutional points of origin. What we face today, in any attempt to have a historically balanced conception of Goldziher and the body of scholarship that he has produced is first, an entirely inappropriate and *ad hominem* attack on Ignaz Goldziher, and second, an equally flawed mutation of Edward Said's principled critique of Orientalism into a personal dispute between him and his nemesis. If Raphael Patai, a recent biographer of Ignaz Goldziher, is chiefly responsible for the former, Bernard Lewis, for years the principle academic nemesis of Edward Said, is equally responsible for the latter. The matter, however, is far more institutionally grounded, and theoretically robust, for these *ad hominem* distortions of principled issues to cloud our historical assessment of Orientalism as a mode of knowledge production in general, and of Goldziher in particular.

* * *

Today a clear assessment of Goldziher and his significance as a scholar must be navigated through two sets of flawed and fallacious assumptions about his person and his achievements as an Orientalist. The first task facing such a fair and balanced assessment is to restore the dignity of his name as a man and a scholar against the background of an entirely tendentious and *ad hominem* attack against him that in the guise of a "psychological portrait" has cast an entirely unfair shadow of doubt on the dignity of his character. Once he is cleared of this unfortunate shadow, the next task is equally to de-personalize the question of Orientalism and reach for a principled critique of its mode of knowledge production, as articulated by Edward Said before it was derailed into the assumption of an *ad hominem* attack on individual Orientalists.

On 22 June 1890, on the occasion of his fortieth birthday, Goldziher began writing his memoirs. He summarized the early part of his life in general strokes, giving for example only eight pages to 1850-1866, that is to say the first sixteen years of his life, including a moving account of his Bar Mitzvah.[20] Other memorable years of his life include 1873-1874, the year that he traveled to Syria, Palestine, and Egypt and studied at al-Azhar, the year that he calls "mein orientalisches, mein muhammedanisches Jahr."[21] One of the longest passages that Goldziher writes in this part of his *Tagebuch* is about his studies at al-Azhar in Cairo,[22] what for the rest of his days he believed was the happiest and most fulfilling time of his life. This section is in sharp contrast to the years he summarizes after his return from Cairo, which commences with the death of his father on 4 May 1874 and includes his failure to secure a proper teaching position and being forced, against his will and in order to provide for his family, to accept a secretarial position at the Israelite Congregation of Pest, a job he bitterly resented until his dying day. Beginning in 1890, when he had started writing his memoirs, Goldziher's notes become contemporaneous with his life and rather consistent until 1919 (1 September 1919 is his last entry), namely just two years before his death on 13 November 1921.

When in 1955, Ignaz Goldziher's son, Károly Goldziher, died in Budapest, the Goldziher family handed over to Alexander Scheiber, the director of the Budapest Rabbinical Seminary, the manuscript of Goldziher's *Tagebuch*, which he in turn edited, annotated, and published in its original German in Leiden in 1978. On this occasion, Goldziher's family also delivered to Alexander Scheiber another manuscript—this one the detailed travelogue that Goldziher had kept during 1873-1874 (between 15 September 1873 and 14 January 1874), while on his memorable journey to Syria, Palestine, and Egypt. Alexander Scheiber subsequently gave this manuscript to Raphael Patai, an anthropologist and biblical scholar, the founder and director of the Palestine Institute of Folklore and Ethnology, and the editor of Herzl Press, who at the time was living in New York and teaching at various universities. Raphael Patai subsequently translated Goldziher's travelogue to Syria, Palestine, and Egypt, called it Goldziher's "Oriental Diary," wrote an extensive introduction to it, in effect summarizing Goldziher's other, more extensive, memoir in German, the *Tagebuch*, and then used the occasion to produce what Patai calls a "psychological portrait." This English translation of Goldziher's original German by Raphael Patai is the only published version of this travelogue.[23]

Goldziher's travelogue to Syria, Palestine, and Egypt abruptly ends on 14 January 1874. But he remained in Cairo until mid-April of that year, returning to Budapest a few days before the death of his father on 4 May 1874. Between mid-January and mid-April, Goldziher continued to write in his travelogue, including a detailed description of his attending a Friday prayer in Cairo. But according to Raphael Patai that part of the *Travelogue* has been lost. Patai's theory about this loss, which seems plausible, is that in 1924, three years after Goldziher's death, a Hungarian Zionist named Ludwig Bató approached Chaim Weizmann (1874-1952), then already the president of World Zionist Organization, to purchase Goldziher's library for the soon to be inaugurated Hebrew University of Jerusalem. Weizmann raised the necessary funds and purchased the library, which apparently included only the printed books and not Goldziher's own manuscripts, which remained in possession of Goldziher's son Károly until the German invasion and occupation of Hungary in 1944, in the course of which Patai believes this portion of the library (and thus the last part of Goldziher travelogue) was lost.[24]

Whereas Alexander Scheiber's preface to Goldziher's *Tagebuch* is very short and modest (just about two and a half pages of the published book) with very useful, factual, and straightforward endnotes, Raphael Patai's introduction has a far more ambitious project of producing what he calls a "psychological portrait." While both these scholars have done the scholarly community a service by making Goldziher's *Tagebuch* and *Travelogue* available, Patai's "psychological portrait" is a singular act of systematic defamation of a prominent scholar with whose politics Patai is in obvious, and rather drastic, opposition. It is imperative to try to rescue Goldziher from this unconscionable falsification of his character and dignity, for it casts an entirely unfair shadow over his character as one of the most distinguished scholars of his generation—loved and admired by his friends, family, students, and colleagues alike. This corrective measure is equally necessary if we are to stay clear of *ad hominem* attacks on scholars and have a fair and balanced assessment of their scholarship.

* * *

"The great Goldziher" was the exclusive honorific term with which the prominent German Orientalist Carl Brockelmann is reported to have referred to Ignaz Goldziher.[25] Born and raised in a learned Jewish family in Székesfehérvár (Stuhlweissenburg) in west-central Hungary, Ignaz Goldziher had mastered the original text of the Hebrew Bible by the time he was five years old. "At seven he and his friends organized religious services every Sunday, at which Náci preached the sermons. At eight he was started on the Talmud."[26] At eight, his mother told him later, he would go to bed embracing and kissing, "like beloved beings," his own voluminous copies of the Talmud. At twelve, he had started reading such major Jewish philosophers as Bahya ibn Paquda, Yehuda Halevi, and Maimonides. He was still twelve when he wrote and published a treatise on the origin and development of the Jewish prayers. Later he recalled, "this opus was the first cornerstone of my bad reputation as a 'freethinker.'"[27] The following year, he persuaded his father to arrange for him to deliver his Bar Mitzvah speech from the pulpit of the synagogue. The speech had a lasting influence on the young Goldziher, who considered it "the beacon of my life."[28] By the time he was fifteen, and before he even had his high school diploma he entered University of Budapest, where he commenced a course of studies in "classical languages, philosophy, German literature and Turcology."[29] He was barely sixteen when he published his first translations from Turkish literature, and by the time he was nineteen he earned his Ph.D. in Leipzig, followed by yet another year of studies in Leiden—by then, "he had no less than thirty published items to his credit."[30] After all these achievements, the prevalent European anti-Semitism still prevented him from securing a paid teaching position at a university, unless he converted (like his own teacher Armenius Vámbéry had) to Christianity, something he refused to do. Failing to secure a solid teaching position, Goldziher was engaged to teach as a *Privatdozent* (an unpaid lecturer) at the University of Budapest, while subsisting on a meager stipend from the Ministry of Culture.

Rescuing Goldziher from this disconcerting condition—being one of the most prominent Islamist of his generation, and yet prevented from assuming his rightful place at a university—a timely governmental grant enabled him to travel to the Islamic world. Between September 1873 and April 1874, Goldziher spent what he later considered the happiest months of his life in Syria, Palestine, and Egypt, enrolling at al-Azhar as a student, a feat rarely (if ever) attained by a non-Muslim. Goldziher kept a meticulous travelogue of this journey, now one of the most fascinating firsthand accounts of his life and career as a scholar. Whatever the bureaucratic purposes of that governmental grant may have been, Goldziher's intentions were entirely directed towards the rare opportunity given him to study Arabic and Islamic sources at a major center of scholastic learning.

A considerable part of the travelogue demonstrates the love and affection Goldziher had for Islamic intellectual history, a fact that combined with some severe criticism of the *formal* aspects of Judaism that he expresses in the same source has provided occasions for Raphael Patai in his "psychological portrait" to criticize Goldziher and project the complicated character of a man who was "infatuated with Islam"[31] and "suffered from an acute anti-Jewish complex."[32] Neither of these two attributes is fair, correct, or corroborated by evidence.

During this sojourn, Goldziher was exceedingly happy and proud to be in the company of Muslim scholars, thought of himself as "a member of the Mohammedan scholars' republic," had an unsurpassed affinity for the subject of his scholarship, considering Islam in fact to have "developed out of the Judaized Meccan cult the mighty world religion of Islam," and then went so far as stating categorically:

> I truly entered in those weeks into the spirit of Islam to such an extent that ultimately I became inwardly convinced that I myself was a Muslim and judiciously discovered that this was the only religion which, even in it doctrinal and official formulation, can satisfy philosophical minds. My ideal was to elevate Judaism to a similar rational level.[33]

In order to understand the meaning and significance of this statement, it is crucial to remember that Goldziher never converted to Islam and to his dying day (and against all odds) remained committed to his own ancestral faith. The statement, instead, must be understood as a simple confession of affinity with a person's subject of lifetime scholarly devotion. The other aspect of this statement is its comparative disposition. Goldziher detested Christianity with a vengeance, traced the horrid roots of European anti-Semitism to its doctrinal formations, and given his own personal and communal experiences in Europe his views of Christianity can hardly be surprising. When members of Damascene Jewry, for example, mistrusted him for they thought he was a Christian missionary, he did not hesitate calling Christianity "the most abominable of all religions."[34] One can easily see that much of Goldziher's love and admiration for Islam is in fact an intellectual extension of his devotion to his own faith, to Judaism. Goldziher's fellow Jewish Hungarians report that there are reasons to believe that towards the end of his life he had religious concerns about having committed his life to Islamic studies rather than Judaic studies. Raphael Patai reports that one of Goldziher's students, Bernard Heller, who later became a professor at the rabbinical Seminary of Budapest, once visited Goldziher a few days before his death,

> and found him seated at the festive Sabbath table with the Bible and an Arabic book before him: "I don't know," Goldziher addressed Heller, "whether it is right that I should still delve into Arabic literature when

> tomorrow I shall stand there where they will ask me, Nasata w'natata be'emuna? (Did you conduct yourself faithfully?)[35]

It is perhaps only natural for Hungarian Jewish scholars like Heller and Patai to have wished that a man of Goldziher's status would have devoted his scholarly life to Judaic rather than Islamic studies—and thus remembered and recorded this story. But if a few days before his death Goldziher is reported to have had "compunctions," as Patai puts it, "whether from the Jewish religious point of view it was permissible for him to have devoted his life to the study of Islam instead of Judaism,"[36] on the very first page of his own memoir, from his own pen, written at the mature age of forty, he tells a rather different story (a point recorded on the very first page of Goldziher's *Tagebuch* but completely missed by Patai in his "psychological portrait"). "Mein Leben," writes Goldziher,

> war von früher Jugend an durch zwei Wahlsprüche geleitet: Der einer ist der Prophetenspruch, den ich mir an meinem Confirmationstage in die Seele gepgrägt: "Er hat Dir verkündet o Mensch, was gut sei, und was Jahve von Dir fordert: Nur dies: Gerechtigkeit üben, Barmherzigkeit bieten und in Bescheidenheit wandeln vor Deinem Gott." Der andere ist der Koran-Spruch: "fa-sabrun gamilun wa-Ilahu-l-musta'anu," d. h. "Ausdauer ist gut: und Gott ist der, zu dem man um Hilfe aufblicken muss."[37]

"My life," says Goldziher,

> from the early youth, has been guided by two principal mottos. One is the prophetic saying that on the day of my conformation I imprinted upon my soul [Micah VI: 8: from the Hebrew Bible]:
>
> He hath shewed thee, O man,
> what is good;
> and what doeth the LORD require of thee,
> but to do justly,
> and to love mercy,
> and to walk humbly with thy God?[38]

The other is the Qur'anic saying [Surah XII (Joseph) in the Qur'an]:

> . . . comely patience. And Allah it is whose help is to be sought . . . .[39]

If we take these words for what they simply say (and abstain from abusing them in order to psychoanalyze their author), Goldziher did not have to (and thus he did not) choose between his ancestral faith and the subject of his scholarship. Those two books on the Sabbath table had been there for quite some time, "*von früher Jugend*" (from early youth) in fact. If at the mature age of forty, Goldziher says that since his early youth two mottos from the Hebrew Bible and from the Qur'an have been the guiding principles of his life, then his lifetime scholarly devotion to Islam and his unflinching commitment to Judaism were integral to each other and part and parcel of the same character. In this respect, Goldziher was no oddity, for he was in a direct intellectual tradition that linked him to Moses Maimonides (1135-1204), who had no problem being the supreme codifier of the Jewish Law (*Mishneh Torah*) while writing his philosophical masterpiece, *The Guide to the Perplexed* (*Dalalat al-Ha'irin*) in Arabic and in conversation with Muslim philosophers in general, while being under the direct influence of al-Ghazali's (1058-1111) *Deliverance from Darkness* (*al-Munqidh min al-Dalal*). Neither Maimonides nor Goldziher saw any contradiction in what they were doing. The problem is not with them. The problem is with taking the fictive construction of a "Judeo-Christian tradition" far more seriously than allowing for the far more historically balanced assumption of a Judeo-Islamic heritage.

To be sure, the sorts of doctrinal questions that Raphael Patai raises are perfectly legitimate issues. Speaking of Goldziher's spiritual elation at participating in a Muslim Friday prayer, Patai asks, "how a religious Jew (Goldziher was and remained throughout his life an observant Jew) could have,"

> done what he did: substitute, even if only for a brief moment, Muslim belief and worship for the Jewishness that was his patrimony. For a person of such persuasion even to enter the place of worship of another faith, let alone participate in a non-Jewish service, is anathema.[40]

To answer this question, Patai resorts to such observations as Goldziher having fallen "under the spell of Muslim public worship that, with its uniform and rhythmically repeated mass prostrations and unison mass proclamation of the oneness of God, is—to this I can attest from my own experience—more impressive, not to say mesmerizing, than the rites of the other two monotheistic religions."[41] But what Patai disregards is that at no point did Goldziher "substitute," let alone abandon, his own religious beliefs and practices, and his intellectual affinity with Islam, momentarily extended into a single act of religious ritual, and remained perfectly compatible with his Jewish identity, faith, and practice. It in fact accentuated and corroborated it.

Patai compares Goldziher's enthusiasm for Islamic rituals he witnessed and in which he participated while in Cairo with his severe criticism of the Jewish services that he saw in Istanbul to conclude that he "suffered from an acute anti-Jewish complex." There is no evidence for that claim. As a confident Jew, there is nothing wrong with Goldziher criticizing aspects of certain "forms of Jewish observance."[42] This criticism of form never went into the substance of Goldziher's faith. He runs away from a service in a German-Jewish synagogue in Istanbul and goes to his room, and what does he do? He "buries himself in the Book of Isaiah," and writes in his *Travelogue,* "here is the Temple I seek."[43] There is no question that Goldziher was full of "boundless admiration for the ideas of prophetic Judaism," but there is no reason to believe that Judaism for him was, even at this young and ambitious years, just a set of admirable ideas. It is impossible to read Goldziher's memoir, both his *Tagebuch* and his Travelogue, without having a sense of his profound faith (not just admiration for prophetic ideas) as a confident and proud Jew. So, in fact, confident and proud of his faith he was that he felt himself entitled to criticize its occasional formal failures. The assumption that Goldziher "suffered from an acute anti-Jewish complex" is entirely false and not corroborated by the facts, nor indeed by Goldziher's lived experiences.

How could one read the following passage of the *Tagebuch* and not see the overriding love and devotion of a man of faith for his own religion, his own ancestral covenant, and yet severely critical of its institutional shortcomings, assured (with the pride of an accomplished young scholar) of his superior knowledge of his own faith?

> I cried bitterly, I lamented; as I recited mechanically the sins as prescribed for me, I howled as I bothered "Our Father and King" with the likewise prescribed requests; I felt elevated as I kissed the Tora, whose legends and myths I mercilessly analyze, whose roster of authors I dare construe with certainty, whose formation as to year and day I make bold to fix with proud assurance. Am I weak or mad? A hypocrite I am not, for my tears flowed too endlessly salty against my will, this much I can say. Explain it, friends; I cannot. But then again I was driven against my will when I heard the reader snorting away at the story of the two burned sons of Aaron—away, away, far away from these vulgar rooms, again over mountain and hill, to Pera. For the synagogue made merry over my tears, laughed at my emotions, jeered at my convulsion—this idols' synagogue, this fasting, godless one, does not deserve my sympathy. They laughed at the stranger who brought his better heart to their infamous horde because he honors the most holy of all days, which symbolizes the idealization of the dust, the contempt for the flesh, the spiritualization of the matter. He finds this idea in their inane songs, in their senseless customs; he grasps the little kernel of spirit which hides in this mud; he identifies his own self with the day of renunciation and disembodiment; he cries honestly, bitterly; he loves with the noble ones of the time; he feels unhappy in the flesh; he cries about it; he trembles as he speaks, "Father-King, we have sinned before you;" he shakes as he grasps the power of the word "Sins"—and this synagogue of the Sephardim, which

he had held higher than it deserved, laughs at him! Away, away from the impure! Here you can no longer stand it.[44]

These cannot be the words of a person who is suffering "from an acute anti-Jewish complex"? Avicenna has a quatrain in Persian (among the few things that he wrote in his own mother tongue), in which he says:

Kofr-e cho mani gazaf-o asan nabovad,
Mohkam tar az iman-e man iman nabovad;
Dar dahr cho man yeki-o ou ham kafer,
Pas dar hameh dahr yek Mosalman nabovad.

[The infidelity of someone like me is no simple matter,
For there is no faith stronger than my faith;
All around the universe there is no one like me, and I am an infidel,
Then throughout the universe there is not a single Muslim.][45]

People like Goldziher and Avicenna are the measure of their faith, not an abstract notion of faith the measure of their experiences. They were, in their persons, mobile synagogues and itinerant mosques, living and breathing temples to the truth of their respective religions.

There is a universal ecumenicalism about Goldziher's religiosity that seems to have escaped the author of his "psychological portrait." A Muslim public prayer was not the only non-Jewish service that Goldziher attended while on this journey. During his short visit to Jerusalem, on 2 December 1873, he also attended a mass in the Church of Holy Sepulcher, of which Patai is fully aware and yet about which he remains curiously silent, seeming to have no moral "compunctions" such as those he expresses about Goldziher's attending a Friday prayer in a mosque in Cairo.[46] This attendance at the Church of Holy Sepulcher was despite the fact that Goldziher was severely critical of Christianity as a religion.

As further evidence that Goldziher "suffered from an acute anti-Jewish complex," Patai refers to his criticism of the rampant commercialism on religious sites he visited while in Palestine. But if Goldziher was critical of the Jewish and Christian "religious industry," as he calls it, and considered its practitioners "swindlers," so did he consider Muslims capable of the selfsame commercialism and had no hesitation in calling them "the great Mohammedan Ramadan swindle."[47] In these passages, Goldziher's religious (Jewish) sensibilities are offended by the crass commercialism of the "religious industry," the term he uses in anticipation of what decades later Theodore Adorno and Max Horkheimer would call "culture industry," to which they too had a justifiably angry reaction.[48]

In understanding Goldziher's expressed joy in traveling to Syria, Palestine, and Egypt, we must also consider the rarity of the occasion, and the opportunity it had afforded the young scholar to see first hand the lands where Islam had historically flourished. Given the infrequency of such adventures into the Islamic world for a European of Goldziher's generation, it is only natural that he take advantage of every second of his journey to learn more about Muslims and their lived culture. One must also remember that Goldziher's principal objection to Wilhelm Bacher, a gifted Biblical scholar whom he deeply admired, was that he was too bookish. This was a rare chance for Goldziher's own knowledge of Islam not to have remained limited to what he had learned in books and in Europe.

What Patai does understand, and articulates quite well, are the sources of Goldziher's anger against certain *formal* aspects of practiced Judaism. "Religion," Patai observes,

> and especially Jewish religion, was for him a great and sacred thing, embodied in the teachings of the Hebrew prophets with their lofty moral ideals. He himself shared this idealism, and when he saw the humdrum observance of ossified rituals, he felt that it was empty, insincere, false, indeed, a "swindle."[49]

Patai's next observation, however, that Goldziher "almost entirely" saved Muslims from "his censorious wrath," and that this is "the most eloquent proof of the extent of the young Goldziher's admiration for the world of Islam, which he extended to its ritual manifestation,"[50] is not entirely accurate for the following reasons: first, neither in his *Tagebuch* and *Travelogue* nor indeed in the vast body of his scholarship did Goldziher refrain from severe criticism of aspects of Islam he disliked (especially of Shi'ism, which he considered "a particularly fecund soil for absurdities suited to undermine and wholly disintegrate the Islamic doctrine of God,"[51] and of certain classes of Turks, whom he showers with utmost contempt—"barbarian, vulgar, and corrupt"—in the early part of his *Travelogue*[52]); second, his admiration for Islam was not out of his religious convictions but due to his scholarly interests, and as all other scholars he was not immune from developing perhaps an inevitable affection for the subject of his scholarship; and above all third, his criticism of practiced (not ideal) Judaism has to do with the fact of his pious, observant, total, and unconditional devotion to his faith.

Patai dismisses Goldziher's expression of love and admiration for Islam as "youthful infatuation."[53] That "youthful infatuation" was the subject of Goldziher's lifetime scholarship. Throughout the scholarly world, Goldziher is known for his unsurpassed critical acumen in dissecting the most sacrosanct principles, doctrines, beliefs, and sacred texts of Islam. Not for a moment in the course of his scholarship did Goldziher lose his necessary critical distance from the subject of his scholarship. He remained consistent, throughout his life, in his critical intimacy with Islam—in fact the very substance of his scholarship was predicated on his distance from it. Goldziher's love and admiration for Islam emerged out of his own profound piety within his own religion, and not despite or against it. Patai completely misreads a superior scholar's natural affection for the subject of his scholarship and consistently seeks to psychologize everything that Goldziher says. Goldziher's affection for Islamic intellectual history never prevented him from being exceedingly and appropriately critical of aspects of Islam of which he did not approve. If one were to detect a non-scholarly reason for Goldziher's love for Islam, it is imperative to see how his affection for the range and depth of Islamic scholastic learning grew through his own superior knowledge of his own faith, for Judaism, and not at its expense. Goldziher saw Islam as an intellectual outgrowth of Judaism (he called Islam "the Judaized Meccan cult" and he meant it in an exceedingly positive and affirmative sense towards both Judaism and Islam). The result is an emotive affinity with Islam on both a confessional and a scholarly plane, and thus far from a "youthful infatuation."

That Goldziher later became exceedingly angry and bitter that he had to work as a secretary for the Israelite Congregation of Pest upon his return from Egypt, or that on occasions he made some rather harsh remarks about this job, is no indication that he had any troubled relationship with his own faith. He refused to betray his faith and convert to Christianity at the heavy cost of endangering and damaging his academic career. He had no problem with being a perfectly proud and confident Jew. Speaking of his friend Wilhelm Bacher (1850-1913), whom he greatly loved and admired as a Talmudic scholar (and with whom, incidentally, he studied Persian and read Sa'di), Goldziher said, "for him Judaism was a literary fact; for me, in 1867, it was already the pulse of my life."[54] Defending his dignity while at the service of a secretarial job that took him away from his scholarship, he insisted, "my house was now Jewish in a higher sense, and I brought up my two children religiously, with prophets and Psalms; all lies were banished and left out of their education. And while I in this manner erected a temple in my home for truly God-believing and Messianic Judaism, the pious men from Bohemia never ceased slandering me and charging me with heresy on ever-broader grounds."[55] Goldziher never forgave his own teacher, the prominent Turcologist Arminius Vámbéry (1832-1913), for having converted to Christianity (after having already converted to Islam), while deriding Goldziher for remaining true to Judaism against all odds.[56] Goldziher's frustration with his secretarial job was the just and perfectly understandable anger of a superior intellect being forced to do a mind-numbing administrative task (while being constantly humiliated by his employers), and had nothing to do with this job being at a Jewish organization. Goldziher was equally contemptuous of his administrative duties when he was made the dean of the faculty in 1917. "I am on the verge of collapse from this slave labor,"[57] he said, using the identical phraseology he used while working for the Israelite Congregation of Pest. Like most great scholars, Goldziher detested administrative duties. This simple and perfectly understandable fact escapes Patai, busy as he is chasing after some dark (self-hating) psychological trait in Goldziher. Patai, without the slightest hesitation, concurs with and seeks to provide a psychological account for, the slanderous remark of an acquaintance of Goldziher who had called him a *"roshe"* (Yiddish for an "evil man"). Goldziher was not evil for disliking the waste of his time on an administrative job (any administrative job) that took him away from his scholarly work. One would have to have an understanding of a man's passion for scholarship before resorting to dark and hidden psychological traits in him, especially for a man who from the age five was mesmerized (not by Islam) but an insatiable intellectual curiosity.

Towards the end of his introduction, Patai does show a bit of understanding in this regard. "No doubt other people too would have reacted with a sense of injury, indignation, and outrage to the experiences that circumstances visited on Goldziher," Patai consents. But he still insists, "the intense hatred with which he reacted must have been due at least as much to the emotional bent of his personality as to the occurrences themselves."[58] It is this persistent attempt at transhistorical psychoanalyzing, by an anthropologist with no psychoanalytical trainings or credentials, that is deeply flawed and utterly irresponsible. Goldziher's devotion to his scholarly pursuits, his occasional criticism of the formal (not doctrinal) aspects of his own faith, and his intense dislike for a secretarial position he had to perform in order to earn his living and provide for his family do not earn him the title of an "evil man," nor do they qualify his relation to Islam as an "infatuation," and certainly are no indication that he "suffered from an acute anti-Jewish complex."

* * *

Neither "infatuated with Islam" nor having "suffered from an acute anti-Jewish complex," nor indeed an "evil man," and thoroughly in command of his own emotions, thoughts, and above all sense of purpose, Goldziher embarked on his journey to Syria, Palestine, and Egypt, having just received his doctoral degree, published extensively on both Islamic and Judaic subjects, and was exceedingly excited at the prospect of meeting and studying with the people he admired most: His

Muslim colleagues at al-Azhar. When soon after his arrival in Egypt, Goldziher met with the Egyptian Minister of Education, Riyad Pasha, he so impressed him with his knowledge of Arabic that the minister offered Goldziher a position in his ministry. Goldziher declined that rather lucrative offer and instead requested permission to attend al-Azhar as a student. The minister was taken aback by this request, for until then no non-Muslim had benefited from that privilege. "I cannot order the mufti to accept you,"[59] the Minister told Goldziher, who in turn asked only for a letter of recommendation and an appointment with the mufti. He would take care of the rest.

Goldziher met with al-Shaykh Abbasi al-Mufti, and presented Minister Pasha's letters to him. He reminisced later that when he arrived to meet with the Shaykh of al-Azhar, the latter was in the midst of a legal discussion concerning the laws of inheritance with other al-Azhar Shaykhs. He continued his juridical discussions while Goldziher waited. Finally, he turned to Goldziher and asked who was he, what his religion was, and how did he know the minister. "My name is Ignaz al-Majari," Goldziher responded, "I was born among the Ahl al-Kitab, and I believe that I shall be resurrected with the confessors of Oneness."[60] Raphael Patai has already noted the intelligence of this response, but he does not know quite why and resorts to some generic explanations based on a very superficial knowledge of Islamic centers of higher learning and thus the circumstances that the young Goldziher faced at al-Azhar. Goldziher's introducing himself as "Ignaz al-Majari," was not just to impress the Shaykh with how far he had traveled to be at al-Azhar, as Patai notes. Goldziher had, while simply introducing himself, approximated his true and correct name and identity in the Arabic and Islamic manner of naming. He was Ignaz and he was from Hungary. He told the Shaykh his name but in a manner that the Dean of al-Azhar would immediately embrace and recognize. He was both true to his identity and yet conversant with the people he most admired in the linguistic idiomaticity of their culture. Goldziher identified himself as a person "born among the People of the Book," not just to be truthful to his own Jewish faith, which Muslims call "People of the Book," but also with a proper pun (which Patai completely misses) on the literal, not the technical, sense of the expression. He is *a man of the book*, meaning a scholar, someone like them, very much the same way that long before he set foot on al-Azhar and once he embarked on his trip to Egypt he thought of himself as "a member of the Mohammedan scholars' republic."[61] As for the expression, "and I believe that I shall be resurrected with the confessors of Oneness," the phrase points not only to his belief in bodily resurrection on the Day of Judgment, but also to a more immediate sense of being resurrected through his scholarship into a truthful recognition of the Oneness of all religions. Patai is correct that the term *Muwahhidun* (those who believe in One God) that Goldziher uses is juxtaposed against *Mushrikun*, but *Mushrikun* are not just the idolaters. It also has a subtle (but perfectly recognizable) reference to Christians as well who believe in Trinity—a doctrine that has always rubbed the absolute monotheism of Muslims the wrong way. It is the unconditional monotheism of Islam and Judaism, of Muslims and Jews, that Goldziher invoked here, doubly making sure that the Shaykh knows that he is a Jew and not a Christian. The trilateral root of *Muwahhidun*, WHD, is also at the root of *Tawhid*, namely Oneness of God, which was integral to the definition of the Mu'tazilah, known as *Ahl al-Tawhid wa al-Adl* ("The People who Believe in the Oneness of God and His Justice)—an elaborate and prolonged theological issue is at the root of that expression. What is most remarkable about this manner of introducing himself is what is most remarkable about Goldziher in general—the subtle and graceful way he had found to remain (without a shadow of a doubt) a pious and believing Jew while deeply respectful of his Muslim colleagues and their scholastic culture. That he managed to strike that balance and yet "mercilessly analyze," to use his own favorite phrase, Islam, as he did Judaism, dissect them both to their most detailed historical particulars, is of course the sign of his superior character as a man and a scholar.

In no uncertain terms, Goldziher had told the Shaykh at al-Azhar that his name is Ignaz, he comes from Hungary, he is a Jew, and he is a scholar. The range of meanings and inferences hidden in that short expression in which he said all of these could not but have impressed the Shaykh tremendously, and thus he proceeded readily to grant Goldziher written permission to attend lectures and seminars at al-Azhar. That the Shaykh of al-Azhar himself was reportedly the son of a rabbi who had converted to Islam[62] is an additional sign of a scholarly camaraderie across religions, nations, and cultures. Without sacrificing one iota of his integrity, identity, or ancestral faith, Ignaz al-Majari was finally at home. There are many moments in his *Tagebuch* when Goldziher says things such as "I termed my monotheism Islam, and I did not lie when I said that I believed the prophecies of Mohammad. My copy of the Koran can testify how I was inwardly turned toward Islam. My teachers seriously expected the moment of my open declaration."[63] But these all remained at the level of a scholar's complete immersion in the subject of his lifelong learning. Based on the evidence of his own *Tagebuch* and *Travelogue*, and given his profoundly pious character as a practicing Jew, Goldziher never even thought of converting to Islam. At al-Azhar he was like a fish in the clear waters of an ocean. But not even the majesty of al-Azhar, where his mind was most at home, made him compromise his integrity as a Jew. It, in fact, accentuated it. Al-Azhar, and by extension

Goldziher's knowledge of Islamic scholastic learning, made him more of a pious, believing, practicing and noble Jew—qualities he in turn squarely invested in his understanding of Islam. It is the nature of that dialectic that has completely escaped the author of his "psychological portrait," busy as he is turning him into "an evil man" who "suffered from an acute anti-Jewish complex."

There were other hoops through which Goldziher had to jump before he was finally admitted to study al-Azhar. With every witty, intelligent, and appropriate answer he provided, he endeared himself to his colleagues and teachers and was welcomed with open arms, especially by a certain Shaykh Mahfuz al-Maghribi who as soon as he laid eyes on Goldziher told him he had a dream that he was coming to study with him, referring to him as "a descendent of the old prophets"[64]—yet another indication that neither Goldziher nor his friends and colleagues hid his identity and ancestral faith. Al-Azhar professors and students alike welcomed, loved, and admired Goldziher as one of their own. He visited them at their residences and they came to pay Goldziher visits. He spent his mornings studying at the library and attending lectures and seminars, and his evenings socializing with his friends and colleagues. He was "led from paradise to paradise,"[65] as he later recalled fondly what to the end of his life he considered the most blissful time of his life. Riyad Pasha, totally vindicated in his recommendation of Goldziher, continued to meet with him and repeat his offer for him to stay in Egypt and pursue a career far more lucrative than what was offered or was expecting him in Hungary. Goldziher politely refused Riyad Pasha's offers.

Neither his preoccupation with his studies nor his acquaintance with high-ranking officials like the minister of education prevented Goldziher from becoming deeply involved with the anti-colonial sentiments current in Egypt at the time. "During the celebrations of the marriage of the daughter of the Viceroy," as Patai characterizes Goldziher's politics, "Goldziher agitated in the bazaars against the advantages enjoyed by the Europeans in Egypt."[66] What Patai calls "agitation" others may call something else, like anti-colonial protest. Goldziher frequented the circles of Egyptian nationalists, prepared historical accounts of a reconstruction of Egyptian culture in opposition to European colonialism.[67] He joined anti-colonial demonstrations in the streets of Cairo, spoke and wrote on behalf of Egyptian nationalism in circles he frequented, refused to attend exclusively European gatherings unless his teachers and colleagues at al-Azhar were also invited—and Patai characterizes all these noble and moral acts as Goldziher's identifying "with traditional Muslim anti-Western Egypt,"[68] representing his principled anti-colonial and pro-Egyptian sentiments, actions, and writings either as "agitation" or else as "anti-Western."[69]

Within weeks after he left Budapest, the twenty-three-year-old Goldziher was demonstrating in the streets and alleys of Cairo against European colonialism alongside his Egyptian friends and colleagues. He was what today we would call an academic activist, a staunch anti-colonial critic of European arrogance in the region of his scholarly interest—and his sojourn to Muslim lands was a rare chance to match his lifelong learning and moral convictions to the test of the lived and material realities of a people and a faith he had devoted his life to understanding. This aspect of Goldziher's character, his anti-colonial activism, Patai has a particularly difficult time understanding. Goldziher's anti-colonial politics and his excitement at visiting the seats of Islamic learning will go a long way in explaining his enthusiasm in this journey than any presumed "infatuation with Islam," or that he "suffered from an acute anti-Jewish complex," to which Patai now adds an "anti-Western" ingredient as well.

Goldziher remained in Cairo until mid-April 1874, returning to Budapest a few days before the death of his father on 4 May 1874. His last and most memorable act while in Cairo was to participate in a public prayer. With the help of a Syrian colleague, Abdallah al-Shami, Goldziher could fulfill this last wish he had and attended a Friday prayer next to Imam al-Shafi'i's mausoleum. "In the midst of the thousands of the pious," he later recorded, "I rubbed my forehead against the floor of the mosque. Never in my life was I more devout, more truly devout, than on that exalted Friday."[70] In summation, Goldziher's time in Syria, Palestine and Egypt to him and in his own words was a "year full of honors, full of luster, full of light."[71]

* * *

To understand the predicament of Goldziher as a superior scholar denied a proper teaching position, as well as his anti-colonial activism in Egypt, it would be very constructive to compare him to his own teacher Arminius Vámbéry, a charlatan Orientalist to the highest degree, a self-confessed spy for the British, a man who betrayed his ancestral faith and out of career opportunism converted first to Islam and then to Christianity, in order to advance his espionage services to colonialism, and a man whom Goldziher detested with a vengeance and whom Patai greatly admires.

Goldziher's return to Budapest was not a happy occasion. His father soon died and he had to assume immediate financial responsibilities for his mother and sister. No teaching position worthy of his stature was forthcoming and thus reluctantly he began working as an administrator. Patai is very sarcastic and critical of Goldziher for resenting this secretarial job. But Goldziher's anger has nothing to do with whatever important function this congregation may have (and must have) served.

Goldziher was a scholar. He had just completed his formal education in Europe, received high degrees, published extensively, and studied at al-Azhar University, a feat never before attained by any European Orientalist. A mind-numbing administrative position (any such position, no matter how otherwise important) was far beneath the dignity of his learning and achievements. Failing to understand this, Patai characterizes Goldziher as being "slightly paranoid,"[72] and wonders why he could not have at least "some measure of satisfaction in occupying the influential position of de facto manager of the largest Jewish congregation in the world."[73]

Goldziher was nowhere near the "de facto manager" of anything. Intellectual inferiors such as Moritz Wahrmann (1832-1892), who was elected the president of the congregation in 1883 and for nine consecutive years terrorized the life of Goldziher, were in positions of power and authority over him and the very livelihood of his family, repeatedly and sadistically subjecting him to deliberate humiliation. The pages of *Tagebuch* are filled with the agonies that Goldziher experienced under Wahrmann and other leaders of the congregation—at some point even driving him to contemplate suicide: "With all my self-control," wrote Goldziher in his *Tagebuch*, "a catastrophe for my inner life was to be feared. In the winter of 1883-84 [that is when Wahrmann became the president of the congregation] I had no more serious wish than to be liberated from this nonlife by death. My nightly prayers had one content: that the merciful God let me not waken again. And when I did wake up in the morning, it was accompanied by feeling of terror and fear that I had again been delivered to the evil life in which I found but shame and torture."[74] Why was he driven to such desperation? "At the meetings of the executive—where I sat as the scribe," Goldziher reports of his having been the "de facto manager of the largest Jewish congregation in the world," as Patai characterizes him, "my incompetence and stupidity were proclaimed hundreds of times by the mouth of this autocrat [Wahrmann]."[75] "You want to be a philosopher," on another occasion Wahrmann ridiculed Goldziher, "If a four-year-old child had given me such an answer I would scold it severely."[76] Goldziher was no "de facto manager" of anything at the congregation. He was a great scholar trapped in a pathetic administrative post, systematically humiliated and abused by his superiors in power and inferiors in intellect.

Occasionally teaching positions would open, such as the one at the Rabbinical Seminary of Budapest. But because in his book *Der Mythos bei den Hebräern* (*Mythology among the Hebrews*) Goldziher had ventured to examine the Hebrew Bible in terms of current theories of myth advanced by Max Müller (1823-1900) he had managed to offend the religious sensibilities of people in charge of that academic position.[77] Goldziher held Arminius Vámbéry, an exceedingly powerful and influential man, directly responsible for his having failed to secure a teaching position. "That I have been totally ignored here," Goldziher believed of his predicament in Budapest, " is the work of vengeance of this evil monster." Calling him the "most cunning of all liars," Goldziher believed that Vámbéry "cannot maintain his grandeur without slighting me." When in March 1905, upon the retirement of a senior colleague, Péter Hatala, Goldziher was finally appointed as a full-time and salaried professor, he was absolutely convinced that it was against Vámbéry's machinations. "Had he been present on the sixteenth [of March 1905, when the faculty unanimously voted in favor of Goldziher], it would certainly not have been unanimous. I would not have got the vote of this malicious ignoramus."[78] This appointment came thirty-five years, from 1870 to 1905, after Goldziher had received his doctoral degree from Leipzig, and thirty-one years after he had completed his round of studies at al-Azhar—and long after decades of enduring a humiliating and demeaning secretarial job to earn a living and provide for his family. Goldziher adamantly believed that Vámbéry not only had absolutely nothing to do with his appointment but that in fact if he could have he would have prevented it from happening.[79] Patai unequivocally takes Vámbéry's side (without providing a shred of evidence except his own deep affection for and political identification with Vámbéry) and, disregarding all fundamental moral and intellectuals issues separating Goldziher from Vámbéry, accuses Goldziher of yet another malevolent character trait, of being ungrateful to his friends and colleagues.[80]

The choice seems to be between Patai's projection of Goldziher as "an evil man" who was "infatuated with Islam," "suffered from an acute anti-Jewish complex," was "slightly paranoid," and utterly ungrateful, or else look a little closer at this Armenius Vámbéry and notice the difference between him and Goldziher. Ignaz Goldziher and Arminius Vámbéry were two radically different people and in fundamental political disagreements—a fact that Patai virtually disregards. As a central Asian expert, Arminius Vámbéry was deeply involved in British colonialism in India, knew Prince of Wales (Edward VII) personally and boasted of having visited him at Windsor Castle. "Vámbéry," as Patai himself reports, "became an advisor to the British government on India and Asiatic policies."[81] Vámbéry was an exceedingly rich man who had made his money by being a "secret agent" for both the British and the Ottomans, as he put it himself proudly, putting his Oriental expertise squarely at the service of British colonialism—by his own repeated admission, to more than one person.[82] "In Hungary one needs no science," Vámbéry told Goldziher condescendingly, "do you think I earned my fortune with Science? Ha, ha, ha! I received an annual salary from the English Queen and from the Sultan, for political matters. England has now increased my salary by 500 pounds sterling a year. This is science."[83] After quoting this passage from Goldziher's *Tagebuch*, Patai corroborates both the extraordinary wealth of Vámbéry and the fact that he was a secret agent in the service of the British Empire and the Ottomans at the same time, from Theodor Herzl's diary (which Patai has also edited). Herzl also reports, entirely independent of any malevolence that Goldziher may have had towards Vámbéry, that Vámbéry had told Herzl that he was a spy for the British and for the Ottoman Sultan at the same time.[84]

Quite independently of Goldziher, Herzl, and Patai, we have another piece of documentation from Vámbéry's own pen, corroborating the reasons why a principled person like Goldziher with a record of anti-colonial activism, would detest him and repeatedly call him a "swindler-rich Dervish."[85] Vámbéry's service to the British Empire had a long and quite adventurous history. In the early 1860s, Vámbéry disguised himself as a wandering dervish and traveled throughout Central Asia and Iran to collect detailed and vital intelligence for his British employers. Vámbéry's own account of these travels, *Voyage d'un faux derviche en Asie centrale, 1862-1864*,[86] provides detailed accounts of his adventures. Disguised as a wandering dervish and calling himself "Rashid Efendi," Vámbéry traveled extensively in the region of vital strategic significance to the British and gathered detailed intelligence, concluding his journey and returning to London to give his reports on 9 June 1864.[87] "I have no doubt," Vámbéry concludes after his long journeys in Iran and Central Asia, "that without any question the Christian civilization is nobler than any other that has ever regulated human societies. It will be a great gift for Central Asia as well." This is so far as his comparative conception of Judaism (his own original faith), Christianity, and Islam is concerned. As for his politics, "I have no clue," he says, catering to the political agenda of his employers, "how England, while possessing India, can tolerate so indifferently the Russian incursions into East. In my opinion the political aspect of the question is more important than it social aspect."[88] With an obvious eye towards his own career in Orientalist espionage, Vámbéry was determined to persuade the British of the danger of Russian incursion into Central Asia, a vital region for protecting the British control of the Indian subcontinent. The British were, of course, not sitting idly by and were far more engaged in Iran, Afghanistan, and Central Asia than Vámbéry knew or divulged at the time. Beginning in the early nineteenth century, the British were deeply involved in the region, including in Iran—and their having dispatched their Orientalist spy Vámbéry to the region was part of their gathering intelligence about the region. As early as the Perso-Russian wars of 1804-1813 and then again 1825-1827, the British were actively involved in Iran and Central Asia—trying to win the

Qajars over against the advances that Napoleon had already made as early as 1805 by allying himself (in the famous Finckenstein Treaty of 3 May 1807) with the Qajars in order to create headaches for the British in South Asia. Pretending to help the Qajars in their fights against the Russians, in compensation for dismissing the French, the British in effect turned Iran into a bumper zone between Russia and India. By the 1830s, when the Qajars had repeatedly invaded Herat, the British had become increasingly concerned that the Qajars were not behaving properly, and saw India, the jewel in their crown, as they called their colonial adventurism, exposed to Russian adventures. On 24 October 1856, the Qajars finally conquered Herat. By 4 December of the same year, the British navy in the Persian Gulf had captured the Kharg Island and were pushing northward all the way up to Ahvaz. By 4 March 1857, a treaty was signed in Paris between Iran and Great Britain. The Qajars left Herat; the British left southern Iran; and soon after created Afghanistan as a buffer state between Russia and India. Vámbéry's travels through Central Asia and gathering of intelligence in the early 1860s all occurred after these crucial events and obviously furthered the British interest in the region.

Contrary to Vámbéry and his illustrious career as a spy, Goldziher was, as a matter of moral and intellectual principle, opposed to European colonialism in general. He had just returned from Cairo where, alongside his Egyptian friends and colleagues, he had been "agitating," as Patai puts it, against precisely the same sort of colonial interests that Vámbéry so lucratively served. Vámbéry and Goldziher were two entirely different people, at the two opposing ends of a moral divide—one a rich spy for European colonialism and an entirely mediocre Orientalist who did not mind converting from Judaism to Islam first and Christianity next when it served his career opportunism, the other a staunchly anti-colonial activist, a poor but justifiably proud scholar, and a man of moral rectitude who as a mater of ethical principle had remained honorably true to his own ancestral faith against all odds. As he states in his *Tagebuch*, Goldziher was propagating the same sort of anti-colonial ideas when he was in Egypt in the early 1870s that a decade later became the rallying cry of the anti-colonial revolt of Arabi Pasha in June 1882.[89] This makes Goldziher an entirely different person than Vámbéry, who on one occasion told Goldziher, "Every man who does not acquire much money is a reprehensible character. I have earned a quarter of a million, half a million kronen, but not with science. Science is shit."[90]

As he fails to understand Goldziher's intellectual affinity with Islamic scholastic learning, Patai equally misconstrues the nature of Goldziher's anger with Vámbéry and thus uses the occasion to heap even more abuse on the subject of his "psychological portrait." Goldziher's critical disposition extended from his scholarship to his political views, which were not only anti-colonial but also altogether anti-establishment. For all his love and admiration for his friend Wilhelm Bacher, he thought that Bacher was too bookish and conformist, that "without being dishonorable, he could adapt his spirit to the dominant trends, of which in the course of time he became a factor."[91] If Goldziher was so gently critical of a man he deeply admired, for being a conformist, what could he think of a wealthy spy who put his Orientalist knowledge at the service of British colonialism, against which Goldziher took to the streets of Cairo, which fact Patai, in his profound affinity with and admiration for Vámbéry, considers as indication of Goldziher's "anti-Western" and pro "traditional Muslim" sentiments and thus "agitations."

There is another principled difference between Vámbéry and Goldziher that again goes a long way in explaining Goldziher's dislike for former without resorting to convoluted psychological witch hunting. Vámbéry's career opportunism led him to act as the intermediary introducing Theodore Herzl (1860-1904) to the Ottoman Sultan to secure permission for Jewish settlements in Palestine. According to Patai, Vámbéry was so close and intimate with Herzl that Herzl called him, "Vámbéry bácsi" ("Uncle Vámbéry"). After Herzl's death, Vámbéry was regularly consulted by David Wolffsohn, then the president of the World Zionist Organization. To his dying day, on the contrary, Goldziher refused to have anything to do with Zionism. In Patai's own words, "although Vámbéry had converted to both Islam and Christianity, he remained a Jew at heart and proudly proclaimed himself a Zionist. In contrast, Goldziher, with his lifelong religious fervor, was opposed to Zionism."[92] These facts speak of fundamental moral and political differences between Vámbéry and Goldziher, and they go a long way explaining Goldziher's anger with Vámbéry, before we need to resort to some deep-rooted, and dark psychological malice on Goldziher's part. When it comes to a career opportunist who did not mind abandoning his own ancestral faith and converting first to Islam and then to Christianity when it served his purposes, and there is no proof that even his presumed Zionism was anything other than the same self-serving opportunism, and who in his own words believed "that without any question the Christian civilization is nobler than any other that has ever regulated human societies," Patai calls him "a Jew at heart." But when it comes to a profoundly pious and practicing Jew who against all anti-Semitic odds in Europe and despite his deep intellectual affinity with Islamic scholastic learning remained true to his faith, Patai considers him having "suffered from an acute anti-Jewish complex."

Goldziher's difficult time during these trying circumstances notwithstanding, he remained exceedingly productive, published extensively, attended international conferences, delivered learned papers, and received accolades of praise and admiration from his peers. His scholarship at this point was by no means limited to Islamic studies. During 1887-1888, he gave a series of public lectures on the "Essence and Development of Judaism."[93] But the highest achievement of this decade, as we saw, was the publication of his two-volume masterpiece, *Muhammedanische Studien* (1889-1890). While his public lectures on Judaism were not very well received—"his presentation was far above the heads of the audience"[94]—his two-volume opus on Islam established him as the undisputed master of the discipline. In his oscillation between two exaggerated extremes, either accusing Goldziher of all sorts of malevolent character traits or else showering him with exaggerated superlatives, and thus projecting the image of a tormented genius,[95] Patai considers the publication of the two volumes of *Muhammedanische Studien* as an indication that "until Goldziher all of this was terra incognita, not only for European scholars but also for the Muslim *'ulama* and intelligentsia. With the publication of this work the scholarly world agreed that Goldziher had *created* the intellectual history of Islam."[96] This absurdity, later repeated by other latter-day Orientalists, simply defies reason. How could Muslims create their own intellectual history, the material that Goldziher studiously examined as the body of his scholarship, and yet not be aware of what it is they have produced? The supreme joy of Goldziher himself was to have (however shortly) lived among those who had created this intellectual history. He felt himself honored to have been accepted by them as a student and as an equal. How could he have "created the intellectual history of Islam"? Goldziher did no such thing. He was a scholar of uncommon erudition. But he did not "create" the intellectual history of an entire civilization. He was no tormented genius—nor was he an evil man.

* * *

Patai's *ad hominem* attacks on Goldziher, completely distorting the historical record and confusing the necessary task of having an accurate conception of his scholarship, assumes utterly slanderous proportions when he turns to Goldziher's personal and private life.

Throughout these troubling years as an independent scholar, Goldziher received numerous offers to teach in Germany, England, and Egypt. He rejected them all and opted to remain in Budapest—his hometown where his family and close friends lived. Patai takes these refusals as signs of Goldziher's perturbed soul that somehow needed to be tormented and heaps even more abuse upon him. "If Goldziher had not had opportunities to break the shackles that tied him to the Israelite Congregation of Pest for thirty years," Patai says in his "psychological portrait" of Goldziher, "his life would have been a most pathetic story of a genius chained. But the fact that he had ample opportunities to liberate himself and never took the decisive step makes that life more nearly pathological than pathetic."[97] Goldziher himself had more immediate and healthy reasons to remain in Budapest, such as his family obligations, particularly towards the orphaned children of his deceased sister, and also his pride of place as a Hungarian. All indications are that he did not wish to pack his family and go to England, Germany, or Egypt. Why should he? Budapest was his city, Hungary his country, of which he spoke with singular affection and possessive pronoun. "He feels that he has a particular mission in my country,"[98] he once wrote of a Baha'i missionary trying to convert people in Budapest to his religion.

Goldziher had two sons, Max and Károly, from his marriage in May 1878 to Laura Mittler. His older son Max committed suicide on 31 May 1900, at the age twenty. The death of his son was a particularly devastating experience for Goldziher, "the darkest day of my life," he wrote in his diary of the day his son died—"my house has been destroyed."[99] When his younger and sole surviving son Károly married Mária Freudenberg in 1913, Goldziher developed a deep affection for his daughter-in-law and thought it a matter of divine intervention that he should have declined all those positions outside Hungary and stayed put to have the grace of this daughter in his life. Patai casts an astoundingly irresponsible shadow of impropriety on Goldziher's affection for his daughter-in-law and accuses him of having fallen in love with her. Characterizing Goldziher's postdated explanation as to why he had turned academic offers coming his ways as "ravings of an enthusiast," Patai believes that "Goldziher, sixty-three at the time, promptly fell in love with her,"[100] suggesting that he had remained in Budapest in order "to be able to experience the elation of falling in love with his divine daughter-in-law"—while emphasizing their obvious age difference in order to add spice to his slanderous suggestions.[101]

Nothing, not a shred of evidence, any passage from Goldziher's *Tagebuch* that Patai's scandalous-ridden language digs out, suggests anything other than a perfectly innocent paternal love that Goldziher had for his daughter-in-law. Goldziher never expresses anything about Mária Freudenberg without adding, "who is now my daughter," or "the good wife of my Karl," or "she is from now on everything for us" (meaning he and his wife and his son). Mária Freudenberg did not live long and died tragically, on 4 December 1918 at the age of twenty-eight (of Spanish influenza). Goldziher's first thoughts on this sad occasion are with his son, "Oh, my dear Karl."[102] Towards the end of his "psychological portrait," and after he has smeared Goldziher's dignity, Patai casually admits that Goldziher's love for his daughter-in-law was "undoubtedly platonic."[103] But why suggest in such a slanderous language anything otherwise first (under a whole section sarcastically subtitled, straight out of a tabloid, "The Divine Mariska,")[104] and then some twenty-three pages after he has accused a man of "falling in love with his divine daughter-in-law" simply add that it was "undoubtedly platonic"? Why not take those expressions of paternal love for what they are? Why not consider the fact that Goldziher did not have a daughter of his own and it was only natural for him to be excited to have a daughter-in-law in his family? Why not remember that thirteen years before Mária Freudenberg entered the Goldziher family, they had lost their eldest son? All members of the Goldziher family must have been elated to have a daughter join them to fill that tragic gap. Why not tell Patai's English-speaking readers what the German-speaking readers were told by Scheiber, the editor of the original German of *Tagebuch*, that Mária Freudenberg was a learned young scholar, a gifted Egyptologist?[105] Why could Goldziher not have a scholarly engagement with his daughter-in-law, fascinated by her achievements, interests, potentials? Why plant a thought on page 32 that Goldziher was not "emotionally involved" with his own wife, suggest there and then that Goldziher was capable of "passionate love," in order to reap the slanderous fruit on pages 52-54 that Goldziher had anything but an entirely innocent and noble sentiments towards his own daughter-in-law? Patai loses not a single occasion to slander Goldziher with this accusation. Long after the "The Divine Mariska" section, and when discussing Goldziher's relations with his students, he still plants such sardonic remarks as, "in 1919, when Goldziher was heartbroken over the death of his beloved Mariska," in the middle of his sentences.[106] This section of Patai's "psychological portrait" of Goldziher tops a systematically slanderous picture that he has painted of him, casting his entire scholarly achievements under a thick shadow of *ad hominem* defamation, simply because Goldziher had committed the unforgivable sin of not being a Zionist.

* * *

The slanderous remarks about Goldziher's feelings and relations to his daughter-in-law is not the last shadow that Patai wishes to cast on his integrity, and thus confusing a balanced assessment of his lifetime achievement as a scholar. His next move is to accuse Goldziher of "superpatriotism," "chauvinism," and even "xenophobia." "Chauvinistic patriotism," Patai writes, "often goes hand in hand with xenophobia, or at least a disdain for foreigners. This was the case with Goldziher."[107] This is quite strange indeed. On one hand Patai accuses Goldziher of having an abiding love for Arabs and Muslims—"infatuated with Islam," "anti-Western"—and then accuses him of xenophobia, "or at least a disdain for foreigners." So which one is it? Is Goldziher a superpatriotic, chauvinistic, xenophobe, or an incurable Arabophile who exempted Arabs and Muslims from his "censorial wrath,"[108] had an "admiration for the world of Islam,"[109] and who was indeed "infatuated with Islam?"[110] Patai did not make up his mind, and in that confusion dwells the persistent demonization of a scholar whose lifetime achievements need a far more serious assessment more than a century after they were produced.

To be sure, Patai raises a perfectly legitimate set of question about Hungarian Jewry and their Hungarian nationalism, which he traces back to "post-Emancipation Hungarian Jewry," emancipated in 1867. Patai raises a series of flag-signs and gives an outline of the odds against which the Hungarian Jewry remained nationalist, a nationalism that "survived," as he argues,

> All the vicissitudes that they experienced in subsequent decades: the wave of anti-Semitism that swept Hungry in the 1880's and culminated in the blood libel of Tiszaeszlár; the attacks and murders that followed the downfall of the short-lived 1919 Communist regime headed by the renegade Jew Béla Kun; the introduction in 1921 of the numerus clasusus law, which stamped the Jews a national minority despite all their protestations that they were but one of the several religious denominations in the Magyar nation and reduced the number of Jews admissible to universities to the proportion of Jews in the total population; and the constant undercurrents of anti-Semitism that characterized Hungarian life in the intervals between these and other such hurtful events. In fact, every anti-Semitic manifestation was countered by the Jews with louder and more emphatic proclamations of their Hungarianism and Hungarian patriotism. This remained the dominant tone of Hungarian Jewish life until the tragic years of World War II and the extermination of 565,000 of the 825,000 Hungarian Jews.[111]

These are all perfectly legitimate questions that one can raise in the aftermath of the Jewish Holocaust. At the time (as indeed at any time), however, Hungarian Jewry, as the rest of European Jewry, had perfectly legitimate claims to their national identities as Hungarians, Germans, Poles, etc. If there is an intensity about nationalism and patriotism it is neither exclusive to Hungarians nor indeed is there any legitimate reason why Hungarian Jewry be exempt from that patriotism. It is only in hindsight and after the horrors of European anti-Semitism culminated in the Jewish Holocaust that one can raise these sorts of historical and sociological questions. But one cannot anachronistically single out Hungarian Jewry, let alone single out Goldziher, accuse them of chauvinism and xenophobia simply because like all other Hungarians and Europeans they felt attached to a country that for generations and millennia had been their homeland.

As a Zionist, Patai does not hide the fact that his anger against Goldziher is rooted in why he refused to endorse the Zionist project. "After the issuance of the Balfour Declaration," Patai notes,

> in which the British government undertook to facilitate the establishment of a Jewish national home in Palestine, Zionist leaders approached Goldziher to ask him to help them establish contacts with Arab notables and scholars with whom he had excellent connections and who had great respect for him, but he refused.[112]

Even this frustration of a committed Zionist as to why a man of Goldziher's status refused to have endorsed his ideology is perfectly understandable. But to turn around and accuse him of "superpatriotism, chauvinism, and xenophobia" is not only anachronistic, but blatantly politically motivated, vindictive, and as such predicated on an entirely flawed line of argument. One could not possibly accuse Goldziher, and hundreds of thousands of other Hungarian Jews, of not caring about their own collective fate, their own well-being. From a Zionist perspective, and from the hindsight of post-Holocaust history, one can even accuse them of a misjudgment and lack of farsightedness. But accusing of superpatriotism and xenophobia not just Goldziher and hundreds of thousands of other Hungarian but millions of European Jewry for their perfectly legitimate claims to their homeland is not just affectedly conceited but also logically flawed.

There are in fact not even any indications that Goldziher opposed the peaceful coexistence of Jews, Christians, and Muslims in Palestine. Patai reports an eyewitness account in which Goldziher purportedly told the Syrian reverend 'Abdul-Ahad Dominique Bashar Mishkuni, a former student:

> I have firmly hoped in my whole life that the time will come when Arabs and Jews making peace with each other, will cooperate in the resurrection of Israel and the Arab people. If you return to your native country, tell your brethren that I have worked all my life for your people and for my people.[113]

From his own pen in his *Travelogue* we also read how upon his visit to Jerusalem he thought

> of the calumniated, persecuted prophetism of the Hebrew Past, of the prophetism of the future, of the new Jerusalem that, "liberated" and rebuilt by spirit and thought, will become the place of pilgrimage of all those who, with free mind, erect a new Zion for the Jehova of freedom that embraces the whole mankind.[114]

This is in November 1873, from the pen of the twenty-three-year-old Goldziher, decades before the Dreyfus Affair (1894) gave momentum to the rise of political Zionism, twenty-three years, to be exact, before Theodor Herzl (1860-1904) published his *Der Judenstaat* ("The

Jewish State," 1896), and almost thirty years before Herzl published his novel, *Altneuland* ("Old New Land," 1902), giving his vision of a socialist utopia in Palestine. Long before Herzl, Goldziher too had his own utopian vision. "He wanted the persecuted Jews," recalls Bernard Heller, "to find a home in the Holy Land, that Jews, Christians, and Muslims might live there in brotherhood together."[115] Goldziher too called that utopia "Israel," and invoked the name of Zion to mark it, but his was a "Zion for the Jehova of freedom that embraces the whole mankind." There is a serious difference between Goldziher's "Zionism" and Herzl's. Patai has obviously selected his, but he cannot demonize Goldziher for having dreamt of another.

Patai, much to his credit, seriously discounts the later efforts of people like Louis Massignon who tried posthumously to turn Goldziher into a "spiritual" or a "cultural" Zionist, and characterizes them as "to say the least, tenuous."[116] But more than tenuous is his own issues with millions of European Jews who simply refused to take Herzl's colonial adventurism (if they were not Zionists) or prophetic visions (if they were) too seriously. That they paid for their decisions dearly and with their own lives and the lives of their loved one's cannot be subjected to a Monday-morning quarterbacking and their natural and perfectly legitimate love for their homelands branded as superpatriotic, chauvinist, and xenophobic. Goldziher's "profound religion," Bernard Heller believes, in exact contradiction to Raphael Patai, "was not mixed with any kind of nationalist element. On this point he made a fundamental statement in his letter to Joseph Bánóczi in 1889: 'Jewry is a religion, and not an ethnographical concept. As for as my nationality is concerned, I am a Trans-Danubian Hungarian, and for my religion I am a Jew. . . . On leaving Jerusalem for Hungary I said that I was returning home."[117] Might that be the reason why Patai turns Goldziher into a xenophobic, superpatriotic, zealot—that he believed Judaism is a religion, not "an ethnographic concept," that he had something of a nationalism about him, but not the right kind of nationalism that suited Patai's perhaps own "psychological portrait"?

* * *

Towards the end of his "psychological portrait" of Goldziher, Patai concludes with what he believes are the "two contrasting aspects of Goldziher's personality: his clear, analytical, scholarly mind, which, of course, is well known from his great works, and his uncontrollable, powerful emotionalism, which ever and again breaks forth from depth of his psyche and, as it were, sweeps him off his feet."[118] Patai's assessment of this apparent paradox assumes yet another psychological malady in Goldziher and proposes that he suffered from something close to a "split personality." The psychological diagnosis of the anthropologist:

"As a matter of fact the explanation is not far to seek. It is found in a lack of adjustment, an absence of harmony, between the cerebral Goldziher and the emotional Goldziher that was to remain a basic characteristic of his life. I would not go so far as to say that he had a split personality, but he certainly came near enough to it."[119]

The alternative reading, instead of a systematically abusive interpretation of Goldziher's *Tagebuch* and the *Travelogue*, would be that these two documents are in fact entirely private spaces that have perfectly innocent functions for their author. Neither *Tagebuch* nor the *Travelogue* was meant for publication. The *Tagebuch* was written exclusively for Goldziher's wife, children, and very close friends.[120] As for the *Travelogue*, when on the occasion of his fortieth birthday, on 22 June, 1890, Goldziher began writing his *Tagebuch* and came to his recollections of his trip to Syria, Palestine, and Egypt he had apparently misplaced (or else did not care to consult) his *Travelogue* and thus did not care even to consult it for exact dates, locations, or the chronology of events, and as a result he makes a few minor mistakes about dates and locations (which Patai is of course quick to catch). These facts indicate that the function of *Tagebuch* and *Travelogue* was entirely momentary, private, and a simple way of unloading the burden of the day that had passed. "I have nobody to whom I could confide the mortifications and humiliations that are my daily bread," Goldziher writes in his *Tagebuch* on the day that his son Max dies, "except to these pages."[121] Neither the *Tagebuch* nor the *Travelogue* was meant to be abusively read by an anthropologist with a penchant for pop-psychology, scandalous sexual innuendos, and above all indulging in radical political disagreement with Goldziher.

There are other aspects of the *Tagebuch* and the *Travelogue* that come together to define their mutual function in providing Goldziher with his perfect sanity and sense of purpose in his life. Patai notes how on one day Goldziher goes on a rampage against people who have irritated him, and only a few days later he forgets what he had said earlier and writes: "I have become apathetic to all marks of honor just as I have, with a will, become apathetic to all humiliation."[122] Patai takes this as an indication of Goldziher's instability. But these remarks point to something entirely different, that the *Tagebuch* (and by extension the *Travelogue*) is really an occasion for Goldziher to spontaneously let off the steam, cramped up inside him during the day, an immediate function even beyond his original purpose of telling his family and close friends his life story. The *Tagebuch* certainly began as a life story to be shared with Goldziher's immediate family and friends, but as soon as he summarizes the early part of his life (with an obvious and perhaps inevitable sense of nostalgia), and continues to write about his current life from 1890 forward the function of the diary almost completely changes and becomes a manner of talking to a friend, a close confident—and even then not on a regular and systematic way. There are days, weeks, and even months that go by and Goldziher does not write anything in his *Tagebuch*. For the entire year of 1905, for example, has only forty-two entries, some of them as short as a single sentence—and that year is a relatively crowded year in his *Tagebuch*. Between 28 August and 5 September 1905 he does not write a single entry in his *Tagebuch*, and after an entry in September for three months he writes nothing until a couple of entries in December. The same is true of 1906 (twenty-six entries), 1907 (ten entries), 1908 (ten entries), 1918 (eighteen), and 1919 (two entries)—meaning that in an entire year he writes as little as twice in his diary. The earlier years of the *Tagebuch*, to be sure, contain more elaborate entries and more frequently—1892 (forty-five entries), 1893 (twenty-one entries), 1894 (forty-nine entries), whereas the later years have fewer entries. Throughout most of the *Tagebuch*, the summer entries (from May to August) are far more frequent than the spring (January-April) and fall (September to December) entries—an obvious indication that during his summer holidays he had more time to set down his private thoughts. The overwhelming majority of Goldziher's time was spent on writing his scholarly essays, with prodigious, voluminous, and astounding rapidity and frequency. These few, infrequent, and entirely innocent reflections of a man in the privacy of his diary cannot be abused to construct a whole scenario about the tormented soul of a "pathetic genius" full of horrid and amoral character traits, coming together to produce "an evil man."

There are other, rather fascinating, ways to read the *Tagebuch*, instead of a single-minded determination to slander its author and imagine him a demonic character. Consider the fact that the lengthy and elaborate entries of the *Tagebuch* in its earlier parts and the shorter staccatos of the later years in a rather peculiar (and most probably unconscious) way resembles the narrative composition of the Qur'an, with short and exclamatory Meccan verses (revealed between 610-622) standing in sharp contrast with long and elaborate Medinan verses (revealed between 622 and 632). Although this order is chronologically reversed in the case of Goldziher's *Tagebuch*, and the longer and more elaborate entries occur earlier in his life and the shorter and terser ones later, the narrative structure of the *Tagebuch* follows exactly that of the canonical composition of the Qur'an, in which the longer chapters come first and the shorter ones later. There is a saying that what Muslims do is not just memorize the Qur'an but Qur'anify their memory. Goldziher, too, knew much of the Qur'an (and the Bible, of course) by heart. On the very first page of *Tagebuch* he quotes a passage of the Qur'an as one of the two guiding principles of his life (the other being from the Hebrew Bible).[123] He refers to his personal copy of the Qur'an being an indication of his piety—"my copy of the Koran can testify how I was inwardly turned toward Islam."[124] Goldziher's intimate familiarity with the Qur'an could not have been entirely irrelevant in the way his mind and memory worked, especially in the unguarded and private spaces of his diary. One must not overemphasize or exaggerate this point, or the fact that Goldziher began writing his *Tagebuch* exactly on his birthday when he turned forty—precisely the age of the Prophet Muhammad (570-632) when he began receiving his revelations. The point is that there are far more insightful and crucial ways of reading the *Tagebuch* without resorting to systematically abusing it to create a slanderous characterization of its author.

As evidenced in his repeated questions as to why, for example, in *Tagebuch* Goldziher did not talk about his trip to the United States in 1904, or why did he not talk about his students more than he did—such as in the case of Bernát Heller who had translated into Hungarian the six lectures Goldziher was supposed to deliver in a later (cancelled) trip to the United States, his *Vorlesungen über den Islam* (later translated also into English as *Introduction to Islamic Theology and Law*)—Patai seems to have his own fixed conception of what a diary ought to be. That, of course, is perfectly fine, but he cannot demand that conception from Goldziher, and read even what he has not written as the sign of a psychological malady. Patai reports how Bernát Heller (with whom Patai studied in the academic year 1929-1930) told him "several times about his great master [Goldziher], whose memory he cherished as that of the kindest person he had ever known,"[125] but, alas, nothing of that kindness seems to have rubbed off on Patai's own pen when writing Goldziher's "psychological portrait." Instead, he uses even this report—the eyewitness account of a close and trusted student speaking fondly of his teacher—to cast a shadow of doubt on Goldziher's integrity, that he failed to mention and praise his students properly in the pages of his *Tagebuch*. Not only in this but also in every other case, Patai uses every opportunity, every occasion that Goldziher's students have testified to his kindness and greatness, to turn the point around and cast doubt on Goldziher's character. Joseph de Somogyi writes in his reminisces of Goldziher how in 1919, when Goldziher and his family were mourning the tragic death of his daughter-in-law, he still managed to give Somogyi private tutorials in Arabic in his home "twice a week, from 4:00 PM to late in the evening." Patai cannot report this without a subordinate clause, adding, "when Goldziher was heartbroken over the death of his beloved Mariska," deliberately using the endearing diminutive "Mariska" for Mária Freudenberg.[126] Frau Mária Freudenberg Goldziher was "Mariska" to members of her close family, not to Raphael Patai.

It does not quite make sense to preface a translation of a scholar's travelogue in a journey he considered the most joyous occasion of his scholarly career with persistently casting him as "an evil man" who was "infatuated with Islam," "suffered from an acute anti-Jewish complex," and who "agitated" in the streets of Cairo because of his "anti-Western" and "pro-traditional Muslim" culture sentiments, and to top it all was not only ungrateful to his own teachers and benefactors but had fallen in love with his own daughter-in-law, was a chauvinist and xenophobe who also suffered from a split personality—and then to compensate for all of these keep repeating a nonsensical cliché that he was a "tormented genius." Why systematically distort and thus seek to destroy a man's monumental reputation as a gifted scholar and keep calling him a "pathetic" or "pathological genius"?

It does not quite make sense, except the fact that in the pages of his "psychological portrait" of Goldziher, Patai has given ample evidence to see how he is far more sympathetic to someone like Armenius Vámbéry, a self-proclaimed spy for the British, an Orientalist squarely at the service of European colonialism, a man who had betrayed his ancestral faith and first converted to Islam and then to Christianity both to further his career as a spy, and who derided Goldziher for having remained true to and faithful to his Judaism—simply because Armenius Vámbéry was sympathetic to Zionism, a friend of Herzl, and an intermediary between him and the Ottoman Sultan to secure permission for Jewish settlements in Palestine, bestowing upon Armenius Vámbéry the honorary position of having remained "a Jew at heart." Meanwhile, Patai turns Goldziher—an exceptionally gifted scholar, a noble, observant, and pious Jew—into a psychological freak, a tormented soul, full of venom against the Jewish community, and guilty of inappropriately amorous feelings towards his own daughter-in-law, simply because he was opposed to European colonialism of all sorts, and was sympathetic to Islam and Muslims. Patai was, of course, perfectly entitled to whatever politics he wished to have and harbor, but to using that politics in order to slander a giant scholar of unsurpassed moral integrity he was not.

Goldziher was neither a tormented genius, nor an emotional pervert, nor an evil man, nor indeed did he harbor anything but the proudest and most noble attachment to his ancestral faith. He was a superior scholar of uncommon learning, one of the most gifted scholars of his time, and a man of enormous moral and intellectual authority, who rightly resented any single second that distracted him from his scholarly pursuits. He was a man of principle, a devout and proud Jew, who opposed European colonialism of all sorts, while producing a massive body of scholarship over a lifetime of meticulous and inquisitive learning.[127]

* * *

Beyond clearing the name of Goldziher as a scholar from such flawed and fallacious assumptions about his person, it is equally important to de-personalize the critique of Orientalism, as best articulated by Edward Said, and thus reach for a principled assessment of its mode of knowledge production, not allowing this critique to be derailed into the assumption of an *ad hominem* attack on individual Orientalists. Goldziher's achievements as an Islamist must be read not just as having come from the pen of a gifted scholar but also as the particular examples, in fact, examples *par excellence*, of a mode of knowledge production called "Orientalism"—and no appreciation of the work of an Orientalist like Goldziher at the height of his remarkable career can of course disregard the magisterial work of Edward Said (1935-2003), *Orientalism* (1978), and his cogent critique of the discipline at the colonial origin of its epistemic formation.

More than a quarter of a century after its publication, Edward Said's *Orientalism* has assumed an entirely iconic status quite independent of the actual idea at the heart of the book. In his own 1995 afterword to *Orientalism*, Said addressed this what he called "Borgesian" mutation of his book into various languages, texts, interpretations, intentions, readings. "In so far as I have been able to follow and understand these subsequent versions," Said wrote, he sought to correct and address them, navigating them through what he saw as a "strange, often disquieting and certainly unthought-of polymorphousness."[128] On this and on many other occasions, Said sought to clarify what he meant, dismiss certain misreadings, expound on his principle contentions, and altogether restate his case. But all of these protests were read against the background of the idea of "the death of the author," which much to Edward Said's own chagrin had been one of the dominating ideas of his own academic discipline, literary criticism.[129] No matter how much and how many times he protested that his book was not a case of "anti-Westernism"—"as it has been misleadingly and rather too sonorously called by commentators both hostile and sympathetic"—or that he did not believe in the existence of a "true Orient" that Orientalists had then misrepresented it, or a score of other such takes on the book, including the accusation that "to criticize Orientalism . . . is in effect to be a supporter of Islamism or Muslim fundamentalism,"[130] it did not matter. The multifaceted social construction of the text had almost completely taken over the text itself, making "the text itself," in fact, a matter of opinion.

Perhaps one of the most unfortunate misreadings of Edward Said's *Orientalism*, not only beyond Edward Said's control but in fact he inadvertently contributed to it, is its having been turned into an *ad hominem* attack on Orientalists as such. This misreading, at least in part, is due to a series of public confrontations between Edward Said and Bernard Lewis, who took upon himself the task of defending the

Orientalists, prompting Edward Said in turn to engage with Bernard Lewis personally—beyond his cogent references to his work in the pages of *Orientalism*.[131] This was perhaps an inevitable political fallout of the publication of *Orientalism* in the United States (recently home to the most mediocre Orientalists as compared to their nineteenth-century counterparts), but most unfortunate also in derailing (certainly in public domain) the more serious discussions of the text, which remained by and large limited to literary-critical and anthropological circles.

Thus while such critics as James Clifford, Aijaz Ahmad, and Sadiq Jalal al-Azm[132] took serious issue with Edward Said, taking both his theoretical and political assumptions and consequences meticulously to task, Bernard Lewis became the spokesman of a whole generation of mediocre Orientalists who were personally offended by *Orientalism* and sought to discredit it with the clumsiest and most theoretically illiterate arsenal, in effect exposing the historical exhaustion of Orientalism as a discipline of engaged scholarship and intellectual vigor—thus providing the widest possible public testimony of the point that Edward Said was trying to make. Said justifiably responded to Bernard Lewis and thus inevitably helped in detracting from the more serious discussion of his own work. Said did not particularly mind this active politicization of *Orientalism*, though of course he disagreed with the theoretical criticisms of his points as well. "Orientalism, " he declared in the 1995 afterword to his book and in response to still more serious critics of his work, "is a partisan book, not a theoretical machinery."[133] In other words the very same political energy that had made Edward Said take the insights of Michel Foucault on relations between knowledge and power, rescue it from its discursive and institutional limitation to theoretical domains, apply it to European colonialism in an unprecedented and politically potent way—thus turning his *Orientalism* into a global phenomenon—was equally instrumental in detracting from its more serious, theoretically consequential, discussions. Edward Said was one of those rare public intellectuals who walked a tightrope between his serious theoretical concerns, groundbreaking in many related fields, and his equally serious political concerns, redefining, in effect, the role and function of a public academic intellectual. The two sides of this critical imbalance inevitably both reinvigorated and compromised each other. It was an awareness of this critical imbalance, perhaps, that led Max Weber to warn against the involvement of academic intellectuals in public affairs—to which, in his life and scholarship, Edward Said offered an alternative model.[134]

The *ad hominem* misreading of *Orientalism* is particularly troublesome because it has turned the disciplinary critic of an epistemic mode of knowledge production into the street battles between opposing political parties, while categorically dismissing a whole constellation of different Orientalists and their at times radically opposing politics into a singular category—thus for example equating Ignaz Goldziher (a gifted and dignified scholar opposing European colonialism of all sorts as a matter of moral and intellectual principle) with Bernard Lewis and his Orientalist pedigree Arminius Vámbéry (a mediocre Orientalist and a self-confessed spy working on behalf of British colonialism in general and European Zionism in particular).

In any understanding of the scholarly output of Goldziher as an Orientalist, it is of course imperative to read him in the context of Edward Said's critique of Orientalism. But one cannot do that before the issues are completely de-personalized and brought back to the principal points of Edward Said's critique of a powerful discipline of knowledge production. One way of diffusing the issue in order to work towards a de-personalization of Edward Said's critic of Orientalism is to turn the calendar back to decades before the appearance of *Orientalism* (1978) in order to stay clear of the quagmire of Pavlovian reactions to that text and take the issues back to their principal positions and critical points. The detection and outline of this theoretical and substantive genealogy of Edward Said's argument is not to detract by any means from his extraordinary achievement in *Orientalism*. It is, in fact, to buttress it with at times identical critical perspectives that either in their embryonic state or else in their expansive theoretical domains anticipate, corroborate, and substantiate Said's thesis. This genealogy also provides a wider spectrum of critical perspective on the practice of Orientalism so that political disagreement with Edward Said on other grounds cannot disguise itself in a shallow and flawed criticism of his *Orientalism*. But above all, it is to clear the field for a principled assessment of Goldziher's scholarship against the powerful critique that Edward Said has leveled against the discipline in which Goldziher conducted his scholarship.

On 19 June 1904, more than half a century before Michel Foucault (1926-1984) had formulated his ideas on the relation between knowledge and power and then Edward Said extended that argument to Orientalism, a twenty-seven year old Iranian scholar named Mohammad Qazvini (1877-1949) left Tehran and, traveling through Russia, Germany, and Holland came to London. Before his death at the age seventy-two, Mohammad Qazvini was universally recognized as the most distinguished Iranian scholar of all time, earning the honorific title of *Allamah* ("Most Learned"), rarely given to any other Iranian scholar of that generation.[135] To this day, Allamah Qazvini is universally revered as a model of scholarly acumen, an exemplar of a vastly learned, exquisitely cultivated, and meticulously precise scholar. His critical edition of medieval texts and his pathbreaking essays and articles are the exemplary models that succeeding generations of scholars have followed in their own work. Even the scraps of notes Qazvini took on various occasions have been meticulously collected, edited, annotated, and published by his students and admirers—so precious, so rare and so revered is every trace of his significance as a scholar. So when we mention the name of Allamah Qazvini, generation after generation of Iranian scholar stand up in reverence of the mighty memory of his unsurpassed excellence as a learned man. This all by way of a brief introduction, so we know whose authority we are about to witness.[136]

Qazvini spent two years in London and then in June 1906 left London for Paris. He spent nine years in Paris and a year after the onset of World War I, on 23 October 1915, he left Paris for Berlin, at the invitation of a close friend, Hossein Qoli Khan Nawwab, who had just been appointed Iranian ambassador to Germany. Qazvini wished to visit German libraries and meet with German scholars, but because of the war, his journey to Germany became a four-and-a-half-year sojourn. Qazvini lived in Berlin, until the end of the war, and then in January 1920, he returned to Paris again, where he remained until 1939 and the commencement of World War II, at which time he finally decided he had seen enough of European wars and went back to Iran. Between 1906 and 1939, Qazvini spent more than thirty years in Europe.[137] Throughout his sojourn in Europe, the singular abiding preoccupation of Qazvini was to visit libraries, read manuscripts, produce critical editions, and meet with prominent European Orientalists. In the short autobiographical account that he wrote and published, Qazvini proudly mentions the names of all the major European Orientalists he met in London, Paris, and Berlin. He mentions such Orientalists as E. G. Browne (1862-1926), whom he dearly loved and admired, and A. A. Bevan, whom he describes as a "specialist in Arabic literature . . . in this field very few people are his match . . . exquisitely learned, and in his work he exercises an astounding degree of precision, caution, even finicky-ness." The same story is repeated in Paris, where he met with the leading French Orientalists, including Barbier de Meynard (d. 1908), Clément Huart (d. 1926), and G. J. E. Blochet (1870-1937). When he went to Berlin, he did the same, and met with Joseph Marquart (1864-1930) and Karl Eduard Sachau (1845-1930), among other prominent German Orientalists. In Berlin his only regret was that he did not have a chance to meet Theodore Nöldeke (1836-1930), "despite my sincere hope to meet him. But at this time he was living in Strasbourg and I was in Berlin, and during the war traveling between cities was quite difficult."[138]

It is important to take note of Qazvini's own scholarly achievements and his explicit admiration for prominent Orientalists of his generation so that some seventy years before Edward Said he too is not dismissed as a dilettante in Orientalist scholarship, or engaged in obscure French theories (there was not a single theoretical bone in Qazvini's scholarship, and he was, in fact, quite antipathetic towards theory. He was a straight-arrow textual critic of unsurpassed precision and diligence). It is this very same Allamah Qazvini, who gave the following assessment of European Orientalism in general:

> Now that I have mentioned these Orientalists, I would not consider it entirely inappropriate if at the end of this [autobiographical] essay I were to mention this final point, which I have learned from my own experiences. The point is this: My dear fellow countrymen should know that in Europe and among the Orientalists the number of fake and would be scholars, and indeed charlatans, is infinitely more than the number of genuine Orientalists and real scholars. Although this is perhaps generic to all humanity, and in every field of knowledge and science, and as such is not exclusive to European Orientalists alone, but nevertheless, in the case of European Orientalists the domain of this problem has an unbelievable expansion. The reason for this, perhaps, is that, as the French proverb has it, "in the land of the blind, the man with one eye is the king." Because of the European public ignorance at large, concerning the issues of the Orient, and the languages and sciences of the Orient, then naturally the field of Orientalism has become a vast and ready domain for imposters and charlatan—people who as soon as they acquire a preliminary knowledge of a couple of Oriental languages, and pass an exam in them, which in most cases those who examine are more illiterate than those are being examined, then by hook or by crook they become a teacher of Oriental languages. At this point the instruction of these languages, and in fact the teaching of a few other languages as well, and all at the same time—such as Persian, Arabic, Turkish, and all the arts and sciences that have been produced in those languages, as well as all the various and innumerable dialects of those languages—all and all are entrusted to these Orientalists.[139]

This is so far as Qazvini's general assessment of Orientalists is concerned. Now, what does he think of their scholarship? Here is what he says:

> These Orientalists then proceed, without the slightest sense of shame or fear of being scandalized, for there is no one to tell, to claim knowledge and authority in all these languages and the arts and sciences written in them, teaching them, publishing books and articles about them, and even coming out with their own new and specific ideas about them. Occasionally these people take a few innocent books in Persian, Arabic, or Turkish, thoroughly distort them, and proceed to publish them, full of blatant mistakes. This is not the case about Latin and Greek languages at all, for the European public at large more or less knows about these languages. So because they might be exposed in public, those who know

> these languages never dare to make such claims, not even one tenth of such claims. They only speak of their own field of specialization in a very small branch of those two languages, and would not dare to utter a word beyond their area of competence.[140]

As to Qazvini's recommendation:

> My point is that my dear fellow countrymen should not be fooled by such authoritative-sounding titles as "Professor of Oriental Languages," or "Member of Such-and Such Society or Academy," and should not accept blindly any nonsense that comes from Europe, signed by such non-entities, without first subjecting it to critical judgment. Their assessments should not be considered as divine revelation, and you must use your divinely endowed reason, which is the sole measure of distinguishing between truth from falsehood, along with the knowledge you have acquired, in everything. Gauge everything with that measure, so that you can distinguish between the right and the wrong path, between the learned guide and the misguided fool.[141]

Qazvini wrote these words on 14 November 1924, based on his experiences accumulated over the preceding two decades in Europe and with European Orientalists. These are the words of a scholar who admires, and considers it an honor to have even met prominent European Orientalists. He has no political axe to grind. He is not Palestinian. The state of Israel is not yet established. He is neither a Zionist nor an anti-Zionist. Postmodernism, poststructuralism, and deconstruction are terms yet to be invented decades after Qazvini made these observations, years after he had died. None of the crowded and crowding issues that subsequently coagulated to confuse the principled questions raised by Edward Said in *Orientalism* are anywhere in sight, nor does Qazvini present his case against these "charlatans," as he calls them, in the theoretically sophisticated language of Edward Said. He simply provides an eyewitness account of a legendary scholar on what he thought of Orientalism and its practitioners except the handful he exempts and mentions specifically by name—and these do not all add up to even two dozen in all of Europe (exactly sixteen scholars altogether). Major European Orientalists whom Qazvini thought were "charlatans" include such luminaries as Louis Massignon and Henri Massé. He accused these and other Orientalists like them of having "phantasmagoric conjectures, illusory theses, drug-induced illusions, and opium-assisted gibberish," as he put it in a letter he wrote to a prominent Iranian literati and close friend (Seyyed Hassan Taqizadeh), on Sunday 30 December 1923—Orientalists who Qazvini thought "after one or two years of studies claim to know all the languages and sciences of the East—claiming not only to understand them but in fact venturing to come up with their own autonomous opinions and ideas and laughable conjectures, all against the common consensus of all Muslims, and the origin of which is nothing but the ignorance of Muslim habits, customs, sciences, and traditions—facts that in Muslim countries not just every simple student of religious seminaries but in fact even pious old women know."[142]

Qazvini's view of Orientalism, uttered at the height of its epistemic power and contemporaneous with the best European scholars that the discipline had generated, is not exclusive to him, and is, in fact, representative of the most learned of his generation of Iranian scholars and literati and those who came later. Hossein Kazemzadeh Iranshahr (1884-1962), yet another major literary intellectual who was a contemporary of Qazvini and shared much of his experiences in Europe, particularly in Berlin where they were together during World War I, published an exceedingly important journal in Berlin (in Persian), called *Iranshahr*. In the very first issue of this influential journal, dated 26 June 1922, Iranshahr published a short essay that he called "Orientalism and Occidentalism." In this essay (again published half a century before Edward Said's *Orientalism*—effectively corroborating his theoretical observations with eyewitness accounts), Iranshahr begins by telling his readers how over the last "two or three centuries" a discipline called "Orientalism" has been generated in Europe.[143] Iranshahr traces the origin of this discipline to European travelers and adventurers who used to write their travelogues and inform their countrymen of what they had seen and witnessed. Originally, Iranshahr suggests, these accounts were in fact read as works of fantasies, and indeed, "many of these works did not have much else to offer." Then Iranshahr writes:

> But later, when European countries expanded the domain of their colonial possessions and conquered much of Oriental lands, the significance and influence of these sorts of [Orientalist] writings became far more powerful. European governments who needed to know about the habits, ethics, as well as the political, economic, and social conditions and organizations of the Orientals began to pay closer attention to these travelers and their works. For this reason, they began also to establish in their capitals Orientalist schools and societies, encouraging the Orientalists and promoting Orientalist journals and periodicals.[144]

Thus, about half a century before Edward Said, Kazem Zadeh Iranshahr clearly and concisely saw and articulated the link between colonialism and Orientalism. To be sure, he did not have Edward Said's theoretical sophistication in arguing the organic link between the epistemic foregrounding of Orientalist knowledge production and the colonial power that engendered it, for in fact Michel Foucault was not even born yet (the first issue of *Iranshahr* in which this article appears is dated 26 June 1926; Michel Foucault was born a few months later on 15 October 1926) to spend a lifetime of his scholarship discovering and articulating that link, from which then Edward Said borrowed and proceeded with his own version of the idea. But the essence of the idea, the connection between colonialism and Orientalism, following in the footsteps of European travelers and adventurers and their Oriental fantasies they created, foretells Edward Said's very table of content in *Orientalism* almost chapter by chapter—fifty years before Said put pen to paper and wrote *Orientalism*.

Upon this premise, Iranshahr then proceeds to tell his readers how by his time the domain of Orientalism had vastly expanded and there were now Orientalists specializing in various fields as Egyptologists, Arabists, Iranists, Sinologists, Armenialogists, etc. Despite his acute political alertness, Iranshahr is not an anti-Orientalist and like Qazvini acknowledges the service that European Orientalists have in fact provided the world of scholarship. So in order to be fair, he reminds his readers that the beneficiaries of the work of these Orientalists have not been just the "political interests," as he puts it, of the Orientalists' respective countries. The Orientalists have indeed, Iranshahr believes, done a wonderful job of discovering the most detailed aspects of these countries, so much so that "for centuries the Orientals themselves need to benefit and follow the Orientalists and learn their methodology as the exemplary model of scholarship."[145] It is imperative to place Iranshahr's insight into the link between colonialism and Orientalism, outlined half a century before Edward Said's theories and scholarship, in the context of his appreciation of Orientalism so he too cannot be dismissed as an "anti-Western," "pro-Islamic fundamentalist," "Palestinian activist," "Professor of terror," who just did not appreciate the finer points of Orientalist scholarship. If anything, Iranshahr and his colleagues in Berlin, particularly their patron Seyyed Hasan Taqizadeh (1878-1969), were the staunchest supporters of the so-called "Westernization" in Iran. Taqizadeh, the principal benefactor of Kazemzadeh and scores of other expatriate Iranian intellectuals who gathered in Berlin during World War I to publish *Kaveh*, another extraordinary journal advocating the cause of "modernization" in Iran, is famous in modern Iranian history for having said, "From the top of the head to the tip of the toe, Iranians must become European."[146] So none of these people can be accused of any ill will towards "the West," or even of having a strong political position on colonialism. They have simply recorded what they thought of Orientalists and Orientalism.

Iranshahr's concluding remark in this short essay is to suggest (anticipating in this respect too Edward Said's repeated insistence) that people in "the East" should also start creating a discipline of

"Occidentalism," in which they will study "the social, political, literary, economic, industrial, and technical aspects of Western nations."[147]

The combined effect of Qazvini and Iranshahr's critic of Orientalism, both in scholarly and political terms (representative of a wider constituency of Iranian scholars and coming from people who are pronouncedly appreciative of the best that the discipline has produced) anticipates Edward Said's much later, and much more theoretically cogent, critic and should once and for all eradicate the false assumption that before Edward Said's *Orientalism* there was no problem with this mode of knowledge production or that scholars were unaware of its systematic services to colonialism—and above all emancipate the domain of criticism from personal politics and *ad hominem* battles between Edward Said and his political adversaries. One can, of course, expand on these precursors of Edward Said and point to the works of scholars like Anwar Abdel Malek ("Orientalism in Crisis," 1963) and Jacques Waardenburg (*L'Islam dans le miroir de l'Occident*, 1963),[148] which, of course, Edward Said knew and cited in his *Orientalism*—or even to Raymond Schwab's *Oriental Renaissance* (1950), for the English translation of which Said wrote a highly appreciative introduction.[149] The point is neither to diminish the rightful significance of Edward Said's *Orientalism* as a monumental text of universal significance, nor indeed to detract from its far superior theoretical apparatus—but in fact to accentuate it, bring it out to the fore and rescue it from entirely tangential political and *ad hominem* issues before we read the work of any prominent Orientalist like Goldziher against the background of the cogent and powerful argument that Said put forward in *Orientalism*. It is imperative to note that observers whom neither Said knew nor they could have known Said or read his *Orientalism*, quite independent of him were severely critical of the Orientalist project, to the point of calling the overwhelming majority of them illiterate "charlatans." This is not what Said says. He in fact is exceedingly appreciative of the scholarly output of the Orientalists. Said's issue centers around the question of "representation"—who represents whom and by what authority and power, and thus knowledge is produced predicated on what tacit epistemic assumptions? But yet, observations that scholars like Qazvini and Iranshahr make expand the domain of a critical perspective towards Orientalism beyond an *ad hominem* exchange between Edward Said and his political nemeses.

* * *

Beyond this expansion and the clarification of the argument of Edward Said in *Orientalism*, we need also to see what Said specifically says about Ignaz Goldziher himself. In *Orientalism*, Edward Said makes three specific references to Goldziher, and they are as follows: The first reference is when Said effectively admits his own shortcomings in not having covered German Orientalism. "Any work that seeks to provide an understanding of academic Orientalism," Said says, "and pays little attention to scholars like Steinthal, Müller, Becker, Goldziher, Brockelmann, Nöldeke—to mention only a handful—needs to be reproached, and I freely reproach myself. I particularly regret not taking more account of the great scientific prestige that accrued to German scholarship by the middle of the nineteenth century, whose neglect was made into a denunciation of insular British scholars by George Eliot."[150] Said then proceeded to provide a perfectly persuasive explanation for this neglect—first because Germany never had a *national* interest in the Orient, and second because despite this absence of colonial concerns (like the French and the British Orientalism), the German Orientalism did project "a kind of intellectual authority over the Orient within Western cultures,"[151] namely the exclusion of German Orientalism was theoretically explainable without exempting it from Said's more general critic of European Orientalism, which is to say he implicated German Orientalism, and quite rightly so, in his general critique of the discipline, while providing something of an explanation as to why he had excluded it, and yet still confessing that there is lacunae in his coverage. Be that as it may, what Said is saying specifically about Goldziher is a confession of the limitation of his coverage, but phrased in a way that does not altogether discredit his observations—and he is (as I will soon explain) perfectly correct in that suggestion.

The second time Said refers to Goldziher in *Orientalism* is in the context of his discussion of the objectification of "the Orient," the "Orientals," and thus the systematic ignorance, for example, of national liberation movements in the former colonies, a theme that Said picks up from Anwar Abdel Malek and expands. Here Said says,

> The Orientalists—from Renan to Goldziher to Macdonald to von Grunebaum, Gibb, and Bernard Lewis—saw Islam, for example, as "cultural synthesis" . . . that could be studied apart from the economics, sociology, and politics of the Islamic peoples. For Orientalism, Islam had a meaning which, if one were to look for its most succinct formulation, could be found in Renan's first treatise: in order best to be understood Islam had to be reduced to "tents and tribe."[152]

Whatever the accuracy of this assertion might be about the other Orientalists (and it certainly is accurate about Bernard Lewis), it is not entirely applicable to Goldziher. The distinguishing factor of Goldziher as an Islamist was in fact his particular attention to social and political factors in the course of the historical developments of Islam, not only as evident in the pages of his *Muslim Studies*, but throughout the rest of his work, particularly his Qur'anic, *Tafsir* (Qur'anic exegesis), and legal scholarship. Ironically, Goldziher is in fact severely criticized by Muslim scholars, especially by Muslim Hadith scholars, for having too much historicized—subjected to social and political factors—the development of their sacred lore.[153] In addition, Goldziher was acutely aware of the most recent developments in the Islamic world, had traveled there, and wrote about such revolutionary movements as Wahabism and Babism with a combination of critical appreciation and extensive analytical detail. As evidenced in the pages of his travelogue to Syria, Palestine, and Egypt, he in fact participated in street demonstrations against European colonialism and refused to have anything to do with (and in fact opposed) Zionism—so he certainly cannot be accused of either ignoring social and political issues or reducing Islam to "tents and tribes." But to be fair to Said, neither Goldziher's *Tagebuch* (1978) nor his *Travelogue* (1987) was available to him when he was writing *Orientalism* (1978)—though the two volumes of Goldziher's *Muslim Studies* (1966 and 1970) and other works, evidence of Goldziher's detailed attention to social and political factors in the development of Islam, were indeed available, as was his *Richtungen der islamischen Koranauslegung* (1920), another major indication of Goldziher's attention to social and political factors in the historical developments of Qur'anic hermeneutics (the *tafasir*).

Be that as it may, there is an element of truth to what Said observes even about Goldziher, namely the disciplinary and epistemic self-sufficiency of Orientalism as a mode of knowledge production, in which Orientalists rarely paid any attention to adjacent disciplines or learned from their methodologies and discoveries. The one work in which Goldziher did pay attention to the theories of myth advanced by Max Müller is his study of Hebrew Bible, *Der Mythos bei den Hebräern (Mythology among the Hebrews)*, cost him dearly in the course of his academic career. As we noted earlier, his contemporaries were utterly scandalized by it, in effect costing him a prominent position that had opened in the Rabbinical Seminary of Budapest, for it had offended the religious sensibility of powerful men in positions to deny him that job.[154] Even earlier in his life, when as a precocious teenager (merely twelve years old) Goldziher published his *Sihat Yitzhaq* ("Isaac's Discourse")—Yitzhaq being his Hebrew name—on the historical origin and gradual development of Jewish prayers, people began to call him, by way of an insult and accusation, that he was a "freethinker" and a "Spinozist."[155] So both in epistemic terms domestic to the discipline of Orientalism and in terms of the social conditions that prevented an Islamist or a scholar of Judaism to venture into uncharted theoretical and methodological domains, Goldziher was very much the creature of his own time—though being a European and writing about Islam gave him a freer hand in applying a vigorous historical analysis to Islamic intellectual history, a feat denied him when it came to Judaic studies because of severe and immediate professional consequences.

One has to also consider that much of the disciplinary formations of sociology, anthropology, political science or economics were in their nascent stages as Goldziher was writing. Said's expectation that Goldziher should have paid attention to "the economics, sociology, and politics of the Islamic peoples" must be balanced by what was available to him from an intellectual history perspective, for by the time that Goldziher was writing, say between his first publication, the very same *Sihat Yitzhaq*, in 1862 and his death in 1921, the disciplines of sociology, anthropology, economics, and political science were very much in their nascent, formative, and mostly positivistic phases. Karl Marx (1818-1883), Max Weber (1864-1920), and Emile Durkheim (1857-1917), as the three major founding figures of social sciences were, of course, contemporaries or near-contemporaries of Goldziher, but he could not have known their works and been creatively conversant with them while engaged in his own scholarship, when even Max Weber did not know of Emile Durkheim's *Les Formes élémentaires de la vie religieuse: le système totémique en Australie* (1912) when he was writing his own *Religionssoziologi Typen der religiösen Vergemeinschaftung* as part of his monumental *Wirtschaft und Gesellschaft* (1921-1922)—and in fact Weber's and Durkheim's respective sociology in general developed quite independent of each other.[156] Although Said's criticism is, of course, perfectly appropriate when it comes to the later Orientalists and their systematic ignorance of these disciplines, which could have complicated their conception of Islamic history but of course did not, one must still keep the contemporaneous formations of these disciplines in mind. As it pertains to the Goldziher's generation of Orientalists, it is not just the question of awareness of the discoveries and discussions among social scientist, but (and here Edward Said is, of course, absolutely correct) the disciplinary self-sufficiency of Orientalism that prevented the Orientalists from looking outside their own discipline.

In short, Goldziher was aware of and attentive to social and political factors while writing on various aspects of Islam, but not to the degree of being conversant with the disciplinary methodologies in the fields of economics, sociology, or political science, in part because these disciplines were very much in process of being systematically articulated at the time, and also in part because Orientalism was, by and large, a self-sustained mode of scholarly operation—which is of course the whole point of Said's criticism.

The third and final time that Said refers to Goldziher in *Orientalism* is in the context of his discussion of how "widely diffused notions of the Orient depended on . . . the almost total absence in contemporary

Western culture of the Orient as a genuinely felt and experienced force." "For a number of evident reasons," Said adds, "the Orient was always in the position both of outsider and of incorporated weak partner for the West." Here the point of Said's argument is to show how in the manufacturing of the Orient, the Orientalist is the "superior judge, learned man, powerful cultural will," while the Orient itself "is all absence," and that in fact "the Orientalist's presence is enabled by the Orient's effective absence." These are all instrumental and exceedingly poignant arguments for Said in order to show how the Orientalist is in fact dialectically cornered into reducing the Orient

> in his work, even after he has devoted a good deal of time to elucidating and exposing it. How else can we explain major scholarly production, of the type we associate with Julius Wellhausen and Theodore Nöldeke and, overriding it, those bare, sweeping statements that almost totally denigrate their chosen subject matter? Thus Nöldeke could declare in 1887 that the sum total of his work as an Orientalist was to confirm his 'low opinion' of the Eastern people.' And like Carl Becker, Nöldeke was a philhellenist, who showed his love of Greece curiously by displaying a positive dislike of the Orient, which after all was what he studied as a scholar.[157]

It is at this point that Said refers to Jacques Waardenburg's *L'Islam dans le miroir de l'Occident* (1963), and relies on his report in order to assert that "Ignaz Goldziher's appreciation of Islam's tolerance towards other religions was undercut by his dislike of Mohammad's anthropomorphisms and Islam's too-exterior theology and jurisprudence"—and after similar observations about the paradoxical views of a few other Orientalists, Said concludes that "the manifest differences in their methods emerge as less important than their Orientalist consensus on Islam: latent inferiority."[158]

As in the previous cases, whatever the accuracy of these particular observations about other Orientalists, initially articulated by Waardenburg and followed by Said, might be (and they certainly are about Theodore Nöldeke and Carl Becker), their application to Goldziher is incorrect and unfair. To be sure, Said's initial observations about the epistemic disposition of Orientalism in general remains meticulously correct. Here, Said is at his absolute theoretical best, dissecting, as he does, the normative constitution of the Orientalist as historical agent, and the simultaneous withdrawal of that agency from "the Orientals," thus epistemically constituted. But the veracity of that theoretical observation is entirely independent of what Waardenburg and, by extension, Said have to say about Goldziher, which remains categorically false.

To begin with, the assumption that no scholar should have a critical perspective towards the subject of his or her scholarship is patently wrong. Goldziher, like any other scholar, not only can but should have a legitimately critical angle on any aspect of the subject to which he has devoted his life. Second, the assumption, implicit in Said's point here to be sure, that the problem with Orientalism was that Orientalists had an unsympathetic perspective on Islam is equally flawed. Some of the worst Orientalists, completely and specifically at the service of colonialism, absolutely adored Islam and had an entirely uncritical and romantic take on Arabs and Muslims. Third, if anything, Goldziher had too much of a sympathetic perspective on Islam, much to the chagrin of people like Raphael Patai, who raised even religious issues as to the propriety of his having devoted his life to a sympathetic understanding of Islam.

We now come to the specific question of Goldziher's "dislike of Mohammad's anthropomorphisms and Islam's too-exterior theology and jurisprudence." Here, Waardenburg (and by extension Said) are entirely wrong in their reading of Goldziher, for the following reasons: first, as a contested issue, the question of anthropomorphism is endemic to Islamic theology in general and from its very inception, dividing the Mu'tazilites and the Ash'arites and wreaking havoc in both theological and juridical terms on Muslim intellectual history—a long (very long) time before Goldziher or the entire field of Orientalism attended to it. Goldziher vicariously participates in this long (and rather exquisite) theological debate, and is perfectly entitled to take one side or another; second, the entire body of Goldziher's work on Islamic theology and jurisprudence is, in fact, argued in terms drawn from *within* Islamic theological and jurisprudential schools themselves. If Goldziher has prejudices, he has, in effect, "Islamic" prejudices, namely Sunni prejudices, for example, against Shi'ism. But these are all indices of his having completely identified with Islamic intellectual history and with Muslim scholars in particular. It is a fact of Goldziher's intellectual legacy that as a pious, believing, and practicing Jew he very much saw himself as a "Muslim scholar," but not in a flimsy and romantic way, and, in fact, directly from the heart of his Judaism. He believed (and repeatedly asserted that) the Islamic intellectual history was simply superior to any other religious intellectual history known to him, and the only one that could "satisfy philosophical minds."[159] One can even go so far as to argue that Goldziher saw something "Jewish" in Islamic intellectual history, as an intellectual potential of Judaism that was more realized in Islam than in Judaism. His decision to work on Islamic intellectual history, rather than his own (of which he was perfectly capable), was in fact an intellectual choice, not a career decision. For Goldziher, "the East" was no career, as Benjamin Disraeli

(1804-1881) had put it in his *Tancred* and Said quotes him appropriately at the very outset of his *Orientalism*. For Goldziher, "the East" was positively detrimental to his career, an anti-career, a very bad career choice. He would have had a far more comfortable professional career if, like his friend Wilhelm Bacher whom he deeply admired, he had devoted his life to a judicious and perfectly neutral study of Judaism, or like Armenius Vámbéry, whom he distinctly despised, had put his infinitely superior knowledge of Islam at the service of British Empire. To this day, and as evidenced by the "psychological portrait" Raphael Patai has written on him, studying Islam was a hazardous decision for an intellectually honest and morally principled man, placing him at the mercy of men infinitely inferior to his monumental stature who turn him into a psychological freak—precisely because he thought of himself as the historical partner of Muslim scholars engaged with exquisite moral and philosophical issues. Goldziher did not create the question of anthropomorphism in Islamic theology. It existed long before he studied it—and he had absolutely every right to agree or disagree with it, and Goldziher's position on anthropomorphism, one way or another, is not the issue that was with Orientalism.

That brings us to the most unfair and entirely inaccurate assessment of Said himself, that Goldziher shared the other Orientalists' belief in the "latent inferiority" of Islam. By now it must be quite evident that this is exactly the opposite of what Goldziher actually believed. So far as Christianity is concerned, Goldziher detested it with a vengeance, calling it an "abominable religion, which invented the Christian blood libel, which puts its own best sons to the rack."[160] He thought only Christianity was capable of missionary activities, for "this is an insolence of which only Christianity, the most abominable of all religions, is capable."[161] So far as a comparison between Islam to Christianity is concerned, Goldziher believed, "Islam signifies a mighty advance in relation to Christianity."[162] As for the intellectual disposition of Christianity, Goldziher thought Christianity "has no forehead to become aware of the insolence that forms its historical character. The forehead of a whore, that is the forehead of Christianity."[163] So much for Christianity! As for Judaism, we just saw how Raphael Patai skewered Goldziher for being too critical not only of his contemporary coreligionists and detesting the fact that he had to do a secretarial job at the Israelite Congregation of Pest, but for being entirely dismissive (to the point of revulsion) of the *formal* (certainly not doctrinal, prophetic, or devotional) aspects of his contemporary Judaism, for running away from synagogues in order to save his own faith. To be sure, Goldziher remained a pious and practicing Jew to his dying day (the supreme sign of the dignity and nobility of his character). But in no shape or form did he believe that Judaism was "superior" to Islam. Quite to the contrary—

"I truly entered in those weeks," as he reminisced about his sojourn to Muslim lands, "into the spirit of Islam to such an extent that ultimately I became inwardly convinced that I myself was a Muslim and judiciously discovered that this was the only religion which, even in its doctrinal and official formulation, can satisfy philosophical minds. My ideal was to elevate Judaism to a similar rational level. Islam, my experience taught me, was the only religion in which superstition and pagan elements were proscribed, not by rationalism but by the Orthodox doctrine."[164]

How can we accuse the man who wrote these sentences of having a consensus with those who believed in the "latent inferiority" of Islam? Goldziher was so profoundly pro-Islamic (without losing his scholarly perspective on it, of course), that his own co-religionists consider him of having been "infatuated with Islam" and "suffered from an acute anti-Jewish complex." The facts of Goldziher's thoughts, ideas, and scholarship do not corroborate Waardenburg/Said's specific assertions. Goldziher is at once accused of being "infatuated by Islam" and then of believing in "latent inferiority" of Islam. He could not have been both, for he was neither. He was neither infatuated with Islam nor did he believe it to be an inferior religion. He thought it one of the greatest religions and civilizations the world had experienced, without either converting to it or else losing his scholarly distance from it—and yet none of these false attributes to Goldziher clear him from the principle criticism of Edward Said in *Orientalism*, which survive these minor mistakes and remains solidly valid. The question is how.

* * *

Once the principle argument of Edward Said in *Orientalism* is cleared of any false *ad hominem* supposition and cast back to its substantive thesis, and his specific references to Goldziher' scholarship evaluated and balanced, what still remains solidly valid and perfectly legitimate is the principal point of his suggestion, that there is a structural correspondence between Orientalism as a disciplinary mode of knowledge production and European colonialism. That central argument, after whatever modifications one may make about specific examples Said has provided, still remains legitimate, for there are plenty of other examples that abound in his book and that along with the consistency, logic, and reasoned premise of his theory still demand attention, and against which one has to measure the specific work of Ignaz Goldziher. Goldziher *was* an Orientalist, the European founding figure in fact of the Orientalist study of Islam. So what Said says in *Orientalism* must still be tallied against Goldziher's life achievements. In fact, towards the end of his references to Goldziher through Waardenburg, Said implicates (without naming him but including him among the five

Orientalists that Waardenburg had studied) Goldziher in having "shaped a coherent vision of Islam that had a wide influence on government circles throughout the Western world," and that as such they were bringing to completion the earlier Orientalist practices beyond a "literary problem" and towards "un ferme propos d'assimiler adéquatement la valeur des langues pour pénétrer les mœurs et les pensées, pour forcer même des secrets de l'histoire."[165] To the degree that Goldziher was an Orientalist he did, in fact, contribute to the production of a system of knowledge that was subject to that political abuse. But would that earn Goldziher the same criticism that he applied to his friend Wilhelm Bacher, that "without being dishonorable, he could adapt his spirit to the dominant trends, of which in the course of time he became a factor?"[166] The answer is certainly not, for Goldziher adapted his spirit to no dominant trend—for he was breathing in it, too close to it to see it, and that is where the more principled criticisms of Edward Said in *Orientalism*, beyond specific examples and *ad hominem* errata, remains thoroughly valid.

The principle reason that the main thesis of Edward Said's *Orientalism* is not in any shape or form compromised by any specific examples that he may have provided and that they do not survive the test of closer examination is not merely the ample alternative examples that support it, nor is it merely due to the internal cohesion and consistency of the argument that he persuasively formulates, but above all because it is deeply rooted in a mighty intellectual tradition from which it has emerged—namely the extended body of literature in the *sociology of knowledge*. Here, Said's *Orientalism* has much suffered not just because of its opponents but also from some of its strongest supporters, both of whom have left this powerful intellectual tradition by and large out of their responses to Said. Here it is important to keep in mind that the theoretical tradition from which Edward Said himself worked out his argument in *Orientalism* is rather eclectic—borrowing from a diverse group of theorists, ranging from Michel Foucault (the relation between knowledge and power in the formation of a *discourse*), predicated on Antonio Gramsci (the relation between power and ideology in the formation of *hegemony*), and then wedded to Friedrich Nietzsche (the relation between metaphor and representation in the formation of *truth*). Said's extraordinary task was to bring these three theorists together and have them coagulate around the central problem of *representation.*[167] The problem with Orientalism for Said was thus a problem of *representation* (and by extension the thorny issue of *the soverign subject*), a much larger literary-theoretical issue, which now Said brought to bear on the specific case of *Orientalism*. In his own words: "The Orient that appears in Orientalism, then, is a system of representation framed by a whole set of forces that brought the Orient into Western learning, Western consciousness, and later, Western empire;"[168] or as he put it years later, towards the end of his life, "I recall quite emphatically making a similar set of points in my book *Orientalism*, when I criticized the representations of the Orient and Orientals by Western experts. My critique was premised on the flawed nature of all representations . . . ."[169] Though much less pronounced in the pages of *Orientalism* than elsewhere, Said's preoccupation with the question of *representation* is also rooted in his lifelong fascination and identification with Erich Auerbach's notion of *estrangement* in his highly influential book *Mimesis*,[170] which both Auerbach and Said thought were instrumental in gaining a greater insight (thus overcoming the problem of *representation*) not just into one's scholarly subject matter but also into the scholar's own culture—with the only critical stipulation being that

> one of the striking differences between Orientalism in the Islamic version and all the other humanistic disciplines where Auerbach's notions on the necessity of estrangement have some validity is that Islamic Orientalists never saw their estrangement from Islam either as salutary or as an attitude with implications for better understanding of their own culture. Rather, their estrangement from Islam simply intensified their feelings of superiority about European culture, even as their antipathy spread to include the entire Orient, of which Islam was considered a degraded (and usually, a virulently dangerous) representative.[171]

Said placed this problem of *representation* in the context of the larger issue of what he called *worldliness*. The significance and centrality of this idea in Said's work is not limited to *Orientalism*, and in fact finds its most succinct expressions in his other, mostly literary-critical, works, particularly the essay, "The World, the Text, the Critic" in his book of the same title.[172] This is how Said understood the notion of *worldliness*:

> The key word here is "worldly," a notion I have always used to denote the real historical world from whose circumstances none of us can in fact ever be separated, not even in theory. I recall quite emphatically making a similar set of points in my book *Orientalism*, when I criticized the representations of the Orient and Orientals by Western experts. My critique was premised on the flawed nature of all representations and how they are intimately tied up with worldliness, that is, with power, position, and interests. This required saying explicitly that my work was not intended as defense of the real Orient or that it even made the case that a real Orient existed. I certainly held no brief for the purity of some representations against others, and I was quite specific in suggesting that no process of converting experience into expression could be free of contamination.[173]

And indeed in his *Orientalism* Said specifically indicates that he is not arguing that there is a "real Orient" that Orientalists have failed to represent, but the problem he is articulating is in the very nature of *representation*. "The methodological failures of Orientalism," Said insists, "cannot be accounted for either by saying that the real Orient is different from Orientalist portraits of it, or by saying that since Orientalists are Westerners for the most part, they cannot be expected to have an inner sense of what the Orient is all about. . . . I certainly do not believe the limited proposition that only a black can write about blacks, a Muslim about Muslims, and so forth."[174]

Through the intellectual pedigree of Nietzsche, Gramsci, Auerbach, and above all Foucault, all synthesized and placed in Said's own articulation of the notion of *worldliness*, and then laser-beamed on the universal problem of *representation*, the central thesis of *Orientalism* was ultimately fused with Said's political punch to give it its global appeal: "If this definition of Orientalism [as representation of the Orient by the Orientalists]," he said, "seems more political than not, that is simply because I think Orientalism was itself a product of certain political forces and activities. Orientalism is a school of interpretation whose material happens to be the Orient, its civilizations, peoples, and localities."[175]

That particular intellectual pedigree informing Said's own insights into the direct epistemic and emotive links between Orientalism and colonialism gave *Orientalism* its unprecedented insights, theoretical prowess, global appeal, and political energy—and yet at the very same time delimited its serious readership, interpretations, and reception very much within a literary-critical body of idiomaticity—namely the enduring problem of *representation* and the barbed barrier of the *sovereign subject*—both of which preoccupied Edward Said to the very end and including his posthumously published book, *Humanism and Democratic Criticism* (2004). Putting the latter-day Orientalists' belligerent and theoretically illiterate response (best represented by Bernard Lewis') aside, Said's own intellectual heritage and subsequent readership are the principle reasons why James Clifford's critique of *Orientalism*—that its author himself while criticizing a particularly powerful mode of *representation* partook uncritically in the humanistic tradition of presuming an all-knowing and sovereign subject that can *represent* with authority—to this day remains the most cogent that it has received.[176] What Clifford was in effect saying was that Said takes from Foucault what he wants (dismantling *representation*) and then abandons him when Foucault becomes a theoretical troublemaker (disallows the critic to assume the authorial position of an omniscient narrator). Later in his life, Edward Said himself in fact agreed with Clifford's main point. "In many ways," Said concurred, "Clifford was right."[177] In other, more exasperated, moments, Said would lash out against such criticisms and say: "Among American and British academics of a decidedly rigorous and unyielding stripe," he says in his 1995 afterword to *Orientalism*, "*Orientalism*, and indeed all of my other work, has come in for disapproving attacks because of its "residual" humanism, its theoretical inconsistencies, its insufficient, perhaps even sentimental, treatment of agency. I am glad that it has! *Orientalism* is a partisan book, not a theoretical machine."[178] In other words, instead of Said not being Foucauldian enough in mistrusting agency, perhaps Foucault was not Saidian enough in allowing for political activism! But on a more consistent level with his enduring theoretical struggles against the question of *representation*, Said sought to overcome the problem of the sovereign subject not by yielding to its poststructuralist dismantling but in fact by going into the opposite direction and radically redefining and expanding humanism by what he called a "democratic criticism," namely the opening up the limited domain of European humanism to a wider range of humanisms, in plural, manifested globally in various literary cultures and humanistic traditions.[179]

An entirely different intellectual tradition from which Edward Said's *Orientalism* derives, and which in fact gives it far more cogency and authority, is that of sociology of knowledge, an aspect almost entirely absent from the critical reception of *Orientalism*. To be sure, the origin of this neglect is in *Orientalism* itself. Edward Said was not a sociologist. He was a literary critic, and it was basically, but not exclusively, as a literary critic that he sought to dismantle the central epistemic hold of Orientalism. To be sure, in *Orientalism*, Said makes a cursory reference to Robert K. Merton's *Sociology of Science* and his notion of "insider and outsider."[180] He also makes another fleeting reference to "Weber, Durkheim, Lukács, Mannheim, and other sociologists of knowledge," but here in the context of in fact taking Weber's notion of "ideal-type" to task.[181] Altogether it is quite clear from *Orientalism* that Said was only tangentially attentive to the long and illustrious tradition of sociology of knowledge and took the principal source of his theoretical insights from an entirely different tradition—from Foucault in particular.

The entirely implicit roots of Edward Said's *Orientalism* in the rich and powerful tradition of sociology of knowledge not only gives it added validity and momentum but posits the very discipline of Orientalism in an entirely different conundrum. Implicit in Said's *Orientalism* is the weight of an intellectual tradition that from Karl Marx to Karl Mannheim has sought to historicize the modes and manners of knowledge production in terms specific to social forces that have occasioned it. Given the major political and ideological diversity among the principle figures in the gradual articulation of sociology of knowledge it is impossible to dismiss the entire discipline as radical or conservative, Marxist or anti-Marxist—and in its entirety it was articulated by European social scientists themselves. The cumulative insights of the sociology of knowledge as a discipline are not something that theoretically illiterate Orientalists like Bernard Lewis and his cohorts can dismiss as whimsical "postmodernist" (as they call them) ideas and thus evade the fundamental dismantling of their discredited and bankrupt operations. What is common, in fact, to all the major theorists and schools of the sociology of knowledge is that their theoretical proposition concerning the social conditioning of knowledge production are far more radical in their implications than what Said had articulated in his *Orientalism*. The advantage (and brilliance) of Said's *Orientalism* is that it added a pronouncedly political impetus to those insights implicit in his book and then concentrated it on a specific historical case with profound consequences for global geopolitics—something that remained entirely dormant (and rather provincial in their reach, however universal in their theoretical implications) in the body of insights produced by sociologists of knowledge.

It is now imperative to remember that long before Michel Foucault (the principle theoretical source of Edward Said in *Orientalism*) began examining the relation between knowledge and power as embedded in various forms of discursive and institutional formations, Max Scheler (1874–1928) and Karl Mannheim (1893–1947) had articulated a major line of sociological inquiry into the modes and manners of the social production of knowledge—including (obviously) the question of power. If we come to Edward Said's *Orientalism* from this long and illustrious tradition of investigating the sociological roots of knowledge formation, it is impossible either to ignore its insights (because of its literary-critical origins) or else readily dismiss them as if it stood only on its own limited ground. A far more variegated and powerful intellectual tradition is at the root of (the rather modest) suggestions of Edward Said in *Orientalism*—suggestions that became radical and revolutionary in part because of the inordinate institutional power of those who were offended by *Orientalism*, and their vested interest was in a rather violent opposition to its suggestions.[182]

More than half a century before Edward Said wrote *Orientalism* (1978), Max Scheler's *Versuche zu einer Soziologie des Wissens* (Munich, 1924) had made far more radical proposition concerning the relationship between knowledge production and its sociological conditioning. The expanded argument of Max Scheler appeared two years later in his *Die Wissensformen und die Gesellschaft* (Leipzig, 1926).[183] A couple of years later, and quite independent of Max Scheler, in Karl Mannheim's masterpiece, *Ideologie und Utopie* (Bonn, 1929), we come across the proposition that social life and economic conditions have a catalytic effect on the nature and function of bodies of knowledge produced within their parameters. Two years later, Karl Mannheim published his groundbreaking essay, "Wissenssoziologie" (Stuttgart, 1931).[184] Both Max Scheler and Karl Mannheim were far more radical in their daring propositions, linking not just the substance but also the forms of knowledge to social forces, than Edward Said ever was in his *Orientalism*. "All human knowledge," declared Max Scheler as the very first axiom (his term) of the sociology of knowledge, "in so far as man is a 'member' of a society in general, is not empirical but '*a priori*' knowledge. The genesis of such knowledge shows that it *precedes* levels of self-consciousness and consciousness of one's self-value. There is no 'I' without a 'we.' The 'we' is filled with contents prior to the 'I.'"[185] This is decades before Foucault postulated the notion of *episteme*, which here in Scheler is simply called "a priori knowledge" that precedes empirical data. Another *axiom* of Scheler in his sociology of knowledge states that "there is a *fixed law that orders* the origin of our knowledge of reality, i.e., our knowledge of what generally 'brings about effects,' and orders the fulfillment of the individual spheres of knowledge, constant in human consciousness, and the correlative *spheres of objects*."[186] This is even longer before Edward Said posited his notion of *worldliness* as the condition that affects the Orientalists' production of knowledge. What Scheler calls "our knowledge of what generally brings about effects" is what in Said becomes the colonial condition of knowledge production. Similarly provocative proposals are evident in Karl Mannheim, who categorically theorized the principal function of the sociology of knowledge as "a theory of the social or existential determination of actual thinking," and thus sought to investigate the "social processes influencing the process of knowledge" and "the essential penetration of social process into the 'perspective' of thought."[187] All Edward Said's *Orientalism* does is an extension of these very principles into the global operation of colonialism and its Orientalist mode of knowledge production, concentrating on one particularly powerful and integral relation between the social (colonial) conditions in which a mode of knowledge (Orientalism) is presumed valid and set in motion.

The origin of Max Scheler and Karl Mannheim's own thoughts on the sociology of knowledge can easily be traced back, as it has been, to Karl Marx (1818–1883) and Friedrich Engels (1820–1895) and *The German Ideology* (1846)—and their elaborate argument concerning the structural link between specific class interests and the modes of knowledge (ideology) best compatible and conducive to them. "The production of ideas, of conceptions, of consciousness," Marx and Engels proposed more than a century before Edward Said wrote *Orientalism*, "is at first directly interwoven with the material activity and the material intercourse of men, the language of real life. Conceiving, thinking, the mental intercourse of men, appear at this stage as the direct efflux of their material behaviour."[188] This is infinitely more radical than a simple proposition that the knowledge that European colonialists were instrumental in producing, or conditioning to be produced, was at their immediate political and financial service. Marx, Engels, Scheler, and Mannheim demonstrated the foundational production of the very *a priori* structure of thinking, at a deep epistemic level, before even a producer of knowledge has put pen to paper. Edward Said's *Orientalism* is a particular example of these insights, generated by major thinkers generations in creative conversation with each other. The specific insights of *Orientalism*, as a result, cannot be readily dismissed as if Said wrote it whimsically just to settle his accounts with Bernard Lewis and other contemporary Orientalists with whom he was in political disagreement. Bernard Lewis and generations of Orientalists like him are simply not in the same league as these thinkers. One must by all means resist the temptation of taking issue with Said as to why instead of elaborating these profoundly important theoretical sources of his insights (that sustain and support his argument) he wasted so many precious pages on Bernard Lewis and his ilk, for it is precisely the immediate contemporaneity of the third chapter of *Orientalism*, "Orientalism Now," that made it so universally appealing, however it may have also made it theoretically wanting in more support.

There is another line of argument that can—quite independently of Marx, Engels, Scheler, and Mannheim—link the rise of the sociology of knowledge as a critical discipline of thought to the American social pragmatist George Herbert Mead (1863-1931).[189] There is yet another persuasive argument, linking Scheler's notion of "the powerlessness of the mind," to Mannheim's "homelessness of the mind," and connecting both to Georg Lukács' central concept of "reification of consciousness," and thus demonstrating the rise of the sociology of knowledge in Weimar Germany, between 1918 and 1933, and connecting it to the cultural and political crisis of Germany at the time.[190] Even longer traditions have been put forward articulating the relationship between modes of human existence and manners of thought and knowledge production, and can be traced back to Francis Bacon (1561-1626) and the French Enlightenment philosophers, or in Saint-Simon's (1760-1825) philosophy of history.[191] Once we come to Edward Said's *Orientalism* from this extraordinary body of critical literature, we see that there is really nothing particularly new or even radical about his theoretical proposition that there is a structural link between Orientalist manner of knowledge production and colonialism. This rather theoretically innocuous proposition—far less radical in its implications than, say, Mannheim's suggestion that all forms of knowledge and institutionalized beliefs are politically modulated—can indeed be linked not only to a major branch of the sociology of knowledge that through Max Scheler and Karl Mannheim is rooted in the works of Karl Marx, Emile Durkheim, and Max Weber,[192] but may in fact completely bypass Michel Foucault and trace its origin to Quentin Skinner's philosophical hermeneutics on political theory and the link that he proposes between social meaning and social action.[193] A similar argument can be made linking the argument of Said's *Orientalism* to an even more critical school of intellectual history, now best represented in the work of Dominick Lacapra.[194]

If we come to Edward Said's *Orientalism* from the angle of the sociology of knowledge, a number of critically corrective lenses will mitigate our reading of it: first, it will be cleared of all its tangential *ad hominem* implications as a polemic between him and his Orientalist adversaries and thus give more room, weight, and significance to the substance of his argument; second it will be rescued from its abusive readings by a populist brand of Arab and Muslim intellectuals who have taken it as a declaration of open season on "the West" (an empty abstraction that they, in fact, thus authenticate and corroborate), a misreading that Edward Said repeatedly sought to correct;[195] third it will provide *Orientalism* with a breathing space against its more serious critics like James Clifford who now need to tackle a much mightier intellectual tradition at the roots of its argument than its "residual humanism;"[196] and fourth it will also make it possible to distinguish between a remarkable man and prominent scholar like Ignaz Goldziher and a self-confessed spy like Arminius Vámbéry, while reading them in the epistemic limitations of a mode of scholarship they shared.

From this perspective, that as a manner of knowledge production Orientalism was deeply rooted in European project of colonialism (as best exemplified by Arminius Vámbéry) does not mean that all Orientalists were willing partners with colonialists, or that all their scholarship was (or is) suspect, or that some devilish European design was at the root of their scholarly project. None of these are contingent on Edward Said's thesis, and all of them are unintended and unexamined misreading of his book. As a scholarly project, Orientalism has produced some of the most magnificent works of scholarship, unsurpassed, at their best, to this day. Edward Said's criticism was directed against the *epistemic* origin of a disciplinary formation, irrespective of its individual results. No knowledge is possible, as entirely independent of Edward Said and long before him Thomas Kuhn had discovered and persuasively argued, except as articulated within a specific *epistemic* (or what Kuhn called *paradigmatic*) frame of reference.[197] What Kuhn considered "the priority of paradigms" in scientific discoveries, straight out of a long tradition of the sociology of knowledge, not only determine the sorts of questions raised, answers provided, and directions of even newer discoveries charted, but upon the exhaustion of the paradigm, Kuhn spoke of a "crisis" that occurs in the scientific discoveries that, in turn, result in a "paradigm change," which for him constituted the very mechanism of new scientific discoveries.[198]

The Orientalist paradigm of knowledge production was productive not only in terms of such paramount features of its epistemic operation as a primarily positivist mode of investigation, textual criticism, philological lineages, literary traditions, received and elaborated notions of canonicity (many of which were equally applied to Greek, Latin, and Biblical scholarship), but also in terms of the colonial relation of power between the discipline itself and its subjects of scholarship—and thus the necessary consolidation of "the Orient" as a knowable object for the Orientalist as a knowing subject. This epistemic aspect of Orientalism is quite independent of the fact that an Orientalist adventurer like Arminius Vámbéry was a bought and paid for spy for British colonialism while Goldziher was adamantly opposed to any kind of European colonialism. Both Vámbéry and Goldziher were operating within the same set of epistemic assumptions about "the Orient"—that it was a "thing," and that it was knowable, and that they were there to know it. So far as Orientalism as a mode of knowledge production is concerned, the individual differences between Vámbéry and Goldziher (morally and intellectually extremely important) is far less important than the fact that they shared the same set of not just identical research and analytical tools but also the same blind spots. But these blind spots (and there is the rub) are as much conducive to the production of that knowledge as the analytical parameter definitive to its creativity—to the degree that a scholar like Goldziher can be anti-colonial in his own personal politics, and still the language of his critical inquiry partakes in a colonially conditioned discourse. All his insights into Islamic intellectual history were contingent on the blind spot of not knowing that predicated on what set of epistemic assumptions and within what discursive formation he was producing them.

Even more concisely than Thomas Kuhn, it was Hans-Georg Gadamer who in his magnum opus *Warheit und Methode* (*Truth and Method*, 1960/1975) argued that understanding is made possible not despite but because of prejudices. Based on his reading of Heidegger's notion of the "fore-structure of understanding" (both similar to and articulated prior to Kuhn's *paradigm* and Foucault's *epistêmê*), Gadamer devoted an entire section of *Truth and Method* to "the problem of prejudice," and after a critical evaluation of the discrediting of "prejudice" by the Enlightenment, he proceeded to articulate it in fact as the very condition of understanding.[199] That Orientalists were prejudicially predisposed (in an imaginative not necessarily political term) towards the Orient that they had epistemically manufactured, as Edward Said persuasively argues and demonstrates, was also instrumental in making their understanding of the Orient possible and, as such, at the very root of the monumental body of scholarship they produced. One may, to give an entirely different example to make the point clear, take fundamental and epistemic issue with say a *mechanical* conception of human body in certain periods of medical science, and argue for the *organicity* of the human body. But that very mechanical conception of human bodily organs has been instrumental in major discoveries and progress in medical science. Rejecting and discrediting a *mechanical* conception of the human body and proposing its *organicity* certainly requires a radically new mode of medical knowledge production but it does not, ipso facto, dismiss or discredit the discoveries and services done within medical science while it operated under a mechanical assumption about human body. While the science of physics, as another example, operated under a Ptolemaic (geocentric) conception of the universe it created magnificent works of scientific discoveries. The Copernican revolution and the positing of a Heliocentric universe was a critical moment of what Kuhn calls a paradigmatic shift in physics, requiring a whole new mode and manner of mathematics and astrophysics, but the knowledge the physics as a science produced while operating under a geocentric assumption are simply superceded by a superior *epistêmê*, without any derogatory assumption about physicist who were still operating under a geocentric assumption.[200]

These examples from fields entirely different from Orientalism help to distinguish between the epistemic and the political dimensions of Orientalism. Long before Edward Said delivered his magnificent *coup de grace*, Orientalism had collapsed under the weight of its own narrative contradictions, or epistemic exhaustion, to be more accurate, of all its productive possibilities, to use the language common among Kuhn, Foucault, Claude Lévi-Straus, and all other post-structuralists. Said, more than anything else, was a post-structuralist in this sense, detecting an epistemic mode of knowledge production (particularly conducive to the European colonial project) and seeking to map out its blind spots, and given the political dimension of his project, its navigation through imperial and colonial *modus operandi*, his *Orientalism* assumed a global significance far beyond anything achieved by the (theoretically ambitious but thematically provincial) sociology of knowledge.

In every epistemic mode of knowledge production, blindness and insight are integral to each other and mutually productive of the minutest particulars of its very hermeneutic underpinning—which never remains constant or static. One of the most significant contributions of Edward Said's diagnosis of Orientalism is that he posited and diagnosed it as a living organism of knowledge production. After Said, it is now possible to make distinction among a variety of phases and mutations of Orientalisms, in plural, that are otherwise treated identically in his *Orientalism*. The Orientalism of the Greeks towards the Persians, for example, was an *Orientalism of enmity and rivalry*; that of Western Europeans towards the Ottomans was an *Orientalism of rivalry and fear*—both of which were categorically different from the *Orientalism of domination* that was coterminous with the rise of European colonialism and that Said first and foremost identified and diagnosed.[201] By the same token, by the time Edward Said published his *Orientalism* (1978), the discipline had pretty much exhausted its inner creative power, done its active or implicit services to European colonialism, produced some magnificent works of scholarship, completely run out of creative and critical energy, and had already begun its mutation (in correspondence with the global relations of power that had necessitated it) into what in the language of post-World War II Cold War was called "Area Studies"—for this reason, there is a noticeable difference between the first two and the last chapter of *Orientalism*, where Said traces the mutation of Orientalism into Area Studies.

One has to make, however, crucial distinctions among the various phases of Orientalism, before and after its by now classical case of the Orientalism of domination, the principal point of Said's investigation. There are significant differences between that Orientalism and Area Studies, for example. They are not identical in their nature and function. As Said's *Orientalism* has made it possible to see the variety of Orientalisms that preceded the Orientalism of colonial domination, it has also made it possible to see its subsequent mutations in the aftermath of the World War II. The Orientalism that Edward Said diagnosed and analyzed was an Orientalism of domination that best corresponded with the European age of industrial revolution and the colonial expansionism that was entirely contingent on it. This was an Orientalism that corresponded best with the invention of "the West" as the categorical imperative of the bourgeois revolutions in Europe. As a category, "the West" came to constitute the civilizational canopy that brought under its protection the European national economies, polities, and cultures. As the European national cultures—the British, the French, the German, etc—supplanted dynastic configurations and histories (and thus the very notion of "Europe" as a cultural category was invented), "the West" supplanted "Christendom" as the civilizational category that symbolically united these nations all together. The difference between "Christendom" and "the West" was that dynastic and ecclesiastical Christianity was taken out of the category and replaced with the European Enlightenment in order to manufacture "the Western Civilization." It was at this point that the army of mercenary Orientalists were dispatched to invent alternative civilizational categories—Islamic, Chinese, Indian, etc, and altogether "Oriental"—all in order to corroborate the anxiogeneric fabrication of an empty abstraction called "the West."[202] It was not just the European asylum houses that emerged to house the unreason, as Foucault argued and demonstrated in his *Madness and Civilization* (*Folie et déraison*) (1961/1965), but a much larger and exotic domain was needed to harbor that unreason for the European Enlightenment to be assured of its primacy of reason. "The Orient" was that larger asylum house of exoticism and unreason for "the Occident" to feel safe and secure in its illusions of sanity and reason (until the horrors of the Holocaust and the systematic genocide of the European Jewry shattered that dangerous delusion).

In the immediate aftermath of the World War II, the global geopolitics of power that had conditioned that kind of Orientalism radically changed, Europe became relatively tangential, and the U.S. and the USSR emerged as the polar opposites of two imperial claims to metanarratives of reason and progress. As a similar relations of power persisted, changed its shape from European colonialism into U.S. and USSR imperialisms, the Soviets went about creating their own version of Orientalism (quite competent and equally colonial in its blindness and insights), while in the US, Area Studies emerged as the site of security knowledge production about nations and cultures on the periphery of the Soviet Empire. If Orientalism of the European colonialism was in the business of manufacturing an Orient compatible with its colonial domination of the globe, Area Studies specialists were employed as the intelligence arm of the U.S. imperial rivalries with the USSR. By the time of the publication of Edward Said's *Orientalism*, old-fashioned European Orientalism had either mutated into disciplinary modes of knowledge production—sociology, anthropology, and political science in particular—or else delegated its erstwhile tasks to the realm of Area Studies. As a mode of knowledge production, Area Studies, now squarely at the service of U.S. imperial competition with the Soviet Union between the end of World War II in 1944 and the collapse of the Soviet Union in 1991, was producing knowledge about "the Orient" on a rather different mode of operation—and principally charged with preventing Soviet expansionism. If Orientalism was strategically oriented, Area Studies was far more policy-driven. Again, the specific case of Bernard Lewis, to whom Edward Said paid an inordinate and altogether distorting attention, was among the few old-fashioned European Orientalists who had lived long enough to link his services to the British colonialism to that of the U.S. imperialism. Perhaps if Edward Said had not allowed Bernard Lewis' specific and rather bizarre case to distort his vision, he would have theorized in more detail the radically changing epistemic operation of old-fashioned Orientalism and Area Studies, for by the time Said wrote *Orientalism*, classical Orientalism that Goldziher best represented had long since combined its blindness and insights, produced some magnificent works of scholarship, served (willingly or unwittingly) its colonial purposes, and its duties done, self-destructed—as all other paradigms and epistemes do: they never go with a bang; they go with a whimper.

With the collapse of the Soviet Union in 1991, the dissolution of the Eastern bloc, and the emergence of a monopolar U.S. Empire also ended the particular services provided by the Area Studies mutation of Orientalism. "The West" now no longer exists. It ended with the fall of the Berlin Wall. With the end of "the West" also ended all its binary oppositions, particularly "the Orient," all having dissolved into an amorphously globalized universe. "The West versus the Rest" is no longer the term of global operation of either the capital or the cultures it keeps producing to sustain its legitimacy—though the binary still persists in the perturbed imagination of ideologues like Samuel Huntington and Bernard Lewis, whom we now witness undergo a third level of mutation: from Orientalist to Area Studies specialist to active propagandist.[203] The instrumental function of Area Studies specialists effectively ended with the collapse of the Soviet Union and the need for an entirely different mode of intelligence gathering, while whatever of old-fashioned Orientalism had entered such disciplines as anthropology or sociology were subject to self-regulatory, intra-disciplinary debates, discussions, ideas, and combatant and conversant theories.

The world marked by the iconic dates of 9/11 is now sought to be dominated by a U.S. Empire with no ideological claim to legitimacy—to which neither old-fashioned Orientalism nor Area Studies specialist of yore are of any use anymore. This is an empire with no hegemony. While European colonialism worked through multifaceted hegemonies (and thus the colonial function of Orientalism), not limited or exclusive to scholarship, but, and as Said noted, also in art, literature, and popular fantasies as well, the flailing American imperialism works without an overriding hegemony and by sheer brute force (and thus the intellectual mendacity of the clique called "the neocons," which in its global strategies of domination seeks to link old-fashioned European Orientalism and erstwhile American Area Studies to the most pestiferous attempts at the ideological justification of the U.S. Empire). If upon the exhaustion of Orientalism as a robust mode of knowledge production at the height of European colonialism the gradual emergence of the United States as a global superpower necessitated and generated a whole new *modus operandi* of intelligence gathering, global strategies, and ideological justification during the Cold War era and termed it "Area Studies," with the collapse of the Soviet Union in 1991 and a decade later the rise of the U.S. global "war on terror," even the phase of Area Studies is no longer valid or useful. The gradual mutation of old-fashioned Orientalists into Area Studies specialists is now further transmuting into a class of barefaced propagandists in close collaboration with think tank strategists—perhaps best represented by Bernard Lewis' *What Went Wrong?* (2003). To witness this astounding historical metamorphosis in person, the career of Bernard Lewis remains exceptionally instructive—for in his person and his long and productive services to British colonialism and American imperialism he has systematically mutated from an Orientalist into an Area Studies specialist and now into a master propagandist, the author of one empty, vacuous, and dangerously delusional set of ideas after another. These dangerous delusions no longer have any connection with the classical case of Orientalism and are identical in their hazardous consequences for the world with the gibberish of people they seek to fight but in fact necessitate—Osama bin Laden and Company. What we are witnessing today is a perilous aspiration with no idea, ideal, or imagination to match or mastermind it—the result is a fake empire running on empty and operating on sheer brute force that as evident from New Orleans in the aftermath of Hurricane Katrina to Baghdad and Kandahar in the aftermath of Hurricane ("Shock and Awe") Rumsfeld is as administratively incompetent as it is ideologically vacuous—imperially self-delusional.

* * *

It is for that set of reasons that reading the magnificent essays of Ignaz Goldziher today is like a walk through a museum of exquisite antiquities, of dead and outdated elegance, the solid thoughts and graceful reflections of a noble man full of graceful sensibilities in his scholarship, beset by brightest blindness and shining with the darkest insights. A combination of his personal brilliance as a scholar and his institutional membership in the discursive particularities of Orientalism come together to demand an entirely different readership for him. The question is how to read Goldziher today, generations after his exquisitely crafted essays were the groundbreaking events of an entire discipline called Islamic Studies. The significance of these essays should not be measured against the historically outdated and theoretically discredited discipline called Orientalism anymore. As that of all other Orientalists, Goldziher's scholarship was integral to a mode of knowledge production at once exceedingly productive and insightful and yet at its very epistemic root predicated on the European colonial interests in what they called "the Orient," a fact entirely independent of two vastly different people like Goldziher and Vámbéry sharing the same designation of "Orientalist." Today, Goldziher must be read as an exemplary scholar of unsurpassed brilliance, a cultural comparatist of uncommon insight, a humanist with a vast catholicity of learning rarely seen among his peers, a politically alert and intellectually diligent activist who opposed colonialism of all sorts as a matter of moral principle, a gifted essayist who put his extraordinary learning at the service of understanding a religion, a culture, a civilization, and above all a people entirely different than his, helping him to gain insight into his own; and ultimately a pious and ethically principled man with a passion for a morally meaningful and purposeful life, which he drew not against but from the very heart of his proud Judaism.

Hamid Dabashi
New York
January 2006

Notes

1. Ignaz Goldziher, *Tagebuch*. Herausgegeben von Alexander Scheiber. Leiden: E. J. Brill, 1978: 59. The English translation is Raphael Patai's in Raphael Patai, *Ignaz Goldziher and His Oriental Diary: A Translation and Psychological Portrait* (Detroit, MI: Wayne State University Press, 1987): 20. Two of my Columbia colleagues, Gil Anidjar and Hossein Kamaly, read an earlier draft of this essay. I have much benefited from their comments and am grateful to them.
2. Goldziher, *Tagebuch*: 251. The invitation had come from an organization he calls, "Gesellschaft der Religionsgeschichte" ("Society for the Study of History of Religion").
3. Decades later a competent and scholarly translation of Goldziher's *Vorlesungen über den Islam* (Heidelberg, 1910) appeared in English. See Ignaz Goldziher, *Introduction to Islamic Theology and Law*. Translated by Andras and Ruth Hamori. Princeton, NJ: Princeton University Press, 1981).
4. "The feeling intellect" is Philip Rieff's phrase, which he selected as the apt title of a selection of his essays, collected and edited by Jonathan B. Imber. See Philip Rieff, *The Feeling Intellect: Selected Writings* (Chicago: University of Chicago Press, 1991).
5. Max Weber, *The Protestant Ethics and the Spirit of Capitalism*. Translated by Talcott Parsons. Introduction by Anthony Giddens. New York: Charles Scribner's Sons, 1958): 182.
6. Ignaz Goldziher's study of the Shu'ubiyya movement in *Muslim Studies*, edited by S. M. Stern, translated by C. R. Barber and S. M. Stern (Chicago: Aldine Publishing Company, 1966: 137-198) needs to be augmented by the equally important essay of Sir Hamilton Gibb, "The Social Significance of the Shu'ubiyya," in his *Studies on the Civilization of Islam*. Edited by Stanford J. Shaw and William R. Polk. Princeton, NJ: Princeton University Press, 1962: 62-73; as well as by Roy Mottahedeh's "The Shu'ubiyya Controversy and the Social History of Early Islamic Iran," International Journal of Middle East Studies, Volume VII (1976). The most recent essay on the subject is by H. T. Norris, "Shu'ubiyya in Arabic Literature" in Julia Ashtiyani, et. al (Eds), The Cambridge History of Arabic Literature: 'Abbasid Belles-Letters (Cambridge: Cambridge University Press, 1990: 31-47. Equally

important is the extensive study of Shu'ubiyya by the Iranian scholar Jalal Homa'i, *Shu'ubiyya* (Tehran: Sa'eb Publication, 1984).

7. For the homage that Goldziher pays his Muslim peers in the discipline of Hadith criticism see his essay, "The Development of Law," in *Introduction to Islamic Theology and Law*, op. cit.: 39-40.
8. Needless to say, later Muslim scholars have continued these heated debates and particularly when it comes to matters of their doctrinal beliefs (concerning the divine origin of the Qur'an, for example), they have taken strong objections to some of Goldziher's scholarly positions. As a non-Muslim scholar, Goldziher was free of such doctrinal convictions and as a result had a freer sense of inquiry. Neither his freedom nor Muslim scholars' convictions means either one of them were necessarily compromised in their scholarship. They simply operated within two different epistemic apparatus. For a critical debate with Goldziher, concerning his Qur'anic scholarship, from a pious Muslim perspective, see Seyyed Muhammad Reza Jalali Na'ini, *Tarikh-e Jam'-e Qur'an-e Karim* (Tehran: Noqreh Publications, 1365/1986): XIII, XVI, XVV, et passim.
9. Many of Goldziher's observations on Islamic law have of courses been extensively amended by the later scholarship, among them Subhi Mahmassani's *Falsafat al-Tashri: The Philosophy of Jurisprudence in Islam.* Translated by Farhat Ziadeh (Leiden: E. J. Brill, 1961); Joseph Schacht's *An Introduction to Islamic Law* (Oxford: Clarendon Press, 1964); and Noel J. Coulson's *A History of Islamic Law* (Edinburgh: Edinburgh University Press, 1964).
10. Ignaz Goldziher, *Muslim Studies*. Edited by S. M. Stern. Translated by C. R. Barber and S. M. Stern. (Chicago: Aldine Publishing Company, 1971: 262.
11. Goldziher, *Introduction to Islamic Theology and Law*, op. cit.: 41.
12. On further scholarship on Islamic theology after Goldziher see L. Gardet and M. M. Anawati's *Introduction a la theologie musulman* (Paris: Vrin, 1948).
13. Goldziher, *Introduction to Islamic Theology and Law*, op. cit.: 174.
14. Goldziher, *Introduction to Islamic Theology and Law*, op. cit.: 186.
15. For alternative readings of the rise of Shi'ism in the context of early Islamic history see my *Authority in Islam: From the Rise of Muhammad to the Establishment of the Umayyads* (New Brunswick, NJ: Transaction Publishers, 1992). It is noteworthy that after a critical examination of some of the exceedingly illiberal aspects of Shi'i law, Goldziher feels obligated to make the following observation: "The Shi'i community has suffered the hardship of an *ecclesia oppressa*, having from the outset struggled against persecution and repression. It has on the whole lacked the freedom to make open profession of its beliefs, and could disclose and practice them only in the conspiratorial secrecy of its members. Its mood therefore tends towards rage against the adversaries who prevailed" etc. (Ibid: 217). While his scholarly criticism leads him to pinpoint certain xenophobic aspects of Shi'i law, his historical imagination leads him to place them in their proper social context.

16. See Goldziher, *Introduction to Islamic Theology and Law*, op. cit.: 241-254. Goldziher also pays close attention to the Constitutional Revolution in Iran (Ibid: 196-202), as well as reformist movements in India (Ibid: 254-267).
17. Goldziher, *Introduction to Islamic Theology and Law*, op. cit.: 244.
18. "During the writing of these pages," writes Goldziher towards the end of his observations about the Baha'ism, "I have had occasion to hear such Biblical proofs [that Abbas Efendi, the leader of the Baha'is, has been promised in the Bible, and that Isaiah 9:6, "unto us a child is born, unto us a son is given; and the government shall be upon his shoulder," foretells him] from the mouth of a Baha'i zealot. This man, originally a doctor from Tehran, has been staying for the last two years or so in the city where I live, in an effort to gain converts to his religion. He feels that he has a particular mission in my country: one more proof that it is not only American soil that the extra-Islamic propaganda of the new Baha'is has in view" (Ibid: 254).
19. See Ignaz Goldziher, *Mythology among the Hebrews and its historical development.* Translated from the German, with additions by the author, by Russell Martineau. London: Longmans, Green, 1877. See also Goldziher's *On the History of Grammar among the Arabs: An Essay in Literary History*. Translated and edited by Kinga Dévényi, Tamás Iványi. Amsterdam: J. Benjamins, 1994; *A Short History of Classical Arabic Literature.* Translated by Joseph de Somogyi. Hildesheim: G. Olms, 1966. Goldziher's classical study of Qur'anic hermeneutics, *Richtungen der islamischen Koranauslegung* (Leiden: Brill, 1920) was a pioneer study in the comparative discourse analysis of varied forms of Qur'anic interpretations—ranging from juridical to mystical.
20. Goldziher, *Tagebuch*: 22-23.
21. Goldziher, *Tagebuch*: 55.
22. Goldziher, *Tagebuch*: 65-74.
23. Patai, *Psychological Portrait*: 9-11. Patai reports that the original German of Goldziher's travelogue to Syria, Palestine, and Egypt is at the Jewish Theological Seminary of America in New York.
24. Patai, *Psychological Portrait*: 26.
25. This according to Raphael Patai who studied with Carl Brockelmann during academic year 1930-1931. See Patai, *Psychological Portrait*: 13.
26. Patai, *Psychological Portrait*: 15.
27. Patai, *Psychological Portrait*: 15.
28. Patai, *Psychological Portrait*: 16.
29. Patai, *Psychological Portrait*: 16.
30. Patai, *Psychological Portrait*: 18.
31. Patai, *Psychological Portrait*: 21, and again "infatuated with Islam" (Ibid: 27).
32. Patai, *Psychological Portrait*: 63.
33. Goldziher, *Tagebuch*: 59, as translated by Patai in Patai, *Psychological Portrait*: 20.
34. Goldziher, *Tagebuch*: 60-61, as translated by Patai in Patai, *Psychological Portrait*: 21.
35. Patai, *Psychological Portrait*: 60.

36. Patai, *Psychological Portrait*: 60.
37. Goldziher, *Tagebuch*: 15.
38. *Holy Bible*, King James Text, Modern Phrased Version (New York: Oxford University Press, 1979): 1249.
39. The full text of the verse is: "And they came with false blood on his shirt. He said: Nay, but your minds have beguiled you into something. (My course is) comely patience. And Allah it is whose help is to be sought in that (predicament) which ye describe" (*The Meaning of the Glorious Koran: An Explanatory Translation* by Mohammed Marmaduke Pickthall. New York: A Mentor Book, no date). Arberry's "sweet patience" (*The Koran Interpreted*. New York: Macmillan Publishing Company, 1955: 255) and T. B. Irving's "patience is beautiful" (*The Qur'an*. Translation and Commentary by T. B. Irving/al-Hajj Ta'lim 'Ali. Brattleboro, Vermont: 1985: 120) are perhaps better translations of the original "fa-sabrun jamilun."
40. Patai, *Psychological Portrait*: 61-62.
41. Patai, *Psychological Portrait*: 62.
42. Patai, *Psychological Portrait*: 62.
43. Patai, *Psychological Portrait*: 62.
44. Goldziher's *Travelogue* in Patai, *Psychological Portrait*: 99-100 (entry of 1 October 1873). Goldziher has similarly moving passages when he visits Jerusalem for the first (and last time). See Goldziher's *Travelogue* in Patai, *Psychological Portrait*: 132-133 (entry of 29 November 1873).
45. As quoted by Zabihollah Safa in his magisterial history of Persian literature, *Tarikh-e Adabiyat dar Iran*. Six Volumes (Tehran: Ibn Sina Publications, 1959-1990), Volume One: 308. Such self-deprecating poems abound in Persian literature. Perhaps the most famous is the Eighteenth century poet Hatif al-Isfahani's celebrated *Tarji'-band*, in which he describes his metaphoric journeys through all religious beliefs and practices finds them all identical. The most famous passage is when he goes to a Zoroastrian temple and becomes ashamed of being a Muslim: *"Man-e Sharmandeh az Mosalmani/Shodam anja beh gusheh'i penhan ("I, ashamed of being a Muslim/Hid myself there in a corner")*. See the original Persian and an English translation in E. G. Browne's *A Literary History of Persia*. Four Volumes (Cambridge: Cambridge University Press, 1969), Volume IV: 184-297.
46. See Goldziher, *Tagebuch*: 65; and Patai, *Psychological Portrait*: 66.
47. Goldziher's *Travelogue* in Patai, *Psychological Portrait*: 119 (entry of 29 October 1873).
48. On "culture industry" See Theodore Adorno, *Culture Industry* (London: Brunner-Routledge, 2001).
49. Patai, *Psychological Portrait*: 67.
50. Patai, *Psychological Portrait*: 67.
51. Goldziher, *Introduction to Islamic Theology and Law*, op. cit.: 186.
52. Goldziher's *Travelogue* in Patai, *Psychological Portrait*: 93-97, et passim (entries of 26 and 29 September 1873 and an undated entry as well).
53. Patai, *Psychological Portrait*: 21, and again "infatuated with Islam" (Ibid: 27).

54. Patai, *Psychological Portrait*: 46.
55. Patai, *Psychological Portrait*: 36.
56. Patai, *Psychological Portrait*: 39.
57. Patai, *Psychological Portrait*: 55.
58. Patai, *Psychological Portrait*: 73.
59. Patai, *Psychological Portrait*: 22.
60. Patai, *Psychological Portrait*: 23.
61. Patai, *Psychological Portrait*: 20.
62. Patai, *Psychological Portrait*: 24. Footnote 12.
63. Patai, *Psychological Portrait*: 27.
64. Patai, *Psychological Portrait*: 25.
65. Patai, *Psychological Portrait*: 27.
66. Patai, *Psychological Portrait*: 27.
67. Patai, *Psychological Portrait*: 27.
68. Patai, *Psychological Portrait*: 27.
69. Patai, *Psychological Portrait*: 27.
70. Patai, *Psychological Portrait*: 28.
71. Patai, *Psychological Portrait*: 29.
72. Patai, *Psychological Portrait*: 29.
73. Patai, *Psychological Portrait*: 30.
74. Goldziher, *Tagebuch*: 107, and Patai, *Psychological Portrait*: 34.
75. Goldziher, *Tagebuch*: 98, and Patai, *Psychological Portrait*: 33.
76. Goldziher, *Tagebuch*: 98, and Patai, *Psychological Portrait*: 33.
77. Patai, *Psychological Portrait*: 31. Patai dismisses Goldziher's *Mythology among the Hebrews* even on scholarly grounds and believes it "to be the only work of Goldziher's scholarly output that did not stand the test of time" (Ibid: 31). The moral courage and intellectual imagination to engage with current theoretical propositions from the heart of one's own religion bear the marks of an entirely different "test of time" and of course character.
78. Patai, *Psychological Portrait*: 44. As evidence of his belief, Goldziher offers an incident in which two days after he was appointed as full professor he run into Vámbéry and he had no idea of Goldziher's appointment and asked him, in yet another condescending remark, when will he finally be appointed as full professor.
79. Patai, *Psychological Portrait*: 40. As evidence of his belief, Goldziher offers an incident in which two days after he was appointed as full professor he run into Vámbéry and he had no idea of Goldziher's appointment and asked him, in yet another condescending remark, when will he finally be appointed as full professor.
80. Patai, *Psychological Portrait*: 44-45.
81. Patai, *Psychological Portrait*: 40.
82. Patai, *Psychological Portrait*: 44.
83. Patai, *Psychological Portrait*: 44.
84. Patai, *Psychological Portrait*: 44, quoting from Theodor Herzl, *The Complete Diaries of Theodor Herzl*. Edited by Raphael Patai (New York: Herzl Press and Thomas Yoseloff, 1960): Volume III: 961.
85. Goldziher, *Tagebuch*: 129, and Patai, *Psychological Portrait*: 41.

86. See Armenius Vámbéry, *Voyage d'un faux derviche en Asie centrale, 1862-1864* (Paris, 1993).
87. Because this book contains extensive and detailed passages on Iran and Central Asia in the nineteenth century, it was later translated into Persian by Fath Ali Khawja Nurian as *Siyahat-e Darvishi Doroughin dar Khanat-e Asiya-ye Mianeh* (Tehran: Elmi va Farhangi Publications, 1986).
88. Vámbéry, *Siyahat-e Darvishi Dorughin*: 534.
89. Goldziher, *Tagebuch*: 71-72, and Patai, *Psychological Portrait*: 27-28.
90. Patai, *Psychological Portrait*: 43-44.
91. Patai, *Psychological Portrait*: 46.
92. Patai, *Psychological Portrait*: 40.
93. Patai, *Psychological Portrait*: 37.
94. Patai, *Psychological Portrait*: 37.
95. "The portrait of the man Goldziher that emerges from the pages of my introduction," Patai writes at the very outset, "is not a totally attractive one. Like many a genius—and he undoubtedly was one—Goldziher had his share of unpleasant character traits" (Patai, *Psychological Portrait*; 10).
96. Patai, *Psychological Portrait*: 36. Emphasis added.
97. Patai, *Psychological Portrait*: 50-51.
98. Goldziher *Introduction to Islamic Theology and Law*: 254.
99. Goldziher, *Tagebuch*: 228-229, as translated by Patai in Patai, *Psychological Portrait*: 50.
100. Patai, *Psychological Portrait*: 52.
101. Patai, *Psychological Portrait*: 54.
102. Patai, *Psychological Portrait*: 55, based on Goldziher, *Tagebuch*: 311. Goldziher is so distraught at this point that his entry for 4 December 1918 begins in Hungarian, which Scheiber translated into German in his footnote 529 and Patai into English: "The Crown of my head is fallen! My Mariska fell victim to the Spanish epidemic. My soul is broken into a thousand pieces. Oh, my dear Karl!"
103. Patai, *Psychological Portrait*: 73; while his accusations are all concentrated in Patai 1987: 50-56, under the suggestive subheading of "The Divine Mariska."
104. Patai, *Psychological Portrait*: 50-56.
105. Scheiber in Goldziher, *Tagebuch*: 10—"einer begabte Ägyotologin" is the way Scheiber describes Maria Freudenberg.
106. Raphael Patai's penchant for making scandalous assumptions about people's sexuality in particular is not limited to thus slandering Goldziher. In 1973 he wrote a book called *The Arab Mind* (New York: Hatherleigh Press, Revised Edition, 2002), in which he devoted an entire chapter, Chapter VIII, "The Realm of Sex," pp: 126-151) to the way he thought "the Arab sexuality" works. In his "Gray Zone" (*New Yorker*, 24 May 2004), Seymour Hirsh implicitly connected the sexual torture of Iraqi inmates in Abu Ghraib to this chapter of Raphael Patai and its central significance to teaching the U.S. military how to deal with Muslims. Other journalists, such as Brian Whitaker (*The Guard-*

ian, 24 May 2004) picked up from Hirsh and wrote a scathing attack against Patai's book. Raphael Patai's supporters came to his defense. The problem, however, with Patai's observations in *The Arab Mind* is not limited to the reported uses or abuses to which the U.S. (or any other) military may have put it. Four years after he published *The Arab Mind*, Raphael Patai also published a book on *The Jewish Mind* (New Jersey: Wayne State University Press, 1977). Long before Patai, Charles A. Moore had edited a volume on *The Japanese Mind: Essentials of Japanese Philosophy and Culture* (Honolulu: The University Press of Hawaii, 1967), announcing in his introduction similar volumes on the Chinese and the Indian "minds." The problem with these sorts of assumptions as "the Arab mind" or the "Jewish mind" (replicated by the fabrication of equally empty and absurd abstractions about "the Western mind") is their outdated analytical language and superseded scholarship, not just their (potential) political bad faith. After more than a hundred years of sociological and anthropological advances (Patai was an anthropologist), no one thinks and writes in such a generic and essentialist language anymore. There are so many class, gender, communal, regional, national, and moral and psychological variants that come dialectically together to constitute a people that one cannot even think in terms of an "Arab" or "Jewish" or "Japanese" mind that works in any particular way—one way or another. These are simply flawed categories, long before suggesting and articulating them can be debated as the indices of a retrograde politics. In addition to "the Arab Mind" and "the Jewish Mind," Patai has made equally untenable and entirely vacuous observations about "the Middle Eastern culture" in his *Golden River to Golden Road* (Philadelphia: University of Pennsylvania Press, 1969). In *Orientalism* (New York: Vintage Books, 1979: 308-309), Edward Said has critically examined a passage of this book as an example of how "the Orient" is constituted as the fixed object of investigation for the Orientalist. But as Said demonstrates the problem with such essentialist attributes is that they categorically disregard a whole variety of factors that have been systemadically essentialized (in this particular case metaphorically sexualized) in order to facilitate a particular mode of analytic. Instead of grand conspiratorial assumptions about people, one has to take to task these flawed analytics on specific scholarly grounds.

107. Patai, *Psychological Portrait*: 70.
108. Patai, *Psychological Portrait*: 67.
109. Patai, *Psychological Portrait*: 67.
110. Patai, *Psychological Portrait*: 27.
111. Patai, *Psychological Portrait*: 68.
112. Patai, *Psychological Portrait*: 69.
113. Joseph de Somogyi, "My Reminiscences of Igance Goldziher." *The Muslim World*, LI (1961): 15; also quoted in Patai, *Psychological Portrait*: 69.
114. Goldziher's *Travelogue* in Patai, *Psychological Portrait*: 132 (entry of 29 November 1873).

115. Bernard Heller, "Goldziher Ignác emlékezete," IMIT 1932, Évkönyve, Budapest 1932: 24-25, as quoted by Joseph de Somogyi, "My Reminiscences of Igance Goldziher": 15.
116. Patai, *Psychological Portrait*: 70.
117. Bernard Heller, "Goldziher Ignác emlékezete," as quoted by Joseph de Somogyi, "My Reminiscences of Igance Goldziher": 15.
118. Patai, *Psychological Portrait*: 71.
119. Patai, *Psychological Portrait*: 71.
120. Patai, *Psychological Portrait*: 73. See also Goldziher's *Tagebuch*, which he begins by saying that he is writing it "für meine Frau, meine Kinder und die allernächsten Glieder meines engern Freudeskreises" ("for my wife, my children, and the close circle of my intimate friends," 15).
121. Goldziher, *Tagebuch*: 228, as translated by Patai in Patai, *Psychological Portrait*: 50.
122. Goldziher *Tagebuch*: 235-239, as translated by Patai in Patai, *Psychological Portrait*: 75.
123. Goldziher, *Tagebuch*: 15.
124. Patai, *Psychological Portrait*: 27.
125. Patai, *Psychological Portrait*: 77.
126. Patai, *Psychological Portrait*: 77.
127. Given the highly speculative, tendentious, and outright slanderous nature of Patai's account of Goldziher's life on the basis of his reading of the German original of Goldziher's *Tagebuch*, it is imperative that a competent English translation of this seminal text be made available to the larger scholarly community. For the very same reasons, Patai's English translation of the German original of Goldziher's travelogue to Syria, Palestine, and Egypt should also be published in its original German. The scholarly community should not be at the mercy of the English translation of a German (the original of which is not published), done by someone so systematically hostile to Goldziher. In fact it is a rather dubious scholarly practice to have kept the original German in manuscript form and published only an English translation of it. A more serious scholar would have first published the German original, or else published a bilingual version. When the English translation of *Tagebuch* and the German original of Goldziher's travelogue to Syria, Palestine, and Egypt are published a larger community of interpreters can read these two extraordinary documents and make its own judgment.
128. Said, *Orientalism*: 330.
129. On the origin and later development of the idea of "the death of the author" in contemporary French thought see Sean Burke, *The Death and Return of the Author: Criticism and Subjectivity in Barthes, Foucault and Derrida* (Edinburgh: Edinburgh University Press, 1992). See also Roland Barthes' "The Death of the Author" in his collection of essays, *Image, Music, Text* (New York: Hill and Wang, 1978): 142-148.
130. Said, *Orientalism*: 330-331.

131. The most memorable such exchanges were in the pages of *The New York Review of Books*. See Bernard Lewis' "The Question of Orientalism" (*The New York Review of Books*, Volume 29, Number 11: 24 June, 1982), and the subsequent exchange among Edward Said, Bernard Lewis and Oleg Grabar (an Islamic Art Historian) in "Orientalism: An Exchange" (*The New York Review of Books*, Volume 29, Number 13: 12 August, 1982). In a subsequent MESA (Middle East Studies Association of North America) meeting in Boston, MA, Edward Said and Bernard Lewis faced each other in a debate.
132. See James Clifford, "On Orientalism," in *The Predicament of Culture: Twentieth Century Ethnography, Literature, and Art* (Cambridge, MA: Harvard University Press, 1988): 255-276; Aijaz Ahmad, *In Theory: Classes, Nations, Literatures* (London and New York: Verso, 1994); and Sadiq Jalal al-Azm, "Orientalism and Orientalism in Reverse," *Khamsin* (1981).
133. Edward Said, *Orientalism* (London: Penguin, 1978/2003): 340.
134. See Max Weber, "Science as a Vocation, " in *From Max Weber: Essays in Sociology*. Translated and Edited by Hans H. Gerth and C. Wright Mills (Oxford: Oxford University Press, 1946): 129-156. For Edward Said's articulation of the role of public intellectual see his *Representations of the Intellectual* (New York: Vintage, 1996). For an excellent study of Max Weber's conception of intellectuals see Ahmad Sadri's *Max Weber's Sociology of Intellectuals*. (Oxford: Oxford University Press, 1992). For reflections on Edward Said's *Representations of the Intellectual* see my review essay in the journal *Critique*, Fall 1994: 85-96.
135. This has of course now changed and there is a whole "Allamah" bestowing industry in the Islamic Republic.
136. For more on Mohammad Qazvini see his own short autobiography in *Doreh-ye Kamel-e Bist Maqalah-ye Qazvini* ("The Complete Collection of Twenty Essays by Qazvini"). Edited by Abbas Iqbal and Ibrahim Pour Davoud (Tehran: Donya-ye Ketab, 1363/1984): 7-30.
137. For additional biographical data on Mohammad Qazvini see Houshang Ettehad, *Pazhuhishgaran Mo'asser* ("Contemporary Scholars"). Two Volumes (Tehran: Farhang-e Mo'asser, 1378/1999), Volume I: 1-52.
138. Qazvini, *Bist Maqalah-ye Qazvini*: 23-24.
139. Qazvini 1984: 24-25. All translations from the original Persian are mine.
140. Qazvini 1984: 24-25.
141. Qazvini 1984: 24-25.
142. See Iraj Afshar (Ed.), *The Letters of Qazvini to Taqizadeh*. Tehran: Javidan Publications, 1974: 102-103). For more details on Qazvini's derogatory views on Orientalists and Orientalism see Hossein Kamaly's "Allamah Qazvini va Mustashriqin," *Golestan*, vol. III (nos. 3 & 4), Fall and Winter 1378 (1999-2000): 125-138.
143. See Hossein Kazemzadeh Iranshahr, "Orientalism and Occidentalism," in *Iranshahr* (Number 1, 26 June 1922): 12-14.
144. Iranshahr 1926: 12-13.

145. Iranshahr 1926: 13. For more on Hossein Kazem Zadeh Iranshahr see Kazem Kazem Zadeh Iranshahr (Ed.), *Athar va Ahval-e Kazem Zadeh Iranshahr* (Tehran: Iqbal Publications, 1971).
146. For more on Seyyed Hassan Taqizadeh see his autobiography, *Zendegi-ye Tufani: Khaterat-e Seyyed Hassan Taqizadeh*. Edited by Iraj Afshar (Tehran: Bahar Publications, 1989).
147. Iranshahr 1926: 13-14.
148. See Anwar Abdel Malek's "Orientalism in Crisis" (*Diogenes* 44, winter 1963) and Jacques Waardenburg's "*L'Islam dans le miroir de l'Occident* (The Hague: Mouton & Co., 1963).
149. See Raymond Schwab, *The Oriental Renaissance: Europe's Rediscovery of India and the East, 1680-1880*. Translated by Gene Patterson-Black and Victor Reinking. Foreword by Edward W. Said (New York: Columbia University Press, 1984).
150. Said, *Orientalism*: 18.
151. Said, *Orientalism*: 19.
152. Said, *Orientalism*: 105.
153. See for example Seyyed Muhammad Reza Jalali Na'ini, *Tarikh-e Jam'-e Qur'an-e Karim* op. cit: XIII, XVI, XVV, et passim.
154. Patai, *Psychological Portrait*: 31.
155. Patai, *Psychological Portrait*: 15.
156. See Talcott Parsons' Introduction to Max Weber's *The Sociology of Religion*. Translated by Ephraim Fischoff (Boston: Beacon Press, 1963): xxvii, for Parsons note to this effect.
157. Said, *Orientalism*: 208-209. Said's apt observations about Theodore Nöldeke can of course be extended to Bernard Lewis tenfold. Lewis exemplifies the later generation of Orientalists who positively loathed and politically plotted against the very dignity of the subject of their lifetime scholarship. A bona fide psychologist (no anthropologist) needs to do a "psychological portrait" of people who spend their lives studying peoples and cultures they loathe. There must a psychopathological explanation for this.
158. Said, *Orientalism*: 209.
159. Goldziher, *Tagebuch*: 59, as translated by Patai in Patai, *Psychological Portrait*: 20.
160. Goldziher, *Tagebuch*: 60, as translated by Patai in Patai, *Psychological Portrait*: 21.
161. Goldziher, *Tagebuch*: 60, as translated by Patai in Patai, *Psychological Portrait*: 21.
162. As quoted in Patai, *Psychological Portrait*: 20.
163. Goldziher, *Tagebuch*: 60-61, as translated by Patai in Patai, *Psychological Portrait*: 61. Again to be fair to Said, neither the *Tagebuch* nor the *Travelogue* was available to him at the writing of *Orientalism* (1978).
164. Goldziher *Tagebuch*: 59, as translated by Patai in Patai, *Psychological Portrait*: 20. Quoting Goldziher's comparative and categorical statements on Judaism, Christianity, or Islam is obviously not to endorse them. But simply to show that Said's assumption that Goldziher thought of Islam as inferior to other religions is false.

165. Said, *Orientalism*: 210. The passage Said quotes in French is from P. Masson-Oursel, "La connaissance scientifique de l'Asie en France depuis 1900 et les variétés de l'Orientalism," *Revue Philosophique* 143, Numbers 7-9 (July-September 1953): 345.
166. Patai, *Psychological Portrait*: 46.
167. By far the most significant of these three for Said is Foucault. "I have found it useful here," Said says early in his *Orientalism*, "to employ Michel Foucault's notion of a discourse, as described by him in *Archeology of Knowledge* and in *Discipline and Punish*, to identify Orientalism" (Said, *Orientalism*: 3, et passim).
168. Said, *Orientalism*: 202-203.
169. Edward Said, *Humanism and Democratic Criticism* (New York: Columbia University Press, 2003): 48-49.
170. Said, *Orientalism*: 258-259.
171. Said, *Orientalism*: 260.
172. See Edward Said, *The World, the Text, the Critic* (Cambridge: Harvard University press, 1983/2004): 31-53.
173. Said, *Humanism and Democratic Criticism*: 48-49.
174. Said, *Orientalism*: 322.
175. Said, *Orientalism*: 203.
176. See James Clifford, "On Orientalism," op. cit.
177. See Said, *Humanism and Democratic Criticism*: 8-10.
178. Said, *Orientalism*, 340.
179. This is the principal project of his first posthumously published book, *Humanism and Democratic Criticism*, op. cit.
180. Said, *Orientalism*: 322.
181. Said, *Orientalism*: 259.
182. It was in the best interest of not just Bernard Lewis (the Arminius Vámbéry of his time) and his ilk but of an entire lucrative industry of knowledge production about "Islam" (and soon "Islamic terrorism") to pretend that they had no idea what this problem of *representation* was, that it was some sort of French mumbo-jumbo, and that they were "experts" on Islam and could tell the U.S. and European governments what to do in their dealing with Muslims. While the academic world went after the goose-chase of solving the essentially insoluble problem of *the soverign subject*, "Islamic experts" made a very lucrative living telling the world (powerful people in particular) what to think of Islam and what do to Muslims. "Persian and Turkish poetry are entirely Muslim," Bernard Lewis tells his readers in *The Middle East: A Brief History of the Last 2,000 Years* (New York: Simon and Shuster, 1995: 258), as an example of his exquisite command of primary sources and what they represent. Ayatollah Khomeini could not have thought and said it better, nor could Moustapha Kamal disagreed more. The astounding illiteracy at the very root of a sentence like that is prototypical of every single sentence that Bernard Lewis utters in his writings—making the Persian and Turkish poets of the last one thousand year (particularly of the last two hundred years) turn in their graves. Bernard Lewis and the industry he represents need not have

worried about the problem of *representation*. They knew everything there was to know about Arabic, Persian, and Turkish languages and literatures and cultures. Allamah Qazvini knew these "charlatans," as he called them quite well: "The instruction of these languages, and in fact the teaching of a few other languages as well, and all at the same time—such as Persian, Arabic, Turkish, and all the arts and sciences that have been written in those languages, as well as all the various and innumerable dialects of those languages—all and all are entrusted to these Orientalists. These people then proceed, without the slightest sense of shame or fear of being scandalized, for there is no one to tell, to claim knowledge and authority in all these languages and the arts and sciences written in them, teaching them, publishing books and articles about them, and even coming out with their own new and specific ideas about them." (Qazvini, *Bist Maqalah-ye Qazvini*: 23). His prophetic soul!

183. For an English translation, see Max Scheler, *Problems of Sociology of Knowledge*. Translated by Manfred S. Frings. Edited and with an Introduction by Kenneth W. Stikkers (London: Routledge & Kegan Paul, 1980).
184. For an English translation of both these sources see Karl Manheim, *Ideology and Utopia*. Translated from the German by Louis Wirth and Edward Shils (New York: Harcourt Brace Jovanovich, 1936). See also Karl Mannheim, *Structures of Thinking*. Translated by Jeremy J. Shapiro and Shierry Weber Nicholson. Edited and Introduced by David Kettler, Volker Meja and Nico Stehr (London: Routledge & Kegan Paul, 1982).
185. Max Scheler, *Problems of a Sociology of Knowledge*. Translated by Manfred S. Frings. Edited and with an Introduction by Kenneth W. Stikkers. London: Routledge & Kegan Paul, 1980: 67. Emphasis in the original.
186. Scheler 1980: 70. Emphasis in the original.
187. Karl Mannheim, *Ideology and Utopia*. New York: Harcourt Brace Jovanovich, 1936: 267-271.
188. See Karl Marx and Fredrich Engels, *The German Ideology*. Edited and with an Introduction by C. J. Arthur (New York: International Publishers, 1947): 47.
189. See for example Tom W. Goff, *Marx and Mead: Contributions to a Sociology of Knowledge* (London: Routledge & Kegan Paul, 1980).
190. See David Frisby, *The Alienated Mind: The Sociology of Knowledge in Germany, 1918-1933* (London and New York: Routledge, 1983). A similar attempt at providing a sociology of knowledge for the rise of the sociology of knowledge, as it were, that corroborates Frisby's observations is provided by Pierre Bourdieu for the emergence of Martin Heidegger's philosophy in Pierre Bourdieu's *The Political Ontology of Martin Heidegger*. Translated by Peter Collier. (Stanford, CA: Stanford University Press, 1991): 7-39.
191. See Gunter W. Remmling (Ed.), *Towards the Sociology of Knowledge: Origin and development of a sociological Thought Style* (New York: Humanities Press, 1973).

192. For cogent observations about similar thoughts in the sociology of Talcott Parsons see Harold J. Bershady, *Ideology and Social Knowledge* (New York: John Wiley and Sons, 1973).
193. For further details see James Tully (Ed.), *Meaning and Context: Quentin Skinner and his Critics*. Princeton: Princeton University Press, 1988.
194. See Dominick Lacapra, *Rethinking Intellectual History: Texts, Contexts, Language*. Ithaca: Cornell University Press, 1983.
195. "Let me begin with the one aspect of the book's reception," Said wrote in his 1995 Afterword to *Orientalism*, "that I most regret and find myself trying hardest bow (in 1994) to overcome. That is the book's alleged anti-Westernism, as it has been misleadingly and rather too sonorously called by commentators both hostile and sympathetic . . . . One scarcely knows what to make of these caricatural permutations of a book that to its author and in its argument is explicitly anti-essentialist, radically skeptical about all categorical designations such as Orient and Occident, and painstakingly careful about not "defending" or even discussing the Orient and Islam"" (Said, *Orientalism*: 330-331).
196. To be sure, the central and thorny issue of the sovereign subject remains valid in Clifford's critic even when we move into the domain of the sociology of knowledge. However, the long tradition of Verstehendesoziologie, namely a sociology that is predicated on the *verstehendemethode* (subjective understanding), central, for example, to Max Weber's sociology, will go a long way addressing that problem. The tradition extends from Wilhelm Dilthey and Max Weber to more recent statements by Theodore Abel and others. For more on this see Marcello Truzzi (Ed.), *Verstehen: Subjective Understanding in the Social Sciences*. (London: Addison-Wesley Publishing Company, 1974.
197. See Thomas Kuhn, *The Structure of Scientific Revolutions* (Chicago: University Of Chicago Press, 1962/1996). In *Orientalism*, Edward Said makes a very brief and tangential reference to Thomas Kuhn. The context is Said's discussion of the distinguished Orientalist Sir Hamilton Gibb's "mind operating with great ease inside established institutions" (Said, *Orientalism*: 275). Later on, however, Said made direct connections between Foucault and Kuhn. "Michel Foucault and Thomas Kuhn," he believed, "have done a considerable service by reminding us in their work that, whether we are aware of it or not, paradigms and epistemes have a thoroughgoing hold on fields of thought and expression, a hold that inflects if it does not shape the nature of the individual utterance" (Said, *Humanism and Democratic Criticism*: 42).
198. Kuhn: *The Structure of Scientific Revolution*, op. cit: 66-67.
199. Hans-Georg Gadamer, *Truth and Method*. Second, Revised Edition. Translated by Joel Weinsheimer and Donald G. Marshal (New York: Crossroad, 1989): 277-285.
200. For a discussion of the epistemic impact of Copernican revolution on a range of moral and intellectual developments see Hans Blumenberg's *The Genesis of the Copernican World* (Cambridge, MA: The MIT Press, 1989).

201. In Said's *Orientalism* all these varied forms of Orientalism are coagulated, while they need to be separated and periodized. For Said's observations on Greek Orientalism on the basis of Aeschylus' *The Persians* see *Orientalism*: 55-56; and on that of Europe towards the Ottomans on the basis of Mozart's *Magic Flute* and *Abduction from the Seraglio* see *Orientalism*: 118.

202. For a more elaborate argument for this point see my "For the Last Time: Civilizations," *International Sociology*. September 2001. Volume 16 (3): 361-368.

203. No other propagandist alive is more responsible for sustaining this delusional opposition between "Islam and the West" than Bernard Lewis. He even forgets the books he himself has already written on the subject and writes new ones. In 1993, Lewis forgot that he had already written a book called *The Middle East and the West* (New York: Harper, 1964) in 1964 and wrote yet another one on *Islam and the West* (New York: Oxford University press, 1994)—essentially the same ideas, almost verbatim similarities, not just in these two books but in practically everything that he writes—"the West" got it right; "Islam" and Muslims did not; there were some accidentally intelligent Muslim reformists who did, but the ignoramus masses and fanatics did not, and thus we are in the mess that we are. This is Bernard Lewis in a nutshell.

THE manuscript of this volume and a great part of its continuations were in my desk for many years. Circumstances unfavourable to sustained literary activity made for repeated postponement and pressure from friends alone forced me into beginning the publication of the material whose early appearance I too confidently anticipated in my foreword to the *Ẓāhiriten.*[1] The profound books by Robertson Smith and Wellhausen[2] on Arabic antiquity reached me after my manuscript had been completed, and—as happens easily when the same sources are used—some of its paragraphs contain material identical with theirs. So far as was possible, without complete dissolution of the context, I have omitted many things from my work, confining myself to references to these authors. But in some cases this would not have been possible without disturbing the context or completely re-writing the passages in question.

In *Muslim Studies*, of which this is the first volume, I intend to bring together a number of treatises on the development of Islam. Some of the material which I have previously published on this
subject in Hungarian and French is here republished in completely x
new form: the text is extended, and references to sources (which had often been omitted in those publications), and discussions concerning these, are added. In this first volume the introductory chapter represents in a new and enlarged form a few pages of my book *Az Iszlám* published by the Hungarian Academy of Science (Budapest 1881); the second excursus is based on my article '*Le culte des ancêtres et le culte des morts chez les Arabes*' which appeared in the *Revue de l'histoire des religions*, vol. X (1884), pp. 332-59. Since here I am more concerned with stressing the Islamic elements, this article was most especially extended in this direction. It will hardly be held against me that some of the data which had been collected for the first time in that publication, but have since been partly assembled elsewhere, quite independently from my study, have not been omitted here. The study contained on pp. 164-98 to which the preceding chapters are to be a preparation owes its existence to the public encouragement given in: '*Zur arabischen Literaturgeschichte der älteren Zeit*' by Baron Victor v. Rosen (*Mélanges asiatiques*, 1880, VIII, p. 750, note 7).

[1] Leipzig, O. Schulze, 1883.

[2] [W. Robertson Smith, *Kinship and Marriage in early Arabia*, Cambridge 1885—the second edition, London 1902, contains additional notes by Goldziher; J. Wellhausen, *Reste arabischen Heidentums*, Berlin 1887, 2nd ed., with additions and corrections, Berlin 1897.]

Oriental script was avoided in this publication and will also be transcribed in its continuations; knowledgeable readers will not be disturbed by the unavoidable vacillations (also between grammatical and popular pronunciation) and they will hardly be noticeable to non-Orientalists.[1]

xi A few further words on the citations in the notes. The meaning of the abbreviations will be self-evident to readers familiar with the literature; but I should like to point out that the letter B in quotations from the traditions refers to the collection of Bukhārī. Of oriental editions I have used the older editions, chiefly those which appeared in the seventies; most of them are described in my preface to the *Ẓāhiriten*. The *Sīrat 'Antar* is quoted from the Cairo (Shāhīn) edition in thirty-two volumes;[2] the *Siqṭ al-Zand* of Abu'l-'Alā' from the Būlāq edition in 1286 in two volumes; this work has since been re-issued in the Orient (Brill's *Catal. périodique* no. 589).

The manuscripts which I have used are described at the appropriate places, but al-Ṣiddīqī's work is accidentally described only on p. 78, n. 7. I am deeply indebted to my dear friend Baron v. Rosen for making available to me his collated copy of the *Kitāb al-Bayān wa'l-Tabyīn* by al-Jāḥiẓ (MS. no. 724 of the St. Petersburg University library); he put this copy at my disposal for a lengthy period some
xii years ago. Baron v. Rosen would render inestimable service to students of the history of Islamic civilization and literature by publishing his laborious and conscientious edition of this most important book which was freely exploited by later authors of *adab* books and especially by Ibn 'Abd Rabbihi and al-Ḥuṣrī (by the latter mostly without indication of his source).

I hope soon to be able to follow up this volume with the second volume, which is to contain a study on the *ḥadīth* and *ḥadīth* literature. For the furtherance of this undertaking I am indebted to my friend Professor August Müller in Königsberg and to my former pupil Dr. Martin Schreiner in Csurgó who made the index to the first volume.

Budapest, October 1888 I.G.

[1] [In the transcription adopted in the present edition traces of the 'popular pronunciation' have been eliminated. The list of errata which follows in the original has been omitted.]

[2] It is odd that the thirty-first volume of this edition is hardly available in the Cairo book shops, at least since 1874. All the copies that I have seen lack this penultimate part, and this deficiency is for the most part concealed by cunning tricks and falsification, so as to hide it from the buyer, at least at the first glance.

CHAPTER ONE 1

INTRODUCTORY: MURUWWA AND DIN

I

It would be a vain undertaking to attempt a description of the religious state of the Arab people[1] before the spread of Islam which would be equally applicable to them all. When comparing the religious attitude expressed in the existent relics of old Arab poetry with those—somewhat contradictory[2]—data which are given in non-Arabic reports on the religious life and habits of pagan Arabs, one is strengthened in the conviction that a generalization of local experiences is wrong in this wide field. The religion of the Arabic tribes and societies was certainly different in different geographical areas. It would be misleading to expect to find the religious life of the Northerners—exposed to the influence of a more refined civilization—in Petra, Syria and Mesopotamia, where Arabs had settled since ancient times, amongst the more primitive tribes of central Arabia. Only in the towns which grew up in this area, and whose traffic put them in touch with more civilized circumstances, was the influence of this intercourse felt also with regard to religion, and from there some influences penetrated also to the barbarian inhabitants of the desert.

When speaking of Arabs here we shall not consider the more developed state of the northern Arabs or the old culture of southern
Arabia, but confine ourselves to the tribes which inhabited central 2
Arabia—though they extended their migrations also to the north; particularly to those tribes who supplied ancient Arabia with the poets[3] from whose vigorous works we have to derive our information about the ideas of this section of the Arab people.

[1] [For the religion of the Arabs before Islam see Wellhausen's study, quoted above, and G. Ryckmans, *Les religions arabes préislamiques*, Louvain 1951; J. Henninger, 'La religion bédouine préislamique', *L'Antica Società Beduina*, ed. F. Gabrieli, Rome, 1959, pp. 115–40.]

[2] Only one example, which is provided by the comparison of the Narrations of St. Nilus (beginning of the fifth cent.) with the account of Antoninus Martyr, who observed the Arabs of the Sinai peninsula in 570: the first says (ed. Migne, *Patrologia graeca*, vol. LXXIX, pp. 612 ff.) that the Arabs have no idols, but the latter mentions (*Perambulatio locorum sanctorum*, ed. Tobler, ch. 38, p. 113) a marble idol, white as snow, which is the centre of big feasts and he tells a fable of the changing colour of this idol.

[3] Cf. Nöldeke, *Die Semitischen Sprachen, Eine Skizze*, p. 46.

These products of that old Arabic mentality which Muhammed felt such a powerful call to influence are being made more readily available to us through current philological work; but they do not give satisfactory information about religious matters. It would not be wrong to conclude—though people are less willing to do so now than formerly—that Dozy was right in inferring from the lack of traces of a deep religious sense in pagan Arabic poetry[1] that 'religion, of whatever kind it may have been, generally had little place in the life of the Arabs, who were engrossed in worldly interests like fighting, wine, games and love.'[2] This at any rate would apply to the time when these poems were composed, i.e. to the time immediately preceding Islam.

It is true that a few outstanding individuals were open to deeper religious stimuli, which however did not spring from the national spirit but were due to special contacts (these people made many journeys to the north and the south; consider for example the extensive area crossed by al-A'shā, one of the last amongst them).[3] But even in the case of these the borrowed religious thoughts did not become organic elements of their inner life, but rather give the impression—for example in the work of the poet Labīd—of
3 mechanically superimposed sentences[4] rather than principles deeply influencing their general outlook. This despite a few pietistic sentiments, was still firmly based in old Arabic life.

The religious sense evident in the monuments of other Arab groups, as for instance those of the civilized provinces of south Arabia, is quite different. Here there is an unmistakable predominance of religious ideas and in comparison the failure to find any religious sentiment amongst the northern Arabs appears even more startling. Even the language of the southern Arabs has a greater variety of religious nomenclature than that of the northern Arabs

[1] This would be true also if the mention of pagan gods were commoner than in fact it is (Nöldeke, *Beiträge zur Kenntniss der Poesie der alten Araber*, p. ix, n. 2). On the other hand I wish to add an example of the expurgation, due to religious scruples, of traces of pagan elements from the remains of pre-Islamic poetry: Zayd al-Khayl mentions the Azdite idol 'Ā'im in one of his poems (Yāqūt, iii, p. 17), but this mention was not tolerated and *lā wa-'ā'im* was changed into *wa'l-'amā'im*, *Agh.*, xvi, p. 57, 2 from below. [For ''Āim see also Wellhausen, *Reste*, p. 66; Ibn al-Kalbī, *al-Aṣnām*, ed. Klinge, p. 25.]

[2] [*Histoire des Musulmans d'Espagne*, I, 22; German transl.:] *Geschichte der Mauren in Spanien*, I, p. 15. [Cf. H. A. R. Gibb, *Studies in the civilization of Islam*, pp. 179–81.]

[3] Thorbecke, *Morgenländische Forschungen*, p. 235, and also [al-A'shā', *Dīwān*, ed. Geyer, 17: 6; 25: 2; and 4: 56 ff. =] Yāqūt, III, p. 86, 16.

[4] This can be verified by looking at the contents of his *Dīwān* in v. Kremer's study of it (*Sitzungsberichte der Kais. Akademie der Wissenschaften*, phil. hist. Cl., XCVIII, 1881, pp. 555 ff).

which, otherwise so rich, is so poor in this respect.[1] A south Arabian prince would in his votive inscriptions thank the gods who made him victorious over his enemies and the warriors erected votive memorials to their divine patron 'for having made them happy with ample killing and in order that he may continue to grant them booty', or for having seen to it that they came to no harm in battle. In general the thankful and submissive feeling towards the gods[2] is the basic tone of the existent south Arabian monuments.[3] The warriors of central Arabia boast of their heroic courage and the bravery of their companions; they do not think of thanking superior powers for their successes—though they do not altogether refuse to acknowledge such powers. Only the thought of the necessity of death—the result of everyday experience against which they could not close their mind—occasionally calls forth the harsh idea of the *manāyā* or *manūna*,[4] i.e. the powers of fate which blindly and unconscious of their aim[5] may inevitably foil all mortal plans.[6] Good fortune enhances the egoism of these warriors, increases their self-confidence and is least apt to stimulate them to religious feelings. Only matters connected 4
with their tribal constitution could awaken in these pagan Arabs a real religious piety.[7] This eventually developed into a kind of ancestor cult, much as the chief attributes of Arabic morality are connected with the customary law which governed their social life.

The rare traces of religious sentiment can presumably not be dissociated from the influence of the south on the north.[8] At Yathrib the indigenous disposition of immigrant tribes from the south

[1] Halévy, *Journal asiatique*, 1872, I, p. 544. Some of the religious nomenclature of southern Arabia was borrowed by the north Arab language. [It seems, however, that here too the contrast is not so much between northern and southern Arabia as between Bedouins and a settled population. The south Arabian inscriptions bear witness of the religious spirit of the settled population of that country.]

[2] E.g. Mordtmann and Müller *Sabäische Denkmäler*, p. 29 and passim.

[3] A good example of many that could be cited is the inscription Osiander No. 4 [=*Corpus Inscriptionum Semiticarum*, iv, 74], see Prideaux in *Transactions of Soc. Bibl. Arch.* V (1877), p. 409.

[4] Also, I think, *manawāt*; P. Aelius Theimes appeals to the *manawāt* in his Latin inscription which was found in Várhely (Hungary) and published by Prof. Torma in *Archaeolog. epigr. Mittheilungen aus Osterreich* (Vienna 1882), VI, p. 110. [*Manawāt* also among the Nabataeans: Wellhausen, *Reste*, p. 28.]

[5] Zuhayr, *Mu'all.*, v. 49.

[6] How very personified *manāyā* was can still be realized in Islamic times in al-Farazdaq (*Dīwān* ed. Boucher, p. 12 ult). W. L. Schrameier has dealt exhaustively with *manāyā* in his thesis *Über den Fatalismus der Araber*, Bonn 1881. [See now W. Caskel, *Das Schicksal in der altarabischen Poesie*, Leipzig 1926; H. Ringgren, *Studies in Arabian Fatalism*, Uppsala 1955.]

[7] These facts were revealed by Robertson Smith in *Kinship and Marriage in Early Arabia*.

[8] Cf. *Journal asiat.*, 1883, II. p. 267.

produced a mood more easily accessible to religious thought which was a great help to Muhammed's success.[1] Generally, however, Muhammed could not expect the mind of his people to be readily responsive to his preaching. He offered them the opposite of their established view on life, their ideals and ancestral traditions. Hence the great opposition that he encountered everywhere. The pagans opposed less the shattering of their idols than the pietistic disposition which they were to accept: that the whole of their life should be determined by thinking of God and His omnipotence which predestines and requites; that they should pray, fast, abstain from enjoyable indulgences, sacrifice money and property, all demanded from them in the name of God. In addition they were to consider as barbaric many things which hitherto had been esteemed cardinal virtues, and were to recognize as their leader a man whose claim to this title seemed unusual and incomprehensible and radically different from the attributes upon which had been founded their glory and that of their ancestors.

II

In the first place, and quite apart from the special contents and direction of Muhammed's announcement, the person of the prophet was little suited to impress people who gave admiration and veneration only to powerful individuals very different from 'God's apostle', who had an unimportant position even within his own lineage. How could the call of such a man find voluntary followers amongst the unbridled desert tribes? The very fact that he was a city dweller might have been repulsive enough for these nomads. The Bedouins did not see in Muhammed any of the qualities that they were accustomed to admire in their sheikhs. Muhammed was no authority in the eyes of these children of the desert, though his transcendental pronouncements may have impressed some of the unbelieving city dwellers. For the tribesmen he had nothing that could be admired because they were unable to understand the concept of a man as God's emissary.

This feeling emerges quite clearly from some tales which arose later from a good knowledge of the character of the Bedouins. During their journey to Mecca the prophet's party met a desert Arab whom they asked for information. In order to give themselves greater importance they told him that 'God's apostle' was amongst them. 'If you are God's apostle,' replied the Bedouin to Muhammed, 'then tell me what is inside the body of this she-camel.'[2]

[1] On the points that helped Muhammed in Medina see Snouck Hurgronje in De Gids 1886 no. 5 (*De Islam*), offprint, p. 32 [= *Verspreide Geschriften*, I, pp. 210-11].

[2] Ibn Hishām, p. 433.

Only prophecies of such a nature would have inspired him with respect for a man who could make them. Sermons about the last judgment, God's will, and other transcendental matters made no impression on him. Each Arab tribe was also much too full of admiration for its members to accept a man as 'the best of all men', who was lacking in those virtues which represented the height of perfection to the Arabs. For such a man Arabs sought first of all amongst their own tribe, among the heroes of its past or present. Abū Rabī' from the Ghanī tribe said as late as in the second half of the first century: 'The best of all people are the Arabs and amongst those the Muḍar tribes, amongst those Qays, amongst those the clan of Ya'ṣur, amongst those the family of Ghanī, and of the Ghanī I am the best man. Hence I am the best of all men.'[1] What then will have been the feelings of these people's ancestors when Muhammed first appeared?

In his revelations Muhammed complains of the difficulty of converting the desert dwellers. 'The Arabs, the dwellers in the desert,
are stronger in their disbelief and hypocrisy (than the city Arabs) 6
and they are much more prone to not knowing the boundaries (laws) which God has revealed to His prophet. Amongst these Arabs there are some who consider what they have to spend (for religious purposes) as a compulsory loan and who are awaiting a change of circumstances.'[2]

There are, however, exceptions—as he says in the next verse—believing Bedouins who willingly spend money for Muhammed's venture and who see in this a means of getting closer to God; but these are a very small minority. Amongst the believers, too, there are some who outwardly confess their belief but have no inclination in their heart towards Islamic morals and dogma[3] and show no understanding of what Muhammed meant by and taught about 'giving oneself to God'.[4] A few details from tradition help to clarify the Bedouin Arabs' relation to religion: 'Brutality and recalcitrance are the characteristics of those bawlers (*faddādīn*), the tent dwellers from the tribes of Rabī'a and Muḍar who drive their camels and cattle' (literally: by the roots of the tails of their camels and cattle.)[5] In their intercourse with the prophet they are accused of coarseness and lack of veneration.[6] It is understandable that even converted

[1] Al-Mubarrad, p. 352.

[2] Sūra 9: 98-99.

[3] Ibid, 48: 11.

[4] Ibid 49: 14.

[5] B. *Manāqib*, no. 2 [*Maghāzī*, 74; Muslim, *Īmān*, 92; Ibn Ḥanbal, *Musnad*, II, p. 258, III, pp. 332, 335, 345, 439].

[6] Examples for this are in B. *Waḍū'*, nos. 60, 61; *Adab*, nos. 67, 79; cf. Ibn Ḥajar, I, p. 993. Notice the word *a'rābiyya* 'bedouin behaviour' in connection with *jafā'*—coarseness in al-Balādhurī, p. 425, 1. 'Umar b. 'Abd al-'Azīz, the sworn

Bedouins did not like to stay in Muhammed's company since they did not relish city life and they returned to the desert after the prophet showed himself unwilling to absolve them from their vow of homage.[1] How little they had lost of their Bedouin character can be seen from the example of the converts from the tribes 'Ukl and 'Urayna, who said to the prophet, after having lived near him for some time: 'We are people used to the udders of our camels, we are not people of the clod and Medina is uncomfortable for us and life there does not become us.' The prophet then gave them a herd, placed a herder at their disposal and permitted them to leave Medina to return happily to their accustomed form of life. Hardly had they reached the Ḥarra when
7 they fell back into their old disbelief, killed the herder and drove the animals with them. They were overtaken by the prophet's cruel revenge.[2]

According to tradition, the prophet once said to his companions: 'He who climbs that mountain (i.e. Murār near Ḥudaybiya) will be delivered of his sins as they were taken from the Banū Isrā'il.' The mounted men of the Banū Khazraj were the first to tackle the task and the rest followed them in large numbers. The prophet promised them forgiveness of their sins. A Bedouin sat watching, mounted on a brown camel: everybody urged him to get rid of his sins by undergoing the trial which the prophet had set. But he replied: 'I consider it more desirable to find my lost camel than that your companion there would pray for the remission of my sins.'[3] Only the expectation of a higher position within Arabic society, or the even meaner motive of material gain, could have moved a thoroughly realistic people to follow the call of this man who spoke to them of incomprehensible things. Some who were impressed by the promise of reward and well-being might have expected that their business would prosper and all their wishes would be fulfilled as a result of confessing Islam, but when experience taught them that all their external affairs were still subject to the same changes and accidents—even after their conversion—they cast Islam aside like an unpropitious fetish. The Koranic verse (22; 11) about people who serve God 'on an edge' is supposed

[1] B. *Aḥkām*, nos. 45, 47, 50.
[2] B. *Zakāt*, no. 68, *Diyāt*, no. 22, *Ṭibb.*, no. 29.
[3] Muslim, V, p. 348. Another version in Wāqidī-Wellhausen, p. 246.

---

enemy of luxury as developed under the Caliphate, finds at least the spartan way of life of the Bedouins praiseworthy. 'Nobody would be more similar to the pious ancients than the Bedouins, were they not different from them in their coarse behaviour (*jafā'*)', al-Jāḥiẓ, *Kitāb al-Bayān*, fol. 47a [II, 164]. [For the tradition: 'Those who live in the desert are coarse', and for other similar tradition see the references in *Concordance de la Tradition musulmane*, s.vv. *bdw* and *jfw*, and Ibn 'Abd al-Barr, *Jāmi' Bayān al-'Ilm*, I, pp. 163–4.]

to refer to such desert Arabs. Bedouins came to Medina—says the traditional exegesis of this passage—who, if their bodies were healthy, their mares had pretty foals and their women gave birth to well-shaped boys, if their property and cattle increased, were satisfied with Islam, to which they attributed these favourable results. But if anything went wrong they blamed Islam and turned away from it.[1]

True Bedouins thus were little attracted by the prophet's preaching of salvation. The language of the Koran was alien to them and they had no understanding of it. 'Glad tidings' and 'redemption' meant other things to them than advice on how to gain eternal salvation. 'Imrān b. Ḥuṣayn tells that he was present when the prophet invited the Banū Tamīm to accept the 'glad tidings,' and the latter refused the prophet's promise with the words: 'You bring 8
us glad tidings, it would be better if you were to give us something.'[2] Whole chapters of the prophet's biographies are regularly concerned with descriptions of the lack of receptivity on the part of the tribes to Muhammed's preaching. It is always stark egoism with which they counter the prophet. When he offered his message to the Banū 'Āmir b. Ṣa'ṣa'a, their leader Bayḥara b. Firās replied: 'If we are to pay homage to you and you defeat your enemies will we come to power after you?' . . . And when Muhammed referred him in this matter of power to Allah's will, who grants or withholds power as He sees fit, he was displeased and said: 'Are our necks to be a target then to the Arabs for your sake? and if you win others are to rule. We have no use for such an arrangement.'[3]

It is because of this attitude of the Bedouins towards rising Islam that the legislation which is traditionally referred back to the prophet shows a tendency to slight and despise the Bedouins. For example, the prophet is said to have forbidden the acceptance of things offered by desert Arabs and had to justify himself to his own entourage when he had the milk that the Aslamite woman Umm Sunbulā offered him as a present poured into his vessels.[4] And even when, after the first strengthening of the Muslim community, the object was to ensure that all its members received their share in the material gain of the wars and raids, the Bedouins were treated worse than the city dwellers. There is evidence of disparagement of desert dwellers as late as the time of the Caliph 'Umar II.[5]

It is true that the traditional accounts which we used in the above exposition, and those which will appear in the further course

[1] Al-Bayḍāwī, I, p. 628, 21 ff.
[2] [B. *Bad' al-Khalq*, 1.]
[3] Ibn Hishām, p. 283.
[4] Ibn Ḥajar, IV, p. 896.
[5] Al-Balādhurī, p. 458

of our survey, are not so strongly attested as to make them acceptable as contemporary data from the time to which they are ascribed by the sources. They can nevertheless serve as valid evidence of the reactions of authentic Arab society to the new teaching. If the Bedouins' reaction to Muslim teaching at a time when the greater part of the traditions came into being—i.e. at a time when Islam was strong, or even dominant—made it possible to give such des-
9 criptions taken from experience as we have seen above, it may be imagined what their reaction was when the call of the dreamer of Mecca followed by a few pious disciples in Medina first penetrated into the desert.

III

Deep as was the antagonism to the personality of 'God's apostle' the Arabs were even more violently opposed to the content and trend of his teachings. At the very heart of Muhammed's preaching lay a protest against many things which had hitherto been valued and considered noble by Arabs. The highest ethical perfection in the eyes of pagan Arabs could often be regarded as the lowest moral decay from an Islamic point of view and vice versa. In much the same way as the Church-Father Augustine, Islam also considered 'the virtues of the pagans as brilliant vices'.

If, therefore, a man were truly converted to Islam, he confessed virtues which were considered vices by the Arabs. No true Arab could agree to renounce his inherited ideas of virtue. When the wife of the hero 'Abbās b. Mirdās learned that her husband had joined the prophet, she destroyed their homestead and returned to her old tribe, reprimanding her unfaithful husband in a poem where she says amongst other things:

By my life if you follow the *dīn* of Muhammed
and leave the faithful ones[1] and the benefactors,
10 This soul has exchanged lowness for pride
on the day when the sharp blades of the swords
hit against each other.[2]

[1] *Ikhwān al-ṣafā*; not the 'Brethren of Purity', as might be pointed out here again to correct a popular error (cf. *Lbl. for orient Phil*, 1886, p. 28, 8 from below. For the early appearance of this phrase which the philosophers of Baṣra chose as their name one can quote *Ḥam.* p. 390, v. 3 (cf. *Opusc. arab.*, ed. Wright, p. 132 note 33), *Agh.*, XVIII, p. 218, 16. [In his article 'Über die Benennung der Ichwān al-ṣafā' ', *Der Islam*, I, 1910, pp. 22 ff. Goldziher adds *Naqā'iḍ*, ed. Bevan, p. 933, l. 6, and points out that the 'Brethren' took their name from a story of Kalīla wa-Dimna where the expression is used]. Cf. from later poetry, *Agh.*, V, p. 131, 3, and this expression must be understood in the same sense in the so-called 'prayer of al-Fārābī' (see Aug. Müller, *Gott. gel. Anz.*, 1884, December, p. 958) [=Ibn Abī Uṣaybi'a, II, p. 137], and in similar usages

Muhammed's teaching was unable to show the legitimation which in Arabic conscience was the measure of all things, the agreement with the traditions of the past: it was those very traditions against which the new teaching preached. Reference to ancestral custom was the most powerful argument against which Muhammed had to defend his new teaching; in a large part of the Koran he writhes under the weight of this argument. 'If one says to them: Follow the law that God sent you, they reply: we follow the customs of our fathers.' 'If one says to them: Come and accept the religion which Allāh has revealed to His apostle, they counter: We are satisfied with the religion of our fathers. They are not concerned that their fathers had neither knowledge nor guidance to lead them.' 'When the evil-doers commit blameworthy deeds they say: Thus we saw things done by our fathers: it is Allāh who orders it so. Say to them: Allāh has never ordered blameworthy deeds.' 'But they will say: We found that our fathers followed in this road and we follow their traces. Say then: Do I not announce something better than what you found your fathers following?'[1] In the Koran sinful peoples of early times do in effect always quote their fathers' customs to the prophets who have been sent to them for their improvement; Muhammed puts this argument into the mouth of the speakers of the various peoples who reject the preaching of the prophets Hūd, Ṣāliḥ, Shu'ayb, Ibrāhīm and others, and in describing these people he has in mind the pagan Arabs, his own opponents. All these people reply to the prophets who are sent to instruct them: This was not known to our fathers, we only do as our fathers did before us.

The Arab liked to stress when speaking of his virtues that in practising them he was striving to resemble his forefathers,[2] he

[1] [The passages from the Koran are: 2: 170 (=31: 21); 5: 104; 7: 28; 43: 23-4.]

[2] *Ḥam.*, p. 742, v. 3.

(*Yatīmat al-Dahr*, ed. Damascus, II, p. 89, 11). In this context also other terms of kinship and appurtenance may be used for *akhū*: e.g. *nadīm al-ṣafā'* (*Agh.*, XXI, p. 66, 7) *ḥalīf al-ṣafā'* (ib., XIII, p. 35, 8) i.e. in the same sense as we find *ḥalīf al-jūd* (V, p. 13, 23) *ḥalīf al-lu'm* (XIV, p. 83, 3 bel.) *ḥalīf al-dhull* (II, p. 84, 16) *ḥilf al-makārim* (XVII, p. 71, 14) or *ḥalīfu hammin, ḥilf al-saqām* (*al-Muwashshā*, ed. Brünnow, p. 161, 18, 24) or *muḥālif al-ṣayd* (Nāb., *App.* 26, 37), as also the verb *ḥlf* is often used to indicate that someone has a quality, a state or colour the name of which follows the verb in the accusative. Other synonyms are also used in this context, like *akhū* and *ḥalīf*, particularly *mawlā* (Labīd, *Mu'all.*, v. 48, *Ḥam*, p. 205, v. 3, *Agh.*, IX. p. 84, 9, XII, p. 125, v. 10, Abu'l-Aswad, *ZDMG*, XVIII, p. 234, 18, 20, Abu'l-'Alā', *Siqṭ al-Zand*, I, p. 197, v. 4) or *tarib al-nadā* (Mutan., I, p. 35, v. 35), *quarīn al-jūd* (*Agh.*, XIII, p. 61, 9). The idea lying at the base of these expressions is expressed in a paraphrastic way in al-Mutanabbī, I, p. 151 as: *Ka-annamā yūladu'l-nadā ma'ahum.*

[2] Ag. XIII, p. 66.

11 displayed in this practice a conservative attitude,[1] refusing to accept anything new which was not founded in transmitted custom, and opposing everything which threatened to abolish an existing custom. Thus it is easily understood that the frivolous Qurayshites, who had first regarded the message of 'the boy from the family of 'Abd al-Muṭṭalib, who repeats the words of heaven' as the harmless phantasy of an overwrought eccentric, turned into spiteful opponents of the new teaching only when Muhammed not only began to attack their gods—to whom they felt no pious devotion—but also 'condemned their fathers who had died unbelievers'; then they began to hate him and to strive against him.[2] 'O Abū Ṭālib,' they complained, 'your brother's son insults our gods, criticizes our habits and declares our custom barbaric and decries our fathers.'[3]

The remonstrances quoted above from the Koran are not typical phrases of the prophet as might be thought from their frequent, almost literal repetition. Evidence of this Arab mentality, strongly opposed to the new teaching, always referring to 'the traces of the ancestors', and appealing to that 'which the fathers were found to do',[4] is to be found for example in a poem where the poet Ka'b b. Zuhayr, who was then still engrossed in paganism, attacks his brother Bujayr for his conversion to Muhammed's teaching.

12 You have left the good road (*al-hudā*)[5] and followed him—woe, where have you been led: to qualities which you share neither with father nor mother, nor do you know any brother who has followed it.

[1] It was considered praiseworthy to practise the virtue of hospitality with the help of household utensils inherited from the ancestors: al-Nābigha, *Append.* 24, 4. This explains why the dying father of Imru'l-Qays entrusts his son, who was to revenge him, not only with such precious legacies as his weapons and horses, but also with his pots (*qudūr*): *Agh.*, VIII, p. 66, 4, cf. Rückert, *Amrilkais der Dichter und König*, p. 10. Pots are the symbol of hospitality and hospitable people are called '*iẓām al-qudūr*: Ḥassān, *Dīwān*, p. 87, 11 = Ibn Hishām, p. 931, 5. Also of war horses as a means to bravery, it is said in this sense that they are inherited from the fathers and must be passed on to the successors: 'Amr b. Kulthūm, *Mu'all.*, v. 81. On hereditary swords: Schwarzlose, *Die Waffen der Araber*, p. 36. The commentators conclude unjustly from B. *Jihād*, no. 85, that the Arabs of the Jāhiliyya used to destroy the weapons of their heroes after their death.

[2] Ibn Sa'd [I, 133, quoted by] Sprenger, I, p. 357. [The correct translation seems to be 'who is addressed from heaven.']

[3] Ibn Hishām, p. 17, cf. 183, 186; al-Ṭabarī, I, pp. 1175, 1185.

[4] On the power of tradition and custom over true Arabs, see L. Derome in the introduction to his French translation of Lady Anne Blunt, *Pèlerinage au Nedjd berceau de la race arabe*, Paris 1882, pp. XLVII ff.

[5] This word is probably used by the pagans ironically: Muhammed and his followers liked to use it to describe their teaching and practice.

To which the Muslim Bujayr replied:

> Father Zubayr's religion (*dīn*)—his religion is a nothing—and the religion of Abū Sulmā (the grandfather) is despicable to me.[1]

But a little later Ka'b also cast aside the gods al-Lāt and al-'Uzzā and became the poetical panegyrist of the prophet and his teachings.

IV

From the point of view of cultural history it is of little account that Muhammed's teaching was not the original creation of his genius which made him the prophet of his people, but that all his doctrines are taken from Judaism and Christianity. Their originality lies in the fact that these teachings were for the first time placed in contrast to the Arabic ways of life by Muhammed's persistent energy. If we consider how superficially Christianity influenced the few Arab circles into which it penetrated,[2] and how alien it was to the main body of the Arab people despite the support which it found in some districts of Arabia, we must be convinced of the antagonism of the Arabs to the ideas which it taught. Christianity never imposed itself 13
on the Arabs and they had no opportunity to fight against its doctrines sword in hand. The rejection of a viewpoint diametrically opposed to their own found its expression only in the struggle of the Arabs against Muhammed's teachings.

The gulf between the moral views of the Arabs and the prophet's ethical teachings is deep and unbridgeable.[3] If we seek slogans to make

[1] *Bānat Su'ād*, ed. Guidi, pp. 4-5, cf. Ibn Hishām, p. 888.

[2] This is true e.g. of Christianity in the tribe of Taghlib, cf. [al-Ṭabarī's and al-Zamakhsharī's commentary on Koran 5 7, and] al-Bayḍāwī, i, p. 248, 2 where a saying which characterizes this state of affairs is ascribed to 'Alī. Nöldeke, *Geschichte des Korans*, p. 7 [2nd ed., I, 10]; Dozy, *Geschichte der Mauren in Spanien*, I, p. 14 [in the French original: I, pp. 20-1]; Fell, *ZDMG*, XXXV, p. 49, note 2. Combine with this saying a verse by Jarīr referring to later times, quoted by al-Mubarrad, p. 485: In the dwelling-places of Taghlib there is no mosque, but there are churches for wine jugs and skins, i.e. many taverns. [The text is slightly different in *Naqā'iḍ*, ed. Bevan, 95: 88=*Dīwān*, ed. al-Sāwī, p. 576.] How superficially Christian laws were absorbed by circles who outwardly professed Christianity has already been pointed out by Caussin de Perceval, II, p. 158 (polygamy); cf. Nöldeke, *Die ghassanischen Fürsten*, p. 29, note. It may be added that the Christian poet al-Akhṭal, who lived at the court of the Umayyad ruler 'Abd al-Malik, divorced his wife and married the wife of a Bedouin: *Agh.*, VII, p. 177. On alleged ruins of Taghlibite churches on the islands of Farasān, see Yāqūt, III, p. 874, after al-Hamdānī [*Jazīrat al-'Arab*, p. 53].

[3] Fresnel set out to prove in his *Lettres sur l'histoire des Arabes avant l'Islamisme*, p. 13, that the Arabs at the time of the Jāhiliyya were on a higher moral plane than after the penetration of Islam (*Journal asiat.*, 1849, II, p. 533); but the proofs which he cited are highly inconclusive.

this contrast clear, we can find none better than the two words: *dīn* and *muruwwa*; the first[1] is the 'religion' of Muhammed, the second the 'virtue' (literally and etymologically the latin word *virtus* corresponds to the Arabic *muruwwa*) of the Arabs.[2]

By *muruwwa* the Arab means all those virtues which, founded in the tradition of his people, constitute the fame of an individual or the tribe to which he belongs; the observance of those duties which are connected with family ties, the relationships of protection[3] and hospitality, and the fulfilment of the great law of blood revenge.[4] Reading their poets and observing the virtues of which they boast, we have a picture of *muruwwa* according to the ancient Arabic concepts.[5] Loyalty to, and self-sacrifice for the sake of all who are connected, by Arab custom, with one's tribe are the quintessence of these virtues. 'If one in my care is harmed I tremble because of this
14 injustice, my bowels are moved[6] and my dogs bark.'[7] 'Faithless' (*ghudar*) is the sum total of all that is most loathsome to the pagan Arabs. It would be wrong to suppose that the exercise of this virtue had its source merely in the semi-conscious instincts of a half savage people; it was regulated and disciplined by perfectly fixed traditional legal ideas.

The social intercourse of the ancient Arabs was based on the principle of right and equity. Their ideas on law are expressed in a statement by one of their poets usually accepted as genuine: 'Truth is established by three ways: oath, contest, and the evidence (of the case itself)'[8]. Such a saying indicates a conscious striving for justice in the higher sense and it inspired at an early date high esteem for the strong sense for justice of the society from which it emanated. (Our

[1] Naturally the loan word *dīn* and not the old Arab word which sounds the same.

[2] The modern language also uses the synonym *marjala* (from *rajul* = *mar'*) for the idea of *muruwwa*: Van den Berg, *Le Ḥadramaut*, p. 278, 5.

[3] *Jiwār*: a distinction was made between two kinds of *jiwār*, i.e. the one founded on guarantee (*kafāla*) and the proper relationship of protection (*talā'*), Zuhayr 1:43. Of refusal of protection it is said: *ḥassa*, *Hudhayl.*, 37:2. The relation of *jiwār* could be dissolved only through a solemn public act, *Agh.*, XIV, p. 99. [For *jiwār* cf S. Fraenkel, 'Das Schutzrecht der Araber', *Orientalische Studien T. Nöldeke gewidmet*, I, pp. 233-301.]

[4] [For blood revenge see O. Procksch, *Über die Blutrache bei den vorislamischen Arabern*, Leipzig 1899; H. Lammens, *L'Arabie occidentale avant l'hégire*, pp. 181 ff.]

[5] 'Honour and revenge', Muir calls the essence of the ethical code of the Arabs ('The forefathers of Mahomet and history of Mecca', *Calcutta Review*, no. XLIII, 1854).

[6] Cf. Jerem. 31:20; Cant., 5:4

[7] *Ḥam.*, p. 183, v. 1.

[8] Zuhayr, 1:40; cf. *Muḥīṭ al-Muḥīṭ*, I, p. 278b; in this *qaṣīda*, juridical reflections are also to be found; cf. only v. 60.

source makes the Caliph 'Umar I[1] express admiration for this verse.) Similarly, a *qaṣīda* is attributed to Salama b. al-Khushrub al-Anmārī[2], addressed to Subay' al-Taghlibī on the occasion of the war of Dāḥis and Ghabrā, which reveals such conscious striving for justice that Sahl b. Hārūn, in whose presence the *qaṣīda* was recited, remarked that one might almost believe that the poet had been familiar with the instruction about the administration of justice given by 'Umar to Abū Mūsā al-Ash'arī.[3]

Islamic teaching was not opposed to a large part of the Arab system of virtues[4]—in particular Islam incorporated into its own teaching[5] the moving loyalty of the Arabs towards those seeking 15
protection. In pagan times the dwelling places of the faithless were marked with flags at general assemblies so that people might be able to avoid them,[6] and Islam's teaching that on the day of resurrection such a flag will be hoisted in front of the perfidious[7] is undoubtedly related to that custom. Nevertheless there were decisive and basic points in the moral teaching of the Jāhiliyya to which Islam was in almost irreconcilable contrast.

At such points the fundamental difference between Muhammed's *dīn* and the Arabic *muruwwa* becomes evident.[8] The study which follows this introductory chapter will deal with the foremost of these

[1] He is also otherwise said to have been an admirer of the poetry of Zuhayr, *Agh.* IX, pp. 147, 154.

[2] [The correct form of the name is Salama b. al-Khurshub.]

[3] Al-Jāḥiẓ, *Kitāb al-Bayān*, fols. 96b-97a [I, 238-9] = Ibn Qutayba, *'Uyūn al-Akhbār* fol. 73a [I, 67]. I owe this last reference to my friend Baron v. Rosen.

[4] The idea that the noble points of the *muruwwa* of the Arabs must remain valid and also in Islam receive so to speak the sanction of religious ethics is expressed by Islam in this principle: *lā dīn illā bi-muruwwa*, i.e. there is no *dīn* (religion) without the virtues of old Arab chivalry (*muruwwa*).

[5] Primarily in Sūra 4:40, then in a large number of traditions which are brought together in Shaykh Aḥmad al-Fashanī's commentary to the Arba'īn collection of al-Nawawī, no. 15 (*al-Majālis al-Saniyya fi'l-Kalām 'ala'l-Arba'īn al-Nawawiyya*, Būlāq 1292, pp. 57 ff.

[6] *Al-Hadirae Diwanus*, ed. Engelmann, p. 7, 4 [*al-Mufaḍḍaliyyāt*, ed. Lyall, 8:9]; on another custom belonging here, cf. Freytag, *Einleitung in das Studium der arab. Sprache*, p. 150. [Cf. al-Marzūqī's commentary on the *Ḥamāsa*, p. 1788.]

[7] B. *Adab*, no. 98.

[8] Under the influence of Islamic views several definitions of the *muruwwa* came into being, which to a greater or lesser extent preserved old Arabic points but which were by and large deeply influenced by religion; see al-Mubarrad, p. 29, *al-Muwashshā*, ed. Brünnow, pp. 31 ff., *al-'Iqd*, I, p. 221, al-Ḥuṣrī I, p. 49. Some of these definitions express a sure consciousness of the contrast between pagan virtues and what Muslims understood by virtue. There were pietists who understood by *muruwwa* in Islam the diligent reading of the Koran and frequent visits to mosques (*al-'Iqd*, l.c.). Generally the view was taken that there could be no *muruwwa* in a man who had acted contrary to Allāh's will (*Agh.*, XIX, p. 144, 11). [Cf. also the article 'Murū'a', by B. Farès, in *Enc. of Islam*, Suppl.]

contrasts. Here we will only mention a detail which made Arabs always conscious of the strangeness of Muhammed's ethical teachings—the attitude towards retaliation.

The pre-Islamic Arabs had no more barbarous views about retaliation for insults than any of the most cultured peoples of antiquity. Revenge and the requital of good[1] are both within the scope of morality for them. If we are to pass a fair judgment upon the fact that the pre-Islamic Arabs did not consider forgiveness and conciliation of enemies a virtue, we must not forget that in this they were at one not only with so-called primitive peoples[2], but also with
16 the most highly civilized peoples of antiquity, such as the Egyptians[3] and Greeks. The greatest teachers of ethics among the last mentioned saw man's vocation as excelling his friends in doing good and his enemies in inflicting evil: 'to be sweet to friends and bitter to enemies, honourable to the first and terrible to the latter'; 'every injustice inflicted on an enemy is counted justice before God and men.'[4] Even the later Stoic ethic does not consider it bad to inflict harm when one has been provoked by insults (*lacessitus iniuria*).

This attitude towards retaliation is found not only among the pre-Islamic Arabs but, even after Muhammed's teaching had taken a hold, amongst those people who, despite the rule of Islam, clung to the attributes of the ancient pagan *muruwwa*.

An old proverb says: 'Good for good, he who starts is the nobler of the two; bad with bad, he who started it is the guilty one.'[5] This principle of repaying injury with injury recalls the self-praise with which poets of ancient Arabia covered themselves or their tribe,[6] and in which the same principle figures most prominently. The dying 'Amr. b. Kulthūm tells his children that there is nothing good in a man who, when he is insulted, does not return the insult;[7] and indeed he himself had adhered to this principle all his life like a good and true Arab. In a famous poem he boasts that his tribe endeavours to outdo in brutality all who treat them badly.[8] Aws b. Ḥajar says: 'I hold good and evil on loan: evil I repay to him

[1] Even a late poet talks of hatred as the twin of gratitude: Freytag, *Chrestom. arab.*, p. 90, 1.

[2] On retaliation as moral principle in primitive societies see Schneider, *Die Naturvölker*, Paderborn 1886, I, p. 86.

[3] Even at the time of the end of paganism, *Revue égyptologique*, II, p. 94, ff.; *Transactions of the Soc. of bibl. Archaeology*, VIII, pp. 12 ff.; Tiele, *Verglijkende Geschiedenis van de Egypt. en Mesopotam. Gods.*, p. 160.

[4] Cf. Leopold Schmidt, *Die Ethik der alten Griechen*, Berlin 1882, II, pp. 309 ff.

[5] In *al-Iqd*, III, p. 129, this saying is ascribed to 'Umar.

[6] Cf. Kremer, *Culturgeschichte des Orients*, II, p. 232.

[7] *Agh.*, IX, p. 185.

[8] *Mu'allaqa*, v. 53.

that does me evil and good I give unto him that treats me well.'[1]
The ancient Arabs do not always even recognize the limit set by that 17
proverb. Zuhayr—a man with a strong sense of justice—praises a hero for the fact that he repays injustice with injustice and that he acts unjustly even when he himself has not been attacked;[2] and in the poem which heads the heroic poems in the collection of the *Ḥamāsa* the poet Qurayṭ b. Unayf rails at the members of his tribe for forgiving injustice done to them and requiting evil with good.[3] This was considered shameful by the ancient Arab, who had a different ideal: 'The man of men is he who thinks early and late how he can injure his enemies and do his friends good,'[4] a principle which is almost a literal repetition of an epigram by Solon.

Examples of such sayings by early Arabic heroes and poets could be considerably amplified: anybody versed in Arabic literature can add a number of texts to those quoted above. It has already been hinted that in Islamic times, too, this view was expressed by circles who adhered to the traditions of the Jāhiliyya. 'Who do not reward good with evil and do not reply softly to hardness'[5] is still in the early days of Islam a high tribute. In 'Umar's time Abū Miḥjan of the Thaqīf tribe boasts that he 'was strong in hatred and anger when slighted.'[6]

But Islam preached a far-reaching reform in this field of human emotion. Muhammed was the first man of their kind who said to the people of Mecca and the unbridled masters of the Arabian desert that forgiveness was no weakness but a virtue and that to forgive injustice done to oneself was not contrary to the norms of true *muruwwa* but was the highest *muruwwa*—was walking in Allāh's
road. And the mentality expressed by the Muslim poet[7] who said: 18
'To reward insults with mildness and forgiveness means leniency and to pardon where one could take revenge is noble' is quite different from that which fired the old Arabic poets to the cult of revenge.

[1] Ibn al-Sīkkīt [*Tahdhīb al-Alfāẓ*] (MS. Leiden no. 597) p. 336 last line [ed. Cheikho, p. 406]

fa-'indī qurūḍu'l-khayri wa'l-sharri kullihi
fa-bu'sā li-dhī būsin wa-nu'mā li-an'umi.

['Gedichte and Fragmente des 'Aus ibn Ḥajar' (*Sitzungsber. der Kais. Akademie der Wissenschaften*, Vienna 1892, no. XIII), 43: 7; the correct text is: *fa-bu'sā ladā bu'sā.*]

[2] Zuhayr, *Mu'allaqa*, v. 39; cf. v. 57 *wa-man lā yazlimi'l-nāsa yuẓlamu* and *Dīwān* of the same poet 17:13. [Al-Najāshī taunts the objects of his satire with their never acting unjustly: *ZDMG*, LIV, p. 461; Ibn al-Shajarī, *Ḥamāsa*, p. 131.]

[3] *Ḥam.*, p. 4, v. 3.

[4] *Ḥam.*, p. 730, v. 2 = Rückert, II, p. 285, no. 725.

[5] Abu'l-Ghūl al-Ṭahawī, *Ḥam.*, p. 13 v. 2 (Rückert, I, p. 5); cf. also al-Farazdaq, ed. Boucher, p. 46, 4.

[6] *Ṭuraf 'Arabiyya*, ed. Landberg, p. 60.

[7] Al-Mas'ūdī, V, p. 101, 3.

He who did not repay an insult in kind was a coward to the Jāhiliyya and brought shame upon the tribe; but those 'who conquer their anger and forgive men' are promised paradise in the Koran (3: 128), and tradition makes Muhammed say that such men are rare amongst his people but could often be found in the older religious communities.[1] According to the Koran, one of the chief conditions of divine forgiveness is that men shall also forgive those who trespass against them and that they shall strive to forget any injustices that they may have suffered (24:22). 'Reward evil with something better' (23:98). Islam could not miss in the description of the prophet's character the feature that 'he did not reward bad with evil but forgave and exercised leniency'.[2] What the Koran teaches here in sharp contrast to the old Arabic views, pious Muslims have later strengthened and elaborated by a large number of traditions; and no work of Muslim scholarship belonging to the branch of theological ethics lacks a chapter on *al-'afw*.

Muhammed severely castigates the *mukāfa'a*, i.e. retaliation (of evil for evil) primarily in one's relations with one's own kith and kin. By *ṣilat al-raḥim* (love of kindred) he understands love which does not counter hatred and lack of love with the same coin.[3] But even beyond this he is depicted by his faithful followers as preaching love and forgiveness. He is represented as saying: 'Shall I tell you whom I consider the worst of you? He who goes by himself to meals and withholds his presents and beats his slaves. But who is worse even than these? He who does not forgive faults and does not accept apologies, he who does not forgive offences. But who is worse even than that? He who is angry with others and with whom others are angry in return.'[4] 'He (who on his deathbed) forgives his mur-
19 derer'—pious Muslims make their master say—'is certain of paradise.'[5] 'But he who refuses to accept the apologies of others is considered as sinful as a tax collector[6] before God.'

[1] Al-Bayḍāwī to the verse, I, p. 175.

[2] Al-Nawawī, *Tahdhīb*, p. 41.

[3] B. *Adab*, no. 14.

[4] Al-Mubarrad, p. 39.

[5] Ibn Ḥajar, I, p. 436.

[6] Ibid., I, p. 524. [Other references in al-Sulamī, *Ādāb al-Ṣuḥba*, ed. M. J. Kister, p. 66, n. 192.] The tax collector, *'āmil al-kharāj*, is an unpleasant figure in Arabic literature (*Agh.*, IX, p. 129, 9), especially the collector of customs duty (*makkās* or *mākis*). The Arabic opinions of this profession and some legends and poems referring to it are to be found in al-Jāḥiẓ, *Kitāb al-Ḥayawān* (MS. of the K. Hofbibliothek, Vienna), fol. 326a [VI, pp. 80 ff., cf. pp. 184 ff]. Muslim legend ascribes a saying to King David in which even collectors of tithes (*'ashshār*) are excluded from God's mercy: *Agh.*, XVIII, p. 159 below. According to another legend the crying of donkeys is a curse against tax collectors and their profession, the croaking of crows is a curse against collectors of tithes: al-Damīrī, II, p. 122. Cf. a Muslim saying on customs collectors in al-Zarkashī,

The point of view of the *muruwwa* thus was totally altered and we shall not be surprised to find in its Muslim definition the requirement that men shall forgive where retaliation would be possible.[1]

V

Most irksome to the Arab sense of freedom were those restrictions which Muhammed and his doctrine sought to enforce upon the Arab people for the sake of religion. During the early times of Islam true Arabs found the fast of Ramaḍān little to their taste, holding that the long fast of the grave should absolve them from all abstinence on earth.[2] Expression is given even later to the true Arab's aversion from the ascetic abstinence prescribed by Islam.[3] During Muhammed's
days the most violent opposition was to the restrictions prescribed 20
in respect of sexual intercourse and wine drinking. Wine and sexual licence were called by them *al-aṭyabān* (the two delicious things). When al-Aʿshā prepared to go to Muhammed to pay him homage his pagan comrades tried to dissuade him by pointing out that Muhammed restricted these *aṭyabān*.[4]

There was such freedom in their sexual life that they were reluctant to relinquish it on the command of Muhammed whose authority was not sacred to them. The authority of the *dīn* was a revelation of God and that of the old Arabic *muruwwa* the old traditions founded on ancestral custom. But the latter was freer in respect of sexual intercourse and was not hedged in with those barriers which Muhammed now sought to erect in the name of Allāh. It is therefore not surprising to hear that the Hudhaylites asked the Prophet to grant them sexual licence even after they joined the Muslim cause.[5] Even after the decisive victory of Islam we encounter attempts

[1] Al-Ḥuṣrī, I, p. 49: *al-afw ʿind al-maqdara* (traced back to Muʿāwiya).

[2] Ibn Durayd, p. 142, 13 is probably only a typical example. It is characteristic that a Bedouin poet (*aʿrābī*) mentions 'the prayer and faster' (*al-muṣallī al-ṣā'im*) with expressions of disgust: *al-ʿIqd*, III, p. 414, 24. These examples can easily be amplified.

[3] Al-Jāḥiẓ (*Bayān*, fol. 128b) [II, p. 322] tells that a man's pious abstinence and much fasting and praying was praised in the presence of a Bedouin: 'Ho, this man seems to believe that God has no mercy on him unless he tortures himself in this fashion' (*ḥattā yuʿadhdhib nafsahu hādhā'l-taʿdhīb*).

[4] Thorbecke, *Morgenl. Forschungen*, p. 244 [*Dīwān*, ed. Geyer, no. 17], another version *Agh.*, VIII, p. 86.

[5] Al-Mubarrad, p. 288, cf. Robertson-Smith, p. 175. The lampoon of Ḥassān b. Thābit quoted in Ibn Hishām, p. 646, 4 ff. refers to this; cf. Sībawayhi, ed. Derenbourg, II, p. 132, 9, p. 175, 11.

Ta'rīkh al-Dawlatayn, ed. Tunis 1289, p. 63, 2, a poem against customs and tax collectors, Yāqūt, II, p. 938, 11 ff. Because of this antipathy *makkās* is almost synonymous with 'swindler': *Agh.*, IX, p. 129, 1. Parallels to this view are to be found in Jewish antiquity (see Edersheim, *The Life and Times of Jesus*, 2nd ed., I, pp. 515-18).

by the Arabs to avoid the Muslim restrictions on marital law. An example from 'Uthmān's[1] time is less typical than a later one from the fifth century A.H. of the continued Arab opposition to the restrictions of Islamic marital law. At that time lived Qirwāsh of the Arabic dynasty of the Banū 'Uqayl in Mesopotamia, who despite their extensive rule continued their nomadic-national traditions—the princes lived in tents. He is best known for his fight against the dynasty of the Būyids. This Qirwāsh is said to have had two sisters as
21 wives at the same time, and when he was called to account he replied: 'How much is there in our customs which is according to religious law?' He congratulated himself that his conscience was burdened only with the murder of five or six Bedouins. As regards city dwellers, God is not concerned about them.[2]

The ascetic limitations of the individual free will in respect of food and drink, demanded by Muhammed in the name of Allāh, was revolting to Arab sentiment. These were completely different restrictions from those of which Sūra 5:102, 6:139-45 speak as pagan traditions and habits.[3] The sacrifices in abstinence which Muhammed wished to enforce were of a rather different nature.[4] To drink excessively was not praiseworthy among virtuous Arabs. 'He drinks twice during the day and four times during the night, so that his face swells and he becomes fat'[5] is a slighting reference to an enemy; and it is complimentary to say of a man that he does not waste his wealth on wine-drinking.[6] Barrāḍ b. Qays, who caused the second Fijār war, was expelled by his tribe, the Banū Ḍamra, and later by other tribes amongst whom he sought protection, because he indulged in drink and excesses.[7] This shows that such persons were not liked even by pre-Islamic Arabs. But it was asking too much that

[1] During 'Uthmān's time the governor of Syria has to enforce Muslim law against a man who wishes to take back the wife he had too carelessly divorced: 'God's business is important, yours and your wife's counts for little; you have no right claim on her (according to religious law)': al-Tabrīzī to *Ḥam.*, p. 191. (Notice also *Agh.*, VI, p. 164, 17.) Before Islam divorce took place for trivial reasons: Zuhayr, 12: 1, *Agh.*, IX, p. 5, 3 below. Of a beautiful woman it is said: a woman who need not fear divorce: *Hudhayl.*, 169:10.

[2] Ibn al-Athīr, year 444, IX, p. 219 ed. Būlāq [ed. Tornberg, IX, p. 403]; cf. *Journal of Royal Asiatic Soc.*, 1886, p. 519.

[3] Cf. also Ibn Durayd, p. 95. It is an exaggeration to conclude as does Barbier de Maynard from *Agh.*, VII, p. 17, 2, that even late in Muslim times the Tamīmites (as late as the second century?) adhered to old Arabic customs in respect of the Baḥīra and Sā'iba camels: *Journal asiat.*, 1874, II, p. 208 note below.

[4] [For the various questions concerning wine in pre-Islamic Arabia and Islam, cf. also A. J. Wensinck's article 'Khamr' in the *Enc. of Islam* and its bibliography.]

[5] Ṭarafa, 16:4, cf. some passages belonging to this context in Freytag, *Einleitung in das Studium der arabischen Sprache*, p. 144.

[6] Zuhayr, 15:34; but cf. Ṭarafa, *Mu'all.*, verses 53, 59.

[7] Caussin de Perceval, I, p. 301.

Arabs should confine themselves to drinking soft date juice,[1] give up wine altogether, and even consider wine-drinking as sin and dishonour. Arabs found nothing less to their taste than asceticism, and sang of their national heroes as 'givers of wine'.[2] Their most celebrated poets and heroes in pagan times sang the praise of the sparkling and foaming cup expressing such sentiments as these: 'When I 22
have drunk wine I risk my whole fortune and my honour increases and cannot be harmed,' i.e. as the scholiast paraphrases it: his drunkenness drives him to express his nobility of soul and keeps him from all baseness.[3] Or: 'You can see that the miserly curmudgeon becomes generous when the cup makes its round to him.'[4] Or: 'When the cup gains ascendency over me my virtues appear and my companions need fear no harm from me and need not worry about my avarice.'[5]

We see that the Arabs, despite the spartan life that the bleak nature of their country imposes on them, are not inclined towards asceticism, and we can understand that Muhammed vainly preached abstinence from the indulgences of paganism. On the whole there is a hedonist undertone in all the expressions of their views on life. 'You are mortal, therefore enjoy life. Drunkenness and beautiful women, white ones like gazelles and brown ones like idols.'[6]

Wine especially encourages virtue, honour, generosity; and it was now to be branded as despicable sin (*rijs*) and the work of Shayṭān, as the Koran calls it, 'the mother of great sins' (*umm al-kabā'ir*), its favourite designation in the mouth of theologians.

This was incomprehensible to the true Arabs, who relished the memory of many a drop which had moistened their lips on their wanderings through Syria and Mesopotamia,[7] where they had enjoyed many an agreeable interlude in the taverns.[8] And it was their most famous men who boasted of wine drinking, preferably when the wine was 'red like the blood of a slaughtered animal',[9] but also when it was mixed with water and honey[10]—since drinking of undiluted

[1] *Naqī'*, *Agh.*, IX, p. 3, 5 from below; cf B. *Nikāḥ*, no. 78.

[2] *Agh.*, XIV, p. 131 penult: *sabbā'u khamrin*. A variant in *'Iqd*, I. p. 44. 15 (where this poem is ascribed to Ḥassān b. Thābit): *shirrību khamrin*.

[3] 'Antara, *Mu'all.*, v. 39.

[4] 'Amr b. Kulthūm, *Mu'all.*, v. 4.

[5] Al-Mubarrad, p. 73.

[6] Imrq., 64:7.

[7] Cf. Guidi, *Della sede primitiva dei populi semitichi*, pp. 43 ff.

[8] *Agh.*, IV, p. 16.

[9] Ḥassān b. Thābit, *Dīwān*, p. 84, 8 [ed. Hirschfeld, 3: 2]; Ibn Hish., p. 522, 8; *Agh.*, X, p. 30 ult., 64, 11, XIX, p. 155, 12; Ibn al-Sikkīt, p. 176 (al-A'shā) [ed. Cheikho, p. 217 = *Dīwān*, 3:9], cf. Guidi, l. c., p. 45.

[10] 'Amr. b Kulthūm, *Mu'all.*, v. 2; *Mufaḍḍ.*, 25: 75, 37: 21; *Agh.*, II, p. 34, 29 [Ḥassān b. Thābit, *Dīwān*, ed. Hirschfeld, no. 1, 6 = Ibn Hishām, p. 829, 7].

23 wine was usually considered a dangerous excess.[1] The true gentleman is he 'whose hands are eager with the arrows of the *maysir* in the winter and who tears down the flag of the wine merchant (because he has exhausted his supplies)'.[2] And the poet who could boast: 'If you seek me in the assembly of the tribe you will find me and if you hunt me in the taverns you will get me'[3] probably described everyday circumstances.

They tried to escape from the women who were always ready with their admonitions[4] by drinking in the early morning[5] before the fault-finders were awake. Such sessions were presumably noisy and gay since there must be some reason for comparing 'the loud neighing of war horses' to the songs of drinking feasts which are accompanied by cymbals.[6] The Arab only abstained from wine when in mourning for one he loved, or when he was under the obligation of blood revenge when he did not touch the cup until he had fulfilled his sacred task. Then he said *ḥallat lī al-khamr*, I am permitted to drink wine. This must have been a sort of religious custom.[7]

[1] *Agh.*, XII, p. 128, 4 (cf. a doublet ib., III., p. 17, 17). Nevertheless the mixing of wine is called in old Arabic 'wounding' (*shajja*, *Mufaḍḍ.*, 10:4, *Agh.*, VI, p. 127, 20, *Bānat Su'ād*, v. 4, ed. Guidi p. 34; *qara'a*, *ZDMG*, XXXVI, p. 622, XL, p. 573 v. 137; *ṣafaqa*, Jawh. s.v. *mrḥ*, cf. 'Alq., 13:41), or even killing: *Agh.* XIX, p. 93, 13, Ḥassān b. Thāb., p. 73 [ed. Hirschfeld, 13:18], cf. Al-Maydānī, II. p. 47, *Agh.*, VIII, p. 169, Ibn Durayd, *Malāḥin*, ed. Thorbecke, p. 14, 5. On living and dead wine, cf. the poem by Ibn Arṭāt, *Agh.*, II, p. 86. Continuing this image the idea of revenge for the murdered (*tha'r*) has been introduced (al-Āmidī, *Kitāb al-Muwāzana*, Istanbul 1287, p. 24, ib. 31). In later poetry mixing of wine is also called sullying it (*Agh.*, V., p. 41, 20). Arabic tradition gives the name of the men who drank unmixed wine: *Agh.*, XXI, p. 100, Abulfeda, *Hist. anteislam.*, p. 136, 4. From wine the expressions *ṣirf* (unmixed), and *mizāj* (mixture) was transferred to other concepts as e.g. death or unfaithfulness: *ṣirfan lā mizāja lahu* (Ḥassān, *Dīwān*, p. 98, 7; 101, 2 [Hirschf., 20: 1, 60: 1]), *Agh.*, XV, p. 79, 13, *ṣarīḥ al-mawti*, *Ḥam.*, p. 456, v. 6, cf. al-*Muwashshā*, ed. Brünnow, p. 85, 19.

[2] 'Ant., *Mu'all.*, v. 52.

[3] Ṭarafa, *Mu'all.*, v. 46.

[4] *Ḥam.*, p. 455, v. 6

[5] Morning was preferred to all other times for drinking: *Agh.*, X, p. 31, 16, XIX, p. 120, 5 from below; Labīd, *Mu'all.*, v. 60, 61.

[6] *Mufaḍḍ.*, 16: 17, cf. 'Ant., *Mu'all.*, v. 18, *Ḥam.*, p. 562, v. 6 *musmi'āt* during drinking.

[7] Evidence now in Wellhausen, *Reste arab. Heidenthums*, p. 116. Also Imrq. 51:9, 10 and *Agh.*, IX, p. 7, 8, ibid 149, 2 (for various objects of the vow to abstinence), introduction to Zuh.'s *Mu'all.*, ed. Arnold, p. 68, Ibn Hishām, p. 543. In this connection is to be understood the turn of phrase: *al-nādhir al-nudhūr 'alayya*, *Agh.*, X, p. 30, 13.

'Cloud water' (*mā'u saḥābin*) is frequently mentioned: Imrq., 17:9; *Ḥam.*, p. 713, v. 3; cf. Nāb., 27:12 and its freshness is stressed in Labīd, p. 120, v. 3. Honey: *Hudh.*, 131:3.

Praise of wine remained an inevitable part of Arabic poetry to 24
such a degree that even Ḥassān b. Thābit, the first Muslim poet and the panegyrist of Muhammed and of his victories, is unable to avoid the words: 'If we commit unseemly deeds—whether a quarrel or railing—we blame the wine (which we drank to excess). We go on drinking it, which turns us into kings'[1] . . . and this in a poem composed about the conquest of Mecca.

The genuineness of this poem is rather doubtful, but in any case the words quoted prove that in the early period talk of wine-drinking was not considered out of place in a religious poem. Later, however, it gave offence and the excuse was invented that Ḥassān had added his *qaṣīda* on the victory of Mecca to a poem which he had composed during his pagan days. It is recounted that the pious poet passed a group of young people who were indulging in wine and when he called the drinkers to account they replied: 'We should have liked to give up wine drinking but your words: "If we commit unseemly deeds . . ." led us back to it.'[2] There are other poems[3] from Ḥassān's pagan days which glorify drinking.

Muslim pietists,[4] of course, did even more to damage the reputation of wine, and this we shall discuss here, since the name of Ḥassān b. Thābit has been mentioned. It seems that these pious men were concerned to prove that the effects of wine had changed with changing times. During the period of paganism it might have had those beneficial effects attributed to it by the old poets; but since Allāh's law of condemnation it had been the cause of all licence. It
seems that this was the idea to be expressed in the following tale, 25
which was not unintentionally attributed to Ḥassān, the poet of the transition from paganism to Islam, and as such the best suited to be the carrier of the idea of the theologians.

'When the pious poet returned home from an entertainment provided by the Nabīṭ family—his son tells us—he threw himself upon the bed, crossed his feet and said: "The two singers Rā'iqa and her companion 'Azza al-Maylā reminded me sadly of the entertainment by Jabala b. al-Ayham in pagan days; since then I have not heard anything like it." Then he smiled, sat up and said: "I have seen ten singing girls, five Greeks who sang Greek tunes to the accompaniment of the harp and five others who sang tunes of the

[1] Ibn Hishām, p. 829, 6.

[2] Al-Suhaylī ad loc., notes, p. 192.

[3] *Agh.*, IV, p. 16 below. Cf. the poems pp. 90 and 99 in his *Dīwān*, ed. Tunis [ed. Hirschfeld, nos. 24, 42, 43], which are characteristic of the pagan poets' passion for wine. Notice p. 39, 8 [Hirschf., 8:25], 'I swear I shall not forget you, as long as drinkers sing about the sweetness of wine.'

[4] The authorities for this account are Khārija b. Zayd, one of the seven Medinian theologians (d. 99) and 'Abd al-Raḥmān b. Abi'l-Zinād, traditionist and Mufti at Baghdad (d. 174).

people of Ḥīra; Iyās b. Qabīṣa, the protector of all the Arabic singers from Mecca and other Arabic lands led them to Jabala. When he sat down for a drinking feast the hall was decorated with treasures and filled with delicious scents and he himself was dressed in priceless robes. But, by Allāh, he never sat down to such a feast without making a present of his precious clothes to myself and the rest of the company. So sumptuous was his manner of living, despite the fact that he was a pagan. Smilingly, without waiting to be asked, he distributed his presents with friendly demeanour and delicate speech. I never heard him utter obscenities or brutalities. Indeed we were all pagans. But now God has revealed Islam to us and has thus abolished all disbelief and we have given up wine drinking and all that is despicable; and now you are Muslims you drink wine made from date and grape juice and when you have drunk three cups you commit all manner of dissoluteness." '[1]

Obviously, this tale was invented because it was noticed that the Arabs did not easily sacrifice the joys of paganism on account of the sermons of peevish pietists in Medina. Even Muhammed had to preach to his faithful that at least they should not pray while drunk:[2] this interdiction is of earlier origin than the later general condemnation of wine, but the necessity for it will prepare us for the Arabs' reaction to the prophet's later ruling. The general interdiction of wine was not much more successful with the Arabs even after Muhammed's death. This was the time when society still
26 retained some traces of paganism; and how could the recognition of the restrictions in the Prophet's law have found sudden acceptance in groups where these traces had yet to be eradicated? Even during the days of 'Umar, the Fazārite Manẓūr b. Zabān still maintained a marriage with the wife of his dead father which he had contracted in pagan days. This Manẓūr was also accused of drinking wine before the strict caliph, who forgave him after he had sworn 'forty oaths' that he was completely ignorant of this religious interdiction. When 'Umar dissolved Manẓūr's incestuous marriage and forbade him further wine-drinking the latter spoke truly pagan words: 'By all that was sacred to my father, I swear: verily a *dīn* which forcibly separates me from Malīka is a great shame. I care nothing further about what fate brings if I am forbidden Malīka and wine.'[3]

There were probably many Arabs who refused to give up drinking and praising wine despite imprisonment and other punishments and who were thus in conscientious opposition to the law. A typical example is the poet Abū Miḥjan al-Thaqafī during the days of 'Umar I.

[1] *Agh.*, XVI, p. 15.

[2] Sūra 4:46; Nöldeke, *Gesch. d.Korans*, p. 147 [2nd ed., I, p. 199].

[3] *Agh.*, IX, p. 56, 7 =XXI, p. 261.

Give me, o friend, some wine to drink; though I am
well aware of what God has revealed about wine.
Give me pure wine to make my sin bigger because only
when it is drunk unmixed is the sin complete.[1]

Though wine has become rare and though we have been
deprived of it and though Islam and the threat of
punishment have divorced us from it:
Nevertheless I do drink it in the early morning hours
in deep draughts, I drink it unmixed and from time to
time I become gay and drink it mixed with water.
At my head stands a singing girl and while
she sings she flirts;
Sometimes she sings loudly, sometimes
softly, humming like flies in the garden.[2]

He was not to be deterred from his pleasures by imprisonment:[3]
indeed, it is characteristic for these people that he gladly gives up wine 27
voluntarily but remains defiant in the face of threatened punishment.[4]

The following poem by Abū Miḥjan was called 'the craziest verse that was ever composed':[5]

When I die bury me by the side of a vine so that my
bones may feed on its juices after death.
Do not bury me in the plains because I am afraid that
then I cannot enjoy wine when I am dead.[6]

Abu'l-Hindī, a poet of the Umayyad times, had a similar thought inscribed upon his tombstone: 'When finally I die fashion my shroud from vines and make a press be my grave.'[7]

[1] *Ṭuraf 'Arabiyya*, ed. Landberg, p. 68, 8; L. Abel, *Abū Miḥgan poetae arabici Carmina*, Leiden 1887, no. 21.

[2] *Agh.*, XXI, p. 216, 15, *Ṭuraf*, p. 69 penult ff., ed. Abel, no. 4. This verse is taken from 'Antara, *Mu'allaqa*, v. 18, which is often cited as an example of original invention by Arabic poets: Mehren, *Rhetorik der Araber*, p. 147, cf. al-Ḥuṣrī, III, p. 36.

[3] Ibn Ḥajar, IV. p. 329.

[4] *Ṭuraf 'Arabiyya*, p. 69, 6, Abū Yūsuf, *Kitāb al-Kharāj* (Būlāq 1302), p. 18, 2. The word *ṭahhara*, 'to clean', is remarkable here, in the meaning of: 'to punish', much as the Qarmaṭians use this word for the death penalty, cf. De Goeje, *Mémoires d'histoire et geographie orientales* (Leyden 1886), p. 53, 133. M. Müller also derives the latin *punire* from the meaning of 'to clean' (*Essays*, II[1], p. 228). [This derivation is, however, unacceptable.]

[5] Al-Damīrī, II, p. 381.

[6] *Agh.*, XXI, p. 215 ff., 218, 10, *Ṭuraf 'Arab.*, p. 72, 5 from below, ed. Abel, no. 15; cf. *'Iqd*, III, p. 407.

[7] *Agh.*, ibid., 279, 12.

It is not only in poetry that the praise of wine continues. In the generation immediately after Muhammed we find a gay drinking fraternity whose members included the son of the pious Abū Ayyūb al-Anṣārī, who sang the following drinking song:

> Fill my cup then and leave the scorners to themselves:
> Revive your bones whose final destiny is decay.
> To miss the cup or be deprived of it is like death,
> But that the cup will come to me is life for me.[1]

Traditions from the earliest days of Islam show us that amongst the representatives of the true Arab character there were people who valued freedom, to whom the new system, with its condemnation and punishment of free enjoyment, was so repulsive that they preferred to leave that society altogether, when it intended to impose upon them the *dīn* in earnest, rather than to lose their freedom. Such a man was Rabī'a b. Umayya b. Khalaf, a much respected man, famous for his generosity. He did not want to relinquish wine-drinking under Islam and even drank during the month
28 of Ramaḍān. For this 'Umar banned him from Medina, thereby making him so bitter against Islam that he did not wish to return to the capital even after 'Umar's death, though he had reason to believe that 'Uthmān would have been more lenient. He preferred to emigrate to the Christian empire and to become a Christian.[2] The same thing is said to have happened in the next century to al-Ṣalt b. al-'Āṣ b. Wābiṣa, who was threatened by 'Umar II, when he was governor of Ḥijāz, with the penalty of whipping; but the proud Arab of the tribe of the B. Makhzūm preferred conversion to Christianity to a regime which proposed the restriction of human freedom in respect of food and drink.[3]

Under 'Umar I an attempt was made to overcome the resistance of the Arabs, and in this respect also the caliph seems to have made serious efforts to eradicate all relics of paganism. Al-Nu'mān b. 'Adī, whom 'Umar had appointed administrator of Maysān near Baṣra, once composed a gay wine song: 'Has al-Ḥasnā' not heard that her husband eagerly indulges in glasses and cumber at Maysān?' And later:

[1] *Agh.*, XVIII, p. 66.

[2] *Agh.*, XIII, p. 112, According to the sources of Ibn Ḥajar, I, p. 1085, he emigrated to Heraclius while 'Umar was still alive and this episode made 'Umar resolve never again to ban a man from Medina. Ibn Durayd, too, makes him embrace Christianity under 'Umar (p. 81), but instead of banning whipping is mentioned.

[3] *Agh.*, V, p. 184.

If you are a good drinking companion pass me the big cup,
for drinking but not the little broken one,
Perhaps the Commander of the Faithful will even be
angered because we are drinking together in the ruined
castle etc.

When 'Umar learnt of this poem he exclaimed: 'Yes, indeed I am angered,' and recalled him. But the poet apologized to the caliph with the words: 'By God, Commander of the Faithful, I have never done any of the things that I mention in my poem. But I am a poet and have an affluence of words which I use in the manner of poets.' 'I swear—replied 'Umar—that you will hold from me no further office even if you did no more than say what you have said.'[1]

The excuse offered by the poet-governor later became typical. The Umayyad rule was ill-equipped to silence wine songs, as it 29
expresses the spirit of opposition to the piety of Medina, which was contrary to the old Arab way of life. In this respect the wine songs of Ḥāritha b. Badr (died 50) are typical: they are to be found in the supplement to the book of the *Aghānī* recently published by Brünnow. Thus the tradition of glorifying wine was not interrupted in Arabic poetry and only rarely is a voice raised against its enjoyment.[2] So we find the phenomenon of a people's poetry being for centuries a living protest against its religion.[3] Pious men were confronted with the apology that all this was but empty talk and not a reflection of real behaviour,[4] since all poets—as the Koran says (26:225)—said things which they did not practise.[5] Thus the wine songs of the Abū Nuwās and kindred spirits became normal phenomena in Arabic literature. The inherited Arabic feeling also found recognition in other forms of literature at this time. We consider the following story so typical that we shall grant it space here, the more so as it is of importance for various points dealt with in these studies. It would be difficult to define when our story, full of glaring anachronisms, really originated, but it is sufficient for its appreciation to say that it seems to picture the vivid protest of the Arab spirit against the theological

[1] Ibn Hishām, p. 786, Ibn Durayd, p. 86, al-Damīrī, II, p. 84 [Muṣ'ab, *Nasab Quraysh*, p. 382].

[2] 'Abd Allāh b. Zabīr al-Asadī, *Agh.*, XIII, p. 46.

[3] Other matters which were disapproved of by theologians, such as profane songs—it is well known what theologians and pietists thought of singers—were placed under the direct protection of the 'companions and successors' as is evident from *Agh.*, III, p. 162. The admissibility of love-songs was also covered with the authority of the Prophet; *al-Muwashshā*, ed. Brünnow, p. 105.

[4] This was thought possible also for love songs: al-Ḥuṣrī, I, p. 220.

[5] Al-Maqqarī, II, p. 343.

reaction[1] which again prevailed at the beginning of the 'Abbāsid
30 period. It must be admitted that it well represents the Arab mentality of the two heroes 'Amr b. Ma'dī Karib[2] and 'Uyayna b. Ḥiṣn, who were converted to Islam, but—as is known from history—soon proved unsteady in it.

'Uyayna once paid a visit to Kūfa, where he stayed for several days. In order to go and see 'Amr b. Ma'dī Karib, he ordered his servant to saddle a horse, and when the latter brought him a mare he said: 'Woe unto you, did I ever ride a mare at the time of the Jāhiliyya and you expect me to do so now under Islam?' Thereupon the servant brought a stallion, and he mounted it and rode towards the quarter of the Banū Zubayd, where he was guided to the dwelling of 'Amr. He stopped by the door and called for Abū Thawr (the by-name of 'Amr). The latter soon appeared in full armour as if he had just come from a battle and said: 'Good morning, O Abū Mālik'. But he replied: 'Has God not ordered us to use a different greeting, namely: Hail unto you?' 'Do not trouble me,' said 'Amr, 'with things of which we know nothing. Sit down because I have for food a lamb walking around.' The guest sat down and 'Amr caught and slaughtered the lamb, skinned it and divided the meat into pieces, threw it into a pot to cook, and when it was ready took a big cup, broke bread into it and emptied into it the contents of the pot. The two men sat down and ate the meal. Then the host said: 'Which beverage do you prefer, milk or that which we used for our meals during the Jāhiliyya?' 'Has not Allāh forbidden this in Islam?' replied 'Uyayna. 'Are you or am I older in years?' asked 'Amr. 'You are the elder,' replied his friend. 'Who has been longer in Islam, you or I?' asked 'Amr. 'In Islam too you are the elder,' said 'Uyayna. 'Well, then,' continued 'Amr, 'know that I have read everything that is written between the two covers of the holy book, but I have not found that wine is forbidden. It is only written: Will you abstain from it? (Sura 5:93) and we both replied to that question: No, and God was silent then and we too were silent.' 'Yes,' said 'Uyayna, 'you are older in years and longer in Islam than I.' Thus they sat down again, sang songs and drank, indulging in memories of the Jāhiliyya

[1] Then wine poets again began to be imprisoned: *Agh.*, XI, p. 147. The poem of the imprisoned poet Ja'far b. 'Ulba (died 125), quoted there, breathes the difference between *muruwwa* and *dīn*, which disallows wine. Similar tendencies are expressed in many anecdotes from these circles, amongst others e.g. *al-'Iqd* II, p. 343 below=ibid., II, p. 400 below. Here the Caliph al-Walīd b. Yazīd is said to have had a man of letters brought from Kūfa and to have addressed him thus: 'By God I did not make you come in order to ask you about God's Book or the teachings of the Prophet, but have sent for you in order to ask you about wine.'

[2] A similar anecdote about him is quoted in al-Suyūṭī, *Itqān* (Cairo 1279), I, p. 35.

late into the night. Now 'Uyayna prepared to leave. 'Amr said: 31
'It would be shameful for me to let 'Uyayna go without a present.' Thereupon he ordered an Arḥabī camel mare to be brought (white) like . . .[1] of silver and had it prepared for the journey and made his friend ride it. Then he called the servant and ordered a sack with four thousand dirham to be fetched; this also he gave to his friend. When the latter refused to accept the money he said: 'By God, this still comes from the present that 'Umar gave me.' But 'Uyayna did not accept it and as he left he spoke this poem:

May you be rewarded, Abū Thawr, with the wages due to nobility;
Verily this much-visited hospitable man is a proper youth.
You invite and give that invitation all honour and teach
us the greeting of knowledge[2] as it was not formerly known.
Then you say that it is permitted to circulate the cup with
wine like the sparkle of lightning at night;
For this you cited an 'Arabic argument' which leads back to
justice all those who were unjust.
You are, by God who sits on the heavenly throne, a fine example
when pietists want to keep us from drinking;
By Abū Thawr's saying the prohibition of wine has been
abrogated and Abū Thawr's saying is weighty and based on
knowledge.'[3]

This story expresses the indignant protests of the circles in which it came into being against the pietistic trend. It originated at a time when piety and theology had gained the ascendancy in public life and is elucidated by the wine-song of Ādam b. 'Abd al-'Azīz, the grandchild of the pious Caliph 'Umar II, one of the few Umayyad princes who escaped the bloody sword of the founder of the 'Abbāsid dynasty.[4] In this song (vv. 11-13) we find the words:[5]

Say to him who scorns you because of this (the wine), the *faqīh*[6]
and respected man:

[1] [In the list of errata in his preface, the author refers for this lacuna to the conjecture of v. Kremer in his *Beiträge zur arabischen Lexikographie*, I, p. 38, under *ḥbr*; translate: 'a bracelet of silver'.]

[2] *Taḥiyyata 'ilmin* in contrast to *t. jāhiliyyatin*. It might be mentioned also that in later traditions the distinction is also made between Islamic and pagan greeting (*taḥiyya*) that the latter consisted in the prostration (*sujūd*) whereas the other consisted of *salām*—like the greeting in Paradise (al-Ghazāli, *Iḥyā*, II, p. 188, 12).

[3] *Agh.*, XIV, p. 30.

[4] Ibid., IV, p. 93, 23.

[5] Ibid., XIII, p. 60, 61.

[6] Instead of this word, we find the variant *wadī'*: Yāq., IV., p. 836, 12. Ḥāritha b. Badr also names those who scorn him because he drinks wine as *li'ām*, *Agh.*, XXI, p. 27, 2; 42, 22.

32 May you leave it then (the wine) and hope for another, the noble wine of Salsabīl (in Paradise, Sūra 76:17),
Remain thirsty today and tomorrow be satiated with descriptions of traces of dwellings.[1]

Now it is no longer the women who scold the spendthrifts who waste their money on wine but it is the *fuqahā'* who scorn the heretics who infringe the law of the Koran. Thus our story was intended as a manifestation of the free Arab spirit[2] against the arguments of those oppressed by the weight of the law (*mukallafūn*), in whose circles there was equal readiness to make propaganda for the prohibition of wine by means of invented stories which referred to the Jāhiliyya.[3] Such an invention is e.g. the story of how the Qurayshite pagan 'Abd Allāh b. Jud'ān despised the drinking of wine, by which it was sought to prove that the most eminent Qurayshites as they grew older spurned this vice even in pagan times. The character of this tradition is sufficiently evident from the fact that the theologian
33 Ibn Abi'l-Zinād (cf. p. 31) is mentioned as its inventor, or at least its propagator. This kind of casuistry is countered with healthy humour by the *ḥujja 'arabiyya*, the Arab argument of the old pagan 'Amr b. Ma'dī Karib.

[1] The last verse is particularly interesting as a parallel to the frequent mockery of the lament about the *aṭlāl* in Abū Nuwās's wine songs (ed. Ahlwardt 4:9, 23:11, 12, 26: 3 ff., 33:1, 34, 53, 60:1, 14, 15 etc.); this lament was taken over from the old poetry (cf. *Agh.*, III, p. 25) and was continued to the latest generations and even to recent times (a remarkable instance is al-Maqqarī, I, p. 925). This attachment to the *aṭlāl* went so far with old Arabs that the word was even used to describe riding animals (*Agh.*, XI, p. 88, 18, XXI, p. 31, 3; Ibn Durayd, p. 106, 7). Instead of pedantic adherence to such old forms, reality should be made the subject of poetry. Derision of the *aṭlāl* poetry can already be found in Tamīn ibn Muqbil (Yāqūt, I, p. 527, 10 ff.) and al-Kumayt, *Agh.*, XVIII, p. 193; some proverbs (al-Maydānī, II, p. 235, 236) seem to have this tendency too. [For ridicule of the convention of lamenting the *aṭlāl* see also Goldziher, *Abhandlungen zur arabischer Philologie*, I, pp. 141 ff.]

[2] The continued protest against the prohibition of wine is evident also from the fact that in the third century sayings were still current which could be used in defence of wine drinking and that the theologian al-Muzanī (died 204) was asked for the reasons why strict scholars of tradition rejected these sayings (Ibn Khallikān, no. 92, I, p. 126 Wüstenfeld). A great many traditions were stored up which were to justify a more lenient practice; the relevant material is in *'Iqd*, III, pp. 409-19. The concession for date wine was made very early (ZDMG, XLI, p. 95). The existence of this distinction is proof that a *modus vivendi* was sought at a very early date. From the first half of the first century it is reported that those who regard wine-drinking as forbidden keep on 're-interpreting this interdiction (*yata'awwalū fīhā*) until they drink themselves' (*Agh.*, XXI, p. 33, 8; 40, 17).

[3] *Agh.*, VIII, p. 5, cf. Caussin de Perceval, I, p. 350. [There is a chapter about those 'who prohibited wine in the Jāhiliyya' in Ibn Ḥabīb's *al-Muḥabbar*, pp. 237 ff.]

VI

The practices which Muhammed required of true believers were also contrary to Arab thinking; and of all the ceremonies and rites of the *dīn* none encountered more resistance than the rite of prayer. The lack of those deep religious sentiments, which in minds attuned to piety make for the need to communicate with the deity and which are the source of devout emotion, would point straight away to the conclusion that among the Arabs prayer would not take a proper hold. In this respect, too, the southern Arabs displayed a rather different national character. There is no parallel in the relics of the spiritual life of the pre-Islamic inhabitants of central Arabia, and while it would be rather daring to use negative indications for more than an assessment of probability, it is of importance for knowledge of the spiritual life of these circles to collect all indications available and to consider their significance.

Given the nature of existing information about the pre-Islamic religion of the Arabs, we are unable to form a positive judgment about the place of prayer in their life; and though we cannot say with certainty that the old Arabs did not pray at all[1] we can say that there is no proof that prayers as an institution of religious service or as an integral part of their rite existed amongst them. The invocation of the gods (cf. Sūra 4:117) probably took place amongst them too, but this does not appear to have been the characteristic focal point of the religious service nor can the description of their services given by Muhammed (Sūra 8:35) prove the existence of anything comparable to the later Muslim *ṣalāt*; but on the contrary, it serves to show us what strange customs existed instead of the rite which Muhammed took from Jews and Christians and taught to his people. 'Their *ṣalāt* by the (sacred) house was nothing but whistling[2] and 34
clapping of hands.'[3]

This description of the forms of their worship reminds us of customs which are also found amongst other peoples of low religious

[1] 'We cannot fail also to be struck with the fact that the lower forms of religion are almost independent of prayer. To us prayer seems almost a necessary part of religion.' [Sir John] Lubbock, [*The origins of civilization and the primitive condition of man*, London 1870, p. 253] translated by A. Passow as *Die Entstehung der Civilisation und der Urzustand des Menschengeschlechtes*, Jena, 1875, p. 321.

[2] From this the legend was later developed according to which the name of Mecca itself was derived from this whistling (Yāqūt, IV, p. 616, 14). In connection with the passage from the Koran, other stories about the circumstances of this whistling and hand-clapping were invented: al-Damīrī, II, p. 387.

[3] Later the ancient period is seen in the light of Islam and then the Hudhaylite is made to report to the Tubba' that the Arabs have a sacred house at Mecca where the *ṣalāt* is held: Ibn Hishām, p. 15, 15.

development. Another practice more akin to magic[1] than to devout
communion with God is the way in which the pagan Arabs sometimes
sought to avert earthly distress. During times of tribulation they
did not turn to their gods in prayer and repentance. Of the few
customs of such kind one in particular may serve to show us how they
sought help in their need. As an aid to its proper appreciation we
might mention a practice which has been reported in recent times
about the inhabitants of the port of Yanbuʿ: During pestilence they
lead a camel through every quarter of the town so that it may take all
the disease upon itself; then it is strangled at a sacred spot and the
people think that the camel and the plague have been finished off at
one blow.[2] One may perhaps assume that this custom is a relic of
pagan days; this is made likely by the fact that the inhabitants of
Yanbuʿ have retained the consciousness and the attitudes of the
Bedouins up to quite modern times.[3] The custom of the ancient Arabs
which we are considering is this: When rain was failing branches of
35 the *salaʿ* (saelanthus) and *ʿushar* (aselepias) trees were tied to the
tails of cattle and set alight: the animals were then driven to the top
of a mountain and thrown down.[4] This custom, which has much in
common with an old Roman one[5] and the practices of many other
peoples (many instructive details can be found in Mannhardt's study
Die Lupercalien),[6] was meant to be efficacious against drought.[7]
To people who were steeped in such ideas the words of the Koran,
'Ask God for forgiveness because He forgives sins and sends abundant

[1] Here belong also the amulets and other magic used for the protection of children and horses and also of adults against diseases: see several passages in Ahlwardt, *Chalef al-Ahmar*, p. 379-80; *Mufaḍḍ.*, 3:6, 27:18; Ibn Durayd, p. 328, 7 (*hinama*); B. *Adab*, no. 55 (*nushra* against knotting, cf. al-Nawawī to Muslim, V, p. 31). Jewesses were concerned with such magic (*ruqya*): *al-Muwaṭṭaʾ*, IV, p. 157; also Bedouin women, *Agh.*, XX, p. 165. Cf. now Wellhausen, p. 144 ff. For the phrase 'against the *manāyā* such magic does not help', see, apart from the passages quoted by him, also *Hudh.*, 2:3, Wright *Opuscula arabica*, p. 121, 14, al-Tabrīzī, *Ḥam.*, p. 233, 17.

[2] Charles Didier, [*Séjour chez le Grand-cherife de la Mekke, Paris* 1857, p. 113 =] *Ein Aufenthalt bei dem Gross-Sherif von Mekka*, transl. by Helene Lobedan, Leipzig 1862, 143.

[3] Maltzan, *Meine Wallfahrt nach Mekka*, I, p. 128.

[4] Reference must be made here to the role of animals in an old Arabic feast, *ʿīd al-sabuʿ* (feast of the wild animal): al-Damīrī, I. p. 450, cf II, p. 52. The expression *yawm al-sabuʿ* in B. *Ḥarth*, no. 4, is supposed to refer to this feast.

[5] Steinthal, *Zeitschr. f. Völkerpsych.*, II, p. 134; F. Liebrecht, *Zur Volkskunde*, p. 261 ff.

[6] *Quellen und Forschungen zur Sprach-und Culturgeschichte der germanischen Völker*, 51. Heft (Strassburg, 1884), p. 136.

[7] Al-Jawharī [and *Lisān al-ʿArab*] s.v. *slʿ*. Cf. *al-Wishāḥ wa-Tathqīf al-Rimāḥ* (Būlāq 1281, p. 80), *Muḥīṭ*, s.v. ,I, p. 981b, al-Damīrī, I, p. 187 ff.: cf. also Freytag, *Einleitung in das Studium der arabischen Sprache*, p. 364 (now also Wellhausen, p. 157). [Cf. also Ibn Fāris, *K. al-Nayrūz*, in ʿAbd al-Salām Hārūn, *Nawādir al-Makhṭūṭāt*, V, pp. 18-9.]

rain from the heavens', as well as the Muslim custom of the *istisqā'* based upon them, must have seemed strange indeed.[1] It must be pointed out that al-Jāḥiẓ, in describing this pagan custom of the Arabs, which he calls *nār al-istisqā'*,[2] mentions that the lighting of the fire was accompanied by loud prayers (*wa-dajjū bi'l-duā' wa'l-tadarru'*), but in the poems which he quotes as evidence of this *istisqā'* fire prayers are not mentioned, nor do they figure in the other accounts of this custom.

It is of importance in judging this problem to note the linguistic phenomenon that Muhammed could find no Arabic word for this institution which he ordered for his community, but had to take the religious term *ṣalāt* from Christianity. If he had found a corresponding word in existence he would have retained it and would merely have equipped it with a new meaning appropriate to his teaching.[3]

One thing can certainly be said: that the Arabs resisted this 36
institution of Muhammed and that the Prophet found it hard work to popularize prayer among his compatriots in the sense understood by him. This aversion is mirrored in the Muslim legend, on the institution of prayer.

This legend[4] attests that those who circulated it pre-supposed a certain antipathy to the new form of worship amongst the pagan Arabs. This, though not founded on contemporary tradition about the Arab adversaries of Muhammed, could nevertheless have been well founded in the everyday experience of Bedouins as the authors of the legend encountered them. Thus we are more concerned about the general contents of the legend and the views reflected in it than its exact wording and its various forms. On the authority of the Prophet himself the legend relates that when Muhammed went to heaven he visited the six lower heavens one after the other and greeted the prophets living there: Adam, Idrīs, Abraham, Moses and Jesus. Then he ascended to the seventh heaven where God ordered fifty daily prayers for his people. Muhammed returned to Moses and told him of God's order. When Moses learnt that God demanded of the Arabs fifty daily prayers he advised Muhammed

[1] Cf. al-Māwardī, ed. Enger, p. 183; *Agh.*, XI, p. 80, 7 from below.

[2] *Kitāb al-Ḥayawān*, fol. 245b [IV, 466] in a chapter on the *nīran al-'Arab*, of which there are fifteen sorts. There are extracts from it without mention of the source in Bahā' al-Dīn al-'Āmilī, *Kashkūl*, p. 189. [The passage is also quoted by al-Marzūqī, *al-Azmina wa'l-Amkina*, II, p. 355; al-Nuwayrī, *Nihāyat al-Arab*, I, pp. 109–10.]

[3] If we find the word *muṣallā* (place of prayer) in a poem transmitted from the Jāhiliyya, such as *Agh.*, XVI, p. 145, 7, this passage, even if the whole were genuine, is a later interpolation; the same is true, of course, of crass falsifications like e.g. al-Azraqī, p. 103, 11 (*qūmū fa-ṣallū rabbakum wa-ta'awadhdhū*).

[4] This is found in B. (ed. Krehl), I. p. 100, *Anbiyā*, no. 6, Muslim, I. p. 234, Ṭab., I, p. 1158 f., Ibn Hishām, p. 271.

to return to God and to tell Him that they were unable to fulfil such an obligation. Muhammed returned to God and God reduced the number by half. But Moses, whom Muhammed again asked for advice, did not agree with this new demand either and persuaded Muhammed to return again to God and say that his people were unable to meet it. Back with God, Muhammed succeeded in reducing the number of prayers to five a day. Moses considered even this intolerable to the Arabs and wanted to make Muhammed continue his bargaining, but Muhammed replied, 'Now I would really be ashamed before God.'

The perhaps not unintentional humour of this legend reflects the supposed antipathy of pagan Arabs to a rite which appeared to them
37 new and senseless. From the history of the war against the tribe of Thaqīf we know that this tribe on its submission tenaciously tried to obtain the concession of freedom from prayers, and when this was not granted the members of the tribe complied with the remark that they would submit to the duty of prayer though 'this is an act of self-humiliation.'[1] Muhammed's anti-prophet Musaylima enticed his followers with the promise to waive prayer.[2]

The first companions and disciples of the Prophet had to keep their prayers more secret from their pagan brethren than any other tenet of their faith. Muslim prayer existed in the community even before the official institution of the rite. It is said that they hid in mountain gorges near Mecca in order to pray, and once when they were surprised in their worship a bloody quarrel ensued. The pious Sa'd b. Abī Waqqāṣ took up the jaw-bone of a camel and with it beat one of the unbelievers who advanced against them till blood flowed. This was—concludes our source—the first blood shed about Islam.[3] The Prophet too is said to have been subjected to the worst insults when the Qurayshites found him in prayer.[4] Amongst those who died in the Islam's war against the heathens, a certain 'Amr b. Thābit is mentioned, whose martyrdom (he died at Uḥud) ensured a place in paradise according to Muslim belief, though he never performed the prescribed prayers.[5]

The scorn of pagans was roused not only by the fact of praying[6] but also by the movements of the body connected with it. This seems to follow from a legend ascribed to 'Alī.[7] The least aversion was shown towards the duty of morning prayer (*al-ḍuḥā*), and in the

[1] Ibn Hishām, p. 916.

[2] Ibid., p. 946.

[3] Ṭab., I, p. 1179.

[4] Ibid., 1198.

[5] Ibn Durayd, p. 262. [Ibn Ḥajar, *al-Iṣāba*, no. 5780.]

[6] The names of the various times for prayer are also derided: al-Baghawī, *Masābīḥ al-Sunna*, I, p. 32.

[7] Notes to the Life of Muhammed, ed. Wüstenfeld, vol. II, p. 53.

early days of Islam, before the duty of prayer was extended to five times a day, the Muslims are said to have observed only two canonical times of prayer: morning and afternoon, the three other times having been added later.[1]

Even after Muhammed's death we find a rather frivolous attitude 38
amongst the Arab tribes in respect of prayers. The Tamīmites gave up afternoon prayers once and for all and gave the following anecdote as the reason for this licence: When the prophetess of the Banū Tamīm allied herself to the false prophet Musaylima and married him, her tribe asked him for the usual nuptial gift. 'I make to you a present,' he said 'of the afternoon prayer (*al-'aṣr*). 'This is now,' the Banū Tamīm said even much later, 'our right and the nuptial gift of a noble lady from our tribe; we cannot give it up.'[2] Even at the end of the third century the most efficacious means employed by the leaders of the Qarmaṭians to win over the Bedouins and other Arabs to their cause was to waive in this province of the movement the Muslim rites, especially fasting and praying and the prohibition of wine. This did not fail to impress the Arabs.[3] A Muslim traveller gives a lively account of this state of affairs and his report in the Qarmaṭian Laḥsa makes us feel as if we were back in the days of the Jāhiliyya. There is a free unbridled life, no taxes or tribute, no prayer, no mosques and no *khuṭba*.[4] Abū Sa'īd, who introduced this state of affairs, well understood the inclinations of the Arabs whom he wanted to win over. There are countless stories, unmistakably taken from true life,[5] which describe the indifference of the desert Arabs to
prayer,[6] their ignorance of the elements of Muslim rites[7] and even their 39

[1] Ibn Ḥajar, IV, p. 700; but cf. B. *Mawāqīt al-ṣalāt*, no. 19, where Abū Hurayra reports the saying of the Prophet, 'The most irksome prayer to the Munāfiqūn is the evening prayer (*al-'ishā*) and the morning prayer (*al-fajr*). O, if only they knew of the merits of these two times for prayer.'

[2] *Agh.*, XVIII, p. 166.

[3] Aug. Müller, I. p. 602.

[4] *Relation du voyage de Naissri Khosrau* etc., ed. Ch. Schefer, Paris 1881, p. 225 ff., cf. De Goeje, *Mémoire sur les Carmathes du Bahraïn et les Fatimides*, 2nd ed., p. 160.

[5] A whole chapter containing Bedouin anecdotes from the city dweller's point of view is to be found in *al-'Iqd*, II, p. 121 ff. Abū Mahdiyya, the prototype of the Bedouin; cf. for him also Ibn Qutayba, ed. Wüstenfeld, p. 271.

[6] When in an Arabic saying of the third century it affirmed that 'he who wants to learn to pray (*al-du'ā'*) should hear the prayer of Bedouin Arabs' (*du'ā' al-'arab*) (al-Jāḥiẓ, *Bayān*, fol. 47b [II, p. 164; ascribed to Ghaylān, second century A.H.]) this does not refer to pious observance of prayer as religious duty (*iqāmat al-ṣalāt*) but to the elegant and concise idiom which the Bedouins use in their occasional requests addressed to God as in all circumstances of their life. In most *adab* books there are examples of such *du'ā'* by Bedouins as patterns for concise and dignified requests. There is on the other hand no lack of examples of Bedouins depicted as entering into naïve communication with the deity, and where they are assumed to be completely ignorant of God's un-

indifference towards the sacred book of God itself and their ignorance of its most important parts.[1] The Arabs always preferred to hear the songs of the heroes of paganism rather than holy utterances of the Koran. It is related that 'Ubayda b. Hilāl, one of the chiefs of the Khawārij, used to ask his men, while they were resting from battle, to come to his tent. Once two warriors came. 'What would you prefer,' he asked them, 'that I should read to you from the Koran, or that I should recite poems to you?' They replied: 'We know the Koran as well as we know you; let us hear poems.' 'You godless men,' said 'Ubayda, 'I knew that you would prefer poems to the Koran '[2]

[1] Cf. e.g. *Agh.*, XI, p. 89, XIV, p. 40. An Arab of the Banū 'Adī mixed up the poems of Dhu'l-Rumma with the Koran, ib., XVI, p. 112.

[2] *Agh.*, VI, p. 7. Even much later they derided and mocked the Koran: al-Jāḥiẓ, *Bayān*, fol. 128a [II, p. 317].

approachable majesty. In the *Mustaṭraf* (lith. ed. Cairo), II, p. 326-7, there are some Bedouin prayers cited by one who heard them: in these God is seen as human and addressed in a naïve way with such expressions as can only be applied to human benefactors: *Abu'l-Makārim, abyaḍ al-wajh*, etc. Compare with these a note in Yāqūt, II, p. 935, 2 where it is said of an inhabitant of the banks of the Dead Sea that he cried to God, *yā rubaybī*, i.e. 'O Little God', as human beings are addressed in the diminutive as a mark of flattery. In a Bedouin prayer in *al'Iqd*, I, p. 207, 3 the prayer says to God *lā abā laka*. Cf. also B. *Adab*, no. 26.

[7] Al-Tabrīzī, *Ḥam.*, p. 800 on the *adhān* of a Bedouin; Yāqūt, I, p. 790.

CHAPTER TWO 40

THE ARAB TRIBES AND ISLAM

I

THERE is a strong and almost unreconcilable difference in respect of the social order between the attitude of Arab paganism, which is based on ancient traditions, and the teachings of Islam. The social order of the Arab people was based on the relationship of the tribes to one another. Membership of a tribe was the bond which united people who felt that they had something in common; but at the same time it also separated them from other groups. The actual or fictitious descent from a common ancestor was the symbol of social morals, the measure by which people were valued. Men who could not boast of ancestors worth mentioning were despised, even if they lived in Arab territory and spoke the Arabic language, and this low esteem forced them to indulge in occupations which lowered them even further.[1] Only the affiliation of strangers to a tribe whose duty it would be to protect them, the solemn call for sanctuary by the pursued who hoped to find refuge in the tents of the stranger tribe, or a solemn alliance which could take the place of common descent were able to establish the obligation of neighbourly love for strangers; it is true that the strict observance of these ties was the foundation of Arab *muruwwa*[2] and infringements branded the individual as well as the whole tribe as irrevocably dishonourable, and marked them with downright shame.[3]

Thus, at the centre of Arab social consciousness stood the know- 41
ledge of the common descent of certain groups. It is easily seen that the glory of a tribe in face of any other tribe consisted of the glory of its ancestors, upon which the claim to honour and esteem of the individual members as well as the whole group was based. The word for this esteem is *ḥasab*. Arab philologists interpret this word as meaning the 'enumeration' of the famous deeds of ancestors,[4] but

[1] Yāqūt, III, p. 391, 3 ff.

[2] It has become superfluous to describe these circumstances in detail since they have been treated exhaustively by Robertson Smith in *Kinship and Marriage in Early Arabia* and Nöldeke's study occasioned by that book (*ZDMG*, vol. XL (1886), pp. 148 ff.) has elucidated some of the doubtful points.

[3] Cf. Labīd, p. 10 v. 1: *idhā 'udda'l-qadīmu* etc.

[4] [Ibn Qutayba, *Kitāb al-'Arab*, in *Rasā'il al-Bulaghā'*, p. 360;] Abū Hilāl al-'Askarī in *Ṭuraf 'Arabiyya*, ed. Landberg, p. 60 penult.

this includes without doubt also the enumeration of these ancestors themselves who figure in the genealogical tree in paternal or maternal descent.[1] The more that can be enumerated, the 'thicker' is the *ḥasab* or nobility.[2] A tribe is mocked if their number is large but their deeds of fame few.[3]

Amongst the causes of self-congratulation amongst the Arabs the fame of ancestors is the foremost.[4] Much as ancestral piety is one of their few religious sentiments, so the fame of the ancestors of the tribe decides for them the position of their clan within the constellation of humanity. This fame was also of importance in the claim to individual esteem, as it was more than a genealogical ornament to Arabs but had great individual relevance to each man. Just as the Arabs took for granted the inheritance of physical characteristics,[5] they also assumed that moral attributes were handed down in the same way. Virtues and vices being passed on from the ancestors, the individual could prove his *muruwwa* best by being able to point out that the virtues which make the true *muruwwa* were transmitted from noble ancestors,[6] or that he had ancestors who had nothing undistinguished to leave to him as the *sunna*[7] followed by the des-
42 cendants.[8] 'He is elevated by the vein—i.e. the blood—of his ancestors'[9] or 'noble veins lift him up' to his ancestor[10] is the usual description of a man's inheritance from noble ancestors. Descent is traced back to an *'irq* . . .'[11] which means to say that a person is able to relate his moral attributes back to his ancestors[12]—an expression

[1] Cf. *Agh.*, I, p. 18, 11 *fa-'addid mithlahunna Abā Dhubābin.*

[2] From this the favourite saying: *al-ḥasab* or *al-sharaf al-ḍakhm*, *Agh.*, I, p. 30, 9 below, XVII, p. 107, 15, XVIII, p. 199, 4; Yāqūt, III, p. 519, 13; cf. *Ḥam.*, p. 703, v. 1.

[3] *Ḥam.*, p. 643, v. 3.

[4] *Bi-annā dhawū jaddin:* Mālik b. Nuwayra quoted by Yāq., IV, p. 794 ult.

[5] *Ḥam.*, p. 639, v. 1.

[6] Ṭarafa, 10:12; Zuhayr, 3:43, 14:40, 17:36; 'Amr b. Kulth., *Mu'all.*, v. 40.

[7] Labīd, *Mu'all.*, v. 81. *Sunna* is a pre-Islamic word: Zuhayr, 1; 60, also its opposite, *bid'a*: *Mufaḍḍ.*, 34:42, cf. *Ḥam.*, p. 747, v. 3. [Cf. Mālik b. 'Ajlān in *Jamharat Ash'ār al-'Arab*, Būlāq 1308, p. 123 l. 3; al-Muzarrid, *Dīwān*, 4:8.]

[8] Zuhayr, 14:8 *ilā ma'sharin lam yūrithi'l-lu'ma jadduhum.*

[9] The verb *namā* with *'irq* or *'urūq* makes several phrases for the expression of this thought: *Mufaḍḍ.*, 12:22, *Hudhayl.*, 220:5, 230:3; cf., *Agh.*, XX, p. 163, 1. A variant of these is also: *zakharat lahu fi'l-ṣāliḥīna 'urūqu* (al-Farazdaq, ed. Boucher, p. 4, 3 from below) 'in him run the veins of the excellent (ancestors)'. The opposite *takannafahu 'urūq al-alā'im*, *Agh.*, X, p. 22, 8. [Cf. also Jarīr, *Naqā'iḍ*, 70:59.]

[10] Al-Mikdām b. Zayd in Yāqūt, III, p. 471, 22 *namatnā ilā 'Amrin 'urūqun karīmatun* (cf. *namathu qurūmun min* etc., *Agh.*, XIII, p. 15, 4 from below II, p. 158, 13 *tasāmat qurūmuhumu li'l-nadā*).

[11] *Hudhayl.*, 125:2.

[12] Cf. *al-ḥasab al-'arīq* in al-Azraqī, ed. Wüstenfeld, p. 102, 16. On *'irq* cf. also Wilken, *Eenige Opmerkigen* etc. (Haag 1885) p. 16, note 15. [For the influence

which is also applied in another context to physical characteristics.[1]

The virtue of ancestors is usually compared to a high and strong building,[2] which they built for their descendants[3] and which it would be shameful to destroy.[4] Their fame is a continuous incentive to emulation by their descendants. A poet from the Ḥarb tribe says of himself that 'Ḥarbite souls'[5] continually call him to do good. Nobility, *ḥasab*, imposes a double obligation to practice good deeds; it lays duties upon these people and they adhere to the principle *noblesse oblige* in the very best sense.[6] Consideration of the past and the tradition of lineage impel the Arab to practise nobility more than do the hope of and striving for future fame.[7] If there are no ancestors of whom a man can boast, he strives to connect his lineage to another 43
even by some bold fiction.[8] Personal fame and merit count for little in his estimation; only inherited fame and inherited merit bestow the proper consecration and confirmation.[9] 'There is a difference between inherited nobility and nobility which grew with the grass.'[10] Therefore a man's bad deeds are readily ascribed to the baseness of his ancestors.[11]

Utterances which are not in keeping with these points of view are exceptional. I refer to some sayings of heroes of ancient times who boast that they do not wish to vaunt their ancestors but to rely on their own virtues and deeds. To these belongs a much quoted poem

[1] E.g., of the stallion *faḥlun mu'arraqun, Agh.*, I, p. 11, 2, which also makes the expression ib. V, p. 116, 9 more readily understood: *Yajri'l-jawādu bi-ṣiḥḥati'l-a'rāqi*. [Cf. al-Quṭāmī, ed. Barth, 26:5.]

[2] Cf. *ḥuṣḍn al-majdi*, 'Amr. b. Kulthūm, *Mu'all.*, v.61; Labīd, *Mu'all.*, v. 86.

[3] *Ḥam.*, p. 777, v. 3, al-Nābigha, 27:34, *Agh.*, XIX, p. 9, 18; cf., *Mufaḍḍ.*, 19:2, 30:21 (*banaytu masā'iyan*), *Agh.*, XVI, p. 98, 5 from below, *ibtinā'al-majd* (cf. XI, 94, 5 from below, 143, 14); of bad attributes it is also said that they were 'built', i.e. those to whom they are ascribed inherited them from the ancestors: al-Nābigha, 31:4, Ḥassān, *Dīwān*, p. 34, 1; 36, 17 [ed. Hirschfeld, 56:5, 212:2], cf. also *bānī Minqarin*, al-Farazdaq., p. 5, 4 from below.

[4] *Agh.*, XIX, p. 99, 6, from below, cf. 110, 14.

[5] *Anfusun Ḥarbiyyatun, Ḥam.*, p. 749, v. 3.

[6] Labīd, p. 58, v. 2. *nu'ṭī ḥuqūqan 'ala'l-aḥsābi ḍāminatan.*

[7] This consideration is especially stressed in Ḥātim, ed. Hassoun, p. 38, 6-7; 39, 6 etc. and also in the poem ascribed to him which is not in the *Dīwān, Ḥam.*, p. 747, v. 2. When judging Ḥātim's virtue from its Arab panegyrists, we find that it was not free of desire for fame: *Agh.*, XVI, p. 98, 15.

[8] Caussin de Perceval, II, p. 491.

[9] Zuhayr, 14, 40; *Agh.*, IX, p. 147, 16.

[10] *Ḥam.*, p. 679, v. 3 = Rückert, II, p. 213, no. 659.

[11] Ḥassān, Ibn Hishām, p. 526, 9 *li-shaqwati jaddihim*, ib. 575, 16.

---

of maternal *'irq* cf. al-Tha'ālibī, *Thimār al-Qulūb*, pp. 275-7 (*'irq al-khāl*) and the dictionaries under *dss* (*al-'irq dassās*), also Usāma b. Munqidh, *Lubāb al-Ādāb*, p. 5.]

by ʿĀmir b. al-Ṭufayl,[1] which is followed by similar utterances from later times.[2]

The boasts (*mafākhir*), which are mainly based on reference to the deeds of ancestors (a field in which the Arabs award the prize to the Muʿallaqa poet al-Ḥārith[3]) are matched by the taunts (*mathālib*) designed to throw as much scorn as possible upon the ancestors of one's opponent or upon his tribe and sometimes even to place their descent in doubt.[4] It is in this respect that a proud Arab can be hardest hit, as it determines his claim to honour and fame. Quarrels
44 between the tribes are therefore accompanied by mutual satire (*hijā'*)[5] recording all that is shameful in the character and the past of the enemy group while making much of the boasts of one's own clan.[6] The satires which concerned themselves even with the inner life of the family[7] were a particularly important part of the conduct of war. Waging war in poetry is considered as the serious start of hostilities between two tribes[8] just as the cessation of fighting coincides with putting an end to the satires.[9] The assurance of peace concerns security not only from hostile attacks but also from boasting provocation (*an lā jughzaw wa-lā yufākharū*[10]). Owing to the peculiarity of Arab culture it is not strange that this part of the fighting was

[1] Al-Mubarrad, p. 93, 6.

[2] Al-Mutawakkil al-Laythī, *Ḥam.*, p. 772, whose verse later became very popular (*Romance of ʿAntar*, XVI, p, 28. often quoted elsewhere too); cf. also al-Mutanabbī, ed. Dieterici, I, p. 34, v. 32 (*lā bi-qawmī sharuftu bal sharufū bī wa-binafsī fakhirtu lā bi-judūdī*) and al-Ḥuṣrī, I, p. 79.

[3] Al-Maydānī, II, p. 31 *afkharu min al-Ḥārith b. Ḥilliza.*

[4] The verb *nasaba* means recording not only ancestors, but also all the glorious or shameful things related to the single links of the genealogical tree. In *Ḥam.*, p. 114, v. 1 Jābir al-Sinbisī says: Verily I am not ashamed when you unroll my tree of descent (*nasabtanī*), provided that you do not report lies about me; ib. 624, v. 4 *nasaba* in general of enumerating attributes; hence *nasīb* the description of the beloved.

[5] [For the satire see Goldziher's extensive study 'Über die Vorgeschichte der Higâ'-Poesie', *Abhandlungen zur Arabischen Philologie*, I, pp. 1-121.]

[6] *Mufaḍḍ.*, 30:38 ff. Rabīʿa b. Maqrūm says about the Banū Madhḥij that he will refrain from recording the shame of the opponents (as is usual in fighting) and confine himself to pointing out famous deeds in the past of his own tribe. Instead of many examples for such boasts reference is made to Ṭarafa, 14:5, as a specimen. For later days an interesting type of tribe satire is to be found in *Agh.*, II, p. 104.

[7] E.g., between man and wife when they belong to different tribes, *Agh.*, II, p. 165. In al-Mufaḍḍal's collection of proverbs (*Amthāl al-ʿArab* ed. Istanbul 1300, p. 9, 4) there is a little tale telling how two wives of the same husband quarrelled: *fa'stabbatā wa-tarajazatā*, they scolded one another and said *rajaz* verses against each other. [Cf. the satires exchanged between Rawḥ b. Zinbāʿ and his wife, Ibn Abī Ṭāhir, *Balāghāt al-Nisā'*, pp. 95 ff.]

[8] Ibn Hishām, p. 273, 10 *taqāwalū ashʿāran.*

[9] *Agh.*, XVI, p. 142, 3.

[10] Al-Tabrīzī, *Ḥam.*, p. 635, 9.

mainly undertaken by the tribe's poets. In the warlike activities of the tribes they were of great importance. This is evident among other things from the description[1] which al-Ḥuṭay'a gives 'Umar of the causes of the successful wars of the tribe of 'Abs during the Jāhiliyya. Together with Qays b. Zuhayr, 'Antara, Rabī' b. Ziyād to whose prudent caution, braveness in attack and circumspection in command they all gladly submitted, it is also mentioned that they let themselves be guided by the poetry of 'Urwa b. al-Ward (*na'tammu bi-shi'r 'Urwa*).[2] It is evident in the context of the story that this cannot refer only to the latter's merits as an exemplary poet.[3] A poet's gifts appear to have been considered from other than artistic standpoints and there are many indications that a connection was traced between these gifts and supernatural influences.[4] It is **45**
typical that on one occasion the poet is mentioned together with the augur (*'ā'if*) and the water diviner.[5] The poets—as can be inferred from their name—are considered 'those who are knowledgable' (*shā'ir*)[6], first of all about the traditions of their tribe which are to be used in war[7] and thus a 'perfect' man (*kāmil*)[8] must in the view of the Arabs be a poet, i.e. must know the glorious traditions of his tribe[9] which he can use for the honour of his own people in war

[1] *Agh.*, II, p. 191, 5 = VII, p. 152, 8.

[2] Cf. what is related of the old poet al-Afwah in *Agh.* XI, p. 44, 9; Zuhayr b. Janāb, ibid., XXI, p. 93, 23.

[3] Cf. Nöldeke, *Die Gedichte des 'Urwa*, p. 10.

[4] E.g. *Agh.*, XIX, p. 84. This recalls the views of some primitive peoples about their poets, cf. *Journal of the Royal Anthropological Institute*, 1887, p. 130.

[5] Al-Maydānī, II, p. 142, 16.

[6] Cf. Ibn Ya'īsh, commentary on *Mufaṣṣal*, ed. Jahn, p. 128, 18. Barbier de Meynard (*Journal asiat.*, 1874, II, p. 207 note) thinks of the supposition of prophetic gifts and compares Latin *vates*. In this connection mention might be made of the sacredness of poets which Cicero, *Pro Arch.*, c.8, mentions of Ennius. [In his study on the *hijā'*, quoted above (p. 48, note 5), pp. 17 ff., Goldziher modifies his explanation and proposes to derive it rather from the supernatural 'knowledge' of the poet, who in early times served as an oracle for his tribe.]

[7] For this view too we find analogy in primitive peoples, see Schneider *Die Naturvölker*, II, p. 236.

[8] *Agh.*, II, p. 169, Ṭab., I, p. 1207, Caussin de Perceval, II, p. 424 (cf. al-Ḥuṣrī II, p. 252: poetry is a sign of nobility). The byname *kāmil* was also given to men of later days; in the beginning of the second century to the Sulaymite Ashras b. Abd Allāh (*Fragmenta hist. arab.*, ed. de Goeje, p. 89, 3).

[9] Ibn Fāris (died 394) in *Muzhir* (II, p. 235): 'Poetry (*al-shi'r*) is the archive (*dīwān*) of Arabs, through it genealogical information (*al-ansāb*) was remembered and the traditions of fame (*al-ma'āthir*) were made known'. The sentence: *al-shi'r dīwān al-'Arab* is mentioned as an old saying of Ibn Jarīr *'an* Ibn 'Abbās (Al-Ṣiddīqī, fol. 122b); from the same source it is quoted also in *al-'Iqd*, III, p. 122 *al-sh. 'ilm al-'Arab wa-dīwānuhā*). It is found also in the following context (Ṣidd., fol. 114a): 'It is said: The Arabs are distinguished from other peoples by four characteristics: the head bindings are their crowns (*al-'amā'im tījānuhā*),

against opponents whose aim is to stress shameful facts of the past of his tribe.[1] Therefore it is said of a poet, whose special function is to serve the tribe in this respect and to promote its honour, that he is a
46 poet of the tribe (e.g. *shā'iru Taghliba* and others), and the appearance of such poetical defenders and advocates was celebrated as a joyous event by a tribe because it meant that 'their honour was protected and their glory defended, their memorable deeds were made immortal and their memory firmly established.'[2]

Sometimes also poets of strange tribes were sought out in order to have them compose—occasionally for high fees—satires against a prospective opponent in battle,[3] and it is not improbable that the biblical story told in Numbers 22:2 ff. is based on the supposition of such conditions. Satires were an indispensable part of war. The tribal poet boasted that he was no mere composer of verses but an instigator of war, who sent forth mocking verses against those who scorned his tribe;[4] and this mockery was so effective because it 'had wings' and 'its words were circulating',[5] i.e. it toured all the encampments and was known everywhere and was even more dangerous because it stuck and could not easily be wiped out—'a bad saying clinging like lard which makes the Copt woman ugly',[6] 'burning like a mark made with hot coal',[7] 'sharp as the tip of a sword'[8] and 'alive even when the inventor has long been dead.'[9]

[1] Labīd, p. 143, v. 6.

[2] Ibn Rashīq (died 370) [*al-'Umda*, Cairo 1907, I, p. 37, quoted] in *Muzhir*, II, p. 236.

[3] *Agh.*, XVI, p. 56, 6 from below. Al-Mundhir b. Imrq. king of Ḥīra, asked several Arab poets in his war against the Ghassānid al-Ḥārith b. Jabala, to compose satires against the enemy: al-Mufaḍḍal al-Ḍabbī, *Amthāl*, p. 50 f.

[4] *Ḥam.*, I, p. 232 Hudba b. Khashram, cf. the forceful expressions in *Hudhayl.*, 120:2.

[5] Ṭarafa, 19:17 *min hijā'in sā'irin kalimuh.* [More passages describing the wide and lasting effects of the satire in Goldziher's monograph (see above, p. 48, note 5), pp. 90-2.]

[6] Zuhayr, 10:33.

[7] Al-Nābigha, 9:2; he compared (29:7) his satires with powerful rocks (probably because of their durability, Ḥassān, *Dīwān*, p. 28, 1 [ed. Hirschfeld, 7:2] *mā tabqa'l- jibālu'l-khawālidu*, Zuhayr, 20:10, etc.); another satirical poet calls his verses 'a necklace which does not perish' (*Agh.*, X, p. 171, 7, from below, cf. Proverbs, 6:21).

[8] Cf. *Agh.*, XII, p. 171, 19, where Jarīr describes his *hijā'*: '. . . dripping with blood, able to go far through the mouths of the rhapsodists, like the edge of an Indian blade which penetrates when it glistens.'

[9] *Ḥam.*, p. 299 = Rückert, I, p. 231 no. 190.

---

the coats are their walls (*al-ḥubā ḥīṭānuhā*), swords are their top clothes (*al-suyūf sījānuhā*) and poetry is their archive.' These sentences appear to be the source of Ibn Fāris' saying, which at an earlier date is also placed at the head of his poems by the poet Abū Firās al-Ḥamdānī (died 337): Rosen, *Notice sommaires des Manuscripts arabes*, 1881, p. 225.

Yea verily they know from of old—says the pagan poet al-Muzzarrid,[1]—

that when the contest becomes severe, I punish with words and shoot arrows.
I am famed for him whom I strike with poems that last for ever[2]
Which are sung by wanderers and which are used to urge along 47
the riding beasts.
With verses which are well remembered
and whose reciters are often met with:
Manifest,[3] they are found in every country,
They are repeated again and again and always increasing in fame
Whenever fierce lips try the song;
And he whom I attack with a line
Is marked as if with a black mole in his face,
And nobody can wash off sůch a mole.'

Thus, in a contest between tribes, the arrows flew from the mouths of poets as much as from the quivers of warriors, and the wounds that they inflicted were deeply embedded in the tribe's honour and were felt for generations. It is therefore not astonishing to learn that poets were greatly feared amongst the Arabs.[4] The effect of the satire in pre-Islamic days is best measured when one considers what power it had even in those days when Islam had—at least theoretically—overcome it and it was consequently officially forbidden. The phenomena of these times, particularly of the Umayyad period when the Arab instincts with all their heathen immediacy survived more or less intact, are particularly instructive about the conditions of the Jāhiliyya, an epoch which, though extending to our Middle Ages, is in many respects virtually prehistoric from our point of view and is elucidated by its after-effects. We shall see that the general indifference of the true Arabs to the equalizing teachings of Islam extended also to matters which depended upon the relations of the tribes with one another.

The satires of a poet could have disastrous effects on the position
of a tribe within Arabic society. One single line of Jarīr (died 110), 48

[1] *Mufaḍḍ.*, 16:57-61 [Lyall's translation 17:57-61].

[2] Cf. al-Farazdaq, ed. Boucher, p. 47 penult.

[3] Cf. Zuhayr 7:7 *bi-kulli qāfiyatin shan'ā'a tashtahiru.*

[4] *Agh.*, IX, p. 156, 10. This awe of poets is even more comprehensible when we consider that they sometimes sent out their biting satires without any outward cause, from pure chicanery against honourable men and tribes. The example of Durayd b. al-Ṣimma is instructive in this respect: he mocked 'Abd Allāh b. Jud'ān, as he admits himself, 'because he heard that he was a noble man and so he wanted to lodge a poem in a worthwhile target': *Agh.*, ibid., p. 10, 24. 'Abd Yaghūth has his tongue cut off by his enemies so that he may be unable to utter *hijā'*: *Agh.*, XV, p. 76, 18.

that classic of the later *hijā'*,[1] against the tribe of Numayr ('Lower your eyes because you are of the tribe of Numayr' etc.) damaged the reputation of this tribe to such an extent that a Numayrite, when asked his tribe, did not dare to name it, but professed to belong to the tribe of Banū 'Āmir from which the Banū Numayr derived. This tribe could thus serve as a warning when poets wished to intimidate opponents with the power of their satire: 'My mockery will bring you shame as Jarīr humiliated the Banū Numayr.'[2] Other tribes suffered the same fate: they were exposed to ridicule and scorn because of but a single line in a verse. Tribes otherwise honoured like the Ḥabiṭāt, Ẓalīm, 'Ukl, Salūl, Bāhila, etc., became the target of shame and mockery because of short epigrams by malicious poets which may be found in many passages of Arabic literature. This fact often seems astonishing when one finds it mentioned by the historians of literature, because in many cases there is merely pointless mockery without wit or any relation to a real fact in the history of the tribe; though on the other hand it must often be assumed that the disparagement is based on some historical fact which is not known to us as well as on the poet's satirical mood.[3]

> I have seen that donkeys are the laziest animals—in
> the same way the Ḥabiṭāt are the laziest among the
> Tamīmites.

Such a satirical verse, however silly and unimportant its content may be, spread among the Arabs with astonishing speed just because
49 of its rudeness and members of the tribe which was attacked had to be prepared to hear it called after them when passing the encampment of another tribe and giving the name of their ancestor in answer to a question about their tribe. Members of a tribe which has been branded by the satire of a poet are forced to deny the true tribal name. The Banū Anf al-Nāqa ('the she-camel's nose') were forced to call themselves Banū Quraysh until al-Ḥuṭay'a dissolved the ban with his words:

[1] A detailed characteristic and critical assessment of Jarīr's satire in relation to that of his contemporary, al-Farazdaq, is to be found in Ibn al-Athīr al-Jazarī, *al-Mathal al-Sā'ir*, (Būlāq 1282), pp. 490 ff.

[2] Cf. also Jarīr on Numayr, *Agh.*, XX, p. 170, l. 2 from below. [Cf. also Ibn Rashīq, *al-'Umda*, Cairo 1907, p. 26.]

[3] Occasionally it was the comic points about the life of an ancestor that stuck to a tribe unendingly. Thus the descendants of 'Ijl (tribal branch of the Bakr b. Wā'il) had to listen to satires about a story told of their presumed ancestor. He was asked to name his horse as all fiery Arab horses had their own names. 'Ijl then destroyed one of the horse's eyes and said: I call it A'war—i.e. one-eyed. The simplicity of their ancestor thus served to mock all 'Ijlites; *Agh.* XX, p. 11. An equally trivial reason is quoted for the Tamīmites being called Banu'l-Ja'rā': *Agh.*, XVIII, p. 199.

Yes, a people is the nose, the tail is another people—
who would call the camel's tail equal to its nose?

Now they could return to their own honest old name.[1] The tribe of Bāhila[2] had the misfortune to be reputed miserly and as late as in the 'Abbāsid period they had to suffer the scorn of poets:[3]

When you call to a dog: You Bāhilite—he whimpers with shame.
Sons of Sa'īd—thus the children of Sa'īd b. Salm
who lived in the time of Hārūn al-Rashīd are addressed
—sons of Sa'īd you belong to a tribe which does not
honour guests.
A people stemming from Bāhila b. Ya'ṣur which is derived
from 'Abd Manāf when asked for their descent (because
they are ashamed of their real descent).
They combine supper with breakfast and when they give food
by your father's life, it is never enough.
And when my road leads me to them it is as if I
visited Abraq al-'Azzāf (north of Medina on the way to
Baṣra), where at night the voice of demons—singular
'azīf al-jinn[4]—is said to have been heard.[5]

The tribe of Taym suffered much from the mockery of al-Akhṭal: 'When I meet the servants of Taym and their masters I ask: which are the servants? The worst in this world are those who rule in Taym and—whether they wish it or not—the servants are masters amongst them.'[6]

Here the spirit of the Arabic Jāhiliyya, which continued to exercise 50
its influence despite the intervention of Islam—which could not favour the *hijā'*[7]—finds expression. During pagan times there were

[1] These things are exhaustively discussed in al-Jāḥiẓ, *Kitāb al-Bayān*, fols. 163 ff. [IV, pp. 35 ff.: the correct reading is Quray', not Quraysh, see IV, p. 38]. A selection is found in *al-'Iqd*, III, pp. 128 ff.

[2] The noble Tamīmite al-Aḥnaf b. Qays is reproached by an Arab who envies his distinction at 'Umar's court with being the son of a Bāhilite woman: *al-'Iqd*, I, p. 143.

[3] Al-Mubarrad, p. 433.

[4] *Agh.*, II, p. 155, 4 from below

[5] See the verse also in Yāqūt, I, p. 84, 9 ff. The place-name is mentioned in addition to the passage quoted in Yāqūt also by Ḥassān, *Dīwān*, p. 65, 15 [ed. Hirschfeld, 178:1], *Agh.*, XXI, p. 103, 21.

[6] *Agh.*, VII, p. 177. The equality of slaves and freemen is also ridiculed by Dhu'l-Rumma [*Dīwān*, ed. Macartney, p. 167], quoted by Ibn al-Sikkīt, Leiden MS. Warner no. 157, p. 165 [*Tahdhīb al-Alfāẓ*, ed. Cheikho, p. 198]: *sawāsiyatun aḥrāruhā wa-'abīduhā*.

[7] The authorities persecuted and punished satirical poets: *Agh.*, II, p. 55 below; XI, p. 152 below; cf. Yāqūt, III, p. 542, 19.

but few poets who disliked the use of *hijā'*, which as we have seen, was considered by the foremost men of those days as a praiseworthy virtue. On the other hand it was considered shameful by the Arabs if their opponents did not deem them worthy of a *hijā'*, as this was taken as a sign of inferiority.[1] A rare, perhaps unique, exception was 'Abda b. al-Ṭabīb, who lived on the watershed between the pagan era and Islam, of whom it is said that he refrained from satirical poetry because he considered its practice base and abstinence from it *muruwwa*.[2] It is mentioned as a sign of close alliance between two people that 'they never climbed the heights of satire.'[3] But even in Islamic times we learn that not even the sacred law of hospitality offered protection from the *hijā'*.[4]

II

The teachings of Islam were in powerful opposition to the social views which gave rise to this state of affairs. We refer not so much to the teachings of Muhammed himself as more generally to the Islamic view of life which resulted from them and which is best expressed in the traditional sayings ascribed to the Prophet. In accordance with these Islam was called upon to make effective the equality and fraternity of all men united in Islam. Islam was designed to level all social and genealogical differences: competition
51 and perpetual strife between tribes, their 'mockings' and 'boastings' were to cease and there was to be no distinction of rank in Islam between Arabs and Barbarians, free men and freed men. In Islam there were to be only brothers and in the 'community (*ummat*) of Muhammed' the distinctions between Bakr and Taghlib, Arab and Persian, were to cease and to be banned as specifically Jāhilī. From the day when Muhammed was proclaimed as 'the prophet of white and black men' and his mission declared as a blessing embracing the whole of mankind, there could be no other claims for preference amongst his followers than those founded on more devout comprehension of and adherence to his mission.

The beginnings of this concept have their roots undoubtedly in that teaching which Muhammed himself imparted during the Medinian period of his work to the few believers who followed him;

[1] *Ḥam.*, p. 628, v. 4.

[2] *Agh.*, XVIII, p. 163 below. Later such examples became more frequent. Miskīn al-Dārimī (died 90) refrains from the *hijā'* but is not against *mufākhara* (*Agh.*, XIII, p. 153, 9 from below): also Nuṣayb (died 108) refrains from satires; for this different reasons are given in *Agh.*, I, p. 140, 8, from below, 142, 13. Al-'Ajjāj (II cent.) boasts that he avoids satire; cf. al-Ḥuṣrī, II, p. 254. Al-Buḥturī (died 284) ordered his son to burn, after his death, all *hijā'* found among his poems. (*Agh.*, XVIII, p. 167).

[3] *Ḥam.*, p. 309, v. 6.

[4] Al-Farazdaq, ed. Boucher, p. 7, 6, cf. *Agh.*, XVIII, p. 142, penult.

and the first impetus to announce them was based less on the desire for a better order of Arab society than on the relationship towards their Qurayshite fellow-tribesmen in which Muhammed and the faithful Meccans accompanying him found themselves owing to the 'emigration'. The necessity of making war against them, an undertaking tantamount to extreme perfidy and dishonour in the ancient Arab view, forced the Prophet to announce the worthlessness of the tribal principle and to find the principle of unity in the profession of a common faith.[1] From this political solution of a problematical state of affairs, grew the teaching propounded in full consciousness of the social advancement contained in it: 'O men, we have created you from man and woman and made you into peoples and tribes that you may recognize one another. Verily before God the noblest is he who fears God most.'[2] Here the equality of all believers before Allāh and the thought that the fear of God is the only measure of nobility,[3] to the exclusion of differences arising from mere descent, is clearly expressed; and Muslim exegesis is unanimous in respect of this interpretation of the Koranic passage, which need not be altered even by our scientific consideration of the text.

Thus a profound breach was made in the ideas of the Arab people 52
about the relationship of tribes to one another; and everything that we know about the social spirit of the Arabs would make us accept the tradition which represents them as resisting this teaching of the Prophet. The tradition tells us for example that the Bakrites, on the point of joining the victorious Prophet, were made to hesitate by the following consideration: 'The religion of the grandchild of 'Abd al-Muṭṭalib,' so they said, 'forbids its followers to go to war with each other; it condemns to death a Muslim who kills another (even if he be of a different tribe). Thus we would have to refrain from attacking and robbing tribes who, like us, accept Islam . . . We will undertake one more expedition against the Tamīmites and then we will become Muslims.'[4] This story may or may not be true, but it certainly grew out of real conditions.

On various occasions Muhammed took deliberate action to further the idea that from now on Islam, rather than tribal affiliation, was to be the unifying principle of society. For example, in Anas's house he inaugurated a brotherhood comprising forty-five (or, according to another authority, seventy-five), pairs each consisting of one of

[1] Snouck Hurgronje, *De Islam*, p. 47 of the offprint [*Verspreide Geschriften*, I, p. 225].

[2] Sūra 49:13.

[3] According to B. *Anbiyā'*, no. 9, Muslim V, p. 215, the nobility of the Jāhiliyya counts also under Islam, but only if the fact of noble descent is implemented by the attributes of a good Muslim: *khiyāruhum fi'l-jāhiliyya khiyāruhum fi'l-islām idhā faquhū.*

[4] Caussin de Perceval, II, p. 604.

his followers from Medina and one from Mecca, and this bond was intended to be so close that the 'brothers' should inherit to the exclusion of blood relatives.[1] This was intended to prove that religion was a firmer basis for brotherly community than membership of the same tribe. It seems that Muhammed carefully guarded against the possibility of old tribal feuds re-awakening in the hearts of those whom he believed he had brought to greater fame than any battle of their pagan forefathers.

This explains the antipathy expressed in old Islamic sources towards poets who were considered the interpreters of the ancient pagan mentality. Not all the enmity against poets and poetry found in old traditions—which could, as is well known, base themselves on Koran, 26:225—was due to the persecution that the Prophet himself suffered from the poets. When, for example, Imru'u'l-Qays is
53 named as the leader of poets in hell, and is said to have had a famous name in the *dunyā* but to be doomed to oblivion in the *ākhira*,[2] poetry is condemned as the organ of pagan mentality. 'It is better for a man that his body be full of pus than that he be full of poems.'[3] In Islamic praxis this view never prevailed,[4] but it did rule the minds of devout men and pietists. Orders to restrict the field of poetry were attributed to the oldest caliphs.[5] 'Umar II was particularly harsh with poets who came to flatter him.[6] Pious men who indulged in ancient poetry, like Nuṣayb at Kūfa (died 108), did at least refrain from reciting old poems on Fridays;[7] and in pietist circles the view was spread in the guise of prophetic traditions that on the day of judgment the Koran would be forgotten in the heart of men and that everyone 'would return to the poems and songs and stories of the Jāhiliyya; whereupon the Dajjāl would appear.'[8] These people were favourably disposed only towards the so-called *zuhdiyyāt*, i.e. ascetic poetry,[9] to which they would have liked to confine the essence of all poetic art. But literary history shows how small was the community who were guided by such ideas.[10]

[1] For sources see Sprenger, III, p. 26 [and I. Lichtenstaedter, in *Islamic Culture*, 1942, pp. 47–52].

[2] *Agh.*, VII, p. 130.

[3] B. *Adab*, no. 91.

[4] Cf. al-Mubarrad, p. 46, 1.

[5] Ṭab., II, p. 213; M. J. Müller *Beiträge z. Gesch. d. westl. Araber*, p. 140, note 2.

[6] *Al-'Iqd*, I, pp. 151 ff., *Agh.* VIII, p. 152.

[7] *Agh.*, II, p. 146, 11.

[8] Al-Ghazālī, *Iḥyā*, I, p. 231.

[9] *Agh.*, III, p. 161.

[10] [For the question of the permissibility of poetry cf. also e.g. al-Muttaqī al-Hindī, *Kanz al-'Ummāl*, Hyderabad 1951, nos. 2825–49 and 3787–3803; *Mishkāt al-Maṣābīḥ*, p. 411; al-Sharīf al-Raḍī, *al-Majāzat al-Nabawiyya*, Cairo 1937, pp. 90, 120, 205.]

III

The relationship of the Arab tribes to one another, with the consequent mutual assistance, strife and the competition of which we have spoken above, meant that there were features of everyday life which had to be rejected owing to the supreme principle that all Muslims were equal. It is likely that the Prophet himself, who, as we have seen, announced this teaching in full awareness of the changes it would involve, was the first to condemn these things. The systematic, and we may even say theological opposition to them is, however, surely due to the evolving effort of generations following the Prophet's initiative—generations which linked the founder's name to their own **54**
work, which was in keeping with his views.

This effort was necessary because of the refusal of Arabs to adjust their feelings to the new order even after they had nominally been converted to Islam. The less the new teaching was understood and followed by those to whom it was directly addressed the more did its devout followers strive to lend it weight by increasingly clear exposition and to attach to it the authority of the Prophet.

Of the phenomena of Arab life which had to be rejected because of the new teaching about the mutual relationship of the members of the believing community, and the abolition of which was to destroy the outward manifestations of the old tribal mentality, we shall deal more especially with three:

(1) the *mufākhara*. (2) the *shi'ār*. (3) the *taḥāluf*.

(1)

Competition between Arab tribes was usually expressed through the mouths of their poets and heroes—and usually these attributes were united in the same person—in the form of *mufākhara* or *munāfara* (more rarely *mukhāyala*),[1] a peculiar form of boasting which is found also amongst other people of low cultural development.[2] This took various forms, of which the most common was that the hero of the tribe stepped in front of the ranks before the beginning of the fight and proclaimed to the enemy the nobility and high rank of his tribe.[3] 'He who knows me,' was a common formula 'knows it,

[1] An interesting story of *mukhāyala* is in al-Mufaḍḍal, *Amthāl al-'Arab*, p. 18. Also in *Agh.*, XVI, p. 100, 3 *mukhāyala* (which is to be read twice instead of the printed *mukhābala*) is explained with *mufākhara*.

[2] For scorn and verbal fights before the real fighting among Negro peoples see Stanley, [*Through the Dark Continent*, London 1878, II, pp. 87–8 =] *Durch den Dunklen Welttheil* (Germ. ed., II, p. 97).

[3] To this refers e.g. *Hudhayl.*, 169:7, cf. ZDMG, XXXIX, p. 434, 5 from below (*idhā qātala 'tazā*).

and he who does not know me may know it now' and so forth.[1] During the fighting too the warrior shouts his *nasab* to the enemy
55 and Muslim tradition does not make the Prophet an exception to this rule.[2] Bedouins call this boasting: *intikhā'*.[3] In this category really belong also the customs mentioned on pages 50 ff. But even in times of peace this competition led by poets was an everyday event in Arab society.[4] Al-Mundhir, King of Ḥīra, asked 'Āmir b. Uḥaymir b. Bahdala, who had claimed the highest rank amongst all present: 'Are you then the noblest of all Arabs in respect of your tribe?' And he replied (as can be seen, the answer is revised according to later genealogical details): 'The Ma'add excell in nobility and number, and amongst them the Nizār, and amongst them the Muḍar, and amongst them the Khindif, amongst whom the Tamīm, and amongst these Sa'd b. Ka'b and of these the 'Awf and of the latter the family of Bahdala. He who does not admit this may compete with me' (*fal-yunāfirnī*).[5] It was, of course, most glorious to win such a competition by means of the intrinsic justness of the cited points of nobility, and it was most shameful if it was said of a tribe that it always lost in such *munāfarāt*.[6] If a self-confident hero of a tribe learnt that somewhere there was a man who was ranked highly he felt called upon to combat that man's claim and did not shirk long journeys in order to defeat him in a *mufākhara*.[7]

Later historians thus assumed that before recognizing Muhammed the heroes of the Banū Tamīm came to him in order to hold a *mufākhara* with him, upon the success of which their conversion would depend.[8] In the same way, later historiography introduced a *munāfara* into the account of ancient Arab history, in the context

[1] Cf. Ibn Hishām, p. 773, 5. In the 'Antar novel this old Arabic custom appears frequently; it echoes in allusions like *Agh.*, XVIII, p. 68, 18, cf. V, p. 25, 15; Ṭab., III, p. 994; *Fihrist*, p. 181, 14. The same type of challenge is usual amongst Bedouins to this day, cf. D'Escayrac de Lautour, *Le Désert et le Soudan* (Germ. ed. Leipzig 1855), p. 119.

[2] B. *Jihād*, no. 165.

[3] Wetzstein, *Sprachliches aus den Zeltlagern der syrischen Wüste* (*ZDMG*, XXII), p. 34 note 25b of the offprint (1868).

[4] A typical story instructive of the various points of view of *munāfara* in pre-Islamic times (*munāfara* of 'Āmir b. al-Ṭufayl with 'Alqama) is in *Agh.*, XV, pp. 52-56.

[5] [Quoted from Abū 'Ubayda by Ibn Qutayba, *K. al-'Arab.* in *Rasā'il al-Bulaghā'*, p. 348, and] al-Tabrīzī to *Ḥam.*, p. 769, v. 2. For this genealogical climax cf. of older sources, *Ḥam.*, p. 459; cf. also *ZDMG*, IV, p. 300, and above p. 15.

[6] Notable is the mockery of Ḥassān b. Thābit against the tribe of the Ḥimās (*Dīwān*, p. 54, 12) [ed. Hirschfeld, 189:6]): *In sābaqū subiqū aw nāfarū nufirū* etc.

[7] *Agh.*, XIX, p. 99, 9 = Nöldeke, *Beiträge*, p. 95, 5.

[8] Ibn Hishām, p. 934 penult. (*nufākhiruka*); *Agh.*, IV, p. 8, 9; Sprenger, III, pp. 366 ff. [and other sources analyzed by W. Arafat in the *Bulletin of the School of Oriental and African Studies*, 1955, pp. 416 ff.]

of an episode of the competition between Hāshim and Umayya, which as is well known was a tendentious anticipation of the rivalry 56
of the two dynasties of caliphs.[1] Here a Khuzā'ite soothsayer is umpire and after hearing the pretensions of both rivals he gives judgment in favour of Hāshim: this is tendentious 'Abbāsid historiography.

Occasionally such competitions led to bloody and passionate tribal feuds as is shown by the traditions about the first *fijār* war between the Hawāzin and the Kināna tribes. The Kinānite Badr b. Ma'shar started the fight by his provocation of the congregated Arabs (at 'Ukāẓ) to whom he pretended that he was the mightiest of his people, and to whom he proclaimed his own tribe to be the most excellent of all the tribes of Quraysh; the fight between the two tribes lasted for a long time.[2] According to a Meccan legend which was still told in the beginning of the third century and which probably contains a grain of truth, a rock near Mecca is called 'rock of mocking' (*ṣufiyyu al-sibāb*) because in pagan times the Arabs on their return from pilgrimage used to stop there and hold competitions in boasting about their ancestors, reciting the relevant poems and throwing inglorious traditions in each other's faces, a practice which often led to fights.[3] Even in early 'Abbāsid times this 'rock of mocking' is said to have been the place of such competitions.[4]

Frequently, the purpose of public *mufākhara* was to end an old quarrel between two people. On such occasions impartial umpires were appointed to judge which of the parties was the winner in poetical boasting. Forfeits were deposited with the umpires to ensure adherence to the judgment.[5] The outcome of the conflict then did not depend, of course, upon the relative justice of the combatants but on their accomplishment in poetical expression, and the ability to gain 57
ascendency in the *tanāfur* is thus part of the glory of the old Arabs.[6]

A variant of the *mufākhara* or *munāfara*[7] is the so-called *muhājāt*:

[1] See the sources in the Muir, 'Forefathers of Mahomet' (*Calcutta Review*, no. 93, 1854), p. 8.

[2] *Al-'Iqd*, III, p. 108.

[3] Al-Azraqī, p. 483 above, cf. 443, 10, 481, 5.

[4] *Agh.*, VIII, p. 109; cf. also the parallel passage, ibid., XVI, p. 162, where, line 16, *sibāb* must probably be read instead of *al-sharāb*, and line 17 *shabīb* instead of *sibāb*. It is not impossible that the story of the rock of mocking as the scene of *mufākhara* during the Jāhiliyya is nothing but the anticipation of later circumstances. The name of the rock is, however, ancient and that would speak for the antiquity of the happenings connected with it.

[5] Cf. Caussin de Perceval, II, p. 565. Typical examples in Freytag, *Einleitung in das Studium der arab. Sprache*, p. 184. Hence the *mufākhara* is also called *rihān*, e.g. *Agh.*, XVI, p. 142, 15; 146, 8.

[6] *Ḥam.*, p. 143, v. 4.

[7] Another variant, (also mentioned in Caussin de Perceval, II, p. 169) is the

if some event had set two people at enmity, so that they persecuted one another with satirical poems, in the manner of the ancient Arabs, they could decide to give a public competition in satire, leaving it to public opinion to decide the winner. Thus, for example, the Tamīmite chief al-Zibriqān b. Badr and the poet al-Mukhabbal, to whom the former would not grant his sister as wife, held a public *muhājāt* after persecuting one another with satirical verses.[1]

All kinds of boasting competitions,[2] in which the combatants vie in proclaiming the fame of their tribe, were sharply condemned by the old Muslim teachers, whose views are expressed in many traditional sayings and stories, of which we will mention one:

After the tribes of Aws and Khazraj, who were rivals in pagan times, had both been absorbed in the unity of the Anṣār through the common bond of Islam, it so happened that they revived memories of paganism and their brave fights at a social gathering: poems were recited—it is claimed by a Jew who hoped in this way to make them
58 relapse into paganism—dealing with the tribal quarrels, and the battle of Bu'āth where the Aws inflicted a serious defeat upon the Khazraj. Listening to the heroic poems was sufficient to rouse the dormant pagan soul and rivalry developed between the members of the two tribes, which soon became so lively that the ancient quarrel was about to be renewed, and the old feud was again declared.[3] The news of this relapse reached the Prophet, who came to the gathering and admonished them: 'O community of Muslims! Has the arrogance (*da'wā*) of barbarism returned while I am amongst you, after Allāh led you to Islam, through which He has enobled you and cut you loose from paganism, with which He has saved you from disbelief and has

[1] *Agh.*, XII, p. 42.

[2] A synonymous designation may be mentioned: *nḥb* III (*Lisān al-'Arab*, in the marginal gloss to Jawh., ed. 1282, III, p. 103) in the meaning of *fkhr* III, which is generally used of normal wagers (Ṭab., I, p. 1006, 9; al-Bayḍāwī, II, p. 102, 12 = *khṭr* III; *Durrat al Ghaww.*, 173, 9). *Khṭr* I is also found as synonym of *fkhr*, e.g. *Agh.*, XI, p. 34 penult. *'inda'l-fakhri wa'l-khaṭarāni, khaṭar* is the prize in the *rihān*: al-Farazd., p. 19, 1. To these synonyms also belongs *tanāḍul*, *Agh.*, XIII, p. 153. A whole treasury of synonyms of this group is found in a poem *Yatīmat al-Dahr*, I, p. 71. [For books on boasting competitions by Abū 'Ubayda, Ibn al-Kalbī, and Abu'l-Ḥasan the genealogist, see *Fihrist*, pp. 80, 166, 170; for one by al-Zubayr b. al-Bakkār, Ibn Abi'l-Ḥadīd's commentary on the *Nahj al-Balāgha*, II, p. 101.]

[3] On fights between these two tribes, as it seems at the beginning of Islam, see al-Tabrīzī to *Ḥam.*, p. 442.

---

munājada, *Agh.*, XVI, pp. 99 ff.; it figures in the legend of Ḥātim. The combatants hold a *munājada*, i.e. a public contest, not with poetic weapons but in respect of their generosity towards guests. He whom the assembled crowd declare the most hospitable is victor and can claim the forfeits deposited with unbiased umpires.

united you with each other?' The Prophet's admonition succeeded and soon the two tribes left, reconciled with one another.[1]

Similarly, other traditions make 'Umar issue the order that poems in which the Anṣār and the Qurayshites compete in the pagan Arab manner may not be recited. A later exegesis of this order makes him say: 'This means the mocking of contemporaries by citing the deeds of the dead and renewing old hatred, when Allāh has abolished ancient barbarism by means of Islam.' 'Umar once heard two men competing by saying: 'I am the son of him who accomplished such and such brave deeds,' and more to the same effect. 'Umar said: 'If you have sense you have ancestors, if you have good qualities you have nobility, if you fear God you are of worth. But if you lack all these an ass is better than you.'[2]

The poetic literature of the oldest Islamic times shows many examples of this kind of survival of the ancient pagan mentality among Arabs. The Ṭayyi'ite Ḥurayth b. 'Annāb (who lived until Mu'āwiya's days) called to opponents from other tribes with whom he was quarrelling about the rank of their descent: [3]

Come along! I call you to the dispute of rank (*ufākhirkum*),
whether Faq'as and A'yā have more honour than
Ḥātim's blood: 59
One of the Qays 'Aylān be a courageous and just umpire
and one of the twin tribe of Rabī'a a good and
honest judge.[4]

Two typical examples of poetic competitions have been transmitted just from the first Islamic period—good examples for a study of the character of these competitions. For brevity's sake mere references must suffice: the *muhājāt* of Nābigha al-Ja'dī (died 79) against several Qurayshites, of which there is a detailed description;[5] and the competition of the poet Jamīl (died 82) with Jawwās, which is also peculiar in that both parties chose the Jews of Taymā as umpires (*tanāfarā ilā Yahūd Taymā'*). They make the following judgment: 'O Jamīl, you may claim what you wish because by Allāh, you are the poet of beautiful face, the noble one; you, Jawwās, may boast of yourself and your father as much as you like; but you, Jamīl, must not boast of your father because he herded cattle with us in Taymā' and the garment in which he was clad barely covered him.'[6] This made the two poets begin their quarrel in earnest.

[1] Ibn Hishām, p. 386.
[2] *Agh.*, IV, pp. 5 and 81.
[3] [Goldziher remarks: 'I quote from Rückert's translation'.]
[4] *Ḥam.*, p. 123, vv. 3-4 = Rückert, I, p. 76; cf. *Ḥam.*, p. 180, v. 2.
[5] *Agh.*, IV, pp. 132 ff.
[6] Ibid., XIX, p. 112.

The consciousness, however, that such language was contrary to Islamic teaching became more assertive later and was expressed in many tales invented by the scholars, of which I will quote one example. 'Alī b. Shafī' recounted: 'I stood in the market of al-Hajar when I saw a man dressed in silk riding upon a noble Mahrī camel, with a finer saddle than I had ever seen before. The man called: "Who will compete with me[1] when I boast of the Banū 'Āmir b. Ṣa'ṣa'a, their knights, their poets, their number and glorious deeds." I said: "I will accept the challenge." And the man replied: "Of whom will you boast?" So I said: "I will boast of the Banū Tha'laba b. 'Uqāba of the tribe of the Bakr b. Wā'il." Thereupon the stranger ran away, pleading the Prophet's admonition and I learnt that the challenger was 'Abd al-'Azīz b. Zurāra of the Kilāb tribe.'[2] Much as this tale shows its apocryphal character it is still instructive of the manner of the *munāfarāt* which continued long after Islam had condemned it.

60 Islam wished to do away with all manifestations of pagan genius and therefore strove to abolish these contests also, even when, instead of boasting nobility of descent, to glorify their ancestors, two people competed in the practice of Arabic virtues. We have already referred (p. 59 note 7) to those contests called *tanājud* or *munājada*. A related term for this contest in hospitality is: *ta'āqur*.[3] True Arabs did not refrain from this custom in Islam either. There is a description of such *ta'āqur* competition[4] between the father of the poet al-Farazdaq, Ghālib b. Ṣa'ṣa'a and the Riyāḥite Suḥaym b. Wathīl. It took place in the vicinity of a well near Kūfa, Ṣaw'ar[5]—such public hospitalities were preferably held at drinking places[6]—where there was the settlement of the Banū Kalb. Ghālib ordered a camel to be slaughtered and regaled all the families of the tribe with it; when Ghālib sent Suḥaym his share the latter grew so angry that he rejected the gift and replied by slaughtering a camel for the tribe himself. This was again imitated by Ghālib and the process was repeated until Suḥaym had no more camels left. Suḥaym was thus defeated and became the target for ridicule in his tribe. However, he could not tolerate this and had a hundred camels brought and slaughtered as proof that he was not miserly.[7]

Such trials of generosity were not approved by the Muslim view.

[1] *Man yufākhirunī man yunāfirunī.*

[2] *Agh.*, VIII, p. 77.

[3] *Agh.*, XXI, p. 102, 21.

[4] Yāqūt, III. pp. 430 f.

[5] Al-Maydānī, II, p. 239, no. 52, expressly has Dawād.

[6] Al-Azraqī, p. 445.

[7] Another version of the same event in *Agh.*, XIX, pp. 5 f. [Cf. J. M. Kister's article "Ghālib b. Ṣa'ṣa'a", *Enc. of Islam*, 2nd ed.]

In a saying ascribed to ʿAlī,[1] the *taʿāqur* is compared to sacrifices made to idols and participation in the eating of such animals is forbidden.

(2)

Another remarkable way of showing tribal attachment was the custom that the ancient Arabs during their battles called out the name of the eponymous hero of their tribe in the manner of a watchword, or in order to ask for help in the heat of battle or in a 61
great danger.[2] The call was: *yāla Rabīʿa, yāla Khuzayma*, etc., 'O tribe of the Rabīʿa, Khuzayma', etc.[3] This documented the unity of the fighters in war and the battle cry, *shiʿār* (recognition) *daʿwa* or *duʿā*[4] (appeal and summons, the latter especially when serving as a call for help), was intrinsically also a symbol of the glorious memories and proud traditions of the tribe, which were to be re-called in moments when individual courage needed strengthening. It was considered of great importance to tribal life. It was every Arab's pride to gain honour for such a call when it was given as a battle cry and to do it justice when it was uttered as a cry for help.[5] No higher tribute could be paid to a tribe than to say that all its men were present when the battle cry was sounded.[6] Therefore the Arab of antiquity could swear by this battle cry as on a sacred concept[7] when roused by tribal pride.

Ḥātim says: 'I testify by our war cry, "Umayma!", that we are children of war; if its fires are kindled we maintain it.'[8] In order to

[1] In the collection of traditions by Abū Dāwūd [*Aḍāḥī*, no. 14] (quoted by al-Damīrī, II, p. 262) the introduction is traced back to the Prophet.

[2] As a call for help they also used the name of the tribal hero who then hurried to the place where he was needed, e.g. ʿAnt., *Muʿall.*, v. 66 (73), the *Dīwān* of same, 25: 1-6; *Ḥam.*, p. 333, v. 5. It is said ʿ*amma al-duʿāʾa*, somebody made general use of the call, i.e. he called on the collective name of the tribe in contradistinction to *khallala al-duʿāʾa*, i.e. he used a special call, the name of a certain hero (see passages in *Lbl. für or. Phil.*, 1886, p. 27). To follow such a call was a matter of honour for an Arab knight even if he were an enemy of the caller (*Agh.*, XVI, p. 55, 4 ff.). If it were a case of blood feud the name of him who was avenged was called: *Hudhayl.*, 35:3.

[3] For these forms cf. Fleischer, *Beiträge zur arabischen Sprachkunde*, VI, pp. 64 ff. (*Berichte der K. sächs. Ges. der Wissenschaften*, phil.-hist Classe 1876), now: *Kleinere Schriften*, I, pp. 390-5.

[4] The calling of the parole is also designated by *waṣala*, I, VIII: Dozy, *Suppl.*, II, 811a, 812b.

[5] ʿAmr b. Maʿdīkarib had a guilty conscience when he heard that Ḥājiz, whom he had wounded, called out *yāla'l-Azd*: *Agh.*, XII, 51, 9.

[6] Even in later poetry, al-Mutanabbī, ed. Dieterici, I. p. 78, v. 35.

[7] See now Robertson Smith, p. 258. *Hudhayl.*, 136:2 also seems to point to the sacredness of the tribal call.

[8] *Dīwān Ḥātim*, ed. Hassoun, p. 28, 4; the second word there must be corrected to *wa-daʿwānā*. Instead of *ishtadda nūruhā* we find in Ibn al-Sikkīt, p. 44, where this verse is cited: *shubba nūruhā*.

indicate a man's tribe, in the old language, one could use the cir-
62 cumlocution: he calls (in battle) this or that name,[1] or one said *istash'ara*, i.e. 'he uses this or that *shi'ār* (parole).'[2] In order to insult Ḥārith b. Warqā and his tribe the poet used the expression, 'Know that the worst of all men are the members of your tribe whose *shi'ār* sounds: *Yasār*.'[3] In the interests of Islam such manifestations of tribal consciousness had to be banned, since they were eloquent witnesses to the tribal segregation which Islam intended to overcome. Islam was compelled to fight the use of the *shi'ār* with even more determination since—as we have seen—it contained some religious elements. Thus it is said of Muhammed—and possibly justly—that he forbade the calls of the Jāhiliyya.[4] Everything that recalled tribal feuds and rivalry, or which might lead to a revival of tribal quarrels, had to be abolished. Thus the historians of the earliest wars of Islam against the pagans tell of a significant change in the battle cry of the Muslims in their wars against their pagan brothers. Now it was no longer the members of different tribes who had to be distinguished, but the faithful from the infidel. Also the former were not supposed to find much to boast about in their memories of their pagan past. At Badr the Muslims cried: *aḥad aḥad*, 'the only one';[5] at Uḥud their word was *amit, amit* 'kill'[6]; at the battle of Mecca and in some other battles their various detachments shouted calls which had a monotheistic sound: *yā banī 'Abd al-Raḥmān, yā banī 'Abd Allāh, yā banī 'Ubayd Allāh*;[7] and in the war against the false prophet Musaylima their battle cry was 'O owner of the Sūra *al-baqara*,'[8] etc. (cf. Judges 7 : 18, 20). The caliph 'Umar[9] is supposed to have given to Abū Mūsa al-Ash'arī the following order: 'If there are feuds between the tribes and if they
63 use the call: "O tribe of N.N." this is the inspiration of Satan. You must kill them with the sword until they turn to God's cause and call upon Allāh and the Imām. I have heard that the members of the tribe

[1] *Hudhayl.*, 202: 1, *da'ā Liḥyāna*, cf. ibid., no. 236; 'Antara, 19:6-7; *Ḥam.*, 80, v. 2 *da'aw li-Nizārin wantamaynā li-Ṭayyi'in*.

[2] Al-Nābigha, 2:15-16 *mustash'irīna*.

[3] Zuhayr, 8:1.

[4] The chief passages are B. *Manāqib*, no. 11, *Tafsīr*, no. 307, to Sūra, 63:6, where the Prophet is made to condemn even the cry *yā la'l-Anṣār* and *yā la'l-Muhājirīn* (not even specific tribal calls), adding *da'ūhā fa-innahā muntina* i.e. 'desist from such calls because they stink.' [Cf. below, p. 73, note 2.]

[5] Ibn Hishām, p. 450. [For the battle-cry *ḥā-mīm* see A. Jones in *Studia Islamica*, 1962, pp. 5 ff.; Abu'l-Shaykh, *Akhlāq al-Nabī*, Cairo 1959, p. 165; *Mishkāt al-Maṣābīḥ*, p. 343.]

[6] Ibid., p. 562.

[7] Ibid., p. 181, Wāqidī, ed. Wellhausen, p. 54.

[8] Al-Balādhurī, p. 89. [The *shi'ār* of 'Alī was allegedly KHY'Ṣ (Sūra 19:1), Ibn Abi'l-Ḥadīd's commentary on the *Nahj al-Balāgha*, V, p. 176.]

[9] Cf. for the battle cries of 'Umar also *Agh.*, IV, p. 55, 2.

of Ḍabba continue to use the cry *yāla Ḍabba*. By Allāh, I have never heard that God brought good through Ḍabba or prevented evil.'[1] But it was Abū Mūsā al-Ash'arī, against whom the shepherds of the Banū 'Āmir, whom he wanted to force into obedience to authority,[2] used the call *yāla 'Āmir*; and immediately al-Nābigha al-Ja'dī, a member of their tribe, famed as poet, came with a band of 'Āmirites, to protect the shepherds from the lawful authorities.[3]

In later times we find arbitrarily chosen *shi'ārs*, partly unintelligible in their references; for example, the parole of an 'Alid leader in 169: 'Who has seen the red camel (*man ra'al-'l-jamal al-aḥmar?*).'[4] It is interesting that we still find this *shi'ār* in modern times as battle cry of the Bedouins.[5]

(3)

In Arab antiquity the exclusiveness of the tribal system was mitigated by the institution of *ḥilf* or *taḥāluf* (confederation).[6] For the purpose of such federation sub-tribes sometimes became detached from the groups to which they belonged by virtue of their genealogical tradition in order to enter a new group by solemn pact.[7] It was possible also for an individual to become the confederate (*ḥalīf*)[8] of a foreign tribe. These confederate groups, however, again 64
made for new segregation, in that they erected a barrier between confederates and all those tribes or tribal groups who had not entered into the pact.

The *taḥāluf* may be considered the original type of Arab tribe formation, inasmuch as a large number of the later tribal names really only served as a collective designation for more or less disparate elements brought together by common interest or casual meeting in the same area. Later the fiction of genealogical unity took the place

[1] Al-Jāḥiẓ, *Kitāb al-Bayān*, fol. 125a [II, p. 293; the correct reading seems to be: 'this is the call of Satan'].

[2] It is well known that the subjugation of the Bedouins under the laws of the state was always the most difficult part of the state administration in the East in old as in modern times. The Khath'am Bedouins were so hostile to the payment of state tax that they made the year when an energetic tax collector (the son of the poet 'Umar b. Abī Rabī'a, end of 1st cent.) from Mecca was in office amongst them the beginning of a new era: *Agh.*, I, p. 34, 1.

[3] *Agh.*, IV, p. 139.

[4] Al-Ya'qūbī, II, p. 488.

[5] 'Cavalier de la jument rouge' in *Récit du séjour de Fatallah Sayeghir chez les Arabes errants du grand desert* etc., Lamartine's *Voyage en Orient* (Paris 1841, Gosselin) II, p. 490. [Cf. E. Bräunlich, in *Islamica*, 1934, pp. 218 ff.]

[6] In South Arab circles *takallu'*; Ibn Durayd, p. 307, cf. *Jazīrat al-'Arab*, p. 100, 9. [For *ḥilf*, and more especially the ceremonies connected with it, cf. also J. Pedersen, *Der Eid bei den Semiten*, Strasbourg 1914, pp. 21 ff; Bräunlich, loc. cit., p. 194.]

[7] Cf. *Ḥam.*, p. 288, v. 5.

[8] Such a one is also called *mawla'l-yamīn*, a relation by oath: *Ḥam.*, p. 187 ult.

of local unity and many of the later 'tribes' thus came into being not by common descent but by common settlement.[1] This process has also been described in other circles in just the same manner as by the Arab genealogists.[2] In historical times too the *ḥilf* pact sometimes resulted in two originally strange tribes being united by a common dwelling place[3] and coming into the closest connection with one another. It was, of course, always the weaker partner who in such cases had to sacrifice some of its local independence and sometimes it was completely absorbed by the more efficient companion, so that, denying its independent tribal consciousness, it professed itself part of the stronger member of the confederation.[4]

Such confederations, if we judge correctly the Arab character, were not made from a feeling of mutual intimate relationship, but were the results of common defensive and offensive interest and sometimes of a common duty of blood revenge; but the most usual reason for such attachments was that a weaker tribe sought protection from a
65 stronger one,[5] that a numerically small group, when persecuted and unable to defend itself from a mightier adversary, joined a strange lineage,[6] or that many weaker groups felt the urge to band together to a new, more imposing, unity. According to information from al-Bukhārī,[7] there existed *ḥilf* associations in which several lineages banded together in order to lay another under an interdict and to stop intermarriage and trade with it until it had fulfilled some condition.

The *ḥilf* group became even more complicated when one confederated group joined in an oath with another such group in order to form an extended *ḥilf* for defence and offence. We know of combined alliances of this kind which survived paganism and

[1] Yāqūt, II, p. 60 on Jurash is instructive. Other points concerning the rise of tribal units are elucidated by Nöldeke, *ZDMG*, XL, pp. 157ff. [Cf. W. Caskel, *Die Bedeutung der Beduinen in der Geschichte der Araber*, 1952; J. Henninger, 'La société bedouine ancienne', p. 80 (in *L'antica società beduina*, ed. F. Gabrieli.]

[2] Cf. Kuenen, *De Godsdienst van Israel*, I, p. 113.

[3] *Agh.*, XII, p. 123 below, 124 above: *wa-kānū nuzūlan fī ḥulafā'ihim.*

[4] *Agh.*, VIII, p. 196, 15. Other examples of this—though from Muslim times —are plentiful in *Jazīrat al-'Arab*, pp. 93, 22; 94, 25; 95, 17; 97, 17. Cf. 109, 17 *yatahamdanūna*, 92, 22 *yatamadhḥajūna*, 112, 16 *yatabakkalūna*, etc. or generally *yamāniyya tanazzarat*, 118, 7. Cf. *Agh.*, XV, p. 78, 10 *tamaḍḍara*, Yāqūt II, p. 632, 12.

[5] As when e.g. the insignificant kinship of the Ka'b joined by *ḥilf* the Banū Māzin: Ibn Durayd, p. 124. The united Khuzā'a joined the Banū Mudlij in order to survive: *Hudh.*, 224; the small Banū 'Āmir joined the more numerous Iyādites: *Agh.*, XXI, p. 271, 4, etc. ['No group ever sought an alliance but for its weakness or small number', al-Balādhurī, *Ansāb al-Ashrāf*, IV/B, p. 8, ed. Schloessinger.]

[6] *Agh.*, II, p. 178, 7 below.

[7] *Ḥajj*, no. 45.

existed as late as the time of the caliph Yazīd I;[1] in general the tradition of the old confederacies continued to live in the midst of the Arabs far on into Islamic times. Al-Farazdaq appeals to the *ḥilf* which the tribes Tamīm and Kalb had entered into in pagan days.[2]

The formation of such confederations was a regular phenomenon in Arab society. Tribes which, presumably in the consciousness of their own strength, did not wish to confederate with others and remained on their own, are exceptional and can be counted on the fingers of one hand.[3] Only the inclination, prevalent amongst the Arab people, to preserve tribal individuality as far as possible[4] could keep these tribes from this process, so usual in Arab tribal life. In any case, it was a matter of pride for the tribe that they were in no need of alliances but could rely on their own swords.[5]

The conclusion of the *ḥilf* which sometimes altered the natural tribal relationships, or extended the duties which were connected
with the natural tribal community to groups which had originally 66
been strange to one another,[6] took place in very solemn manner. Solemn oaths, accompanied by traditional ceremonies, were designed to help, through the memory of the forms and circumstances of the alliance, in keeping the obligations contracted by it from being broken. The recorded ceremonies on such an occasion are reminiscent in general of the usual forms which are observed when making oaths and which have been related also in regard to other semi-primitive peoples.[7] 'Dark red flowing blood' and other—usually pleasantly scented—liquids played a major role, and Robertson Smith has diligently collected the material referring to this;[8] fire strewn with salt was used just as in the great oath of *al-hūla*.[9] It seems, however, that such solemn, and sometimes gruesome, ceremonies were only employed when the alliance was of a permanent character. The most enduring ones can be recognized from a special collective name which

[1] Ṭab., II, p. 448.

[2] *Agh.*, XIX, p. 25.

[3] See the Arab dictionaries, s.v. *jmr*; *al-Iqd*, II, p. 69 [Ibn Ḥabīb, *al-Muḥabbar*, p. 234].

[4] This tendency is reflected in the legend of a tribal group which called itself al-Qāra (tribal branch of the Banū Khuzaym). In very remote times these people were to have been absorbed by the Kināna group, but they strongly objected: al-Maydānī, II, p. 39 below; Ibn Durayd, p. 110, 16 [al-Balādhurī, *Ansāb al-Ashrāf*, ed. Hamidullah, I, pp. 76-7, Ibn Ḥazm, *Jamharat Ansāb al-'Arab*, p. 179; Ibn 'Abd al-Barr, *al-Inbāh*, p. 75].

[5] Cf. al-Farazdaq, ed. Boucher, p. 46, 2.

[6] Such alliances also affected family law, e.g. in respect of the law of inheritance: Ibn Hishām, p. 934 above; cf. Robertson Smith, p. 47.

[7] Plutarch, *Publicola*, ch. 4.

[8] *Kinship and Marriage*, pp. 46 ff., 261.

[9] See my additions to R. Smith's material in *Literaturbl. für orient. Philologie*, 1886, p. 24. [Cf. also Pedersen, *Der Eid bei den Semiten*, pp. 151–2.]

the associated groups carried from then on, names which sometimes pushed the individual names of the members of the confederation into the background. The oldest example of such enduring brotherhood is perhaps the association of a large number of Arab tribes which met during their wanderings in Baḥrayn and formed a defensive and offensive confederacy under the name of Tanūkh.[1] After discounting all the unhistorical data invented by philologists and antiquarians of the second century,[2] we can accept the fact of this brotherhood of tribes as the genuine historical kernel of the traditions and fables connected with it. Another old confederacy of which, however, less is known either in fiction or fact is that of the Farasān, a name adopted by a brotherhood made up of several tribes.[3]

It was not always tribes of different descent who allied themselves by confederation. The various clans of large tribes often had such
67 different interests that their relationship was easily undermined and sometimes we find them involved in decade-long bloody feuds. Therefore confederacies could spring up between the lineages of a great tribe who were brought together by common interests. Thus several clans of the Banū Tamīm united under the name of *al-libad*, i.e. 'those who keep together',[4] and another association called itself *al-barājim*, i.e. 'finger joints'.[5] The names of the associations were often taken from the ceremonies observed during the conclusion of the pact, as in the case of 'blood lickers',[6] 'perfumed ones'[7], 'burnt ones',[8] *ribāb* (who dipped their hands in *rubb*).[9] The name *al-ajrabāni* ('the two with scabies') is interesting. It was given to two united tribes because it was said of them that they would damage anyone resisting them, much as a man with scabies infects all with whom he comes into contact.[10]

However, there were also *hilf* associations of a less permanent nature undertaken for a particular purpose and not marked by a name, nor, we may assume, by solemn ceremonies at the conclusion of the association. Such an alliance in all probability was the one between the Asad and Ghaṭafān which is mentioned in a saying

[1] *'Ala'l-tawāzur wa'l tanāṣur*, Ṭab., I, p. 746.

[2] Nöldeke, *Gesch. der Araber und Perser*, p. 23, note 2; Sprenger, *Alte Geographie Arabiens*, p. 208.

[3] Ibn Durayd, p. 8. [For some of the confederations enumerated here cf. C. von Arendonk's article 'Ḥilf' in the *Enc. of Islam.*]

[4] Ibid., p. 23.

[5] Imrq., 57:1, Ibn Durayd, p. 134, cf. *Agh.*, I, p. 84, two sorts of *barājim*.

[6] Also an individual is called *lā'iq al-dam*, *Agh.* XVIII, p. 156, 7.

[7] See Robertson Smith, l., c., Ṭab., I, p. 1138.

[8] *Lbl f. or. Phil.*, l. c., p. 25, al-Jawharī, s.v.*mḥsh.*

[9] Cf. however *al-'Iqd*, II, p. 59. Just as many tribal names originally without genealogical significance were made by later fictions into the name of ancestors, so we also find Banū Ribāb, *Agh.*, IX, p. 14, 20.

[10] *Agh.*, IV, p. 155, 6 from below.

ascribed to Muhammed,[1] or the one between the tribe of 'Abs—who at the time of the hero 'Antara were abandoned by their nearest kin, the Banū Dhubyān—and the Tamīmite Banū Sa'd; the latter pact, however, broke down quickly because of the greed of the Banū Sa'd.[2] The different groupings which resulted from temporary *ḥilf* relations seem to have been decisive for the politics and diplomacy of the desert, and it was presumably common for tribes to negotiate for the denunciation of old alliances—for which the formula of *khal'* 68
was invented[3]—in order to enter new *ḥilf* combinations.[4] This, according to Arab ideas, was only possible in cases where the undertaking had not been entered into as a permanent one and where no solemn oaths had been sworn. Such pacts were viewed less strictly and this fact motivated the need for the terrible customs at the conclusion of permanent alliances. Old Arabic poetry is full of examples of reproaches against tribes whose members had broken their oath, or had been negligent in performing the duties to which it bound them,[5] or had failed to provide the protection they owed by the bonds of nature or of alliance.[6] On the other hand virtuous tribes and people are often praised for keeping to their oaths of fidelity and alliance and to the duties which these imposed,[7] and in the frequent self-praise of Arabic poets and heroes this point of *muruwwa*[8] is ever-recurring. This would not have been mentioned as so praiseworthy if infringements had not been frequent.[9] The social views of the Arabs were too much based on the fact of true kinship for a symbolical relationship, based on alliance between groups not closely connected by genealogy, to be really considered of equal importance with blood ties.

> Be brothers with whom you like at peace-time but you must know
> That in war all are alien to you except your kin.

[1] Muslim, V, p. 213 *al-ḥalīfayn Asad wa-Ghaṭafān*; in the parallel passage in al-Bukhārī, *Manāqib*, no. 7, this designation is missing in all versions.

[2] 'Antara, no. 25, ed. Ahlwardt, p. 216.

[3] Al-Jawharī s.v. *khl'*.

[4] Introduction to al-Nābigha, no. 26 (p. 212).

[5] One of many examples is *Mufaḍḍ.*, 13:26.

[6] A similar reproach is made to allies in a South Arabic inscription, *ZDMG*, XXIX, p. 609.

[7] E.g. al-Ḥādira, ed. Engelmann, p. 7, 5 ff.

[8] *Agh.*, XIX, p. 93, 4 from below, 50,vv. 4-5; *Mufaḍḍ.*, 7: 9-11.

[9] Generally it must be said that faithfulness to alliances, though praised as the most prominent Arab virtue, remained an ideal which many Arabs contravened. It is, however, an exaggeration to look at the affair as Kay does in his article 'History of the Banu Okeyl' (*Journ. Roy. As. Soc.*, New Series, XVIII, p. 496).

It is your relative who helps you willingly if you call on him while blood is shed.
Do not therefore cast out your relations even if they have done you injustice,
Because even if they spoil things they also make them whole again.[1]

69 The social formations within Arab tribal life represented by the *taḥāluf* must have been as repulsive to representatives of Muhammed's ideas as was the particularism of the tribes, since it facilitated feuds between tribes and had to be superseded by the brotherhood of all men in Islam. Apart from this general ideal brotherhood, the particular brotherhood of various tribes was to have no place. Thus arose the principle ascribed to Muhammed: *lā ḥilfa fi'l-islām*, i.e. that there could be no confederations in Islam.[2]

This principle was also made to serve another end. All obligations of faith based on relations which existed during the Jāhiliyya were made null and void by Muhammed. Many a deed against fellow tribesmen and allies was committed by the oldest followers of Muhammed on the order or with the tacit agreement of the Prophet. This was accounted perfidy by the Arabs but was sanctioned by Islam.[3] There is, however, another version of the cited traditional saying in reply to a question that Qays b. 'Āṣim put to the Prophet about the *ḥilf* relationship. 'There is no *ḥilf* in Islam,' the Prophet is reported to have said, 'but respect the alliances of the Jāhiliyya.'[4]

IV

A document which deserves the notice of cultural historians gives the clearest exposition of the Muslim teaching of the equality of all men. We must point out again that it is regrettable that data on the
70 oldest teaching of the Muslim church, not to say of the Prophet himself, must be gathered from collections in which Islam has put together the words and deeds of its founder. This reservation also applies to those

[1] *Ḥam.*, p. 367.

[2] B. *Kafāla*, no. 2, *Adab*, no. 66.

[3] Interesting in this connection is the poem of Abū 'Afak in Ibn Hishām, p. 995.

[4] *Agh.*, XII, p. 157: *lā ḥilfa fi'l-islām wa-lākin tamassakū bi-ḥilf al-jāhiliyya.* [See also al-Ṭabarī's commentary on Koran IV, 37 and Wensinck, *Handbook of Early Muhammedan Tradition*, s.v. 'League'.] That Islam rejected the *ḥilf* while the *jiwār* is recommended as a connection sacred also in Islam is an additional proof of the fact that *jār* and *ḥalīf* are not completely synonymous as Robertson-Smith assumes, p. 45. That the two concepts must be differentiated is evident also from *Agh.*, II, p. 79 ult. Only where exact definition of the relationship does not matter and it is only desired to indicate that a person lives under the protection of a tribe, can *jār* occasionally be interchanged with *ḥalīf*, e.g. *Agh.*, ibid., 167, 1 (*jār*) line 14 (*ḥalīf*).

collections which in the opinion of Islamic scholarship are the result of the most scrupulous criticism. That part of our 'studies' which is concerned with the literature of tradition in Islam and its history will show the reader how unsafe it would be to derive the teachings and acts of Muhammed from that which the old Muslim authorities transmit as such. Nevertheless these traditions are of great value for the knowledge of the development of the teaching of Islam, for which they are considered the most important sources by those who profess that faith. For us they are primarily documents which show how the oldest teachers of Islam set out to teach in the spirit of the founder.

There are many documents from this circle which comprehend and elaborate the idea mentioned in the Koranic passage 49:13, with all its implications; and it will be our task to fit them into the chronological framework in which they belong. Here we just wish to indicate them generally and quote the most important. None is more important or more diligently spread by those whose argument it serves than the speech which the Prophet is said to have made in Mecca on the occasion of his farewell pilgrimage (*ḥajjat al-wadāʿ*). The Prophet is said to have taken advantage of this solemn moment[1] to bring home to his faithful those teachings of Islam which he valued most and more especially those which were suited to demonstrate the changed social circumstances of Arab society. This speech might almost be called the Islamic Sermon on the Mount. It would be difficult to define which parts of this religious testament of the Prophet can be considered as authentic.[2] On the whole it is the work of later days; around an authentic kernel (because Muhammed did after all presumably preach something to his disciples on that solemn occasion) there grew various gradual additions, and the whole was then edited as the farewell speech. We shall see that even after the conclusion of the usual text tendentious additions have been superimposed.

It is of great critical importance that al-Bukhārī[3] reproduces, after various informants, several smaller pieces[4] which later, when 71
the composition of a long farewell speech by the Prophet was undertaken, could easily be put to good use. But not all the parts of the version of the speech that we have before us can be found in such fragments, and the passage with which we are concerned

[1] Some accounts do not give this specific point of time.

[2] Cf. Snouck Hurgronje, *Het Mekkaansche Feest* (Leiden 1880), p. 145 [*Verspreide Geschriften*, I, 96].

[3] B. *Maghāzī*, no. 79, cf. *Ḥajj*, no. 132, *Adab*, no. 42.

[4] The passage where, in accordance with Koranic ideas, fear of God is postulated as the sole title to nobility, is often found as an independent tradition (*ḥadīth al-taqwā*—as Muslims call it) apart from the context of the *wadāʿ* speech, e.g. *Anbiyā*, no. 9, cf. *al-Muwaṭṭa'*, II, p. 319, as a saying by 'Umar: *karam al-mu'mini taqwāhu wa-dīnuhu ḥasabuhu*.

here is not to be found amongst these old elements. It is true that it is mentioned as an independent speech by Muhammed, having no connection with his other commandments, in the collections of traditions by Abū Dāwūd and al-Tirmidhī; but in the versions transmitted by these collectors the chief point of the doctrine is the rejection of boasting about ancestors who were not in the possession of the true belief, rather than the negation of racial differences. It is impossible to decide whether this trend of the instruction in question is the original one; but it must be remarked that its full force is only brought out by an addition which is not included in the usual versions of the speech. It can, however, be stated that Muslim theologians preferred that development of the tradition of the *taqwā* which condemned boasting of the fame of ancestors insofar as it was the cause of competition between the descendants of different ancestors. The Shī'ite tradition produces this speech as the testament (*waṣiyya*) of the Prophet to 'Alī.[1]

On the other hand people continued to attribute to Muhammed, on the occasion of his farewell pilgrimage, other statements which are not included in the texts used here.[2] At any rate this old piece of Muslim teaching on belief and morals, which was well established as early as the second century A.H. as the pilgrimage speech of the Prophet, does contain the expression of what the teachers of Islam
72 thought it right to spread in the name of the founder as being in accordance with his intentions. All the different versions of this old document of Islamic views, in spite of small deviations of the text, agree in essence that Muhammed recommended to his faithful with great emphasis, as a cardinal virtue of Islam, the renunciation of all conflict based on genealogy, 'O congregation of the Qurayshite,' the Prophet announces, 'Allāh has taken from you the boasting of the Jāhiliyya and its pride of ancestors. All men descend from Adam and Adam was made of dust. O men, we have created you from man and woman,' etc. (the above-mentioned passage in the Koran).[3] 'The Arab has no advantage over a non-Arab except through the fear of God,' was an addition to the original version.[4]

[1] Al-Ṭabarsī, *Makārim al-Akhlāq* (Cairo 1303), p. 190.

[2] Such a passage is found, e.g., in al-Baghawī, *Maṣābīḥ al-Sunna*, I, p. 7, transmitted by 'Amr b. al-Aḥwaṣ: 'Verily nobody repents but for himself and not a father for his child or a child for his father. Verily Satan has lost hope that he will ever be adored in your cities, but he will be obeyed in those of your provinces which you count for little and he will rest content with that.' Others have incorporated into the pilgrimage speech the interdiction of the *mut'a* marriages: al-Zurqānī to *Muwaṭṭa'*, III, p. 29, below.

[3] Ibn Hishām, p. 821, Wāqidī (Wellhausen), p. 338.

[4] The speech is cited with this addition by the Shu'ūbites in Ibn 'Abd Rabbihi, II, p. 85. Also al-Jāḥiẓ, *Bayān*, fol. 115a [II, p. 33] knows the addition which we find also in al-Ya'qūbī, II, p. 123 who starts this passage of the speech with the words: 'Men are equal like the surface of a full bucket.'

For the sake of completeness we must also mention the additions to which we have alluded above and which are added to the instruction of Muhammed in the versions of Abū Dāwūd and al-Tirmidhī. After condemning the boasting of the Jāhiliyya and emphasizing the common descent of men from Adam, who himself was created from dust, and the fact that all glory can only be derived from *taqwā* (trust in God), we find there: 'Let men cease boasting of people who are but coals of Hell's fire. Verily, they are accounted for less by God than dung-beetles which stink in men's noses.'[1]

In this way the old Islamic teaching of equality among Muslims and the unimportance of racial and tribal differences, which—as we saw—was based on a doctrine expressed also in the Koran, was further developed over the centuries and was transformed by the continued work of the traditionists into a basic teaching of Islam. Stories were invented in order to show that taunting a man with his descent was contemptible. Thus 'Amr b. al-'Āṣ—who can hardly appear as a stalwart Muslim in our eyes, accustomed to a historical point of view—is said to have replied to the scornful speech of Mughīra b. Shu'ba by ridiculing his tribe. Thereupon 'Amr is correc- 73
ted by his son 'Abd Allāh who, in shocked astonishment, reproaches him with the Prophet's words. 'Amr repents and as sign of his remorse and repentance frees thirty of his slaves.[2] People never tired of quoting sayings of the Prophet which develop this idea in various ways, either in the form of spontaneous instruction or as a commentary on various events. For example, the canonical collections of traditions[3] contain the following story by some of Muhammed's contemporaries:

'We passed Abū Dharr in al-Rabadha (near Medina) and saw that he was enveloped in a top gown while his servant had a very similar coat. We told him that if he united both garments he would have a top and under-garment for himself. Thereupon Abū Dharr said: "Once upon a time I had an exchange of words with one of my brothers in faith, whose mother was a foreigner. I ridiculed him because of his maternal descent. But he complained of me to the Prophet, who rebuked me with the words: 'You, Abū Dharr, are still haunted by the Jāhiliyya.' When I sought to defend myself with the excuse that if someone were insulted he had the right to gain satisfaction by insulting the parents of the aggressor, the Prophet repeated: 'You still have the Jāhiliyya inside you; verily it is your brothers who made you subject to God. So feed them with what you eat and clothe

[1] The different versions of this saying are found in al-Damīrī, I, p. 245.

[2] Al-Dhahabī in Abu'l-Maḥāsin, *Annales*, I, p. 73. [In fact what 'Amr did and for which he was blamed was to use the tribal call (*da'wat al-qabā'il*); thus what the passage illustrates is the prohibition discussed above, p. 64.]

[3] Muslim, *Īmān*, no. 7 (IV, p. 113), almost literally the same B. *Adab*, no. 43.

them with what you wear, do not burden them with what they cannot bear, and if you do burden them, help them yourselves.' " ' In another tradition we find: 'He who boasts the boasts of the Jāhiliyya, him you may bite with the shame of his fathers.'[1] 'The freed man is made of the remnant of the same clay as the man who freed him.'[2]

These facts show how the equalitarian teaching of Islam extends a step further than the original teaching of the equality and fraternity of all Arabs, by teaching the equality of all men who confess Islam. The first step in this process was Muhammed's own presentiment of the
74 universality of Islam[3] as also his recognition of the difference of men's language and colour, which he considers as sign of divine power.[4] The further development of these rudiments and unconscious stirrings, was a natural consequence of the great conquests which brought a large part of the non-Arabic Orient into the orbit of Islam. If Islam aimed at consistency it then had to extend its teachings, which it had applied in the first instance only to Arabs, to all those other races which now formed part of the Muslim community. Undoubtedly the new teaching was, apart from pietist circles among the Arabs, chiefly furthered by foreigners, Persians, Turks, etc., for whom their position within the community built on Arab foundations was a vital question. They had a particular interest in establishing the new teaching because the esteem which they might expect from their Arab co-religionists entirely depended on its recognition. They presumably originated all those traditions which are intent on re-enforcing the teaching of the equality of all believers irrespective of race; 'Do not insult a Persian, because nobody insults a Persian without God taking revenge upon him in this world and the next.'[5] Such traditions were not invented only for the sake of the gifted white races; the children of the dark continent,[6] too, were to be protected from slight and contempt, particularly as Islam had cause to be grateful to the black Ethiopians for the protection which their king had given to the first followers of the

[1] MS. no. 597 of the Leiden Univers., fol. 134 [omitted in Cheikho's occasionally expurgated edition of the *Tahdhīb al-Alfāẓ*. Cf. also *Mishkāt al-Maṣābīḥ*, p. 418; *Kanz al-'Ummāl*, I, pp. 230, 362. For traditions against boasting with genealogy cf. al-Suyūṭī, *al-Durr al-Manthūr*, VI, pp. 98–9.]

[2] Al-Mubarrad, p. 712. Before that there are many sayings of the Prophet about the equality of the *mawālī*.

[3] Cf. for this Snouck Hurgronje, *de Islam*, l.c. p. 46 [*Verspreide Geschriften*, I, p. 225].

[4] Sūra 30:21.

[5] Al-Tha'ālibī, *Der vertraute Gefährte des Einsamen*, ed. Flügel no. 313. [This text is in fact part of Rāghib al-Iṣfahānī's *Muḥāḍarat al-Udabā'*, ed. Cairo 1287, I, p. 219.]

[6] On the judgment about the indigenous population of Egypt see Yāqūt, I, p. 306, 4.

Prophet. Probably some such feeling was partly responsible for the invention of the kind of legend of which we shall now give some examples.

Once—so it is related—an Ethiopian entered the Prophet's room and said: 'You Arabs excel us in all matters, you are of finer build, more pleasing colour, and God has honoured you by rousing the Prophet amongst you. What do you think: if I believe in you and your mission, will I find a place in paradise with the believing Arabs?' 'Yes, certainly,' replied the Prophet, 'this will be so and the black skin of the Ethiopian will spread a brilliance on the road of a thousand years.'

Similarly, another tradition says that there always live seven pious 75
men on earth for whose sake God maintains the world; if they did not exist the earth would break down and everything living on it would be annihilated. Abū Hurayra relates that the Prophet once addressed him thus: 'Look, by this door enters a man, one of the seven pious ones to whom the world owes its continuance.' And in came an Ethiopian.[1]

When inquiring into the times at which these sayings of Islamic tradition originated, we come to the conclusion that those which preach the equality of the non-Arabic races converted to Islam belong to a later period than those merely aiming at the abolition of tribal differences among the Arab people. This sequence corresponds with the gradual advance of the spread of Islam. But the need for more and more of these traditions[2] points to the fact that the mere Koranic teaching and the teaching of the old traditions in this respect were insufficient to oust inherited national vanity from the Arab soul. Arabs of noble blood did not easily accept the idea that their noble descent did not entitle them to preference over others whom the common bond of transcendental ideas was to make their equals.

The relationship of Arab consciousness with Islam is forcibly expressed by the declaration of a knight of the tribe of Ṭayyi' Zarr b. Sadūs. This hero accompanied Zayd al-Khayl when the latter offered the homage of his tribe and its subjection to the laws of Islam. But Zarr was not inclined to sacrifice Arab pride to Islam like his companion. 'I see here a man who wishes to gain ascendancy over all people, but nobody shall rule over me but myself.' He preferred to go to Syria and to join the Christian empire.[3]

[1] MS of the Leipzig University, D.C. no. 357. [No. 873 in the catalogue by K. Vollers. The passage is presumably from the last piece of the MS., about the number seven by al-Suyūṭī, Brockelmann, II, p. 154, no. 219 and Supplement.]

[2] Similar also is the principle which 'Umar laid down to an Arab: 'When non-Arabs (*al-a'ājim*) practise religion, but we (the Arabs) are unable to do so, they are closer to Muhammed than we on the day of judgment. He who falls behind in the practise of religion cannot be ennobled by his geneology'; al-Māwardī, ed. Enger, p. 346.

[3] Ibn Hishām, p. 112, *Agh.*, XVI, p. 49.

The example of the Ghassānid prince Jabala VI b. al-Ayham is particularly instructive for an appreciation of this way of thinking.
76 This prince, who on the occasion of a *ḥajj* sought to assert his privileges over a common Arab, is said to have been told by 'Umar: 'Verily you are both united in Islam and you have no preference before this man, other than the greater fear of God.' 'I thought,' said Jabala, 'that I would increase my status by accepting Islam,' and when 'Umar rejected this point of view he returned to Christianity and went to the court of the Emperor of Byzantium where he was greatly honoured. Whatever historians may be obliged to detract from the credibility of the details of the story[1]—a credibility further undermined by the fact that it is told in the language of the theologians[2]—it does nevertheless mirror faithfully the thoughts of Arab aristocrats about the Islamic teaching of equality. It is likely that any true Arab, in whom paganism died hard, thought and felt in the early times of Islam much as Jabala, who was close to Christianity, is represented here as saying and doing.

The same contrast between Arabism and Islamic teaching also appears in the continued validity of concepts based on the old tribal system. We have already seen that the mocking of enemy tribes did not disappear from poetry even under Islam,[3] and the many traditions in which theologians condemn *mufākhara* and *munāfara* and many anecdotes which aim at ridiculing Arab boasting (p. 62) show that it was still thought necessary to fight against the survival of pagan Arab views.

The separate consciousness of the tribes remained so vital in the social and political concepts of Muslim society that in the earliest
77 period of Islam the various tribes had to be grouped separately in war too,[4] and in towns which grew up as a result of official colonization, for example Baṣra and Kūfa, the tribes had to be settled in separate quarters.[5] The heads of the various tribal quarters together

[1] Nöldeke undertook the historical evaluation of this tale, *Die ghassānischen Fürsten*, p. 46.

[2] *Agh.*, XIV, p. 4. The tale is frequently told by the Muslims, cf. e.g. *al-'Iqd*, I, pp. 140-43 where it is evident that it ultimately goes back to a *mawlā* of the Banū Hāshim; this fact is relevant to its point of view. In Ibn Qutayba (see Reiske, *Primae lineae historiae regnorum arabicorum*, p. 88) the event is differently related: it does not take place in Mecca but in Damascus, and the judge is not 'Umar but Abū 'Ubayda, the prefect of Damascus. [The text is found on p. 316 in Wüstenfeld's edition.]

[3] In the *Dīwān* of Abū Nuwās (died *c.* 190) the first chapter of book VI contains 'Ridicule of the tribes, the nomad and settled Arabs.'

[4] Ṭab., II, p. 53. Or perhaps this special arrangement was aimed at making possible the proportional payment of the warriors.

[5] Kremer, *Culturgeschichte des Orients*, II, pp. 209 f., Yāqūt, III, p. 495, 19, cf. al-Wāḥidī on al-Mutanabbī (I, p. 147) 57:33. [See also L. Massignon, 'Explication du plan de Kufa', *Mélanges Maspero*, III, Cairo 1940, pp. 341 ff.; Ch.

formed the municipal authority.[1] Only when individual tribes were represented by only a few people was it possible—and even then only after strong resistance—to accommodate the members of various tribes together.[2] Even for the purpose of religious worship —eminently suited to destroy or at least smoothe out tribal particularism—this segregation was maintained, and we learn of special mosques for different tribes in the conquered provinces.[3]

The same issues appear in the more intimate relationships of social and spiritual life. When two men from different tribes have a private quarrel we may be certain that the discussion of the case does not pass without reciprocal mockery about the tribes to which they belong. A member of the Qurayshite Umayyad family wanted to claim the poet al-Farazdaq's bride al-Nawār, though the poet thought he could prove that he had a clear claim because he had paid the bride price. 'Abd Allāh b. al-Zubayr sided against al-Farazdaq and he did not hesitate to reproach him with descent from the Tamīm, whom he called the *jāliyat al-'Arab*, i.e. the banned tribe, in memory of the fact that 150 years before Islam they had robbed the Ka'ba and had therefore been ejected by all other Arabs. This caused the poet to answer the Qurayshite with a panegyric of the Tamīm tribe, in which 78
they appear as the glory of all Arabs.[4] Even at the beginning of the 'Abbāsid period the judge 'Ubayd Allāh b. al-Ḥasan was able to reject a witness from the tribe of Nahshal because the witness did not know a poem praising his tribe: if he were a good man he would know the words which extolled the nobility of his tribe.[5] In the fourth century the poet al-Mutanabbī thinks it necessary to keep his true descent secret because—as he tells his friend—he is in

[1] Ṭab., II, p. 131 *ru'ūs al-arbā'* in Kūfa, *ru'ūs al-akhmās* in Baṣra.

[2] Yāqūt, II, p. 746, s.v. Rāyat.

[3] E.g. the mosque of the Banū Kulayb in Kūfa; al-Mubarrad, p. 561, 13, of the Banū Qarn in the same town, Ibn Durayd, p. 287, 6, of the Banū Bārik (probably of the whole Khuzā'a tribe) also in Kūfa, *Agh.*, VIII, p. 31, 21, of the Anṣār in Baṣra, *Fragmenta hist. arab.*, p. 56, 3 from below and 57, 13. Later conditions are presumably anticipated when a Masjid Banū Zurayq is mentioned in Muhammed's time, B. *Jihād*, nos. 55-57.

[4] *Agh.*, VIII, p. 189. In the Umayyad period the indigenous Syrians called the immigrant Ḥijāzīs *jāliyat al-'Arab*, ibid., p. 138, cf. *Agh.*, XIV, p. 129, *Ḥam.*, p. 798, v. 1.

[5] Al Mubarrad, p. 255, 19. A similar anecdote is related in respect of other persons, *Agh.*, XI, p. 135.

Pellat, *Le milien basrien et la formation de Gāḥiẓ*, pp. 22 ff.] This way of segregating the tribes was carried by the Arabs into the furthest provinces. When the second ruler of the Idrīsid dynasty built Fez at the end of the second century he designated special quarters for the individual Arab and Berber tribes: *Annales regum Mauritaniae*, ed. Tornberg, I, pp. 24-25.

close contact with Arab tribes and is afraid that one or other of these may be hostile to the tribe from which he is descended.[1]

Strangely enough, to the many features which were taken over from the pagan epoch and which continued to manifest themselves in Islam, there was added in the Islamic period a new circumstance calculated to jeopardize the carrying out of the Muslim teaching on the abolition of tribal differences in Islam. The emergence of this new factor in the best period of Islam resulted in tribal feuds which far excelled the small tribal conflicts of pagan times which after all were never more than petty quarrels. The new element in tribal hostility that we must here consider is alive and effective in all fields of Muslim society at all times and to this day: I refer to the rivalry between the northern and southern Arabs.

The hostility of these two factions is so self-evident and well known that the poet al-Mutanabbī[2] was able in a malicious poem that mocked the defeat of the rebel Shabīb, who had revolted against the Ikhshīdite Kāfūr, to use the witty turn of phrase: 'as if men's necks said to the sword of Shabīb: your companion is a Qaysī (northern Arab) but you are a Yemenite' (he was defeated and threw away his sword). The point of the sentence is that 'the Yemenite' (*yamānin*) is a well known epithet of the sword. The Qaysī is unable to remain
79 together with the Yemenite.[3] In the fourth century al-Hamdānī relates that at Ṣan'ā' the Nizārite families who lived there had joined forces with lineages descended from Persian ancestors (*al-abnā'*) and completely segregated themselves from families descended from south Arab tribes.[4] The Muslim pilgrim 'Abd al-Ghanī al-Nābulusī, who travelled in 1101 A.H., says of al-Ṣāliḥiyya, a place by the Syrio-Egyptian border, that when he went there the town had two separate quarters, Qaysite (north Arab) and Yemenite (south Arab), and that there were perpetual feuds between the two.[5] The same picture is found shortly after the Arab occupation of Andalusia, where these tribal groups had to be settled in different parts of the country[6] in an attempt to prevent civil wars, which occurred nonetheless.

Muṣṭafā b. Kamāl al-Dīn al-Ṣiddīqī[7] writes in the year 1137 A.H.:

[1] In Rosen *Notices sommaires des Mss. arabes du Musée asiatique*, I, p. 226, [from the colophon of a MS. of the *Dīwān*. Cf. also Goldziher, 'Verheimlichung des Namens', *Der Islam*, 1928, pp. 1–3.]

[2] Ed. Dieterici, p. 672 (254:6).

[3] On the interpretation of the verse see Ibn al-Athīr, *al-Mathal al-Sā'ir*, p. 392.

[4] *Jazīrat al-'Arab*, p. 124, 20.

[5] *Kitāb al-Ḥaqīqa wa'l-Majāz* (MS. Leipzig Univer. Library D.C. no 362), fol. 152b.

[6] Dozy, *Recherches sur l'histoire et la littérature d'Espagne* (3rd ed.), pp. vii, 10, 79.

[7] MS of the Oriental Institute at St Petersburg (Rosen's Catalogue no. 27), fol. 85a.

'The fanatical hatred between the Qaysite and Yemenite factions continues to this day amongst some ignorant Arabs, and even now wars between them have not ceased, though it is well known that such actions belong to those of the Jāhiliyya and are forbidden by the Prophet.' And even in quite modern times the quarrel between Qaysites and Yemenites survived in various parts of the Islamic world. Robinson relates: 'Throughout the provinces of Jerusalem and Hebron, the inhabitants of the different villages are broken up into two great parties, one called Keis (Keisîyeh), and the other Yemen (Yemenîyeh). ... No person of whom we inquired, could tell the origin or the nature of this distinction; except that it goes back beyond the memory of man, and does not now pertain in any degree to religious worship or doctrine. It seems indeed to consist in little more than the fact that one is the enemy of the other. In former times blood was often shed in their quarrels; but now all are quiet. Yet this inbred enmity shows itself in mutual distrust and calumny.'[1]
Without forcing the analogy, this description reminds us of Caesar's 80
account of the social structure of Gaul, with its dichotomy between Aedui and Sequani. *Eadem ratio est in summa totius Galliae: namque omnes civitates in partes divisae sunt duas.*[2] The Englishman Finn, who during his consular activities in Jerusalem, which lasted for eighteen years, gained much valuable experience of the land and people of Palestine, reported that there were also outward distinguishing characteristics between the two factions. Qaysites wore dark red turbans with yellow stripes and their opponents preferred lighter colours. This colour preference extended to animals. Qaysites considered dark-coloured horses stronger than light ones and also believed that dark cocks always outdid lighter ones. The remark by Finn that two tribal parties also differed in their pronunciation of Arabic is interesting. Qaysites pronounced the sound with which their party name begins like a hard *g*. The much feared clan of the Abū Gōsh belonged to the Yemenite group.[3]

But the relationship between the two groups in modern times is but a pale shadow of what it used to be in the early days of Islam. This spirit is expressed in the feeling of solidarity which the members of the groups show for one another and in the many tokens of enmity which are shown in the intercourse between the parties. It was no exception to the general rule when the Yemenites of Emesa in the middle of the first century had such strong racial

[1] [*Biblical Researches in Palestine*; London 1841, II, pp. 344-5. Goldziher quotes the German edition]: *Palaestina und die südlich angrenzenden Länder*, II, p. 601.

[2] *De bello gallico*, VI, 11.

[3] *Stirring times or record from Jerusalem Consular chronicles* (London 1878), pp. 226-9.

sentiments that they supported the poet al-Aʿshā, from the tribe of Hamdān, as one of their own people who came to Syria, and, on the initiative of the Anṣārī al-Nuʿmān b. Bashīr,[1] made a collection among their compatriots. More remarkable than such manifestations of solidarity are the marks of hostility against people of the rival group. Whatever society itself lacked in hatred, especially at the beginning of this enmity between northern and southern Arabs, was soon made up by poets, who were the prophets of tribal hatred. In Khurāsān at the time of the governorship of al-Muhallab and his son Yazīd the Rabīʿa Arabs formed an alliance with
81 the Yemenites. This did not strike anybody as odd except the fanatical poet Kaʿb al-Ashqarī, an Azdite who demanded in the most virulent tone the segregation of Rabīʿa from the Yemenites.[2] The poet Bakr b. al-Naṭṭāḥ (died 200) says at the end of the second century in his dirge for Mālik b. ʿAlī,[3] who was killed in the war against the Shurāt: 'They (the murderers) took from Maʿdd what they had (in pride) and have implanted racial arrogance into the hearts of all Yemenites (because of the death of their northern Arab rival).'[4] This implied that there is joy when the rival race loses a good man.

Social life, politics and literature mirror with equal vividness the hostility of the two large sections of the Arab nation. Even within tribes belonging to the same group it happened that one tribe considered another unequal and scornfully rejected intermarriage.[5] The Qurayshites in particular cherished such feeling of exclusiveness towards other tribes that it was a special claim to glory if a tribe could boast that they were not barred from intermarriage with the Qurayshites.[6] It was necessary for the family of the Banu'l-Azraq, who had settled at Mecca, to invent the fable of a written privilege by the Prophet to justify their intermarriage with the Qurayshites.[7] Other tribes were ruled by similar considerations. When al-Farazdaq heard that a man of the Ḥabiṭāt was wooing a Dārim

[1] *Agh.*, V, p. 155; XIV, p. 121.

[2] *Agh.*, XIII, p. 60 above.

[3] He belonged to the Khuzāʿa, a tribe about whom there was some doubt whether they belonged to the northern or southern group. [Cf. *Enc. of Islam*, s.v.; Ibn ʿAbd al-Barr, *al-Inbāh*, p. 92.]

[4] *Agh.*, XVII, p. 158, 3 from below.

[5] On inferior marriages in paganism, see *Hudhayl.*, 147. Because of the old Arab views on exogamy the accusation that the father of ʿUrwa b. al-Ward married a stranger (*gharība*) (*Dīwān*, ed. Nöldeke, 9: 9) can refer only to the inequality of the Banū Nahd into whose family he married (cf. 16 and 19). For later times see *Ḥam.*, p. 666, v. 2., Jarīr in Ibn Hishām, p. 62, 11, Notes to Ibn Durayd, p. 196.

[6] *Agh.*, XXI, p. 263, 4.

[7] Al-Azraqī, p. 460, above. The special arrogance of the Qurayshites is characterised by the saying that a *daʿī* of the tribe of Quraysh is nobler than a true noble from any other tribe: *Agh.*, XVIII, p. 198, 3 below.

girl (he himself belonged to this tribe) he rejected this as an imposition:

The tribe of the Misma' are equal to the Banū Dārim—
the Ḥabiṭāt might find a wife amongst their own equivalents.[1]

And in this case two families of the Banū Tamīm were concerned. 82
Even in quite recent times it is reported that the inhabitants of Yanbu' (semi-Bedouins from the Juhayna tribe) only very rarely condescend to marry women from Mecca 'and it inevitably follows that, despite the high rank which Meccans occupy by their birth amongst all other Arabs, children of such marriages are nevertheless considered somewhat inferior.'[2] Even more generally the tension between northern and southern Arabs could make marriage between the groups appear as unusual at least.[3] The poetical literature of the first two centuries reflects this social atmosphere very faithfully. Voices like that of Nahār b. Tawsi'a (died 85) were rare:

My ancestor is Islam, I have no other—
let others boast with Qays and Tamīm.[4]

Just as the poets of old were the heralds of their tribe's fame and the interpreters of the tribe's proud sentiments in the face of other tribes, their art now announced the fame of their tribal grouping and mocked the rival race.[5] If a poet now sought to deride another he was not content, for example, 'with mocking the Azd tribe but accuses all the Yemenites,' and in the process we find accusations like that of the Māzinite Ḥājib b. Dhubyān in his *hijā'* against the Azdite Thābit Quṭna (end of the first century):

The Zinj are better when they name their ancestors
Than the sons of Qaḥṭān, the cowards and uncircumcised.[6]

[1] Al-Mubarrad, p. 39=*Dīwān*, ed. Boucher, p. 46, 4 from below.

[2] Maltzan, *Meine Wallfahrt nach Mekka*, I, p. 129. In the fact mentioned above the circumstance that the Juhayna considered themselves as Southern Arabs presumably played no part. Cf. also Burton, *A Pilgrimage to Mecca and Medina*, Leipzig 1874, II, p. 256, below.

[3] *Agh.*, VII, p. 18, 18.

[4] Al-Mubarrad, p. 538, 15. [See also Ibn Qutayba, *Shi'r*, p. 342, who quotes two additional lines: 'He who has a suspect genealogy helps those by whom he wants to be accepted, which should attach him to one with a pure genealogy. Nobility does not consist in having illustrious ancestors: the pious man is in truth the noble.' The first line is discussed in al-Zamakhsharī's *al-Mufaṣṣal*, §101. Cf. also C.A. Nallino, *Raccolta di scritti*, I, p. 141.]

[5] The northern Arabs thought they were abler in poetry than the southerners: this judgment is also applied to the southerner Imrq., cf. *Agh.*, VII, p. 130.

[6] Cf. p. 88, note 5. To this day the northern tribes accuse Qaḥṭān of lies: Doughty, *Travels in Arabia deserta*, II, p. 41.

These are men whom you see when the fighting is high,
Worse in treading the path of dastardly behaviour
than a shoe.
Their women are common to all lecherous men,[1]
Their protegees are a prey to all who ride or go on foot.[2]

83 The poet al-Kumayt (died 126) gave the most vivid expression to this national poetic competition, and he himself was only one of the many representatives of northern Arab anger against the southern Arabs. In his time the 'poets of the Muḍar' were involved in poetic quarrels with a poetic advocate of the southern Arabs, Ḥākim b. 'Abbās al-Kalbī.[3] But the southerners were hardest hit by the 'golden poem' (*al-mudhahhaba*) of Kumayt, a work of 300 lines,[4] the gist of which is contained in the following line: *wajadtu'l-nāsa ghayra'bnay Nizārin/ wa-lam adhmumhumu sharaṭan wa-dūnā* ('I have found men with the exception of the two sons of Nizār (Muḍar and Rabī'a, the ancestors of the Northern Arabs)—I do not wish to slight them—low and common.')[5]

The southern Arabs had also their poetic defenders. In the year 205—the poem itself gives an exact date in verse 4—'Amr b. Za'bal had to repel a 'famous *qaṣīda*' which the Baṣran poet Ibn Abī 'Uyayna had published to ridicule the Nizārites and to glorify the Qaḥṭānites.[6] How long the Kumayt's satire was effective amongst his adversaries is seen from the fact that a century after him the southern Arabs found a defender in 'Irāq in the bold satirist Di'bil (died 246) of the tribe of Khuzā'a.[7] This poet set himself the task of moderating the arrogance of the northerners by recording the glorious historical position of the south Arab people, and of strengthening the self-confidence of the Yemenites by describing their historical traditions—the invention of which had reached its height in those days.[8] This effort so stung the northern Arabs that the contemporary prefect of Baṣra commissioned the poet Abu'l-Dalfā' to counter the poem of Di'bil with a north Arab satire which he then circulated under the name of 'The Shatterer'.[9] A spirit which is so far removed from

[1] For this phrase see *Ḥam.*, p. 638, v. 5.
[2] *Agh.*, III, p. 51.
[3] *Agh.*, XV, p. 116, 9 from below.
[4] Al-Mas'ūdī, VI, pp. 42 ff.
[5] Ibn al-Sikkīt, *Kitāb al-Alfāẓ* (Leiden MS. Warner no. 597), p. 162 [ed. Cheikho, p. 195]; *Kitāb al-Aḍdāḍ*, ed. Houtsma, p. 16, 11 A. To judge from the metre and the rhyming letters, *al-'Iqd*, III, p. 301, is also a fragment of this poem.
[6] *Agh.*, XVIII, p. 19. How much this poet was concerned with racialism is also seen in p. 22, 3; 27, 19.
[7] *Agh.*, XVIII, pp. 29 ff.
[8] Al-Mas'ūdī, I, p. 352; III p. 224.
[9] *Agh.*, ib., p. 60.

Islam as that of Abū Nuwās will not be missing amongst those practising this poetry of old tribal rivalry; he took the part of the southern Arabs.[1]

Thus we see that at the time when the Caliphate was already 84
becoming an instrument in the hands of foreign praetorians the rivalry between northern and southern Arab tribes was still very real to Arab society and was still of topical importance. As late as the fourth century there are echoes of this racial poetry in the work of a poet from Antioch, resident at Baṣra, Abu'l-Qāsim 'Alī al-Tanūkhī, who in panegyric on his tribe produced the hyperbole:

Quḍā'a is the son of Mālik, the son of Ḥimyar—
there is nothing higher for those wishing to ascend to a high grade.[2]

The framework of prophetic and tendentious traditions was misused for racial rivalry, much as for any other party interests in Islam. Scholars of both parties set their pens to paper in order to cover the aspirations of their group with the hallowed authority of sayings by Muhammed. It almost seems that the southern Arabs were more diligent in this respect, since the greater part of these tendentious traditions is in the service of their ambitions.[3] We shall later see that sayings aiming at the glorification of the Anṣār also belong to this series. Many sayings show the Yemenites as representatives of the spirit and religion in Islam, in contrast to Rabī'a and Muḍar, who are described as brutal, harsh and unfeeling.[4] The Ḥimyar are even called *ra's al-'Arab* 'the head of the Arabs', and to the other southern Arab tribes: Madhḥij, Hamdān, Ghassān, etc., an honourable position in the body politic of Islam is also allotted: one becomes the head of this body, another its skull, shoulder-blade or hump.

There are fewer traditions favouring the northern Arab tribes in
general,[5] except for the glorification of the Qurayshites, or rather of 85

[1] Al-Ḥuṣrī, II, p. 277.

[2] Al-Mas'ūdī, VIII, p. 307.

[3] There is a collection of them in the introduction of the commentary by 'Adī b. Yazīd on the *Qaṣīda Ḥulwāniyya*, a fragment of which (beginning: *Fa-in i'tarada mu'tariḍ*) is found in Cod. Petermann, Berlin, no. 184, fols. 13b-15. [There is another MS. of the commentary by 'Ghāzī'—sic—b. Yazīd on Muḥammad b. Sa'īd al-Kātib's 'Ḥulwānian Qaṣīda, being the self-exaltation of the Qaḥṭānīs over the 'Adnānīs and the demonstration of the excellence of the Yemenites over the Nizārīs' in Cairo, Cat.[2], III, 210; V. 44, cf. Brockelmann, Supplement, II, p. 903.] A further collection taken from al-Suyūṭī's *al-Jāmi' al-Kabīr* is in Muṣṭafā b. Kamāl al-Dīn al-Ṣiddīqi's book, fols. 60b-63a, 71a-77a, 81b-85a.

[4] The most important passage of the series is B. *Maghāzī*, no. 76, *Bad' al-Khalq*, no. 14.

[5] E.g. al-Ya'qūbī, I, p. 259: 'do not scorn Muḍar and Rabī'a, because they

some of their families (in the dynastic interests). Some of these tendentious traditions have found their way into the canonical collections.[1] It is remarkable that the traditions of the two sides are almost identical and that the Qurayshites are praised by one group in almost the same words which the other use in respect of the Anṣār. It would serve no useful purpose to quote examples here. It might just be mentioned that the sentence,[2] undoubtedly taken from the Gospel, in which the Anṣār in relation to other men are likened to salt[3] can also be found as praise of the Qurayshites.[4]

Even more harmless are the anecdotes found from time to time in *adab* literature[5] which clearly show tendencies in favour of one or the other Arab groups. There is, for example, the anecdote about the wooing of the two rivals Yazīd b. ʿAbd al-Madān and ʿĀmir b. al-Ṭufayl, on which occasion Yazīd is said to have spread before his rival the whole of the southern glories;[6] or the story ascribed to the caliph al-Manṣūr about an incident in ʿUrwaʿs biography where a man who in the same business shows his wit and also his mental limitations attributes his perverse character to the fact that his cleverness comes
86 from his father's side, the Hudhayl, and his stupidity from his mother's, the Khuzāʿa.[7]

[1] Muslim, I, pp. 13 ff. on the excellence of the *ahl al-Yaman* in matters of the faith, further the chapters *Manāqib al-Anṣār* in the canonical collections. To this belongs also B. *Tawḥīd*, no. 23, where the disbelief of the Tamīmites is opposed to the zeal of the southern Arab tribes. [For traditions glorifying the southern Arabs, see e.g. Ibn Wahb, *Jāmiʿ*, p. 1; al-Yazīdī, *al-Amālī*, Hyderabad 1948, p. 102; al-Nabhānī, III, p. 506.]

[2] B. *Manāqib al-Anṣār*, no. 11.

[3] The interpretation of the parable, because there is very little salt in proportion to the food, is based on a misunderstanding. This misunderstanding already influenced the text of the tradition. The comparison 'like salt in food' is very popular in later literature, cf. Ibn Bassām in Dozy, *Loci de Abbadid.*, II, p. 224; ibid., 238 note 68.

[4] Al-Ṣiddīqī, fol. 67a, tradition of Ibn ʿAdī: 'The Qurayshites are the best of all men; men are useful only because of them, much as food becomes palatable only with salt.' Here the influence of the Gospel is unmistakable.

[5] E.g. *al-ʿIqd*, II. pp. 152 ff. This sort of anecdote is presumably the story quoted by Robertson Smith, p. 268, from al-Mubarrad, p. 191.

[6] *Agh.*, XVIII, p. 160.

[7] *Agh.*, II, p. 195.

---

were Muslims', or in another version, 'because they confessed the *dīn Ibrāhīm*.' Other traditions invented in regard to the northern tribes can be seen in book VII of Ṣiddīqī. How obvious are the party tendencies in these traditions appears from the following saying of the Prophet in al-Ṭabarānī: 'When differencies of opinions appear between men, right is on the side of Muḍar' (al-Ṣiddīqī, fol. 80a). [This tradition is recorded in Ibn Qutayba's *Kitāb al-ʿArab* (in *Rasāʾil al-Bulaghā'*), p. 375, in al-Kalāʿī's *al-Iktifā'*, ed. Massé, I, p. 67, and in al-Nabhānī's *al-Fatḥ al-Kabīr*, Cairo 1350, p. 69. For the idea that Muḍar was a Muslim cf. Ibn Saʿd, I, p. 30; al-Balādhurī, *Ansāb al-Ashrāf*, ed. Hamidullah, I, p. 31; al-Ḥalabī, *Sīra*, I, p. 20; al-Suyūṭī, *al-Jāmiʿ al-Ṣaghīr*, II, p. 199.]

Such anecdotes are tendentious inventions which the rival groups made up in order to deride each other. It is certainly interesting that between the northern and southern Arabs even psychological and ethical differences were supposed to exist. An 'Āmirite refused to believe that the lover Majnūn, who was said to have died of love-sickness and who was said to be an 'Āmirite, was a historical person. 'The 'Āmirites are men of stronger spirit (*aghlaẓu akbādan*) than this love-lorn hero. Such things are possible only amongst the Yemenites, who have weak hearts, dulled brains and bald heads; but this is unthinkable of the Nizār.'[1] To the account of the sudden death of the Hudhaylite poet Abū Khirāsh, who died in his over-zealous exertions for Yemenite guests as a result of a snake-bite, there are added reflections on the greed of Yemenites, so that 'Umar is made to say on this occasion: 'If it were not so shameful I would forbid hospitality to Yemenites altogether and send an edict to this effect to all provinces. Such a Yemenite is hospitably received and offered the best one has; nevertheless he remains still unsatisfied and rejects what is offered, demanding the impossible as if he were the host's creditor, and he scorns his host and makes all kind of trouble.'[2]

To this type of story also belong contrived competitions set in the court of one or another caliph. Al-Madā'inī, one of the most diligent investigators of Arabian antiquity (died 225), describes such a competition which is said to have taken place before the Caliph al-Manṣūr.[3] A disputation, which is also of philological importance and was first found by Bargés,[4] can be added to the stock of these literary products where fiction is less obvious than in the invented 87
stories previously quoted, because the scene is not put back into pre-Islamic times.

These, however, were bloodless fights. The rivalry of the two tribal groups manifested itself in more dangerous form than in poetic and belletristic quarrels, in the political life of Islam even in provinces far distant from the centre of government. For the appointments to the most important offices and the administration of the conquered provinces, the consideration of tribal differences between the north and south Arabs was very prominent, and from the middle of the first century the unsatisfied ambitions of the tribal groups

[1] *Agh.*, I, p. 167, 16. In poetry too the Yemenites are ascribed a particular gift for love-songs; the words are *ghazal yamānin wa-dall ḥijāzī*, ibid., p. 32, 12. The Prophet is supposed to have said: *ahl al-Yaman aḍ'afu qulūban wa-araqqu af'idatan*, *B. Maghāzī*, no. 76.

[2] *Agh.*, XXI, p. 70.

[3] Ibn al-Faqīh, ed. de Goeje, pp. 39-40; the previous discussion on Yemen seems to cover the main points that southerners used to quote in their favour. [The caliph is al-Saffāḥ. Cf. also al-Mas'ūdī, VI, pp. 136–7.]

[4] *Journal asiatique*, 1849, II, pp. 329 ff. [The story is in fact identical with the preceding one.]

which were for the time being in the shadow often became the cause of bloody civil wars. If the governorship of an outlying province, e.g. Khurāsān, was given to a southerner, the northerners complainingly asked 'whether the tribe of Nizār had become too small that such a post had to be given to a Yemenite,'[1] and vice versa.

I think that these circumstances are responsible for many *ḥadīths*, of which the following is an example: one of the Anṣār asked the Prophet whether he would not use him in the administration as he used the other (who was not of the Anṣār). Thereupon the Prophet replied: 'After my departure you will experience preferences (of your rivals) but wait patiently until you encounter me by the cistern (*al-ḥawḍ*).' Or another such story: The Prophet wanted to allot the province of al-Baḥrayn to the Anṣār but they refused this fief unless the Prophet made a similar gift to their brothers the Muhājirīn (Meccan Qurayshites). So the Prophet said: 'You do not want it? Then endure patiently until you meet me at the cistern (*al-ḥawḍ*) because verily you will witness also after my death preferential treatment (of your rivals).'[2]

Here belong also stories in which it is thought right that the Anṣār should have been given material advantage in the early period of Islam, because they had protected Muhammed, whereas the Qurayshites had made war upon him.[3] The circumstances to which the tradition owes its existence are even more obvious in sayings like this: 'My companions, who belong to me as I belong to them and with whom I shall enter paradise, are the people of Yemen who have been driven to the edge of the provinces and cast from the gates of the
88 government; one of them dies and his need is (sealed up) in his heart, he cannot satisfy it.'[4] In order to express the continued aspirations of the Yemenites, the victory hoped for by their party is put into the distant future, and a promise is attributed to the Prophet that these hopes will be fulfilled in the person of the Qaḥṭānī, who will appear in the future.[5]

It is impossible to consider such sayings and reports other than in the context of the racial rivalry of the first two centuries of Islam, which we have just described. The whole history of the Umayyad period in east and west is governed by this rivalry, and even after the fall of the Umayyads such rulers as wished to make use of the motto

[1] Ṭab., II, p. 489.

[2] B. *Manāqib al-Anṣār*, no. 8. [Cf. also other references in M. J. Kister's discussion of the *ḥadīth* in *Journal of Economic and Social History of the Orient*, III, pp. 332-3.]

[3] E.g. the story quoted by al-Māwardī, ed. Enger, p. 223; cf. ibid., 347, 4. [The motivation is discussed below, p. 93.]

[4] Al-Ṣiddīqī, fol. 84a.

[5] Snouck Hurgronje, *Der Mahdī*, p. 12 [= *Verspreide Geschriften*, I, p. 156; see also Muṭahhar b. Ṭāhir al-Maqdisī, *al-Bad' wa'l-Ta'rīkh*, II, pp. 183 f.]

ʿDivide et impera' had an effective tool in this tribal competition when they wanted to balance one group of restless subjects against another. The cunning adviser of the ʿAbbāsid Abū Jaʿfar al-Manṣūr deliberately provoked a disastrous fight between the two parties, and when the caliph asked his reasons Qutham b. al-ʿAbbās propounded the following political concept: 'I have roused dissension among your troops and divided them into parties, each of which will take good care not to revolt against you for fear that you might overcome them with the help of their rivals . . . Therefore separate them from each other and if the Muḍar rise in insubordination you may beat them with the Yemenites and those of Rabīʿa and the Khurāsānians; and if the Yemenites rebel you can suppress them with the Muḍarites, who remain faithful.' The ruler followed the policy of his adviser and—as our source adds—owed the stability of his empire to this course.[1] We find in fact that even under Hārūn al-Rashīd the policy was followed of rendering harmless the northern and southern Arab tribes in outlying provinces by playing them off against each other[2] and this racial rivalry, which had fateful consequences in social life also,[3] continued even later,[4] until the foreign soldiery put a stop to the political aspirations of the Arabs once and for all.

It is not the intention of this study to go into more detail about the 89
history of these struggles, which have only been hinted at above in order to show the lack of success of the Muslim teaching of equality among the Arabs. It is still Dozy's masterly description (in Vol. I of his *History of the Moors in Spain*) which gives readers the best introduction to the development of these struggles and their effects on the shaping of Muslim political life.[5]

V

There is, however, one feature of this phenomenon in the history of Islam which we shall have to consider at some length: the origin of the antagonism described above between those Arab tribes which belong to the northern half of the peninsula by descent and those which settled there but derive their descent from southern Arabia, whence their ancestors had migrated in ancient times.

Some scholars, clinging to the Arabic historical traditions, which

[1] Ṭab., III, pp. 365 f.

[2] Al-Yaʿqūbī, II, p. 494: *ḍaraba'l-qabā'ila baʿḍahā bi-baʿḍin.*

[3] The rift between ʿAdnānites and Qaḥṭānites was so great that the most commonplace incident was enough to cause civil war with all the horrors of street fighting: Abu'l-Maḥāsin, I, p. 463.

[4] Al-Yaʿqūbī, pp. 515, 518, 567 etc.: cf. the description of the movement under the ʿAbbāsids in Müller, *Der Islam in Morgen u. Abendland*, I, pp. 490 f.

[5] [Cf. for the preceding also A. Fischer's article 'Ḳaḥṭān' in the *Enc. of Islam.*]

put the struggles between Maʿadd and Yemen in the early time of the Jāhiliyya,[1] have continued until recent times to follow the view that the rivalry between north and south Arabic tribes goes back to Arab antiquity or at least to the epoch immediately preceding Islam. Dozy has even developed an attractive ethno-psychological scheme to explain this racial antagonism.[2] In effect it must be admitted that the consciousness of a difference between northern and southern Arabs existed also in old times and this explains—bearing in mind the character of the Arabs—why members of one group like to ascribe bad qualities to those of the other group whenever there is a hostile incident, much as members of the same race did in quarrels amongst their own tribes. Just as the Kindite Imru'u'l-Q̧ays prides himself on his Yemenite descent—provided, of course, that the poem is
90 authentic[3]—so does al-Nābigha in angry mood revile the perfidy of Yemenites.[4] A Hudhaylite poet in the period before Muhammed gives vent to utterances against the Ḥimyar, with whom intermarriage is not considered suitable and of whom strange customs are mentioned which seem to be ignoble in the eyes of the northern Arabs.[5] However, we shall soon see that such points of view apply only between those north and south Arabs where habitat does in fact provide this difference.[6] It must on the other hand not be overlooked that though the genealogical term Maʿadd is not yet quite as strongly contrasted with the southern Arabs as it is later,[7] but defines a much wider concept,[8] nevertheless when poets of early times wish to express the concept of 'Arab' fully, they, like Nonnosus who is often quoted in this con-

[1] Ibn Badrūn, p. 104; Yāqūt, II, p. 434.

[2] *Gesch. d. Mauren in Spanien*, I, pp. 73 ff. [in the French original: I, pp. 113 ff.]

[3] *Innā maʿsharun yamānūna*, 61: 2.

[4] Al-Nābigha, 30: 9 *lā amānata li'l-yamānī*, cf. 31: 3 where the southerner is opposed to the Sha'āmi geographically only; cf. B. *Manāqib al-Anṣār*, 21 (Yemenite Kaʿba against Kaʿba *shāmiyya*) and passages like Yāqūt, III, p. 597, 11.

[5] *Hudh.*, 57; 80:6 The accusation made in 57:2a is also used by al-Farazdaq, who is probably following an old tradition, against the tribe al-Azd, ed. Boucher, pp. 31, 2; 86, 6.

[6] This is true especially of the poem *Ḥam.*, p. 609, in which the Tamīmite poet expresses his disgust of the Yemenite land and its inhabitants; it would be highly relevant to our subject if the time of its writing could be determined with certainty.

[7] Abū Nukhayla, *Agh.*, XVIII, p. 141, 13, calls the caliph Hishām: *rabbu Maʿaddin wa-siwā Maʿaddin*; Abū Nuwās (in Rosen, *Chrestomathie*, p. 526 ult.); Basshār b. Burd, *Agh.*, III, p. 38, 7.

[8] Nöldeke, *ZDMG*, XL, p. 179; Robertson Smith, p. 248. Already Rückert, *Amrilkais der Dichter und König*, p. 52, saw this fact. Caussin de Perceval, II, p. 247, who clings to Maʿadd as a specific north Arab patriarch, is compelled to bestow forced interpretations on a verse (al-Nābigha, 18:1-2, cf. ib. 6:18, 8:17 and many verses of the Kindite Imrq.), when the name Maʿadd is used of tribes which in later genealogies appear as south Arab. [Cf. also *Enc. of Islam*, s.v. 'Maʿadd'.]

nection, mention together with Ma'add tribal names like Ṭayyi' and Kinda, which are considered as southern Arabic.[1]

It is most vexatious to all those who have to make use of the tradition of old Arab poetry, that in deciding the question of the genuineness of the relevant passages—as distinct from data which are obviously of apocryphal character for internal reasons[2]—they often
have to rely on the subjective impression which the poems in question 91
make on the reader. Great suspicion must always be exercised; and if this is true of the traditional poems it applies even more to those stories which are told by philologists and antiquaries of the second and third century, who often projected later conditions into their description of pagan society. How far this went in respect of the point we are now considering is seen, for example, from the information of Abū 'Ubayda about the pagan hero Sulayk b. Sulaka, of whom he says that he never harrassed Muḍarite, but only Yemenite, tribes with his plundering attacks.[3]

Even if we assume that all traces from pre-Islamic times of conscious racial difference between north and south Arabs must be seen as genuine tradition, this is not evidence of the existence in those old times of the racial hatred which appears later between those who call themselves northern and those who call themselves southern Arabs. In antiquity there is no suggestion of the later generalization that all tribes of southern origin which had been established in the north since ancient times formed a unity against all the others, and there is in fact evidence that tribes whose southern character was later taught with axiomatic certainty did not hesitate to mingle with so-called northern ones.[4] The inner life of the tribes also shows that the racial contrast could have existed only between the northern and southern (Sabaean) groups in a geographical sense and did not extend to the relationship of those Arabs of whom it was later rightly or wrongly claimed that their ancestors had migrated from the south. The everyday feuds between tribes did not take into account any consideration of the north and south in alliances or wars. There are many examples of this, and we shall merely mention
one illustration. The clan of Jadīla of the Ṭayyi' tribe, which is known 92

[1] Imrq., 41:5, cf. Labīd, p. 80, v. 4.

[2] For example the verse cited by Abū 'Ubayda of the pre-Islamic Ḥājib b. Zurāra (*Agh.*, X, p. 20, 16) is impossible; it contains the expression: *wa-qad 'alima'l-ḥayyu'l-ma'addiyyu*—the Ma'addite tribe; this *nisba* assumes already the previous theoretical work of genealogists; old poets say: *qad 'alimat Ma'addun* or at the most, like 'Amr b. Kulthūm, *Mu'all.*, v. 94: *wa-qad 'alima'l-qabā'ilu min Ma'addin*. From the scholium to Ḥārith, *Mu'all.*, v. 94, it is evident that the originality of the word Ma'add in such verses cannot always be taken for granted.

[3] *Agh.*, XVIII, p. 134, 2.

[4] *Mufaḍḍ.*, 32:8 ff., this is the source of the passages which Robertson Smith, p. 247, quotes from geographers.

from later genealogies to comprise southern Arabs, was in a *ḥilf* relationship with the northern Arab Banū Shaybān and fought with them against the northern Banū 'Abs.[1] That during the struggle by the Ṭayyi'ites and their allies against the Banū Nizār the latter's descent is mentioned in a hostile manner[2] is not due to antagonism against northerners as such, but must be seen in the same light as any tribal feud in which enemies would be violent in abuse of the descent and nobleness of their opponents, whether northerners or southerners. It is also decisive that the earlier parts of Muhammed's speech of farewell would no doubt have said a word about the disappearance of this particular racial hatred in Islam if it had really existed.

Nöldeke has the credit for being the first to have expressed scepticism of the great antiquity of this generalization of the north-south Arab racial antagonism, and thus to have caused a correction of our views of the Arabs of ancient times. In discussing south Arab traditions he pointed to the causes of the genealogical exploitation of the racial differences by southern Arabs.[3] Halévy went even further and expressed the view, at the end of his work on the Ṣafā inscriptions, that the Arab tradition of the migration of southern Arab tribes into the northern region must be considered a fable; in his view a southern origin for those tribes which lived in the northern region is out of the question.[4]

Though the origin of this racial antagonism cannot then be put back quite so far as was previously believed, it must yet be admitted that the possibility of its development at a later date was inherent in the character of the pagan Arab. The instincts which prevailed among the Arabs with regard to tribal consciousness only needed some new impetus to be focused on to the field of north and south Arab *'aṣabiyya* and to develop further within it. This new trend of tribal rivalry
93 did not add anything to the character of the Arab people but was the natural consequence of its character under the influences of new moments in its history. The most immediate cause of this new opposition and of this new formulation of tribal pride was the rivalry between the Meccan aristocracy, who boasted of their Qurayshite descent and in whose views the religious aura of the Anṣār seems to have been of little value,[5] and the Medinian Anṣār, who were also

[1] 'Antara, 22.

[2] *Ḥam.*, p. 79.

[3] *Götting. gel. Anz.*, 1866, I, p. 774. This view is more profoundly substantiated in Nöldeke's review of Robertson Smith's work, to which we often refer in our study (*ZDMG* XL).

[4] *Journal asiatique*, 1882, p. 490 and *Compte rendu* of the Sixth Congress of Orientalists (Leiden 1884), p. 102.

[5] Otherwise the verse of al-Akhṭal, in Mu'āwiya's time, would be impossible: 'All nobility was taken by Quraysh—and there are low minds under the headgear of the Anṣār' [*Dīwān*, p. 314, l.4=] *al-'Iqd*, III, p. 140.

thought to be inferior by descent.[1] The manifestations of this rivalry are known from the early history of Islam. It is easily understood that the Anṣār were looking for titles which they could oppose to the Meccans' desire for hegemony, and it is not impossible that already amongst them there were in being the germs of that boasting about the southern past which was later so lavishly unfolded in literature, especially after party—and race—genealogists entered this field.

One may expect that this rivalry would express itself, particularly in its earliest days, in panegyrical and satirical poems by the poets of the respective parties. Unfortunately we have insufficient data to demonstrate positively to what extent this was so in the earlier years. The poems of the Anṣār were collected;[2] but such a collection, which would presumably offer some material on this question, does not seem to be extant.

Anṣār poetry is most amply preserved in the poems of Ḥassān b. Thābit. We cannot decide whether those poems by Ḥassān in which, in order to glorify the Anṣār, he points to the great historical past of south Arabia and the power and authority that its inhabitants displayed in the old days,[3] are genuine, or are later fictions which must be placed with those poetical products which were invented for the same purpose and which can be met with by the dozen in the commentary on the so-called Ḥimyarite *qaṣīda*,[4] and the like of which 94
philologists and genealogists delighted to produce.[5] It must in any case be granted that the pre-eminently Anṣār poet was considered a suitable singer of the praises of the south Arab past, a fact which can be taken as an additional proof that the glory of the south was a predominantly Anṣār interest. One may well see in this quarrel between the Anṣār and Qurayshites the source from which the rivalry between northern and southern Arabs gradually derived. In the course of time the expression *al-Anṣār* became almost a genealogical description[6] which was never the case with its original opposite:

[1] The Qurayshites consider the Medinians as *'iljs*: *Agh.*, XIII, p. 148, 8: XIV, p. 122, 11.

[2] *Agh.*, XX, p. 117, 13 mentions such a collection.

[3] Especially *Dīwān*, p. 77 [ed. Hirschfeld, no. 161]=Ibn Hishām, p. 930, 11 ff; p. 87 [Hirschf., no. 9]=Ibn Hishām, p. 931, 4 ff; 99, 14 [Hirschf., 78: 1] =Ibn Hishām, 6, 4 from below; also the *qaṣīda* beginning on p. 103 of the *Dīwān*, particularly 104, 14 ff. [Hirschf., 6: 18 ff.] aims at the glorification of the Anṣār by pointing out that they have inherited their laudable attributes from great ancestors.

[4] A few samples in Kremer's extracts: *Altarabische Gedichte über die Volkssage von Yemen* (Leipzig 1867).

[5] Abū 'Ubayda transmits a poem by a pre-Islamic poet which refers to southern Arabic poems: *Agh.*, X, p. 20, 10-11. The authenticity of the historical elegy Zuhayr no. 20 is very doubtful.

[6] Cf. *Agh.*, VII, p. 166, 14. The Anṣār also differ from the Qurayshites in outward appearance: XX, p. 102, 8.

al-Muhājirūn. Since, after Medina had been flooded by members of other tribes, they seem to have settled in special parts of Medina and its environs,[1] the maintenance of their unity was much facilitated. Ma'add and Muḍar—sometimes also Nizār[2]—are chiefly contrasted with the Anṣār,[3] just as in the *Mufākhara* against the Anṣārī 'Abd al-Raḥmān, son of Ḥassān b. Thābit, reference is made to the deeds of the Banū Tamīm.[4]

The competition of the tribes against the Anṣār is the point from which this contrast was later extended to those groups which—
95 presumably chiefly in order to join the Anṣār group—considered themselves to have originated in south Arabia. The north-south antagonism has its roots in the rivalry between Qurayshites and Anṣār. The consciousness and character of this origin remained alive for a considerable time after the beginning of racial conflict among the Arabs. In the first quarter of the third century the Bedouin poet Nāhid b. Thawma from the tribe of Kilāb b. Rabī'a frequented Baṣra; a *qaṣīda* of his has been handed down in which he defends the northern Arabs against a poetic representative of the southerners, and in conclusion refers to the fact that the Prophet and the oldest heroes of Islam were northern Arabs. This glorification of the northern tribes was, it is said, read in the presence of a descendant of the Anṣār who is reputed to have said: 'He (through his reference to the Prophet and his companions) has silenced us, may God silence him.'[5] So at the time of this competition or the time from which the account about it comes, the southern cause was still considered to be a special concern of the Anṣār. Moreover, the fact that when one spoke of the excellent qualities of the southern Arabs, one had, in the first instance, the Anṣār in mind, can be evidenced by many examples. The saying ascribed to Muhammed: 'The divine spirit comes to me from Yemen' was supposed to refer to the Anṣār.[6]

[1] *Al-Muwaṭṭa'*, I, p. 391 below: *qarya min qura'l-Anṣār*.

[2] Abu'l-Aswad, *ZDMG*, XVIII, p. 239 below.

[3] Muḍar opp. Anṣār, Ibn Hishām, 885, 8=*Dīwān Ḥassān*, p. 46, 15 [ed. Hirschfeld, 131: 11]. In the work of the same poet the opponents of the Anṣār are simply called Ma'add: *Dīw*., p. 9, 1 [Hirschf., 1: 17]=Ibn Hish., 829,4: 'We have daily quarrels, insults and mocking from the Ma'add'; similarly p. 91, 7 [Hirschf., 25: 2]: 'We have protected and harboured the Prophet whether the Ma'add liked it or not.' That Ma'add here already refers to a limited tribal group is seen from the fact that on p. 82, 10 [Hirschf., 49: 2] in a satire against the Banū Asad b. Khuzayma they are accused of wavering in the midst of the Ma'add and from the following verse it is evident that they wished to be counted among the Quraysh; also p. 83, 5 [Hirschf., 198: 3], the Thaqīf are admonished to cease counting themselves as Ma'add since they are not descended from Khindif. Ma'add opp. Ghassān, p. 86, 4 from below [Hirschf., 4: 25] cf. 99, 14 [Hirschf., 78: 1]=Ibn Hishām, p. 6, 4.

[4] *Agh*., XIII, p. 153, 5 from below.

[5] *Agh*., XII, p. 35, 6.

[6] Al-Ṣiddīqī, fol. 74a.

There is no doubt that this rivalry was based on religious arguments from the earliest stages of its development, and the historical points which both sides adduced in boastful self-glorification are later additions. We have just heard on what the northern Arabs prided themselves. The Anṣār side were not backward in rebutting this forceful argument. 'We have given birth to him (*waladnāhu*) and his grave is with us,' or even more definitely: 'We have given birth to a great one of Quraysh, we have brought forth the good prophet of the family of Hāshim,' argues Ḥassān,[1] probably referring to the 96
circumstances that through his grandmother Muhammed came from the Medinian family 'Adī b. al-Najjār (they were thus his *khāls*) and he lived among that family for some time when he was six years old.[2] The best argument which the Anṣār found to counter the incontrovertible argument about the Prophet's northern descent,[3] which the northerners used also in their own favour in the administration,[4] was to point out that 'the Prophet lived and preached some ten years amongst the Qurayshites, waiting in vain for a follower; that he offered himself to the visitors in the market of Mecca, but found none who would take him in,[5] and nobody who would make propaganda for him, until he finally found a community in Medina, that of the Anṣār, who made his cause so completely theirs that they treated their best friends as enemies if they were hostile to Muhammed.[6] For this reason opponents appear to have found repugnant even the name Anṣār, which expresses this claim to glory. 'Amr b. al-'Āṣ is made to say to Mu'āwiya: 'What is this name? call them instead by their genealogy,' meaning that they should not use this honorary name but name themselves according to their descent.[7] The Anṣār

[1] *Dīwān*, p. 24, 5 [from below, ed. Hirschfeld no. 13:15] 91, 12 [Hirschf. no. 25: 7]. This also appears in the alleged dialogue between Sayf b. Dhī Yazan and 'Abd al-Muṭṭalib, which is invented in favour of the southern Arabs, al-Azraqī, p. 101, 7: *wa-qad waladnāhu mirāran w'Allahu bā'ithuhu jihāran wa-jā'ilun lahu minnā anṣāran*; especially in view of the passage quoted from al-Azraqī. For the expression *waladnāhu* cf. *Agh.*, VI., p. 155, 4; but it might also be understood as 'we have protected him like our own child'; cf. 'Amr b. Kulth., *Mu'allaqa*, v. 92 and also Ḥārith, *Mu'all.*, v. 63; al-Fākihī, *Chroniken der Stadt Mekka*, II, p. 49, 13.

[2] Ibn Hishām, p. 107; cf. Yāqūt, I, p. 100, 21; Sprenger, I, p. 145.

[3] *Agh.*, III, p. 27, the boasts of a Yemenite are cut short by referring him to the call of the Muezzin which just began to be heard and which does not tell the praises of a southern Arab. This argument is also advanced in the story *Agh.*, IV, p. 43, 6 from below, cf. also Yāqūt III, p. 330, 6.

[4] Al-Māwardī, ed. Enger, p. 352, 3 from below.

[5] *Yu'wī*, cf. Sūra 8: 73.

[6] Al-Azraqī, p. 377, poem by the Anṣārite Ṣirma (according to others by Ḥassān, Ibn Qutayba, ed. Wüstenfeld, p. 75, 4). Cf. *al-'Iqd*, II, p. 143, the conversation of Mu'āwiya with an Anṣārite.

[7] *Agh.*, XIV, pp. 125, 127; this passage is important for the appreciation of the Anṣār.

also pointed to the many false prophets which the northern Arab tribes have produced, and stress again and again that followers rather than relatives of the Prophet deserve all glory.[1]

Islam, inasmuch as it was unable to abolish the old tribal competition, did in effect provide it with new material, as the merit of the various tribes in the Muslim cause, and their zeal in its support could
97 now be included in the arguments.[2] But people were not satisfied with the glory of piety, they wished also to be the most heroic of all Arab tribes.[3] If we consider the means which used to be employed in Muslim party strife, we shall not be surprised to see Anṣārī partisan tendencies manifest also in the interpretation of the Koran;[4] furthermore, there were no scruples about inventing false Koranic verses which served to extol the Anṣār as against the Qurayshites and even the emigrants.[5]

The early activity of genealogical scholars runs parallel with the beginnings of this rivalry between the Anṣār and the Qurayshites based on internal political feuds in the early days of the Caliphate. To them is largely due the extension to all the tribes deriving their origins from South Arabia of claims which the Anṣār originally made for themselves alone. This derivation itself, in the early period, was often based not so much on inherited genealogical traditions as on subjective inclinations, and even the will of influential people. Thus for instance Abū 'Ubayda reports that in the time of Yazīd I the affiliation of the tribe of Judhām was decided by such considerations.[6] This uncertainty and wantonness was countered by the disciplining effect of the work of the genealogists (based partly on truth and partly on fiction), but this too was the cause of differences of opinion and subject to personal inclinations and prejudices. Thus there grew up the fabulous tales of the southern Arab saga, in which such people as 'Ubayd b. Shariya in the time of Mu'āwiya I, and Yazīd b. Rabī'a ibn Mufarrigh (died 69) in the days of Mu'āwiya's successor, had a great share. Arab critics ascribe the invention of legends and poems of the Tubba' princes more especially to this latter poet, who derived his genealogy from Ḥimyar.[7]

[1] The best resumé of these arguments from a later period is at the end of the Ḥulwānī *qaṣīda*, MS. of the Royal Library in Berlin, Petermann no. 184, fols. 113-120.

[2] An example in Ibn Ḥajar, IV, p. 174.

[3] *Al-'Iqd*, I, p. 45.

[4] 9: 109 *muṭahharūna* is referred to the Anṣār. 44: 36 was used for the glorification of the southern Arabs (*qawmu Tubba'*). Cf. Cod. Petermann cit., fol. 14a.

[5] Nöldeke, *Gesch. des Korans*, p. 181 no. III [2nd ed., I, p. 243]. The second part, in which the Anṣār are praised, shows a heightening in comparison with the first which praises the Muhājirūn.

[6] *Agh.*, VIII, p. 182 below [al-Balādhurī, *Ansāb al-Ashrāf*, ed. Hamidullah, I, pp. 36–7; al-Hamdānī, *al-Iklīl*, ed. Löfgren, I, p. 64.]

[7] *Agh.*, XVII, p. 52, 12 ff.

In order to define the *terminus a quo* of the existence of a well-established consciousness of the hostile difference between the two Arab groups we should look for the earliest expression of this consciousness in the most faithful interpreters of the mentality of Arab
society. In al-Farazdaq (died 110) the various designations of the two 98
racial groups are used in opposition, and it is assumed that it is generally known and acknowledged that these genealogical descriptions comprise the whole of the dichotomous Arab nation.[1] For the beginnings, however, we are referred to a somewhat earlier time and must use the following data. The poet 'Abd Allāh b. al-Zabīr (died 60), a fanatical follower of the Umayyads, accuses the Muḍarites of having looked on while Mukhtār had the house of Asmā' b. Khārija destroyed, when the latter, suspected by the 'Alids of having actively participated in the killing of al-Ḥusayn, was fleeing from his pursuers:

> If Asmā' were of Qaḥṭān, hosts with yellow cheeks
> would have bared their thighs.[2]

'Ubayd Allāh b. Qays al-Ruqayyāt, a follower of the Zubayrides (died 70) seems to use the expression Mudar to denote the genealogical peculiarity of the northern Arabs in contra-distinction to another group;[3] and also in al-A'shā from the southern Arab tribe of Hamdān (died 85) we already see signs of this special consciousness.[4] Above (p. 81) we have already heard the voice of a poet from the same period who speaks in the same vein.[5]

These indications would point to the second half of the first century as the time at which the beginning of the antagonism between northern and southern Arabs must have taken root in the consciousness of Arab society.

VI

This antagonism, which expressed itself in literature too in
increasingly bitter terms, was calculated to rouse the disapproval of 99

[1] Qaḥṭān plus Nizār, *Dīwān*, ed. Boucher, p. 28 penult., Ḥimyar plus Nizār, p. 86, 8, *mini'bnay Nizārin wa'l-yamānīna*, 59, 10, Azd plus Nizār, 68 ult.

[2] *Agh.*, XIII, p. 37, 22 ff, 31.

[3] In the poem edited by Dozy, *Noten zu Ibn Badrūn*, p. 67, 3 from below. [*Dīwān*, ed. Rhodokanakis, *Sitzungsberichte der Kais. Ak. der Wissenschaften*, CXLIV, Vienna, 1902, Appendix, 28:4.] The Asadite poet al-Ḥakam b. 'Abdal also belongs to this time (flourished in the middle of the first century) and he too expresses the contrast between Qaḥṭān and Ma'add clearly, *Agh.*, II, p. 153, 14.

[4] *Agh.*, V, p. 159, 10, cf. also 10 from below, 'Adnān and Qaḥṭān.

[5] Reference can also be made to *Agh.* XVII, p. 59 below, 62, 11, where Yazīd ibn Murfarrigh, (see above, p. 94) appeals to the Qaḥṭānī consciousness of the Yemenites in Damascus in order to find protection from persecution to which he is subjected by the government.

the theologians, who saw in its basis an infringement of the principle of equality postulated by Islamic teaching, the more so as the northern Arabs finally went so far as to state that even Jews or foreign *mawālīs* were preferable to southern Arabs.[1] That this was not a mere theoretical assertion but was indeed applied in practical life is seen from a report that in the middle of the second century the Qurayshites did not wish to recognize the Azdites (southern Arabs) who lived in 'Umān[2] as Arabs. In order to combat at its roots a racial quarrel which had received fresh stimulus from the theories of the genealogists, whose system in its turn arose out of the rivalry between Qurayshites and Anṣār, sayings of the Prophet were quoted which were designed to work against the genealogical theories. In these sayings a common origin is alleged for both southern and northern Arabs: in Ismā'īl as their common ancestor the two groups meet.[3] Genealogists imbued with the theological spirit followed this line of thought and attempted to find deeper foundations for it, and make it sound more probable by a process of harmonization; they taught that Qaḥṭān was a son of Ismā'īl[4] which was, however, too easy a way of cutting the Gordian knot.[5] A compromise was made by those theologians who call all Arabs Banū Ismā'īl but make a few exceptions, such as the Thaqīf and the Arabs of Ḥaḍramawt.[6] The exclusion of the Thaqīf was probably partly due to the indelible memory of the horrors of al-Ḥajjāj b. Yūsuf. The same consideration was responsible for a large number of sayings by Muhammed and 'Alī which, contrary to those genealogists who make Thaqīf descend regularly from Nizār,[7] degrade the tribe of the tyrant[8] whose
100 genealogy was linked to Abū Righāl.[9] He himself was said not to be a descendant of Ismā'īl, the father of the Arabs, but of the godless

[1] *Ansāb al-Ashrāf*, ed. Ahlwardt, p. 254.

[2] *Agh.*, XX, p. 100, 14.

[3] B. *Manāqib*, no. 5; cf. the passages in Robertson Smith, p. 247.

[4] See Kremer, *Über die südarabische Sage*, p. 24.

[5] The descent of the southern Arabs from Ismā'īl was also taught in respect of the history of the language, in order to contradict the older tradition, according to which Ya'rub, a son of Qaḥṭān, was the first to speak Arabic; this role was now allotted to Ismā'īl as the ancestor of all Arabs. The relevant traditions and opinions are collected in al-Suyūṭī, *Muzhir*, I, p. 18.

[6] Al-Ṣiddīqī, fol. 38b (Ibn 'Asākir). [See for Thaqīf al-Balādhurī, *Ansāb al-Ashrāf*, ed. Hamidullah, I, pp. 25–9; Ibn 'Abd al-Barr, *al-Inbāh*, pp. 89–92; for Ḥaḍramawt, ibid., pp. 58, 59, 91, 120.]

[7] A few through Iyād, others through Muḍar, al-Ya'qūbī, I, p. 258, 10, 260, 11; cf. genealogical legends on the Thaqīf in Yāqūt, III, pp. 496-99.

[8] *Agh.*, IV, pp. 74-76. Here all the data for this question are brought together.

[9] The Muslim tradition about Abū Righāl and his role in the expedition of the Abyssinian Abraha against the Ka'ba is influenced by this anti-Thaqafī tendency and was newly revived through the hatred of al-Ḥajjāj, see Nöldeke, *Gesch. der Perser und Araber*, p. 208, note.

Thamudaeans.[1] In the same vein the theologians also put into circulation the tale that the dying Prophet named three Arab tribes whom he disliked: the Banū Thaqīf, the Banū Ḥanīfa[2] and the Banū Umayya.[3] The mere mention of the latter shows the tendentious anti-Umayyad character of this tradition, which was presumably invented in pro-'Abbāsid circles in order to damage the opposing dynasty. The following saying of the Prophet is related on the authority of Ibn 'Umar: 'In the tribe of Thaqīf there will arise a liar and a spoiler (*mubīr*).'[4] The liar is al-Mukhtār b. Abī 'Ubayd, the spoiler al-Ḥajjāj b. Yūsuf.[5] That in pre-'Abbāsid days the tribe of Thaqīf was of better repute is seen from the fact that al-Farazdaq, who was by no means a friend of al-Ḥajjāj, considered descent from Thaqīf laudable.[6]

[1] A contemporary poet is already said to have mocked his origin. He is called *'ilj min Thamūd*, a Thamudaean Barbarian, *Agh.*, XX, p. 13. The prejudice against the Thaqīf continues amongst modern Bedouins, who call them Yahūd, see Doughty, *Travels*, II, p. 174.

[2] The condemnation of the Banū Hanīfa is probably connected with the fact that the Khārijite chief Nāfi' b. al-Azraq belonged to them.

[3] [Al-Ḥākim, *al-Mustadrak*, IV, p. 481.]

[4] Cf. *Ansāb al-Ashrāf*, p. 58, 3 from below and 61, 5. Al-A'shā speaks of the two liars from the tribe of Thaqīf, *Agh.* V, p. 159, 8 from below.

[5] Muslim, V, p. 224; al-Baghawī, *Maṣābīḥ al-Sunna*, II, p. 193; Ibn Badrūn, p. 193.

[6] *Dīwān*, ed. Boucher, p. 44 penult.

101 CHAPTER THREE

'ARAB AND 'AJAM

I

WE come now to another sphere where the Muslim teaching of the equality of all men in Islam remained a dead letter for a long time, never realized in the consciousness of Arabs, and roundly denied in their day to day behaviour. We have already quoted some traditions, and we shall find a few more in this study, which go even further than the overcoming of tribal differences among the Arabs and postulate the equality of the Arabs with all Muslim non-Arabs in Islam. The need which arose for such sayings to be ascribed to Muhammed and the oldest authorities of Islam proves how little heed was paid to these principles in the ordinary course of affairs; such sayings aimed at checking the ever increasing arrogance and racial presumption of the Arabs also in this respect. They were invented by pious theologians who wished to impose the consequences of the Koranic teaching in all spheres of life, as well as by non-Arabs who, without being guided by theological considerations, wished in their own interests to stem the pride of their conquerors by appealing to the highest authority. It was not difficult for the non-Arabs to contribute in this manner to the enriching of the sacred literature, for we shall soon see what a decisive position they held very early in the spiritual life of Islam. Such sayings betray at first glance from which of these two groups they originate. A typical example is the last sentence of the farewell sermon of Muhammed (see above p. 72 note 4), which the newly converted Muslims added with the intention of producing evidence to show that the Prophet demanded equality not only of all Muslim Arabs but of Arabs and non-Arabs as well.

102 Various points in the biography of the Prophet and the old Muslim tradition are meant to support this idea and simultaneously to contradict the Arab concept of the inferiority of all non-Arab peoples. The traditionist al-Zuhrī thus relates that when, on receiving the news that the king of Persia had died on the very day that Muhammed had prophesied, Bādhān the governor of the Persian king in south Arabia sent a Persian deputation to pay homage to the Prophet, they were assured by him of their complete equality with the members of the Prophet's family.[1]

[1] Ibn Hishām, p. 46.

It must be assumed that the theological data to which we have here referred owe their existence to a need of the religious opposition against the deeply-rooted opinions of the Arabs. The clear consciousness of the inferiority of other independent nations is, however, hardly very old among the Arabs,[1] for there is no ancient poetical text known expressing such a view. If these poets make mention of non-Arab nations they do not employ the contemptuous tone which would undoubtedly have been used if the Arabs had been convinced of the inferiority of foreign races. The contacts of the ancient Arabs with Persians and Greeks and their political relations with these peoples were hardly of such a nature as to make the Arabs think of them as inferior; on the contrary, they were likely to make the Arabs feel that their standing was much below that of these peoples. Wherever Persians are mentioned the epithets applied to them relate for the most part to external points only, for example to their clothing[2] and head covers,[3] which seemed strange to the Arabs, or their slender bodies.[4] Arab poetry mentions Persian sword sheaths and mails, which are described with a word taken from the Persian (*musarrad*).[5] The flash of lightning at night is likened to the 103
light of Persian lamps,[6] in the same way as other passages make the same comparison with the lamps of Christian monks (*rāhib*). The character of these foreigners is not described to their disadvantage. The fact, however, that because of their language they are referred to as stuttering barbarians[7] does not exactly show an intention to honour them; and the fact that marriage of an Arab woman with a

[1] Sūra 3: 106 *khayru ummatin* refers to the religious community, not to the Arab nation.

[2] Imrq., 40: 31 *al-fārisiyyu'l-munaṭṭaqu*, *Mufaḍḍ.*, 42: 4 *ka'l-fārisiyyīna mashaw fi'l-kumam*, 'Alq., 13: 41 *mafdūm*—to cover the mouth with the *fadam* if we follow Fraenkel's *De vocibus etc. peregrinis*, p. 3, 12. The striped trousers of the fire priests are later made the subject of comparisons by Jarīr [*Dīwān*, ed. al-Sāwī, p. 587, quoted by] al-Jawālīqī, ed. Sachau, p. 154, 10.

[3] In al-Azraqī, p. 493, 10.

[4] Ṭarafa, 14: 17 *qubbun ka'l-'ajam*.

[5] Frænkel, *Die aramäischen Fremdwörter im Arabischen*, p. 241; Schwarzlose, *Die Waffen der alten Araber*, pp. 208, 340.

[6] *Maṣābīḥu 'ujmin*, *Hudh.*, 134: 3. The same picture, Imrlq., 22:1, *ka-nāri mājūsa*—according to a variant quoted in Ahlwardt's apparatus (*hirbidhi*) also 20:49, refers to Persian priests. Cf. Tamīm ibn Muqbil [*Dīwān*, Damascus 1962, p. 150, 22, quoted] Yāqūt, III, p. 337, 5 (cf. also *Dīwān*, 1:20, Persian fortresses; 36:5, coins; 40:5, bridles].

[7] 'Ant., 27:2 *a'jamu ṭimṭimiyyun*, the same expression is used by the poet *Mu'all.*, v. 25, for the Ethiopians, Kremer, *Südarabische Sage*, p. 38. Cf. *ṭimṭimun ḥabashiyyun*, *Agh.* XVI, p. 156, 18; plural: *ṭamāṭimu sūdun*, XXI, p. 12, 17. Mocking of the Persian language by a Bedouin in the Islamic period (*kalām al-khurs*, language of the dumb), Nöldeke, *Beitr. zur. Kenntniss d. Poesie d. alten Araber*, p. 198, 11 [from al-Buḥturī's *Ḥamāsa*; ed. Cheikho, p. 268, 13]; cf. *laghṭu 'ajam*, *Agh.* VIII, p. 136, 9.

Persian was considered as a *mésalliance*[1] can be considered as a stage in the development of antagonism to the Persian race towards the end of the pagan era. We find, however, if we may trust the source in question, that a part of the Banū 'Ijl formed such close alliance with Persian settlers from Iṣṭakhr who had immigrated into Baḥrayn, that they were soon assimilated to the Persians.[2] Such merging would have been impossible during the days when antagonism had been roused.

The hostility against the Persian race which is unmistakably present in the early Islamic period was greatly stimulated by the courageous uprising of a large section of the central Arab tribes against the tyrannical rule of the Persians, who through their vassal state of Ḥīra exerted a humiliating pressure upon the Arabs, and the heroic fight against and defeat of the Persian empire in the battle of Dhū-qār (611 A.D.)[3] which was one of the three most outstanding military events of pre-Islamic Arab history.[4] There was also
104 invented a saying of the Prophet in which this battle is described as epoch-making in the relationship of Arabs and Persians,[5] and the popular legend which wonderfully elaborated the episodes of this event[6] preserved into later times the importance of that day and prefigured in it the victory of Islam over the Persians.[7] The sentiment which now prevailed among the Arabs was greatly fostered by the subsequent wars of Islam against the Persians. The contempt of the foreign nation was enhanced by the supremacy now gained by the Arab tribes over the state which had once controlled them. If Arabs who were defeated in battle, and especially those who became prisoners of war, were deemed inferiors in the national hierarchy, how much more inferior must have appeared, after its political collapse, the foreign nation with its alien institutions and family orders, the exact opposite of those of the Arabs, on which all fame was based in Arab eyes.

Thus the national hatred which had its beginning shortly before Islam was much encouraged by the conditions and relations created in Islam.

[1] Cf. below, Section IV of this chapter.

[2] Abu'l-Mu'allā al-Azdī, Yāqūt, II, p. 179, 20 ff. But *min 'ajam* in the notes to al-Jawālīqī, ed. Sachau, p. 64, 9, is probably: *ibn 'Ijl*, cf. *Agh.*, XVIII, p. 164, 14.

[3] Robertson Smith, p. 288, had already pointed out the connection, but perhaps one might refer back to the *Yawm al-Mushaqqar*, Caussin de Perceval, II, pp. 576 ff. *Yawm Dhī-qār* as the Banū Shaybān's day of glory over Khusraw, al-Farazdaq, ed. Boucher, p. 59, 8.

[4] *Agh.*, X, p. 34, 19.

[5] Al-Ya'qūbī, I, p. 246, 7 [*Naqā'iḍ*, p. 640, 18; Ṭab., I, p. 1016, 1].

[6] *The Romance of 'Antar*, XVI, pp. 6-43.

[7] The war cry of the Arabs was *yāla Muḥammad*, according to the popular legend.

II

It would be unnecessary repetition, after Alfred v. Kremer's[1] exhaustive exposition of the relations between the various strata of the Muslim people after the conquest of foreign provinces (that is, the full Arabs, the non-Arabs and the clients, *mawālī*, sing. *mawlā*[2]) to discuss this subject again. But in order to make the connection with the theme of the next chapter we must just recapitulate some of the things which are sufficiently dealt with in his exposition, and we shall use this opportunity to add a few facts to the evidence with which he did so much to elucidate the subject.

The expression *mawlā* at the latest stage of its evolution means people descended from foreign families whose ancestors, or even they themselves, on accepting Islam, have been adopted into an Arab 105
tribe, either as freed slaves or free-born aliens. Like many other technical terms of the science of law and social teaching this term underwent some development before it crystallized into the meaning that it has in the circle which we now have to consider.[3] In earlier days *mawlā* meant any relative, without distinction of the nature of the tribal association.[4] Quite early, however, a distinction seems to have been made between *mawla'l-wilāda*, a relative by birth, i.e. by blood, and *mawla'l-yamīn*, i.e. one who became a relative by oath,[5] or in other words the confederate or *ḥalīf*[6] (see above p. 65) who has been associated to a tribe by a sworn sacrament, *qasāma* (cf. Robertson Smith, p. 149). The contrast between these two types of relationship is sharply expressed when *mawlā*, a person assimilated to the tribe by affiliation, is distinguished from *ṣamīm*, i.e. the original true member of the tribe[7] or from *ṣarīḥ*[8] (with the same meaning). In

[1] *Culturgeschichte des Orients unter den Chalifen*, II, pp. 154 ff.

[2] [For other meanings of the word cf. the article 'mawlā' in the *Enc. of Islam*.]

[3] A collection of examples in *Kitāb al-Aḍdād*, ed. Houtsma, pp. 29 f. Ibn al-Athīr mentions sixteen different meanings of the word in his *Nihāya* (quoted by al-Qasṭallānī, III, p. 87, *Zakāt*, no. 61.).

[4] Imrq., 13:5 *lā nasabun qarībun wa-lā mawlan*, according to the variant in al-Ya'qūbī, I, p. 251 penult (the *Dīwān* has *shāfin* without a variant), al-Nābigha, 9:6; Ḥārith, *Mu'all.*, v. 18; 'Urwa, 15:2; *Ḥam.*, p. 216, v. 327, v. 4-6, 629, v. 2; Labīd, p. 5, v. 5, 48, v. 3, 55, v. 4; al-Maydānī, II, p. 139, 7 from below. Also in the Koran, 33:5, *mawālīkum* is used as a synonym for *ikhwānukum*, cf. *akhūnā wa-mawlānā*, B. *Sulḥ*, no. 6.

[5] *Ḥam.*, p. 187 ult. [Cf. al-Nābigha al-Ja'dī, ed. M. Nallino, 12:40-1: *mawāliya ḥilfin lā mawālī qarābatin*.]

[6] *Agh.*, XIX, p. 144, 12-13; the verb *wly* III is used of the *ḥilf* relation *Hudh.*, 122:2.

[7] *Mufaḍḍ.*, 30:22; Yāq., III, p. 520, 2; cf. Ibn Hish., p. 528, 15 *ḥilfuhā wa-ṣamīmuhā*. [Jarīr, in *Naqā'iḍ*, p. 323, 11; cf. Dhu'l-Rumma, *Dīwān*, 87:59.]

[8] 'Abd Yaghūth, *Agh.*, XV, p. 76, 4; Ḥassān, *Dīwān*, p. 81, 10 [ed. Hirschfeld, 62:3,] in a *hijā'* of the Thaqafites: *fa-laysū bi'l-ṣarīḥi wa-la'l-mawālī*; *ṣarīḥ* is also contrasted to *ḥalīf*, *Agh.*, II, p. 170, 9.

those earlier days the word *mawlā* did not yet mean specifically a non-Arab client of an Arab tribe.[1] If one wished to speak of the *mawālī* in the most derogatory way they were called 'tails' (*dhanabāt*)[2] and 'fins' (*za'ānifa*)[3] or 'intruders' (*dukhlulun*, sing.),[4] of whom one
106 expects less courage and honour than of the real members of a tribe fighting for its honour and glory, and whom one is even inclined to suspect of treason to the most sacred duties of the tribe because of their alien origin. Such an increase in numbers (*'adad*) was probably quite welcome to weak tribes, but it was considered particularly praiseworthy if a tribe could manage without such elements.[5]

The changed social conditions which resulted from the victories of Islam demanded an even more thorough definition and classification of the concept of *mawlā*. Foreign prisoners were brought home from the wars who eventually were set free and incorporated into the tribe of their previous owners as *mawālī*, thus complementing the Arab nation. They were, however, not clients by oath. The earliest theoretical consideration of this type of *mawālī*—whose position in the tribe whose serfs they had been was discussed also in the old literature of tradition—in addition to the two types mentioned above, is found in an edict which is ascribed to 'Umar II, but was probably fabricated at a later date and is addressed to one of 'Umar's governors. This edict lays down that: there are three types of *mawālī*: (1) *mawlā raḥimin*, i.e. a blood relation, (= *m. al-wilāda*); (2) *m. 'atāqa*, i.e. a freed man who, through the act of emancipation, becomes the client of his former master; and (3) *m. al-'aqd*, i.e. probably a free Arab who by special legal act becomes a member of a tribe to which he belongs neither by birth nor by previous affiliation as slave (= *m. al-yamīn*). The document to which I refer postulates differences in the law of inheritance for each of these three types, though like many Muslim institutions they are presumably of only theoretical significance, since quite other norms were used in practice.[6] This threefold division of the class of the *mawlās* answered the needs of the situation in which it was made. It presumably takes account of old linguistic usage in calling tribal Arabs *mawlā* too, but the second category contains the seeds of the new use of the word.

The extensive Islamic conquests amongst alien non-Arab races called for a special term by which to describe such non-Arabs who,

[1] Noteworthy in this connection is *Agh.*, X, p. 36, 21.

[2] *Ḥam.*, p. 249, v. 4; cf. *Agh.*, XXI, p. 145, 2, where one can find various expressions for the concept of such tribal appendages.

[3] Even later, *Agh.*, V, p. 130, 10.

[4] Imrq., 27; 1.

[5] *Mufaḍḍ.*, 32, 21 *laysa fīhā ashā'ibu*, cf. al-Jawālīqī, ed. Sachau, p. 20, 3.

[6] *Al-'Iqd*, II, p. 334.

after their country was conquered, were converted to Islam and, freed from the state of prisoners of war and slaves, were incorporated into a purely Arab family by affiliation. For this the old word 107
mawlā was used which now becomes more especially the opposite of 'Arab by descent.' In order to describe the whole of an Arab tribe one says, for example, 'the tribe Bāhila *'urbuhā wa-mawālihā'*, i.e. the true Arabs amongst them and the foreigners assimilated to the tribe: *mawālī*.[1]

The old customary Arab law gave exactly the same rights and duties to those affiliated to the tribe as to proper members. Exceptions appear to have been made in a few special cases only. In Medina, for example, the blood-money (*diya*) for someone who was merely affiliated to the tribe appears to have been but half that for a full member.[2] This phenomenon is explained, however, by the fact that the tribes had no set amounts for the blood money but made their own individual assessments in different ways.[3] Generally, however, the rule of the equality of *mawlās* with the members of the tribe was observed.[4] In this respect principles of the following type were valid: *al-walā' luḥma*[5] *ka-luḥmat al-nasab*, or *al-walā' nasab thābit*, i.e. 'the relationship of clientage creates firm ties' or even 'blood relationship like that based on common descent';[6] *mawla'l-qawm minhum* or *min anfusihim*, i.e. 'the *mawlā* of a tribe should be considered like one of its original members.'[7] In this sense a *mawlā* of the tribe of Quraysh, when asked about his affiliation, does not call himself a *mawlā* but says that he belongs to Quraysh.[8] This principle seems to have been extended to outside relations of the tribe, as for

[1] Ṭab., III, p. 305, 17.

[2] Caussin de Perceval, II, p. 658; *Agh.*, II, p. 167; it is true that there the reference is to the *ḥalīf*.

[3] The Ghaṭārīf of the Azd tribe, demand for the murder of one of their members, double the ordinary blood money, *Agh.*, XII, pp. 50, 54; Labīd, commentary, p. 144, 16.

[4] 'Antara, 26, 11 is based on hatred of *mawālīs* and there is reason to think that this passage is not genuine.

[5] On *luḥma*: Robertson Smith, p. 149. For the opinion expressed there see also Josua, 9:14; for the expression *luḥma* cf. *Agh.*, VIII, p. 152, 7 *bi-luḥmatihi wa-ahli baytihi*.

[6] Cf. Dozy, *al-Bayān al-Mughrib*, p. 17 of the introduction; various explanations in al-Zurqānī to *Muwaṭṭa'*, III, p. 262. [See also al-Jāḥiẓ, *Risāla fī Banī Umayya*, *Rasā'il*, ed. Sandūbī, Cairo 1933, p. 299; al-Sharīf al-Raḍī, *al-Majāzāt al-Nabawiyya*, p. 133; al-Haythamī, *Majma' al-Zawā'id*, IV, p. 231.]

[7] B. *Farā'iḍ*, no. 23; al-Tha'ālibī, *Der vertraute Gefährte des Einsamen*, ed. Flügel, pp. 266 ff. [i.e. in reality Rāghib al-Iṣfahāḥi, *Muḥādarat al-Udabā'*; ed. Cairo 1287, I, pp. 218–9]. See also *Kanz al-'Ummāl*, X, p. 203, nos. 1562–4; al-Samarqandī, *Tuḥfat al-Fuqahā'*, I/1, Damascus 1964, pp. 628–9.]

[8] It is not surprising that the *mawālī* made use of this principle; *Agh.*, XXI, p. 131, 4.

108 example, when the *mawlā* of a family who stands in *ḥilf* relationship with another tribe becomes the *ḥalīf* of that tribe.[1]

If these democractic principles had been transferred in their literal application to the new sort of *mawālī* this new element would at once have found a position in Islam which would have accorded with the Muslim doctrine of equality. A few of the rulers who were devoted to religion did in fact see the new situation in these terms.[2] But on the whole this democratic view of the relations between the newly acquired aliens and the Arabs was not agreeable to the Arabs, obsessed as they were with their aristocratic traditions. Apart from this aristocratic prejudice, envy and jealousy also contributed to the reluctance of the members of ancient Arab families to acknowledge the equality of the foreigners. The proud and boastful Arabs resented especially the fact that it was the foreigners, who had entered Islamic society and had been incorporated into the Arab people, who not only gained riches[3] but also, on account of their intellectual abilities, soon acquired the greater influence in society as far as the material aspects were concerned.[4] It could be said of the *mawlā* Muslim b. Yasār (died 100) that no one was more respected in his day than he.[5] The foreigners also took the lead in intellectual fields through their furtherance of the specifically Arabic and Muslim sciences, which they pursued with greater eagerness, diligence and success than the chosen Arab people with their one-sided gifts. It is also true that old noble families, whose descendants were known in Muslim times as *dihqāns*,[6] countered the racial pride of the Arabs with a pride in their own ancestors which insulted Arab society. This at least appears to have been so from an apocryphal tradition which seems to stem from contemplation of this situation: 'Six kinds of men go to hell
109 without being asked any previous reckoning: the rulers because of their injustice, the Arabs because of their racial fanaticism (*'aṣabiyya*), the *dihqāns* because of their arrogance (*al-dahāqīn bi'l-kibar*), the merchants because of their lies, the scholars because of their envy, and the rich because of their meanness.'[7]

[1] Ibn Qutayba, ed. Wüstenfeld, p. 161 below.

[2] Kremer, l.c., p. 155.

[3] An example from the middle of the first century, Ibn Qutayba, p. 89, 3. [Cf. the ch. about the high sums paid by *mukātab* slaves for their emancipation, Ibn Ḥabīb, *al-Muḥabbar*, pp. 340–7; for Fīrūz Ḥuṣayn cf. also al-Mubarrad, al-Kāmil, pp. 655–6.]

[4] While the Arab rides a lazy mare, the *mawālī* ride fine chargers. 'This was not our custom in the days of the Prophet'—Abu'l-Aswad al-Du'alī had already made this complaint; al-Balādhurī, p. 354.

[5] Ibn Qutayba, p. 121, 3.

[6] For their position and influence see Kremer, *Culturgeschichte*, II, pp. 160 ff. For the early date of their importance in the Muslim state, Ṭab., II, p. 458, is noteworthy.

[7] Al-Ṣiddīqī, fol. 85a.

The shrewd Persians succeeded in working up from the lowest status to the most important positions in the 'Abbāsid empire, thanks to their skilful use of existing circumstances.

The biography of the last vizier of Ma'mūn affords a typical example of the way in which striving Persians knew how to gain administrative posts by their superior skill.[1] There were many such examples in earlier days as well. But the foreigners not only led in administration[2] but—as has been said already—they were foremost too in the specifically religious sciences. Kremer says: 'It seems almost as if these scientific studies (reading of the Koran, exegesis, science of tradition and jurisprudence) were mainly indulged in by clients during the first two centuries,'[3] whereas the true Arabs felt more drawn to the knowledge of their old poetry and to its development and imitation.[4] But, we may add, here too they were often outdone by the foreigners, whose scholars considerably furthered and indeed really opened up this sphere of Arab culture, by literary and historical studies about the ancient Arabs, and by detailed criticism of the tradition, etc. It would be superfluous to mention the many names whose very sound is evidence of the debt Arabic grammar and lexicology owe to non-Arabs. Even if we do not entirely accept Paul de Lagarde's statement that 'of the Muslims who achieved anything in scholarship none was a Semite',[5] it can certainly be said that the Arabs lagged considerably behind the non-Arabs in the specifically religious studies and in the studies concerned with the knowledge of the Arabic language. For this the Arabs themselves were largely to blame. 110
They looked down with sovereign contempt upon the studies zealously taken up by the non-Arabs, and thought that such trivialities were unsuitable for men who boasted great ancestors, but belonged to the παιδαγωγός who wished to hide his obscure genealogy behind such facades. 'It is not suitable for a Qurayshite,' says a thoroughbred Arab, 'to immerse himself in sciences other than the knowledge of the old traditions (of the Arabs) or at best the art of drawing the bow and attacking enemies.' When a Qurayshite once noticed an Arab child studying the grammatical work of Sībawayhi he could not help exclaiming: 'Bah! this is the science of schoolteachers and the pride of beggars,' because it was considered ridiculous that someone who was grammarian, prosodist, arithmetician and learned in the law of inheritance—for the last science a knowledge

[1] *Al-Fakhrī*, ed. Ahlwardt, p. 273.

[2] Few are likely to have shown such modesty as is attributed to Makḥūl. When 'Umar b. 'Abd al-'Azīz offered him the office of judge he is said to have refused with the remark: 'The Prophet said: "Only a man respected by his own people is to judge men" but I am a *mawlā*' (*al-'Iqd*, I, p. 9 below).

[3] *Culturgeschichtliche Streifzüge*, p. 16.

[4] Kremer, *Culturgeschichte*, II, p. 155.

[5] *Gesammelte Abhandlungen*, p. 8, note 4.

of arithmetic was necessary[1]—instructed small children in all these sciences for sixty *dirhams* (unfortunately we are not told for which period).[2]

Even before Islam it was mainly Christians[3] and Jews[4] who were the teachers of the Arabs in schools where the latter learned to read and write, and it is a fact that in Medina,[5] where the Jews were the schoolmasters, writing was more practised than in the purely pagan parts of the peninsula. The perusal of holy scriptures which the pagans lacked made Jews and Christians more capable of learning these arts than the bookless Arabs, amongst whom the art of writing,
111 though not entirely unknown, was only exercised by an elect few,[6] primarily educated poets and more especially those whose intercourse with Ḥīra and the Ghassānid court helped them to acquire this accomplishment. Contact with Persians[7] and Greeks had established a culture there which far exceeded the normal level of Arab civilization and probably became the source from which select Arabs gained

[1] Cf. *Österreich. Monatsschrift für den Orient*, 1885, pp. 137, 156. Hence the frequent juxtaposition in biographies of scholars: *fāriḍ ḥāsib*, Ibn Qutayba, ed. Wüstenfeld, pp. 117, 4, 263 ult.; *al-faraḍī al-ḥāsib*, Ibn al-Athīr, X, p. 201 (anno 511), etc., e.g. *al-faqīh al-aḥsab.*

[2] Al-Jāḥiz, *Bayān*, fol. 92b. Cf. similar stories from other sources, in Kremer, op. cit, II p. 159. [For this and the following, cf. Goldziher's article 'Education' in Hasting's *Enc. of Religion and Ethics.*]

[3] *Agh.*, V, p. 191. Al-Muraqqish is sent by his father to the school of a Christian in al-Ḥīra to learn to write; and the letter of Uriah, which the poets al-Mutalammis and Ṭarafa were to bring to the ruler of Baḥrayn, could only be read by a Christian youth whom they met on their way; al-Ya'qūbi, ed. Houtsma, I, p. 240. Amongst the Iyād—amongst whom Christianity had spread (the bishop Quss b. Sā'ida was an Iyādite)—writing was widely known, as the poet of the tribe Umayya b. Abi'l-Ṣalt stresses with approval (Ibn Hishām, p. 32, 6.). [Bishr, brother of Ukaydir, ruler of Dūmat al-Jandal, is said to have taught Meccans to write, Ibn Durayd, *al-Ishtiqāq*, p. 223; Ibn Ḥazm, *Jamharat Ansāb al-'Arab*, p. 403.]

[4] In Medina Jews taught writing to the Aws and Khazraj; al-Balādhurī, p. 473.

[5] Ibn Qutayba, pp. 132, ult, 133 ult, 166, 16; cf. Yāqūt, I, p. 311, 18.

[6] Cf. Kremer, *Über die Gedichte des Labyd*, p. 28. That poets liken the traces of deserted camps to mysterious characters rather shows that writing was strange to them. This is also indicated by the word *al-waḥy*, which is often found in this context, e.g. Zuhayr, Append. 4:1. Add to the passages mentioned by Fraenkel (*Die aramäischen Fremdwörter im Arabischen*, pp. 244 ff.) a few characteristic verses: *Agh.* XIX, p. 104, 14; Abū Dhu'ayb in Ibn al-Sikkīt, p. 276 [ed. Cheikho, p. 329=*Hudhayl.*, ed. Cairo 1945, I, p. 64] (*ka-raqmi'l-dawāti yazburuha'l-kātibu'l-ḥimyariyyu*); Ṭarafa, 12:2, 13:1, 19:2, Yāqūt, III, p. 58, 21 (Ba'īth). The passage by 'Antar quoted by Fraenkel (27:2) is imitated by 'Alī b. Khalīl, *Agh.* XIII, p. 15, 9 below, *ka-raqmi ṣaḥā'ifi 'l-fursi.* [See collections of passages on writing by F. Krenkow in *A Volume of Oriental Studies presented to E. G. Browne*, pp. 264–6 and Nāṣir al-Dīn al-Asad, *Maṣādir al-Shi'r al-Jāhilī*, pp. 23–103 passim.]

[7] Interesting is *kuttāb al-'ajam*, *Ḥam.*, p. 763, v. 1.

theirs. A large part of the nomenclature connected with the art of writing consists of foreign loan words, as can now be seen from the material collected by Fraenkel.[1] The poet Laqīṭ sends home a written greeting (*fī saḥīfatin*);[2] the conditions of peace between Bakr and Taghlib were written down, but probably by the people of the king of Ḥīra, under whose auspices the treaty was concluded, and on that occasion the loan word *mahāriq* (sgl. *mahraq*), which is used in the relevant account, is interesting.[3] It is indicative of the rarity of scribes that an old poet describes a wise man, from whom he quotes a sentence, as one 'who dictates writing to be noted down upon parchment by the scribe'.[4] An idea of how undeveloped the art of writing was, even amongst those who were acquainted with it at that time in the Ḥijāz,[5] can be gained from the primitive writing materials used for recording the Koran.[6] How few men were able to write in those days can be seen from the account that prisoners taken in the battle of Badr paid for their freedom by giving lessons in writing in lieu of paying ransom.[7] Amongst those who can be called 112
true Arabs—those who remained untouched by foreign contacts and influences—very few have acquired such knowledge; this was especially true of the Bedouins, who to this day despise the arts of reading and writing,[8] much as in the days of the poet Dhu'l-Rumma, who all his life kept secret the fact that he could write. He said to someone to whom he had incautiously given himself away: 'keep it secret because we consider this as shameful (*fa-innahu 'indana 'ayb*).'[9]

From this it is easily understandable that the true Arabs preferred to conform in their spiritual life exclusively to the old ideals of the

[1] *Die aramäischen Fremdwörter im Arabischen*, pp. 244 ff.

[2] His poems ed. Nöldeke, *Orient and Occident*, I, p. 708; al-Ya'qūbī, I, p. 259, 10.

[3] Ḥārith, *Mu'all.*, v. 67.

[4] *Hudhayl.*, 56:15.

[5] Fraenkel, p. 245, below.

[6] Sherds are used as writing material even for the poems of Abu'l-'Atāhiya, *Agh.*, III, p. 129.

[7] Al-Mubarrad, p. 171, 19.

[8] Cf. Robinson, [*Biblical Researches in Palestine*, London 1841, II, p. 178; German transl.] *Palaestina und die südlich angrenzenden Länder*, II. p. 42: 'but as even this (that the sheikh of the Ta'amirah Bedouins knew how to read and write) is an exception to Bedawy custom, the Ta'amirah stand degraded by it in the eyes of their brethren.' How low the standard of literacy is even to-day, even amongst those Bedouins who can lay any claim to it, is seen from *ZDPV*, IX, p. 247. When Wallin's desert poet swears' by the twenty-nine letters of the alphabet', *ZDMG*, VI, p. 190, v. 1, he shows also by this that he is no real Bedouin poet (cf. Wetzstein, *Sprachliches aus den Zeltlagern*, etc. p. 6 of the offprint).

[9] *Agh.*, XVI, p. 121.

'perfect Arab'[1] leaving the care of the higher sciences, which answered the need aroused by the new religion, to the foreigners, the newly adopted 'Ajam—as he called them—even at that stage of civilization which came in the wake of Islam. This, however, does not mean that the Arabs turned away from science altogether. The history of Islamic scholarship mentions many true Arabs—like, for example, al-Mu'arrij from the Bedouin tribe of Sadūs (died 195)—who were quite eminent scholars. He described his own career in the following manner: 'I came from the desert and knew nothing of the rules of the Arabic language, my knowledge was purely instinctive and I first learnt the rules in the lectures of Abū Zayd al-Anṣārī al-Baṣrī.' This man later undertook long journeys as far as Marw and Nīsābūr, where he spread much knowledge, which he also recorded in his writings.[2] But the Arabs had to change their entire nature, and to immerse themselves
113 in foreign culture, in order thus to transform themselves into men of the theoretical sciences. Only a small minority were able to do this and they were easily overtaken in the intellectual field by the newly adopted foreigners who had only to apply their native desire for learning to the new circumstances brought about by the conquest.

It is thus in fact one of the most instructive chapters of the cultural history of Islam to trace the steady progress of the *mawālīs* in Islam's intellectual life. If we are to believe Arab historians, Persian participation in Arab culture goes right back to pre-Islamic times. The predecessor of Bādhān, the governor of Yemen, whom we have previously mentioned as Muhammed's contemporary, was Khurrakhusraw, the son and successor of the governor Marwazān. This Khurrakhusraw is said to have become completely Arabized in Yemen; he recited Arabic poems and educated himself in Arab fashion; his assimilation to the Arabs (*ta'arrabuh*, according to our authority) was the cause of his re-call.[3] Amongst the Islamic theologians there are also some men of Persian origin whose ancestors made contact with the Arabs not only through Islam, but because they belonged to those Persian troops[4] who came to Arabia under Sayf b. Dhī Yazan.[5] Under Islam the Arabization of non-Arab

[1] See above p. 49, note 8. Those circles which, under the influence of their literate surroundings, valued acquaintance with writing also before Islamic times, as in Medina, counted this knowledge also as an attribute of the 'perfect'; al-Balādhurī, pp. 473-4.

[2] Ibn Khallikān, no. 755.

[3] Ṭab., I, p. 1040. From the time of the Prophet must be mentioned Fayrūz al-Daylamī (died under 'Uthmān), cf. Ibn Qutayba, ed. Wüstenfeld, p. 170.

[4] *Banu'l-aḥrār*, cf. *Agh.*, XVI, p. 76; Ibn Hishām, pp. 44-46; Nöldeke, *Geschichte der Araber und Perser*, p. 223.

[5] The famous theologian Ṭāwūs b. Kaysān al-Janadī (died 106) is traced back to such origins (Abu'l-Maḥāsin, I, p. 289); also Wahb b. Munabbih (died 114), one of the main authorities for the Biblical legends in Islam, Ibn Khal-

elements and their participation in the scholarly activities of Muslim society advanced rapidly, and there are few examples in the cultural history of mankind to rival this process. Towards the end of the first century there is a grammarian in Medina named Bushkest, a name which sounds quite Persian.[1] This man, who occupied himself with teaching his subject, took a prominent part in the Khārijite rebellion of Abū Ḥamza, and because of this he was tracked down and killed by the followers of Merwān.[2] A number of the most famous Muslims were descended from Persian prisoners of war. The grandfather of
Ibn Isḥāq, whose biography of the Prophet is one of the most 114
important sources for the history of the origins of Islam, was a prisoner of war named Yasār; this was true also of the father of Abū Mūsā b. Nuṣayr, who reached a high position in Andalusia. The fathers and grandfathers of many others who excelled in politics, science, and literature, had been Persian or Turkish prisoners of war who became affiliated to Arab tribes and who by their completely Arabic *nisbas* almost made people forget their foreign origin.[3] But on the other hand it was not impossible for such Arab *mawālī* to retain a memory of their foreign descent, though it was not very common. The Arab poet Abū Isḥāq Ibrāhīm al-Ṣūlī (died 243) kept in his family name al-Ṣūlī a reminder of his ancestor Ṣol-takīn, a Khurasānian prince who was defeated by Yazīd b. al-Muhallab and lost his throne. Converted to Islam, he became one of the most zealous partisans of his conqueror. He is said to have written upon the arrows that he sent against the Caliph's troops: 'Ṣol is calling you to follow the Book of God and the Sunna of His Prophet.' The famous Arab poet was descended from this Turk.[4]

Even to mention only the most outstanding examples of the participation of the 'Ajam element in the learned life of the Muslim world and its role in the religion of Islam would involve digging deep into the history of Arabic literature. A statistical assessment of these matters would certainly be to the disadvantage of the Arabs. We will, however, permit ourselves to illustrate the influence of non-Arabs on the Muslim state and science, by means of a synchronized list of the most able men of Islam in the time of the Umayyad caliph 'Abd al-Malik. This will be easy, since we only need to quote the words of an Arab writer who was deeply interested in this phenomenon. Ibn al-Ṣalāḥ relates in the book of his travels that al-Zuhrī,

[1] *Agh.*, I, p. 114, 9 from below.
[2] Ibid, XX, p. 108, 5; 110, 18 ff.
[3] Al-Balādhurī, p. 247, gives an interesting list of such men.
[4] *Agh.*, IX, p. 21, Abu'l-Maḥāsin, I, p. 747.

likān, no. 795 (IX, p. 150). Learned descendants are ascribed also to Bādhān himself; Yāqūt, II, p. 891, 2.

the famous theologian, once appeared at the court of the caliph 'Abd-al-Malik and introduced himself to the Commander of the Faithful. The following remarkable conversation is said to have ensued between the ruler and the scholar:

C: 'Where do you come from, al-Zuhrī?'
Z: 'From Mecca.'
C: 'Who had authority over the people there while you were present?'
Z: ''Aṭā' b. Rabāḥ.'
C: 'Is this man an Arab or a *mawlā*?'
115 Z: 'A *mawlā*.'
C: 'How did he succeed in getting such influence over the inhabitants of Mecca?'
Z: 'Because of his religiosity and his knowledge of tradition.'
C: 'This is right, men who fear God and are knowledgeable in tradition are fitted to be eminent among men. But who is the most eminent man in Yemen?'
Z: 'Ṭāwūs b. Kaysān.'
C: 'Is he of the Arabs or of the *mawālī*?'
Z: 'Of the *mawālī*.'
C: 'How did he gain his influence?'
Z: 'With the same qualities as 'Aṭā'.

The caliph asked these questions about all the provinces of Islam, and al-Zuhrī told him that the leadership of Muslim society was in the hands of Yazīd b. Abī Ḥabīb in Egypt, of Makḥūl—son of a prisoner of war from Kābul, set free by a Hudhaylite woman whom he served—in Syria, Maymūn b. Mihrān in Mesopotamia, al-Ḍaḥḥāk b. al-Muzāḥim in Khurāsān, al-Ḥasan b. al-Ḥasan in Baṣra, and Ibrāhīm al-Nakha'ī in Kūfa; all of these were *mawālī*. When the caliph expressed his astonishment at such conditions, which would lead to the *mawālīs* seizing power over the Arabs and bringing them into subjection, al-Zuhrī said: 'This is so, Commander of the Faithful. It is because of the commands of God and His religion: he who obeys them rules, he who neglects them is defeated.'[2]

'Every people,' the Prophet is represented as saying in order to express public opinion, 'has auxiliary forces and those of the Quraysh (meaning here the Arabs in general) are their *mawālī*.'[3] The Prophet

[1] In our story Makḥūl is described as a Nubian slave (*'abd nūbī*). Ibn Khallikān, no. 74, derives his origin from Sind; his name is originally Shahrāb b. Shādhil. He was a teacher of al-Awza'ī and became famous because of the acumen of his judgements.

[2] Al-Damīrī, II, p. 107. A similar story is told in *al-'Iqd*, II, pp. 95-6, but the dialogue there is between the governor 'Īsā b. Mūsā and the theologian Ibn Abī Layla.

[3] Aḥmad b. Ḥanbal quoted in al-Ṣiddīqī, fol. 67b: *inna li-kulli qawm mādda wa-māddat Quraysh mawālīhim.*

made 'Umar present the Qurayshites to him, and when he learned that there were also allies and *mawālī* amongst them he said: *ḥulafā'-unā minnā wa-mawālīnā minnā*, i.e. 'Our allies and *mawālī* belong to us; have you not heard that on the day of resurrection the God-fearing amongst you (irrespective of descent), will be those who are
closest to me?'[1] Al-Bukhārī has a whole paragraph expounding that 116
judicial and administrative offices can be given to *mawālī*. It is typical that the report contained there (that already in the oldest days of Islam *mawālī* were considered equal to Qurayshites of the highest standing) stems from Nāfi' (died 116) the *mawlā* of Ibn 'Umar.[2] Such reports were designed to justify to the Arabs the positions of foreigners in political life.[3] 'Umar is made to answer an accusation that he made a *mawlā* governor of Wādi'l-Qurā with: 'He reads the book of God and knows the laws. Has not your Prophet said that God lifts up some through this Koran and lowers others?'[4] Thus did the pietists acquiesce in the ascendancy of foreign elements.[5]

No pious co-religionist would ever have reproached one of the above-mentioned Muslim scholars of foreign extraction with being of lower standing than the true Arab because of his foreign origin. The fact that these foreign authorities could find such a firm foothold in the ecclesiastical language of Islam, in the same way as the truest descendants of Ishmael, so that they even contributed to the scientific study of this language more than the members of the race of which it was the native tongue, gave them legitimate opportunity to bridge the racial difference even more easily. This also has, of course, to be expressed by no less a person than Muhammed himself: 'Oh men,' he is made to say, 'verily God is one God and the ancestor of all men is the same ancestor, religion is the same religion and the Arabic language is neither the father nor the mother of any one of
you but is nothing but a language. Therefore all who speak Arabic 117

[1] Ibid., fol. 69a. [This tradition occurs in al-Bukhārī, *al-Adab al-Mufrad*, Cairo 1379, p. 40; *Kanz al-'Ummāl*, X, p. 203, no. 1564.]

[2] B. *Aḥkām*, no. 25, cf. above, p. 105, note 2.

[3] Cf. the passage from al-Maqrīzī, *Khiṭaṭ*, II, p. 332, quoted by Kremer *Culturgeschichte*, II, p. 158, note 2.

[4] In al-Fākihī, *Chroniken der Stadt Mekka*, II, p. 36.

[5] Amongst the anecdotical stories which are designed to combat Arab *hauteur* towards the *mawālī*, there is an anecdote of al-Shu'bī of the encounter of 'Abd Allāh b. al-Zubayr with a *mawlā* named Dhakwān (probably an anachronism if it refers to the pious *mawlā* of the tribe of Ghaṭafān who died in 101; Abu'l-Maḥāsin, I, p. 274) at the court of Mu'āwiya. The proud Ibn al-Zubayr disdained to render the *mawlā* an account 'there is no answer for this slave', but the latter reinforced his argument, 'this slave is better than you', with Islamic sentences favouring *mawālī*. The story also makes the Caliph take the *mawlā's* part. See *al-'Iqd*, II, p. 138, and ibid., p. 152, where there is a story intended to teach that the *mawlā* can have a greater share in the happiness of the other world than true Arabs.

are Arabs.'[1] 'He of (the inhabitants of) Fāris who accepts Islam is (equal to a) Qurayshite.'[2]

How deeply this fact was felt early in Islam, and how eager people were to come to grips with it, is seen from the fact that traditions were invented in which Muhammed himself is made to have prophetic foresight of these conditions of Islam. 'We sat,' Abū Hurayra was made to relate, 'with the Prophet when the Sūra of *al-Jumaʿa* was revealed to him . . . Amongst us was Salmān the Persian. The Prophet laid his hand upon Salmān and said: 'If belief were in the Pleiades, men of this people[3] (the Persians) would reach it.'[4] Later this saying was made to refer to science and transformed into: 'If science were attached to the ends of the sky a people of the men of Fāris would reach it.'[5] The following dream of the Prophet is related: He dreamt that black and white cattle were following him and the white ones were so numerous that the black ones were hardly noticeable. When the Prophet asked Abū Bakr to interpret this dream the latter said: 'the black ones are the Arabs and the white ones the non-Arabs (*ʿajam*) who were to be converted to Islam after them; they will be converted in such large numbers[6] that the black ones will not be noticed any more.'[7]

III

We have again seen traditions which are quite unmistakably the product of those circles which endeavoured to protect themselves from the jealousy of the true Arabs by inventing and spreading such maxims. We must repeat here that the representatives of the old pagan Arab ideas turned a deaf ear to the teaching of the Prophet, propagated with pleasure by the pietists and Persians, about the equality of men irrespective of whether they were northern or southern Arabs,
118 Arabs or ʿAjamīs. A son of a sister of the Caliph had to bear the

[1] Ibn ʿAsākir in al-Ṣiddīqī, fol. 90b. I mention the tradition in this context, though it probably is a later invention (Ibn ʿAsākir lived 499-564); there is no doubt that pious Muslims thought like this in earlier times too. [The quotation is from *Ta'rīkh Dimashq*, Damascus 1349, VI, p. 450.]

[2] Ibid., fol. 38b: *man aslama min Fāris fa-huwa Quraysh*. [Read *Qurashī*. The tradition is quoted from Ibn al-Najjār by al-Suyūṭī, *al-Jāmiʿ al-Ṣaghīr*, II, p. 163.]

[3] In a later version specifically: of the ʿAjam (al-Damīrī, II, p. 525.)

[4] B. *Tafsīr*, no. 301, to Sūra 62.

[5] In Ibn Khaldūn, I, p. 478. [Cf. also Ibn Ḥanbal, *Musnad*, ed. Shākir, no. 7937; al-Haythamī, *Majmaʿ al-Zawā'id*, X, p. 645; al-Tibrīzī, *Mishkāt al-Maṣābīḥ*, p. 576.]

[6] Flügel reads *li-shirratihim* and translates: 'because of their badness'; this is to be corrected into *li-kathratihim*, 'because of their great number.' [This is in fact the reading in the ed. of Rāghib; see next note.]

[7] Al-Thaʿālibī, *Vertr. Gefährte*, no. 313. [In fact Rāghib al-Iṣfahānī, *Muḥāḍarat al-Udabā'*, I, p. 219.]

ridicule of his contemporaries because his female ancestors were of Ethiopian origin.[1] The *mawlā* Ziyād al-A'jam[2] (middle of the first century) was mocked because of his obscure descent by the Arabs, who wished him ill,[3] and he did not escape being taunted with incest, the sin of which the Persians were commonly accused.[4] It is true that this *mawlā* had made himself at home among the Arabs; he had persecuted many an Arab tribe with pitiless *hijā'*[5] and had dared to circulate satirical verses about the descent of pure Arab tribes. Nor did he avoid those Arabs who had mocked him; he retaliated with merciless satire: 'When the dress of a Yashkurī touches yours you may not pronounce God's name before you have cleaned yourself; If shame could kill a tribe it would doubtless kill the Yashkur tribe.' 'I am amazed,'[6] he replied to a taunt, 'that I do not whip an 'Anazī who mocks me.'[7]

According to a saying by an Arab of the Banū Shaybān, even the blood of a *mawlā* is quite different from that of an Arab by decsent, so that when the blood of both is shed the difference can be seen after their death.[8] Only as a very rare exception is there a friendly word for the *mawālī* from the representatives of the Arab nation, especially from the poets.[9] Arab poetry, particularly that of the Umayyad period, is full of scorn and derision for those in whose veins the blood of Arab ancestors does not flow. The poet al-Akhṭal thinks that his best way of humiliating Arabs is to call them people of Azqubād (a place in the district of Maysān),[10] i.e. to deny them the status of Arabs and relegate 119
them to Persia,[11] as a not very honourable place of origin. It is typical that—even at a much later date—the *mawlā* Abu'l-'Atāhiya taunts

[1] Ibn Durayd, p. 183. [See the conversation between this 'Abd al-Raḥmān b. Umm al-Ḥakam and Abū Khidāsh in al-Balādhurī, fol. 362 r. 'Amr b. al-'Āṣ was contemptuously nicknamed on account of his mother, a captive woman: Ibn 'Abd al-Barr, *al-Istī'āb*, p. 434.]

[2] He was, however, given this epithet not because of his origin but because of his stuttering, *Agh.*, XI, p. 165; XIV, p. 102; *al-'Iqd*, III, p. 296.

[3] *Ḥam.*, p. 678, v. 2. The poet al-Mughīra b. Ḥabnā' particularly has the habit in the *hijā'* between them to expose him as a foreigner who insinuates himself into Arab society, *Agh.*, XI, p. 166, 16 ff., 167, 20; 168, 8 *'ilj mu'āhad.*

[4] *Agh.*, XIII, p. 62, 6.

[5] E.g. Ibn Khallikān, no. 298 etc.

[6] *Agh.*, XI, p. 171 below. This satire is used much later in a collection of satires against Arab tribes, *Journal asiat.*, 1853, I, p. 551.

[7] In Sībawayhi, ed. Derenbourg, II, p. 313, 13.

[8] *Agh.*, XXI, p. 209.

[9] I refer to the short poem by an anonymous author in *Ḥam.*, p. 514.

[10] Yāqūt, I, p. 233, 6.

[11] Al-Tabrīzī, Comment. to Ibn al-Sikkīt [*K.al-Alfāẓ*] (Leiden manuscript no. 597) p. 465 [ed. Cheikho, p. 580, in al-Akhṭal's *Dīwān*, ed. Ṣalḥānī, p. 193, 6; the reading of the place-name is, however, doubtful since there are many variants], cf. also *Agh.*, XVII, p. 65, 23 where Ibn Mufarrigh says to the family of Ziyād b. Abīhi: *wa-'irqun lakum fī āli Maysāna yaḍribu.*

an Arab opponent, the poet Wāliba, who was the teacher of Abū Nuwās, by saying that he will be well advised to join the *mawālī*, as he is not worthy to stand amongst the Arabs.[1] Nevertheless it was considered as an elevation in rank to become a *mawlā* of an Arab tribe rather than to belong to the Persians. Isḥāq al-Mawṣilī (under Hārūn al-Rashīd), who called himself a descendant of the Banu'l-Aḥrār, was subject to insult as long as he was not affiliated to an Arab tribe, by the Arab Ibn Jāmi', who said that no one need fear contradiction who called Isḥāq the child of a whore. Only his affiliation to the tribe of the Khuzayma protected him from such taunts and he could say: 'Even if the Aḥrār are my tribe and rank, scorn is averted from me only by Khāzim and the son of Khāzim.'[2]

As a *mawlā* he at least found support and defence in the tribe to which he was affiliated, though he was far from being deemed the equal of the Arabs.

Feelings towards *mawālī* who were not even clients of a pure Arab family, but—as happened frequently—stood in the relationship of clientage to another *mawlā* family of good social status, were even more contemptuous. Al-Farazdaq mocks 'Abd Allāh al-Ḥadramī, who had dared to criticize his poems: 'If 'Abd Allāh were a *mawlā* I would make a satire on him, but 'Abd Allāh is *mawlā* of other *mawālī* (and therefore too low a target for my scorn!)'.[3]

If one reads the relevant chapter in the philological work of al-Mubarrad one is easily convinced that in its sentiment towards the *mawālī* that age had in no way altered from the views of those pagan heroes who praised their desert as the source of all ethical perfection. If a person proves himself an exception—and this only in 'Abbāsid times—by showing sympathies for the *mawālī*,[4] this is considered
120 worthy of note as a miracle. And the ill-natured tone of poets is only a reflection of the social ostracism of the *mawālī* of which von Kremer has given us so detailed a picture.[5]

Even on the tombstones of *mawālī* this peculiarity of their genealogical position is clearly indicated: 'Z. b. Y. *mawlā* of X. . . .'[6] It seems that in Kūfa (our testimony refers to the second century)[7] *mawālī* were made to pray in a special mosque; and in provinces where they lived in large numbers (our example is from Khurāsān) they appear

[1] *Agh.*, XVI, p. 149.

[2] *Agh.*, V. p. 56 below.

[3] Ibn Qutayba in Nöldeke, *Beiträge z.K.d. Poes.*, p. 32; 49, 10 [*al-Shi'r wa'l-Shu'arā'*, p. 25]. [See al-Jumaḥī, *Ṭabaqāt al-Shu'arā'*, p. 7.]

[4] *Agh.*, XX, p. 96, Yūsuf b. al-Ḥajjāj.

[5] *Culturgeschichtliche Streifzüge*, pp. 21 ff.

[6] In Wright, 'Kufic Tombstones in the British Museum' (*Proceed. of Soc. Bibl. Arch.*, IX, 1887, p. 340).

[7] Ṭab., III, p. 295 *masjid al-mawālī*. [Cf. for Jurjān *Der Islam*, 1964, pp. 8, 10, 13.]

to have formed a corporate unit.[1] Mistakes in language by *mawālīs* were derided in the most offensive manner and people appeared outraged when a foreigner presumed to criticize an Arab in matter of Arab language and poetry;[2] it was completely forgotten that they had provided for the Arabic language the most eminent grammarians and the most eager researchers into the treasures of the old language and literature.[3] The full-blooded Arabs were convinced that Arab poetry was a field quite inaccessible to the *mawlā*. A Bedouin once said in the mosque at Baṣra, concerning Bashshār b. Burd (died 168), a famous Arab poet who came from a Persian lineage of Ṭukhāristān and was a freedman of the tribe of 'Uqayl: 'How do *mawālī* achieve poetry?' We cannot believe that the sharp answer of the poet he attacked cured the pride of the son of the desert.[4] *Mawālī* were thought capable of some deficiencies in character which were believed impossible in an Arab. 'He who is looking for shame, infamy and disgrace—verily amongst the *mawālī* he finds their neck and extremities (i.e. he finds them there complete from head to foot).'[5] They are thought capable of giving false testimony recklessly, and a number of stories are told of how clever judges recognized their attempts at this crime.[6] This contemptuous attitude is matched by 121
the legal treatment of the *mawālı* at that time, when Arab racial pride was still unbridled. We have indications from which it would seem that under the Umayyads, until 'Umar II, *mawālī* who participated in the wars of Islam were, if possible, deprived of their share of the booty which belonged to the tribe to which they were affiliated. Though this procedure was not the general rule,[7] Arab chauvinists (*'aṣabiyya*) were glad to abide by it and so assert the old Arab conception.[8]

IV

Considering the value that every Arab placed on the nobility of his descent, which filled him with pride and a feeling of honour, it is not

[1] In *Fragmenta hist. arab.*, p. 19, Ḥayyān al-Nabaṭī (beginning of the reign of Sulaymān) is called 'The chief of the *mawālī* (in Khurāsān)'.

[2] *Agh.*, V, p. 61 below.

[3] *Al'-Iqd*, I, p. 295, and al-Jāḥiẓ, l.c., in many passages more especially in *Bāb al-alḥān*; in another work by al-Jāḥiẓ [or rather Pseudo-Jāḥiẓ] there is also a collection (*al-Maḥāsin wa'l-Aḍdād*) MS. Imperial Library Mixt. no. 94, fols. 5b ff. [ed. van Vloṭen, pp. 8–9].

[4] *Agh.*, III, p. 33.

[5] Al-Mas'ūdī, VI, p. 150, 1.

[6] Al-Mubarrad, p. 254.

[7] Because we find, e.g. that in the old days the Muslims of Ethiopian origin were registered in the *dīwān* of the Banū Khath'am, Ibn Qutayba, ed. Wüstenfeld, p. 88, 11.

[8] Al-Ya'qūbī, ed. Houtsma, II, p. 358, 8; 362, 19. [Cf. Ṣāliḥ Aḥmad al-'Alī, *al-Tanẓīmāt al-Ijtimā'iyya wa'l-Iqtiṣādiyya fi'l-Baṣra*, Baghdad 1953, p. 66.]

astonishing that if a man were descended from a female slave or, as the saying went, of a girl who had to lead the flock to pasture,[1] he became an object of contempt to every proud Arab.[2] It was thought that only the son of a free woman was able to protect the honour of his tribe, to help the suffering and oppressed, and thus to fulfil the duties of *muruwwa.*[3] If it could be shown that there was a slave-girl in the genealogy of a tribe this shame was kept alive for generations. *Inna ummakum amatun,* i.e. 'Your ancestor is a slave,' were the words with which the poet abused the Banū Nujayḥ from the tribe of Dārim;[4] and descent from a 'black woman' (the story of 'Antara is well known) could be mentioned as a particular cause for shame.[5] The children of a connection between an Arab and a slave or freed woman were legitimate,[6] but the proud Arabs could not bear
122 to see them as equals, though experience seemed to suggest that such offspring were intellectually gifted above the average.[7] Muhammed (Sūra 4:3) did partly break this prejudice by putting a legitimate marriage with a freed slave and marriage with a free-born Arab woman on the same level. But as with all opinions connected with their tribal constitution, the representatives of ancient Arab thinking did not wish to cede the point. The old Arabs remained quite untouched by the consequences of Muhammed's and Islam's teaching of equality in regard to this question which so deeply affected everyday life. Just as it continued to be a title to special glory if one was born *ibnu ḥurratin,* the son of a free mother,[8] or *ibnu bayḍā'i'l-jabīn,* the son of a mother with white forehead,[9] so Arabic poetry still abounded, even in Islam, in satires alleging rightly or wrongly that a man was the son, or at least descended from the son, of a slave-woman.[10] A mocking appellation of people who had slave women amongst their ancestors was *mukarkas.*[11] It is not surprising to learn that a favourite slave-girl was subjected to continuous taunts from

[1] *Mufaḍḍ.*, 24:20.

[2] Cf. the opprobrious appellations: *ibnu turnā, ibnu fartanā, Hudh.*, 107:13 and commentary (for the explanation of this odd word there is material in *Agh.*, IV, p. 45). Cf. *Hudh.*, ibid., v. 30 'my mother is a slave, if etc.'

[3] Ṭarafa, 9:8.

[4] Ibn al-Sikkīt, p. 163 [*Tahdhīb al-Alfāẓ*, ed. Cheikho, p. 196]. Cf. also particularly Ḥassān, *Dīwān*, p. 17, 11-12 [ed. Hirschfeld, no. 53]; 20, 4 below [Hirschf., 46:2].

[5] Ḥassān, p. 19, 2 *wa-ummuka sawdā'u mawdūnatun* [= Hirschfeld, 196:2].

[6] Cf. in general about these conditions Robertson-Smith, p. 73.

[7] Al-Mubarrad, p. 302. According to al-Aṣma'ī, the children of non-Arab women are the bravest (*al-'Iqd*, III, p. 283, 14).

[8] *Hudhayl.*, 270:30.

[9] *Agh.*, XI, p. 154, 3 below.

[10] Cf. *Ansāb al-Ashrāf*, p. 223.

[11] *Agh.*, XXI, p. 32, 22.

her Arab master's wife, who would boast of noble descent and proclaim the names of her father, uncle and brother.[1]

In the actual happenings of everyday life there is no more telling example of this kind of sentiment than the behaviour of a certain al-Qattāl ('the murderer') of the Kilāb tribe, a wild fellow, whose name alone indicates his savage habits and who under the reign of the Umayyad caliph Marwān b. 'Abd al-Ḥakam was a true representative of the old robber knights, quite unrestrained by Islam. This Qattāl was determined to prevent his uncle from marrying his favourite slave-girl; 'because we belong to a tribe who hate their children to be born of slaves.' He went so far as to kill this slave and the legal proceedings against him because of this murder show an interesting example of exhumation and dissection for forensic reasons.[2] We will judge the Arab resistance to the Islamic teaching 123
of equality rather more mildly when we consider that Islam itself contained many residues of the ancient pagan views in respect of the legal position of slaves.

It cannot be denied, and this has been repeatedly stressed in descriptions of Islam, that the Islamic spirit helped to make good treatment of slaves a duty and inner duty[3] and to encourage an attitude which had its roots in the oldest documents of Islam.[4] It is true that the canonical schools of law—with the exception of the Ḥanbalites—taught that the testimony of a slave was invalid, but in this they contradict the older doctrines of the traditionists, who recognize its full validity and make statements like the following: 'All of you are nothing but slaves and bondwomen'.[5] But even a far-reaching apology for Islam would have to admit that its founders did not rise to the doctrine of the full moral equality of slaves. Insofar as ethical judgment is concerned the slave remained an inferior being. This is manifest nowhere more clearly than in the Islamic concept of the slave's responsibility for his actions. Muhammed taught that an immoral slave-woman received only half the punishment that would apply to a freeborn woman in a similar case (*fa-'alayhinna*

[1] *Agh.*, V, p. 151, 5.

[2] *Agh.*, XX, p. 165, cf. the verse of Qattāl in Sībawayhi, ed. Derenbourg, II, p. 98, 7; 198, 6; the second half there differs from *Agh.*, ibid., 162, 6 from below. [Cf. Ibn Ḥabīb, *al-Muḥabbar*, p. 227.]

[3] Against the unjust and biased judgments of most of the travellers we may refer among recent publications to Oscar Lenz, *Timbuktu*, I, p. 204, Snouck Hurgronje in the *Verhandlungen der Gesellschaft für Erdkunde zu Berlin*, XIV, p.151 [*Verspreide Geschriften*, III, pp. 60-1], and his essay 'Een Rector der Mekkaansche Universiteit' (*Bijdragen tot Taal-, Land- en Volkenkunde*, 1887, no. 5), p. 33 of the offprint [*Verspr. Geschr.*, III, pp. 97 ff.].

[4] B. *'Atq*, nos. 15, 16, *al-Muwaṭṭa'*, IV, p. 217. [Cf. Wensinck, *Handbook of Early Muh. Tradition*, s.v. 'Slaves'.]

[5] B. *Shahādāt*, no. 13 and also al-Qasṭallānī, IV, p. 437.

niṣfu mā ʿalaʾl-muḥṣanāt)[1] and from this derives the principle that the *ḥadd* of a slave must always be only half the punishment prescribed for a free person.[2] Mālik b. Anas refers to the practice of the caliphs ʿUmar and ʿUthmān, when teaching that a slave who infringes the prohibition concerning wine only receives half the number of lashes which a freeman would get if found guilty of this sin.[3] Such
124 small matters unmistakably express the fact that the equalitarian teaching of Islam was not consistently followed in theory or in practice and that the age-old prejudices of society had left their traces in this field. This matter is only referred to in order to elucidate the Arabs' prejudice against marriages such as that which aroused the aristocratic fanaticism of Qattāl.

It took a very long time for these prejudices to be completely overcome. However, their disappearance had the consequence of diminishing the dignity of women. In order to give a theoretical basis to the equality of people whose maternal descent was by ancient Arab standards not noble or equal to their paternal descent people became used to taking the view which a poet expresses in the following words: 'Do not scorn a man because his mother is of the Greeks, or black or a Persian, because the mothers of men are but vessels to which they have been entrusted for keeping; for nobility fathers are important.'[4]

The literatures of many other peoples present analogies for the same idea. Legouvé[5] has a great number of parallel passages from Indian and Greek literature which show this point of view, which, however, corrupted the life of no society more than that of the Muslim East, though it originally developed in the fight against a prejudice.[6]

The irrelevance of maternal descent was already fully established in the middle of the ʿAbbāsid period.[7] Of the ʿAbbāsid caliphs only three, al-Saffāḥ, al-Manṣūr, and al-Mahdī were the sons of free

[1] Sūra 4:30.

[2] Cf. an example *Agh.*, XIII, p. 152, 8 from below. Casuists consequently teach that the punishment of stoning cannot be awarded to slaves as it cannot be halved, al-Bayḍāwī, I, p. 205, 1.

[3] *Al-Muwaṭṭāʾ*, IV, p. 24.

[4] *Al-ʿIqd*, III, p. 296.

[5] *Histoire morale des femmes* (3rd ed.), pp. 214-220.

[6] That the words by the anonymous poet quoted above are more than his own thoughts, but represent universal opinion, is seen from the fact that in the popular book *Sīrat ʿAntar*, II, p. 63, Mālik, who demands from Shaddād equal rights for ʿAntar, son of a black slave-woman and tries to persuade the hesitant Shaddād to introduce this as a *sunna* amongst the Arabs, uses the following argument: 'The woman is but the vessel in which honey is kept; when the honey is taken out, the vessel is cast aside and no longer bothered with.' From the point of view of the Arab patrician, Shaddād rejects this argument with: 'Dagger-wounds would be more congenial to me, Mālik, than such talk.'

[7] Kremer, *Culturgesch. d. Orients*, II, p. 106.

mothers; the mothers of all the rest were slaves.[1] But we have to consider what paved the way to this development.

The importance of the question of the status of children born of 125
non-Arab mothers increased with the number of captive women[2] who were acquired by Arab magnates in the wars between Arab Muslims and nations of different race. Within this question there were several ramifications according to different social circumstances: the non-Arab woman could be, for example, a slave taken prisoner in war or the daughter of a *mawlā*, etc. The question was soon resolved according to Muslim teaching (see for example, Koran, 2:22) and reference could be made to the Prophet's own marriages. Al-Ḥusayn, the Prophet's grandson, married a Persian captive—it is said she was a Persian princess—whom he had gained as his share of the spoils of war, and from this marriage stemmed Zayn al-'Ābidīn. This marriage and its fruit caused religious men to say in later years that all men would wish to have slaves for mothers.[3] The theologians recalled that even Ismā'īl, the ancestor of all Arabs, was the son of the foreign slave Hagar, whereas the free Sarah was the ancestor of the despised Jews.[4]

But this pietistic sacrifice of Arab family ideals did not reconcile the old aristocratic circles. There is a story about the above-mentioned marriage of al-Ḥusayn which, though unhistorical, reflects clearly the conflict between the Arab and Islamic views in this field. The caliph Mu'āwiya, it is related, had a spy at Medina who reported to him on the conditions and events in that town. Once the spy sent the following report to the caliph. Al-Ḥusayn, son of 'Alī, freed and married one of his slaves. Thereupon the caliph sent this letter to 'Alī's son: 'I am told that you passed over women of your own standing of Qurayshite blood, and married a slave, though it would
be more seemly to continue your lineage through your own kind and 126
more to your credit to ally yourself with them. You have considered neither your reputation nor the purity of your future offspring.' Al-Ḥusayn answered this document with the following words: 'I have received the message you have written to me—your rebuff concerning my marrying a freed woman and scorning my equals. There is, however, no goal in nobility and nothing desirable in descent

[1] Cf. *ZDMG*, XVI, p. 708.

[2] Arab women were not to be treated as prisoners in Islam, B. *Maghāzī*, no. 70, cf. al-Tabrīzī on *Ḥam.*, p. 17, 11. The principle mentioned there refers to Arabs as is evident from the full wording in *Agh.*, XI, p. 79 *la sibā'a fi'l-islām wa-lā riqqa 'alā 'arabiyyin fi'l-islām*. But Ḥārith, *Mu'allaqa*, v. 31, calls the women captured from the Tamīm tribe, maids (*imā'*), cf. *Agh.*, XXI, p. 97, 1.

[3] Al-Ya'qūbī, II, p. 364, cf. Ibn Khallikān, no. 433, ed. Wüstenfeld, V, p. 4.

[4] *Al-'Iqd*, II, p. 145 below, at greater length ibid., III, p. 296; al-Ya'qūbī, l.c., p. 390.

beyond the Prophet of God. She whom I married was once my property (*mulk yamīnī* in reference to Sūra 4:3, etc.) and is now beyond my power through an act (of emancipation) with which I hoped to achieve God's reward, and I have re-introduced her to my house in the spirit of the *sunna* of the Prophet. Yes, God has through Islam abolished inferiority and shame of low descent. For the Muslim only sin brings shame and the only infamy is the infamy of barbarism.' When Mu'āwiya had read this letter to the end he handed it to his son Yazīd. After he, too, had read it he said: 'It is too bad the way in which this Ḥusayn sets himself up against you.' 'O no,' replied the caliph, 'it is the sharp tongues of the Banū Hāshim[1] which split rocks and ladle water from the sea.'[2]

The historical accounts do not mention Mu'āwiya's admonishment, and the information is suspect also because in other places Ḥusayn's role is given to his son 'Alī and the admonishing caliph's to 'Abd al-Malik.[3] There is no doubt that this is a tendentious invention which nevertheless has value as a document of cultural history. In their way, in this story the theologians give a picture of the conflict between the mentality of the pious Muslim and that of the race-proud Arab which was still very strong among the true Arabs of the Umayyad times. The poet al-Farazdaq uses the phrase: *yā ibn al-fārisiyya*, i.e. 'O son of a Persian woman',[4] as an insult, much as in the much later popular romance of 'Antar, a person who is disliked is derided
127 with the epithet *ibn al-ifranjiyya* (son of a Frankish woman)[5] and the same al-Farazdaq must submit to mockery from his rival Jarīr because his great grandmother had been a Persian slave.[6] But even these facts show how difficult the adherence to old Arabic racial prejudices became in the face of changed circumstances in the Muslim state and the progressive racial mixture of the population.[7]

Arab opinion in the early days of Islam was even more strict about a freeborn Arab woman marrying a foreigner. The conditions in large Muslim towns must often have given topical interest also to the question whether an Arab woman should become the wife of a

[1] Cf. 'the tongues of the Quraysh', al-Fākihī, *Chron.d.Stadt Mekka*, II, p. 39, 16.

[2] *Zahr al-Ādāb*, I, p. 58 according to older sources.

[3] *Al-'Iqd*, III, p. 296.

[4] *Agh.*, XIX, p. 7, 4, according to ibid., II, p. 77 the mother of Ibn Mayyāda, satirized here, was a Berber, but according to others a Ṣaqlabī woman.

[5] *Romance of 'Antar*, III, p. 170. 'Antar's rival, 'Ammāra, is called this besides other mocking names.

[6] Ibn Qutayba, *Kitāb al-Shi'r wa'l-Shu'arā'* (MS. of the Imperial Library in Vienna) fol. 97b [ed. de Goeje, p. 290].

[7] In much later days the aim of the *Romance of 'Antar* was to fight against the last survivals of the Arab prejudice through 'Antar—one of the heroes of whom the remark of Renan, *Histoire du peuple d'Israel*, I, p. 328 applies; this is the real cultural-historical importance of this remarkable popular book.

mawlā.[1] In the old days it was pretty well established that the marriage of an Arab woman with a foreigner, even of the highest rank, was impossible.[2] Al-Nu'mān, king of Ḥīra, and his Arab subjects resolutely refused to marry an Arab woman to the mighty king of Persia. 'They are miserly with their women to other nations, they prefer deprivation and nudity to satiety and luxury, they choose desert storms rather than the scents of Persia which they call a prison.'[3] The much discussed and beautiful poem which the Kalbite wife of the first Umayyad caliph, Maysūn bint Baḥdal, is said to have written[4] 128
and which contrasts desert life with the luxurious life of the cities,[5] sounds like a poetical elaboration of the *Weltanschauung* expressed by this statement. This poem also concludes with the words: 'and a handsome youth from my tribe, even if he be poor, is preferable to a well-fed barbarian (*'ilj*)'.[6] Of course, the implication here is that 'the barbarian' is the caliph.

How absurd it seemed to the people of the first century that a *mawlā* should marry a free Arab woman is seen from an interesting episode in the biography of the poet Nuṣayb (died 108).[7] This man was so esteemed in the tribe whose client he was that his son obtained the consent of his deceased patron's uncle when he asked for his niece in marriage. But Nuṣayb himself had to admit that such a marriage would seem unnatural and impossible in the eyes of the Arab aristocrats, and he had his son beaten for such a daring aspiration and advised the girl's uncle rather to find her, in his own interest, a youth from a true Arab tribe. The daughter of the poet al-'Ujayr from the tribe of the Salūl, a highway robber like many other Arab poets (died 80), strenuously objected to a marriage with a respected *mawlā* and her brother vigorously supported her refusal.[8] There were only a few *mawālī* who, because of special merits, were

[1] In the earliest days of Islam, when the fight for the new belief made brothers of the small community without much regard to the genealogies of the fighters, this question did not arise. Typical of these conditions is the example of Sālim, a fighter at Badr, a *mawlā* with a very involved genealogy who was adopted by his patron Abū Ḥudhayfa and given the latter's niece for wife; Ibn Qutayba, ed. Wüstenfeld, p. 139; *al-Muwaṭṭa'*, III, p. 91. On the type of emancipation mentioned here (*sā'ibatan*) see *Muw.*, ib., p. 264.

[2] It was shameful to be a *muqrif* i.e. descended from an Arab mother and a *mawlā*; schol. to *Ḥam.*, p. 79, v. 1, cf. *mudharra'* (generally a child of a *mésalliance* even if both parents are Arabs); al-Farazdaq in *al-'Iqd*, III, p. 296.

[3] *Agh.*, II, p. 30.

[4] Redhouse, *Journal of Roy. As. Soc.*, 1886, pp. 268 ff.

[5] [Ibn al-Shajarī, *al-Ḥamāsa*, p. 166;] Abulfeda, *Annales*, ed. Reiske, I, p. 398; cf. al-Damīrī, II, p. 297.

[6] Much similarity can be observed between the ideas expressed in this poem and in that attributed to the pre-Islamic poetess Rāma bint al-Ḥuṣayn from the Asad tribe (Yāqūt, III, p. 813, 4-6).

[7] *Agh.*, I, p. 136.

[8] *Agh.*, XI, p. 154.

deemed entirely equal to true Arabs: one such was Ḥumrān b. Abān (died 75), of whom the caliph 'Abd al-Malik said that he should be regarded as a brother and an uncle; and this man also succeeded in marrying into Arab tribes, as did his children.[1] But this was the exception rather than the rule. The more usual conditions seem to be illustrated in the report that the Qāḍī Bilāl b. Abī Burda punished the descendant of a *mawlā*, 'Abd Allāh b. 'Awn (died 151), with a whipping because he had dared to marry an Arab woman.[2] Only in the days of the deepest degradation of the Arabs[3] could the
129 'Abbāsid Commander of the Faithful, al-Qā'im bi-Amr Allāh, have given his daughter as wife to Ṭogrulbeg; even then, this demand at first made the Qurayshite prince shudder,[4] and two hundred years earlier it would have revolted even the simplest of Arabs. Even people who did not object to the marriage of Arabs with non-Arab women rejected this situation in which the woman of higher position was to change her rank as a member of a free tribe and become the wife of one of lower social rank. Few voices dissent from the outcry against this degradation. When Ibrāhīm b. Nu'mān b. Bashīr al-Anṣārī gave his daughter to Yaḥyā b. Abī Ḥafṣa, quite an eminent Arab poet and a client of the caliph 'Uthmān, probably merely because of the large bride price of 20,000 dirhams, this occurrence was bitingly ridiculed by Arab contemporaries.[5] Later (at the beginning of the second century) when a family from the tribe of Sulaym settled in Rawḥā' in the district of Baghdad because famine had forced them to leave their homesteads, the head of the family gave his daughter to a *mawlā*, and the poet Muḥammad b. Bashīr from the tribe of Khārija considered this event so important that he travelled to Medina in order to inform the governor, who ordered that the marriage should be dissolved. The young bridegroom was also given 200 lashes and his beard, hair and brows were shaved off—a common act of public ignominy—which presumably hurt the poor barbarian more bitterly than the satirical poem in which the poet who had denounced him sang, with malicious humour, of the lashing he had caused.[6] The Sulaymite family had in fact committed

[1] Ibn Qutayba, p. 223 above.

[2] Ibn Qutayba, p. 245 below.

[3] It is worthy of note that the Arabs in Syria retained this attitude even to this century towards the Turks. The last Arab village chief thought it shameful and undignified to give his daughter to a high Turkish officer during the country's invasion by Ibrāhīm Pasha; D'Escayrac de Lautour, *Le désert et le Soudan* (German ed. Leipzig 1855) p. 155 [pp. 334–5 of the French original].

[4] Ibn al-Athīr, anno 454, ed. Būlāq, X, p. 7, cf. Aug. Müller, II, p. 83.

[5] Al-Mubarrad, p. 271; *al-'Iqd*, III, p. 298 mentions Khawla bint Muqātil b. Qays b. 'Āṣim instead of the daughter of Ibrāhīm al-Anṣārī.

[6] *Agh.*, XIV, p. 150. The poem ends with the words: 'What other right have the *mawālī* than that slaves should wed with other slaves?'

a deed which was repugnant to the aristocratic ideas of the Arabs because, even in times of need, true Arab families rejected connections even with Arabs whom they did not consider as fully their equals.[1]

Thus the intermarriage of Arabs with *mawālī* was considered a 130
mésalliance and the question was even debated whether pious non-Arabs could have Arab women as wives in paradise.[2] That such a connection was—at least in this world—regarded as abnormal is seen also from the literary fact that the philologist and genealogist al-Haytham b. 'Adī wrote a special work on those *mawālī* who had married into Arab families.[3] The question whether such connection was permissible remained for a long time a point of debate in Arab society and the theologians were also forced to consider it,[4] a proof of the difficulty of overcoming the prejudices of Arab aristocrats, despite Koran and *Sunna*.[5]

It is quite important for knowledge of the continued survival of the old Arab ideas in the theological development of Islam to look at the position of this question in legal literature which, though not an infallible mirror of the views of those for whom it was written, may yet be instructive concerning their aims and moral level. An example is the theological treatment of the question with which we have been concerned in this chapter. It is well known that Islamic law demands that the *walī*, i.e. guardian of the girl, without whose intervention marriage cannot be contracted, makes sure that the future spouse is 'worthy' (*kufu'*—we cannot yet use the word 'equal') of the girl.[6] The nature of this 'worthiness' was very much disputed in theological circles in the second century[7] and the main point of the argument was whether it included genealogical equality. It is not surprising that the pious Medinian Mālik b. Anas, the father of Islamic jurisprudence, excludes genealogical considerations from the question of worthiness; for him only religious issues are important, and the more pious man is the more worthy. The famous doctrine of Muhammed's farewell
sermon is of course the foremost argument in deciding this question.[8] 131
From the legal point of view one had to provide also for the case in

[1] *Ḥam.*, p. 117, Jaz' b. Kulayb al-Faq'asī, cf. above p. 80, note 5, and below in connection with Haytham b. 'Adī.

[2] Al-Mubarrad, p. 712, 11.

[3] *Fihrist*, p. 99, ult.

[4] Cf. al-Ṭūsī's *List of Shya books*, no. 53.

[5] [Salmān allegedly quoted a prohibition by the Prophet of marriages between *mawālī* and Arab women: al-Jāḥiẓ, *al-'Uthmāniyya*, Cairo 1955, p. 220; al-Haythamī, *Majma' al-Zawā'id*, IV, p. 275. Contrasting attitudes are ascribed to 'Umar: al-Jāḥiẓ, pp. 211, 10; 216, 4; cf. 221, 13-5. Cf also p. 124, note 8.]

[6] Cf. Kremer, *Culturgeschichte*, I, p. 521.

[7] The points of difference are not exactly reproduced in al-Sha'rānī, *Mīzān*, II, p. 125.

[8] Cf. the reproduction of the proof in al-Qasṭallānī, VIII, p. 21.

which a slave (*mukātab* or *'abd*) had a free Arab woman for wife.[1] Such a connection was socially highly objectionable according to old Arab views. But the pious views of the Medinian theologians, with which in this respect the Shī'ites were in agreement,[2] could not prevail as they were in contrast to the prejudices of society, and the Muslim law-givers knew well how to adapt Islam to the demands of society and the needs of the day. The first question which Arab parents addressed to the man asking for the hand of their daughter,[3] or to the man who asked for her on behalf of a friend,[4] remained that of worthiness (*al-kaf'*), and even if worthiness was proved they used to take into consideration special tribal points of view as well.

In the early days of Islam the exclusive spirit of the Jāhiliyya had not changed much in this respect inside Arab society. During the pagan era a father was not sure of his life if he permitted his daughter to marry even a free Arab, if the tribe for some reason considered the connection unworthy.[5] Such prejudices did not cease. The Qurayshite 'Abd Allāh b. Ja'far had to suffer the bitter reproaches of the Umayyad princes because he had given his daughter to the Thaqafite al-Ḥajjāj, though this man was in a highly honoured position; and the Thaqafite was finally forced to divorce his Qurayshite wife.[6] Some Arabs were so proud of their noble maternal and paternal descent that they did not admit that anybody could be worthy of them. This is expressly reported of the poet of the Banū Murra, 'Aqīl b. 'Ullafa (died 100).[7]

The theologians came to terms with these prejudices. We know from a good source what Abū Ḥanīfa thought about this question.
132 Muḥammad b. Ḥasan al-Shaybānī (died 189) a pupil of the 'great Imam' uttered the following doctrine in the latter's name: 'The Qurayshites are equal to one another; (other) Arabs are of equal standing with each other; and of the *mawālī* this is true: those whose grandfather and father were Muslims are equal (to the Arabs) but if they have no bride-price (*mahr*) to offer they are not equal.'[8] Here the

[1] *Al-Muwaṭṭa'*, III, pp. 57, 262.
[2] Al-Ṭabarsī, *Makārim al-Akhlāq* (Cairo 1303), p. 84.
[3] *Agh.*, XIV, p. 151, 4.
[4] Ibid., X, p. 53, gives instructive details of these conditions; cf. also I, p. 153, XIII, p. 34 below, XIV, p. 64, 10 ff.
[5] *Agh.*, XXI, p. 142, 14.
[6] *Al-'Iqd*, I, p. 146, another version, ibid., III, p. 292.
[7] *Agh.*, XI, p. 89, 2.
[8] *Al-Jāmi' al-Ṣaghīr* (Būlāq 1302), marginal edition to *Kitāb al-Kharāj* by the Qāḍī Abū Yūsuf, cf. Brill, *Catalogue périodique*, no. 359, p. 32. The book received its present form, with the division into *abwāb*, at the beginning of the fourth century by the Qāḍī Abū Ṭāhir al-Dabbās in Baghdad (cf. introduction). [Similar maxims are attributed to the Prophet: al-Haythamī, *Majma' al-Zawā'id*, IV, p. 275; al-Suyūṭī, *al-Jāmi' al-Ṣaghīr*, II, p. 68. Cf. also the contrasting opinions in Abū Sulaymān al-Khaṭṭābī, *Ma'ālim al-Sunan*, III, pp. 180–1.]

complete equality of a *mawlā* with the Arabs and of the Arabs with the Qurayshites, which Mālik had required, is discarded even in theory. This teaching was faithfully repeated in the Ḥanafite *madhhab* and was more strictly circumscribed in the derived codices by the direct enunciation of the principle that, in assessing equality, genealogical conditions (*al-nasab*) have to be considered.[1] The Shāfi'ī school also stresses the *nasab* as one of the five points which must be considered when assessing *kafā'a* (worthiness).[2] There is nothing to prevent the assumption that this represents the teaching of al-Shāfi'ī himself. More especially, genealogical equality is much stressed in respect of the women of the Prophet's family and it was the particular task of the *naqīb al-ashrāf* to take care of this.[3] Pious traditionists of course paid no heed to these concessions to Arab racial prejudices and endeavoured to express the true Muslim doctrine. In the third century, al-Bukhārī, by the process usual in his collection of making the objective material of traditions bear out a particular subjective doctrine through tendentious chapter headings,[4] prejudges the question which was in his time probably still much disputed. He thus heads a chapter, the contents of which can hardly be used as an argument for or against the above question, *Bāb: al-akfā' fi'l-dīn*, i.e. 'Chapter: Equals; i.e., in reference to religiousness.'[5] Muslim seems to have avoided the question altogether.[6] In 133
later more advanced days the *kafā'a* question seems to have been considered as wholly antiquated and traces of this are also to be found in belletristic literature.[7]

V

The above facts show us sufficiently the prevailing sentiments of the Arab aristocracy in the first two centuries of Islam. It is not surprising that the scorn and rebuffs by the aristocratic Arabs that daily offended the *mawlā* in private and public life finally resulted in a reaction of the *mawlā* class against this contempt of the worth of its members. In this section we shall see what direction this reaction took.

[1] E.g. *al-Wiqāya*, ed. Kazan 1879, p. 54, commented ed. 1881, p. 125.

[2] *Minhāj al-Ṭālibīn*, ed. Van den Berg, II, p. 332.

[3] Al-Māwardī, ed. Enger, p. 167.

[4] Cf. my *Ẓâhiriten*, p. 103.

[5] B. *Nikāḥ*, no. 15.

[6] Its place would be Muslim, III, p. 365. A proof of how seriously pious Medinians took the doctrine of equality in marriage law, is seen in the fact that Mālik extended the Muslim's right to live married to four women simultaneously also to slaves, whereas other jurists—including Abū Ḥanīfa and al-Shāfi'ī—only allowed two women to slaves, four being the privilege of freemen; *al-Muwaṭṭa'*, III, p. 26. and al-Zurqānī, on this passage.

[7] *Fākihat al-Khulafā'* p. 49. [For the *kafā'a* see also D. Santillana, *Istituzioni di diritto musulmano melichita*, I, pp. 206 ff.]

Many *mawālī* took the easy way out by practising deception to remove the reason for their brusque treatment by the Arabs. They were presumably the most cowardly and mean amongst them. If their foreign non-Arab origin were the cause of rebuffs, fictitious genealogies would remove this obstacle to equality. Since anyhow the *mawālī* had changed their foreign names to ones with an Arab sound[1] when converted to Islam, tribal names, assumed without right, and genealogical lies were now to cause the difference between them and full Arabs to disappear altogether.

134 Not only was it in accordance with the tendency of those who were of the Arab nation to stigmatize this as despicable, but the intended deception also incurred the disapproval of pious circles, the theologians, irrespective of national considerations. Muhammed had already condemned genealogical lies in Koran 33:4[2] and he is said to have accused those who pretended to trace their descent from other than their true father of disbelief, and to have threatened them with exclusion from Paradise.[3] Certainly, however, this condemnation originally referred to one particular type of deception, which was a result of the undisciplined marital conditions in paganism: a child whose father remained unknown because of the mother's freedom in sexual intercourse was allotted to one or other of those who could have been the father, who was then obliged to recognize the child as his.[4] For this adoption the relevant passage in al-Bukhārī uses the

[1] The grandfather of the poet Isḥāq al-Mawṣilī was called Māhān; his son changed this into Maymūn (*Fihrist*, p. 140, 11, *Agh.*, V, p. 1 below). The father of Muhallab b. Abī Ṣufra was originally called Bashāra (Yāqūt, II, p. 387) or Basfarūj (*Fragm. hist. arab*, ed. de Goeje p. 49). Fashrā', *Agh.*, XIII, p. 64, is presumably a mistake; there also the Persian names of this family are to be found. One sees that in such changes of name attention was paid to similarity of sound. An interesting change is that of the name of the Iranian scholar Zarādusht b. Ādharkhar into Muḥammad al-Mutawakkilī (Yāqūt, III, p. 185, probably in honour of the caliph Mutawakkil under whose auspices the learned Persian, to whose oral reports Ḥamza al-Iṣfahānī often refers, was converted).

[2] According to some exegetes, Sūra 68:13 also refers to this; others believe that such connection of the Koranic verses is not reconcilable with the Islamic tendency to take no account of genealogical points; Ibn Durayd, p. 108. In this connection the name given to the intruder is typical: *zanīm* (from *zanama*, pieces of flesh hanging from the ears and necks of sheep and other animals). Shazzāz, a *mawlā* of the Tamīmites is mocked: the red one (see appendix), the *zanīm*; *Agh.*, XIX, p. 163, 19; *'abdun zanīmun la'īmu'l-jaddi min 'ammin wa-khāli*, XIII, p. 53, 12; Marwān al-Aṣghar mocks the poet 'Alī b. al-Jahm: *zanīmu awlādi'l-zina'i*, *Agh.*, XI, p. 4, 11; *muzannam*, *Agh.*, XXI, p. 187, 7. In later language *zanīm* simply means bastard (Dozy s.v.) and is equal to the Hebrew *mamzēr*; in metaphorical usage the word means also a shameless person as is evident from no. 176 of the Responsa of the Ge'ōnīm, ed. Harkavy (Studies and Communications of the Imp. Libr. St Petersburg, IV, p. 72, 23).

[3] B. *Farā'iḍ*, no. 36, cf. *Manāqib*, no. 6.

[4] *Nikāḥ*, no. 36, cf. especially *al-Muwaṭṭa'*, III, pp. 202 ff.

expression *iltāṭa* (*lāṭa* VIII). This word[1] (and the related *nāṭa*, to hang on) is generally used of the reception of a stranger and his complete genealogical assimilation by another tribe, and has usually an overtone of mockery. 'You are a *da'ī* who was tied (*nīṭa*) to the family of Hāshim as a drinking vessel is tied behind the rider.'[2] The comparison with 'a drinking vessel which is hung on' is common in this context[3] 135
just as the 'drinking vessel of the rider' is generally used to denote a matter which is treated as despicable or at least of no importance. This is best illustrated in the saying ascribed to the Prophet: 'Do not treat me like the drinking vessel of the rider (*ka-qadaḥi'l-rākibi*): the rider fills the vessel and then puts it aside and covers it with his luggage. If he needs a drink he drinks from the vessel, if he wants to wash, he washes in it, and if he does not need it at all he empties it; (you must not treat me thus) but mention me at the beginning, the middle and the end of the prayer.'[4] As we have seen this image is a favourite description of unjustified claims to belong to a tribe to which one is really a stranger. This practice must have been common in the pagan era (by way of adoption)[5] as well as in the early days of Islam;[6] otherwise it would hardly have been this very circumstance which was used in the *hijā'*—with or without justification—to injure troublesome opponents.[7] During paganism some people had adopted

[1] *Al-Muwaṭṭa'*, ibid., p. 206 penult., in IV (*yulīṭu*), *Agh.*, XI, p. 171 ult. The mother of the poet Suwayd al-Yashkurī was, before her marriage to Abū Kāhil, married to a Dhubyānī; when he died she was pregnant with Suwayd and her second husband adopted the child (*istalāṭa Abū Kāhil ibnahā*); in an even more general sense in Ibn Hishām, p. 64, 2.

[2] Ḥassān b. Thābit, *Dīwān*, p. 37 penult. [ed. Hirschfeld, 226:7] = *Agh.*, IV, p. 6, 8 (*da'ī Agh.*, = *hajīn*). Similar comparisons using the same expression, (*nīṭa*, *manūṭ*) ibid., p. 83 ult., 97, 5, from below [Hirschf., 228:3; 221:3], *Agh.*, XXI, p. 208, 2. Cf. the word *tanwāṭ* of this root in a variant to *Ḥam.*, p. 249, v. 4. '*Allaqa* is used in the same meaning, e.g. *Agh.*, XII, p. 46, 19.

[3] *Al-sikā' al-mu'allaq*, *Agh.*, VIII, p. 31, 18, used by the poet al-Aḥwaṣ against Kuthayyir (died 105) who, though belonging to the Khuzā'a tribe, wanted above all to be recognised as Qurayshite of the Banū Kināna and submitted to many poetical, but also some real, beatings with this end in view.—In later days Abū Nuwās (in *al-'Iqd*, II, p. 302, 3) made the comparison: 'As the *wāw*, which is without justification added to the word 'Amr(u)'.

[4] Qāḍī 'Iyāḍ, *al-Shifā'* (lith. ed. Constantinople 1295), II, p. 56.

[5] *Tabannā*, B. *Nikāḥ*, no. 15, al-Azraqī, p. 469, 7; it put the adopted on a par with true children in matters of inheritance also.

[6] It is surprising to learn, *Agh.*, XI, p. 80, that it happened with the express approval of 'Umar that Yazīd b. 'Ubayd, who in the Jāhiliyya had become a slave of the Banū Sa'd, incorporated himself and all his family into that tribe and disdained to return to his own.

[7] Several of Ḥassān's satires are very instructive in this respect, especially *Dīwān*, p. 34, 5 [ed. Hirschfeld, 59:3] where Sa'd b. Abī Sarḥ is scorned because 'Abū Sarḥ was impotent and begot no child and now after his death you claim to be his son.' It is known that it was told of al-Walīd b. al-Mughīra that his father declared him to be his son only when he was eighteen years old; a

136 their prisoners of war[1] or their slaves, perhaps because they wished to enhance tribal prestige with an increase of the number (*'adad*) of its sons and members or to gain for the family the property of a wealthy *mawlā* (we have an example of this from the middle of the Umayyad period).[2] For such adoption the verb *istalḥaqa* was used.[3]

By generalizing in a way those sayings ascribed to Muhammed which we have quoted above the theologians represent such corrections of genealogical facts as being sharply condemned by the Prophet himself: 'Doubly cursed is he,' the Prophet is made to say, 'who claims descent from anyone but his rightful father or who insinuates himself into any tribe other than that of his patrons.'[4] Muhammed praises three of his companions[5] because, though not Arabs by descent, they were most faithful followers of his teaching: the Persian Salmān, the Abyssinian Bilāl and the Greek Ṣuhayb b. Sinān. This Ṣuhayb,[6] however, who came to Mecca as a slave, traced his descent back to the Arab Namir b. Qāsiṭ, and when he was reproached by 'Umar
137 invented a convenient hypothesis to justify his genealogical claim.[7]

[1] Cf. the example of Shanfarā, *Agh.*, XXI, p. 134.

[2] *Agh.*, I, p. 134, 11 ff., the example of the poet Nuṣayb (died 108) whom his patrons want to adopt for such purposes; but the poet, realizing the intention, does not consent. The above-mentioned consideration that the *'adad* of the family should be increased, explains the frequent legal cases about the inheritance of the *walā'*, as seen from examples in *Muwaṭṭa'*, III, p. 263.

[3] *Agh.*, I, p. 7 ult., 8, 4.

[4] Al-Mubarrad, p. 10, cf. B. *Jizya*, no. 10 *man tawallā ghayr mawālīhī*. [Cf. al-Haythamī, *Majma' al-Zawā'id*, IV, p. 232; *Kanz al-'Ummāl*, X, nos. 1563–8, and also VI, nos. 725–31, 734–46.]

[5] Cf. also Muslim, V, p. 209, B. *Buyū'*, no. 100.

[6] This name was presumably given him in view of his descent (name taken from colour, see appendix to this volume). Cf. *ṣuhb al-sibāl* in the dictionaries s.v. and a verse of Dhu'l-Rumma in Ibn-al-Sikkīt, p. 165 [ed. Cheikho, p. 198; *Dīwān*, 23:22], cf. Kremer, *Culturgeschichte*, II, p. 155. The beards of the Persians seem to have given the Arabs many opportunities for mockery; in the 'Antar romance, from whose Persians episodes a whole anthology of derisive names for Persians could be made, they are among other things ridiculed, as 'broad-beard with tufted moustache' (*'arīḍ al-dhaqn mantūf al-sibāl; 'Ant.*, V, p. 134, 3). This last name (cf. *madhlūl al-sibāl*, XVII, p. 110, 11) is presumably the opposite of *maftūl al-sibāl*, describing the Arab hero (XI, p. 25, 3); cf. Landberg, *Proverbes et dictons*, I, p. 258. The shaven beard of Persian fire priests is derided in *Ḥam.*, p. 820, v. 3. (Cf. 'Long beard' as a scornful form of address, Ṭab., III, p. 1310, 15; while *aḥaṣṣ al-liḥyati* ('with sparse beard') is the shameful name with which an anonymous poet insults the Banu'l-Hujaym of the Tamīm tribe; *Agh.*, XVIII, p. 170, 20. It is also found, however, that the hero must have a long beard, *Agh.*, XVII, p. 90, 4.)

[7] Al-Mubarrad, p. 366. [Cf. Ibn Sa'd, III/1, p. 162; Ibn 'Asākir, VI, p. 453; Ibn Ḥajar, *Iṣāba*, III, p. 255.]

---

passage of the Koran is referred to this (al-Bayḍāwī, II, p. 348, 4). Ḥassān's satirical verses pp. 94-95 [Hirschf., nos. 173-4, 181, 183] against Ibn al-Ziba'rī put this event into its proper place and should be read in this context.

The true Arabs were only being faithful to their traditional views[1] in indignantly repudiating such genealogical pretensions. Theology[2] and tribal pride—otherwise heterogenous and opposing forces—were united in their disapproval of lies which seemed despicable to either. To those who taught that descent was irrelevant the endeavour to think up untrue descents for wordly reasons must have been doubly reprehensible.

The Arabs called a person who falsely claimed descent other than the true one *da'ī*, i.e. 'usurper, intruder'; this was a shameful thing to be,[3] and the epithet was a sure form of insult.[4] But it seems that the ambitious *mawālī* incurred this opprobrium even where their status was connected with circumstances that were honourable from the Islamic point of view. The family of Abū Bakra in Baṣra, who were among the first Muslim settlers at that place and participated largely
in its founding,[5] did not scruple to claim a fictitious genealogy though 138
their ancestor had been a client of the Prophet himself. A poet from Baṣra ridicules this vain undertaking in the following epigram:

> Family of Abū Bakra, awake! Sunlight is not eclipsed by the light of a little lamp;
> Verily clientship with the Prophet is a nobler connection than is descent from the Banū 'Ilāj.[6]

[1] Al-Nābigha, 24:2, and also 212, 5.

[2] The introduction of Ziyād b. Abīhi, the fanatical enemy of the 'Alids, into the tribe of Abū Sufyān gave the pious Muslims a special opportunity to be indignant with such falsifications; al-Ya'qūbī, II, p. 295. It was the target for ridicule and disapproval also for non-religious reasons, *Agh.*, XVII, p. 57.

[3] *Ḥam.*, p. 652, v. 1. This point is utilized by Arab satirical poetry, cf. p. 671, v. 4. An example is the satirical poem of Farazdaq against Ayyūb al-Ḍabbī, who was said to have been really a Zinjī and insinuated himself into the tribe of Ḍabba, *Agh.*, XIX, p. 24. In the competition of the two rival poets, Ibn Qanbar and Muslim b. al-Walīd (in Hārūn al-Rashīd's time), the latter, who called himself a descendant of the Anṣār, is told: *yā da'ī al-Ansār* (*Agh.*, XIII, p. 9).

[4] An original example is the insult of Mūsā b. al-Wajīh against Yazīd b. al-Muhallab, governor of Khūrāsān (see above p. 126, note 1) who had scolded him for pretending to be a Ḥimyarite with *yā da'ī* and the reply was 'O son of a woman from Marw, whose geneological lies are more obvious than yours? Are you not the *mawlā* of 'Uthmān b. al-'Āṣ al-Thaqafī? Was not your grandfather a Magian named Basfarūj, which you made into Abū Ṣufra?', *Fragm. hist.arab.*, p. 49. A combination of this insult is: *da'ī ad'iyā'* i.e. someone who lies himself into a tribe which itself claims a fictitious genealogy and is therefore *da'ī* itself. Thus the poet Ibn Harma is ridiculed for having unjustly related himself to the Khulj whose genealogy was not certain (cf. Robertson Smith, p. 16); *Agh.*, IV, p. 102, Ibn Durayd, p. 244.

[5] Ibn al-Faqīh, p. 188.

[6] Ibn Durayd, p. 186. There are presumably valuable data on this in the first part of the *Kitāb Ansāb al-Ashrāf* by al-Balādhurī, of which Ch. Schefer of Paris has a MS.; cf. De Goeje's account of its contents in *ZDMG*, XXXVIII,

In assessing these conditions no account should be taken of cases where genealogical lies were dictated not by vain ambition but by the need to survive, as for example in the case of the Khārijite 'Imrān b. Ḥiṭṭān, who had to flee from a'l-Ḥajjāj's anger like a hunted animal and changed his tribal alliance in self-defence. 'To-day I am Yemenite,' he said of himself; 'when I meet a Yemenite; and if I meet a Ma'addite I am of the tribe of 'Adnān.'[1]

The Khārijite confession is the one which did the most to encourage emancipation from rigid tribal affiliations. Thus it is particularly valuable to become acquainted with the relevant sayings of the Khārijite poet and martyr before we begin our description of the Shu'ūbiyya. No Muslim party was more predisposed to take seriously the Islamic teaching of the equality of races and tribes in Islam[2] than the Khārijites, who thought Nabataeans and Abyssinian slaves just as well suited as the proud Qurayshites to gain the leadership of the Islamic community in free elections by the people. Amongst the many divisions of the freely developing Khārijism there was a party whose founder, Yazīd b. Unaysa, carried the equality of 'Arab and 'Ajam so far as to proclaim the doctrine that God would send another prophet from amongst the 'Ajam, together with a book of divine
139 revelation which is already extant in heaven and which would abrogate the religion of Muhammed.[3] In the context of these convictions, the words of the poet of this party who replied to those who asked him whether he belonged to Rabī'a and Muḍar or to the Banū Qaḥṭān, 'We are the sons of Islam, and God is one, and the best servant of God is he who is grateful to him.'[4] are a clear echo of the Prophet's teaching during his farewell pilgrimage. The despised *mawālī* did in fact gladly join this party, which best guaranteed their human rights.[5] Already under Mu'āwiya I there was a Khārijite rebellion of *mawālī* led by a certain Abū 'Alī from Kūfa who was a *mawlā* of the Banū Ḥārith. 'We have,' said the rebels, 'heard a wonderful Koran which guides on the right path; we have accepted

[1] Al-Mubarrad, p. 532, 13. He says in another poem, p. 533, 6: 'He does not cease to question me to gain knowledge, about me but men are either deceived or deceivers.'

[2] Al-Shahrastānī, p. 101, below.

[3] This did not prevent people who had not understood this point in the Khārijite teaching remaining faithful to Arab prejudices. The poet al-Ṭirimmāḥ was a Khārijite, and yet we find him a fanatical Yemenite partisan, *Agh.*, XV, p. 113, 6 from below.

[4] *Agh.*, XVI, p. 154, 6 from below, cf. Dozy [*Histoire des Musulmans d'Espagne*, I, p. 142; German transl.:] *Gesch.d. Mauren in Sp.*, I, p. 89.

[5] Kremer, *Culturgesch. d. Orients*, II, p. 157.

p. 389. The caliph al-Mahdī officially restored the proper affiliation of this family by proclaiming them again as *mawālī* of the Prophet's house, *al-Fakhri*, p. 214.

its teaching and have added no companion to God. This God has sent the Prophet to all mankind and has not withheld him from anyone.'[1] This is presumably the earliest attempt of the foreign element to reject, even if only cautiously, the doctrine of Arab superiority. This viewpoint also explains how it could happen that even old historians of Islam made the representatives of the Shu'ūbiyya into Khārijites;[2] we shall return to this when treating of Abū 'Ubayda in the last chapter.

But it was only much later that the prevailing trend allowed the old Arab tribal barriers to be pierced. In particular al-Ḥajjāj, a fanatical enemy of the *mawālī*, seems to have taken the sayings directed against the intruders seriously. For example, he threatened Ḥimrān b. Abān (in Baṣra), a prisoner of war from 'Ayn al-Tamr who had been freed by 'Uthmān and who attempted to pass as an Arab of the Namir tribe, with death if he did not admit his true descent and desist from his attempts at insinuating himself among 140
the Arabs.[3] There were presumably many such examples, which did not, however, prevent constant and determined attempts at intrusion by descendants of the non-Arabs in the various provinces of Islam.[4] This is proof that the harshness and brutality with which men like al-Ḥajjāj punished such deceptions did not last long and were an exception to the general rule. We find the *da'īs* in the highest political positions; it is sufficient to mention Muhallab b. Abī Sufra and his son.[5]

It was not difficult for Arabs of doubtful genealogy to correct their pedigree, particularly at the beginning of the 'Abbāsid period. Abū Nukhayla, a light-hearted poet of doubtful descent (*mashkūk fī nasabihi*)—the story of his being driven from home by his parents was presumably only invented to conceal his true origin—built himself a house in the area of the Banū Ḥimmān avowedly in order *an yuṣaḥḥiḥa nasabahu*, i.e., to correct his genealogy and gain the right to call himself al-Ḥimmānī. The elders of the tribe supported him in this undertaking.[6] Nobody appears to have objected to al-Ghiṭrīf b. 'Aṭā', brother of the slave-girl Khayzurān, who became the wife of the caliph al-Mahdī and gave birth to Hārūn al-Rashīd, passing as a member of the Arab tribe of the Banū Ḥārith b. Ka'b,[7]

[1] Al-Ya'qūbī, II, p. 262; cf. Ibn al-Athīr, III, p. 179.

[2] Cf. Brünnow, *Die Charidschiten unter den ersten Omajjaden* (Leiden 1884), p. 31, note 4.

[3] Al-Balādhurī, p. 368, cf. Yāqūt, III, p. 597.

[4] A typical example from Andalusia in Ibn Bashkuwāl, ed. Codera, no. 771, p. 357.

[5] See above p. 126, note 1.

[6] *Agh.*, XVIII, p. 145.

[7] Yāqūt, III, p. 489, 12.

despite his obvious foreign descent.[1] He was sufficiently respected (he became governor of Yemen and Khurāsān) to dare to do this. But less important people than this brother-in-law of the caliph al-Mahdī and uncle of Hārūn could also make such attempts. A *dihqān* from Kūfa, in the reign of Hārūn, undertook a long journey when he felt that he had become rich enough to equal the Arab aristocrats. On his return he introduced himself to society as a descendant of the Banū Tamīm: 'He goes to bed as *mawlā*,'—taunted his former friend, the poet 'Alī b. Khalīl, 'and awakens claiming to be an Arab.'[2] Or as another poet puts it:

> To-day you are descended from Hāshim, bravo! and to-morrow you are *mawlā* and the day after you are a confederate of an Arab tribe.
> If this is true you are all mankind, o Hāshimī, o *mawlā*, O Arab.[3]

141 In earlier, stricter times the *mawlā* relationship was disciplined by a rigorous customary law; it was hard for a client of a tribe to change his patron. But even in early times it appears to have been possible by formal buying to withdraw a *mawlā* from the clientship of his original patron and to incorporate him into another clientship.[4] Against such attempts the traditional decree *al-walā' li-man a'taqa* was directed, i.e., as client a man is subordinate to the person who has freed the former slave.[5] Later it was not particularly difficult to become the *mawlā* of a different tribe wherever and as often as one wished. The example of the poet Abu'l-'Atāhiya shows how people could join different tribes as *mawlā* at any moment.[6] The caliph al-Mutawakkil even decreed that a favourite of his court who belonged to the Banū Azd should renounce this relationship and become *mawlā* of the caliph.[7] This would have been impossible in the good old days of Arab tribal strictness.

What was possible in this respect is seen from the example of the poet Ibn Munādir (beginning of the 'Abbāsid period), a true *mawlā* who, despite his frivolity and unchastity, succeeded in becoming an authority in the field of *ḥadīth* philology. Even the famous authority on tradition, Sufyān b. 'Uyayna, consulted him about linguistic difficulties in traditions which nobody could so easily unravel as this

[1] Al-Ya'qūbī, II, p. 481.
[2] *Agh.*, XIII, p. 18.
[3] *Al-'Iqd*, III, p. 301.
[4] *Agh.*, I, p. 129, 17, indicates this.
[5] B. *Shurūṭ*, no. 13.
[6] *Agh.*, III, p. 141.
[7] Al-Ya'qūbī, II, p. 597

mawlā of Sulaymān b. Qahramān. This patron of Ibn Munādir had himself originally been the *mawlā* of Ubayd Allāh (governor of Sijistān under al-Ḥajjāj) a son of Abū Bakra, of whom we have just heard (p. 129) that though originally a slave of the tribe of Thaqīf, he was a freed-man of the Prophet. 'Ubayd Allāh now tried to pass himself off as a full-blooded Thaqafī. Sulaymān insinuated himself into the tribe of Tamīm, and Ibn Munādir told people that he was of the tribe of Sulaym. 'Thus,' says our source, 'Ibn Munādir is the *mawlā* of the *mawlā* of a *mawlā* and at the same time a *da'ī*, client of a *da'ī*. This has never been repeated in history.'[1] This fact is sufficient to show 142
the indifferent leniency with which these conditions, previously so much more strictly judged, were treated in 'Abbāsid times. In the course of time such conditions became more and more common,[2] though they did not escape the strong criticism of genealogists and the scorn of satirists.

It was not only barbarian revolutionaries and rebels who assumed Arab genealogies in order to make dynastic claims;[3] courtiers of the caliph also indulged undisturbed in the flourishing business of genealogical falsifications. Amongst the viziers of the caliph al-Mu'tamid there was the Persian Ismā'īl b. Bulbul, who, during the reign of this prince, wielded much influence in state affairs, hardly anybody in higher circles taking it amiss that he was a *da'ī*, trying everything in his power to pass as descendant of the Banu Shaybān. In speech and writing he indulged in the most choice linguistic finesses in order to pass more easily as a full Arab.[4] It took a mocker like Ibn Bassām (died 303), who made epigrams even against his own father, to touch satirically upon the genealogy of this pseudo-Shaybānite vizier.[5] On the other hand there were some panegyrists who made the assumed descent of the intruder the subject of servile praise: 'They say: Abu'l-Ṣaqr (this was the by-name of Ibn Bulbul) boasts that he is descended from the Shaybān; I told them: By no means, Shaybān boasts of him. Many a father was elevated in nobility

[1] Al-Jāḥiẓ in *Agh.*, XVII, p. 9. It also happened that two brothers of the same family quarrelled about the claim to Arab tribal affiliation, one brother denouncing the intrusion of the other, who wanted to deny his foreign descent at all costs; *Agh.*, XX, p. 67 (Ḥasan b. Wahb (died 250) and his brother Sulaymān b.W.).

[2] An example *Agh.*, XVII, p. 84, 11.

[3] The most remarkable example of this is that of the rebel 'Alī Ṣāḥib al-Zinj with his 'Alid genealogy. He called himself 'Alī b. Muḥammad b. Aḥmad etc. b. al-Ḥusayn b. 'Alī b. Abī Ṭālib. According to Abū Bakr al-Ṣūlī this rebel simply copied the genealogy of another man; the Muḥammad b. Aḥmad with whom the list of his ancestors began was a contemporary only three years older than himself; al-Ḥuṣrī, I, p. 259.

[4] Ibn al-Mu'tazz, ed. Lang, *ZDMG*, XL, p. 572, v. 131.

[5] Al-Mas'ūdī, VIII, p. 259, 3, cf. p. 108, 2 and al-Ḥuṣrī, I, pp. 245 ff.

by his son who descended from him.'[1] Only the descendants of the families of the old Persian immigrants into southern Arabia appear to have prided themselves on the consciousness of their Persian descent and to have aimed at no assimilation with the Arabs. As late
143 as the third century these families are still distinguished as Abnā'.[2] But they participated eagerly in the intellectual life of the Arabs and produced many an excellent Arabic poet[3] and famous Islamic theologian.[4]

VI

What we have considered so far have merely been the clever manoeuvres of individual importance. But we see the methods through which these ambitious Persians tried to enhance their own personal value, being employed in the course of Islamic history by whole peoples and races. Peoples who were brought under Arab rule and who wished to have a part in the preferential position of the Arabs before all other races in the Islamic world easily invented Arab genealogies for themselves. This for instance was done by the Kurds, for whom it was comparatively easy because, like the Arab Bedouins, they were nomads.[5] A Berber group in North Africa named Barr b. Qays as their ancestor, taking no account even of the fact that this Qays whom they claimed as tribal ancestor died without children.[6] Ibn Khaldūn dealt exhaustively with these genealogical fables of the Berber tribes[7] and from the various versions of these one can recognise the endeavours of the genealogists to give this self-confident people, who strove against the Arabs to an unusual degree, an equal place inside Islam. The author of the history of the Almoravids, Almohads and Almerinids mentions in the introduction to the last part of his work the legends about the Arab descent of the Berbers, and the emigration of their ancestors from Arab lands; and he also cites verses invented to strengthen these fables.[8]

144 The negro peoples who had accepted Islam also connected themselves genealogically with the Arab people. The traditions of the Bornu represent their pre-Islamic rulers as being descended from south

[1] *Al-Fakhrī*, p. 299. For such turns of the Arabic language (*taftakhiru bihi'l-ansābu*) cf. al-Āmidī, *Muwāzana*, p. 140.

[2] *Jazīrat al-'Arab*, pp. 55, 13; 88, 13: 104, 2; 114, 15. It is interesting that the racial conscience and national tendency of these Persians was so active that they falsified the Radā'ī *qaṣīda* in favour of Persian national bias (ibid., 234, 10), though this *qaṣīda* speaks well of the Persians in any case (241, 7-8).

[3] Ibid., p. 57, 17.

[4] See above, p. 108.

[5] Al-Mas'ūdī, III, pp. 253 f.

[6] Al-Balādhurī, p. 225.

[7] *Histoire des Berbères*, ed. De Slane, I, pp. 107 ff. On the motives which made the Berbers claim relationship with the Arabs, Ibn Khaldūn has some pertinent remarks, l.c. II, p. 4, transln., vol. III, p. 184.

[8] *Annales regum Mauritaniae*, ed. Tornberg, I, pp. 184-6.

Arabian heroes; the Muslim dynasty traces descent from 'Uthmān; and also the Fula negroes claim Arab descent.[1] Popular legend and etymology show real orgies of invention in giving effect to this aspiration which is so widespread among the lowest nations in Islam.

We find tendencies with a similar aim also amongst the Persians. And this leads us to the discussion of another manifestation of the reaction of the non-Arab elements against Arab arrogance. The Persians retained great pride in their glorious past long after they were conquered, and guarded zealously the traditions of this past, so that they would not, and could not, give up such traditions by deliberately wiping out their glorious memories. When individual Persians proved untrue to their descent and, despite Arab protest, insinuated themselves into Arab tribes by means of clumsy fables, it was only the frivolity of individuals who were concerned in these more or less successful undertakings, and the descent of the whole Persian people was never involved. But it was not only individual *mawālī* who were scorned; the arrogance of the Arabs affected the whole nation. To the desire to bring the Persian nation closer to Arab descent is due the exploitation of those legends which claim that the Persians descended from Isaac[2], the brother of Ismā'īl, whom the Arabs called their ancestor. This assertion is without doubt the invention of the systematic genealogists[3] who liked to embroider their science with biblical touches, but no one was more glad of it than were the Muslims of Persian descent. Whereas on the one hand it showed that the Persians were brothers of the Arabs and as such could claim full equality with them, it contained on the other hand some indication that in a sense they were above them because their ancestor was the child of a free born mother, whereas the ancestor of the Arabs was the son of a slave woman.[4] The ancestor of the Arabs, **145**
Ishmael, is thus confronted with Isaac[5] as the ancestor of the Persians or the non-Arabs in general; [6]hence comes an increased tendency to

[1] G. A. Krause, in *Ausland*, 1883, p. 183.

[2] From a son of Isaac called Nafīs, in particular, many Persian lineages are descended, Ibn al-Faqīh, p. 197, 5.

[3] The poet Jarīr (died 110) can use it already as a well-known theory; Yāqūt, II, p. 862, 21 ff., *Agh.*, VII, p. 65 from below, where *sādatin* must be corrected to *sārata*. [*Dīwān*, ed. al-Sawi, p. 242, 10 ff].

[4] But Arab fanaticism represented them as being descended from Lot; Ibn Badrūn, p. 8.

[5] It is noteworthy that in the *Kitāb al-'Ayn* (cited by al-Nawawī, commentary to Muslim, I, p. 164) and also in the *Sunan* of Nasā'ī (commented ed. of Dimnatī, Cairo 1299, p. 19) a son of Abraham called Farrūkh is mentioned, who is said to be the Abu'l-'Ajam (patriarch of non-Arabs). For the sons of this patriarch see al-Bayḍāwī, I, p. 85, 24.

[6] The Greeks, too, are said to be descended from him [al-Mas'ūdī, *Murūj*, II, p. 244=]; Ibn Badrūn, p. 470. 'Al-Ismā'īliyya wa'l-Isḥāqiyya' (Ishmaelites and Isaacites) means 'Arabs and non-Arabs'; *al-'Iqd*, II, p. 91, 13.

make Isaac feature more prominently in ancient history.[1] Not Ismā'īl, as the Arabs claim,[2] but Isaac, as the Bible teaches, is said to have been the son of Abraham whom the obedient patriarch was willing to slaughter on Allāh's demand. (*al-dhabīḥ*).[3] The legend of the spring of Zamzam in Mecca was approached with similar intent. Long before accepting Islam the Persians whose Abrahamite descent is stressed also on this occasion[4], claim to have made pilgrimages to this holy spring in honour of Abraham, and they have continued this pious custom to the time of Sāsān b. Bābak.[5] Such legends[6] were not put about by the Arabs in order to claim an international past for the Zamzam fable,[7] but owe their existence to the reaction of non-Arab elements in Islam.

It is true that the theologians who, as we have previously observed, furthered as much as they could the teaching of the equality of all nations within Islam gladly accepted such legends. In a late tradition
146 they represent the Prophet himself as saying that the people of Fāris are members of the prophetic family and pointing to the relationship of Ismā'īl to Isḥāq.[8] Nevertheless this genealogical fable is not of Arab origin, but was put about by the reaction of the non-Arab elements in Islam. In particular it was advanced by the circle who in Islamic history represented the strongest and most self-confident reaction of Iran against the contempt of the exponents of the old Arab views: this is the party of the *ahl al-taswiya*, i.e. the confessors of equality (of nationalities), or al-Shu'ūbiyya, as it is usually called. In the next chapter we shall deal with the nature of this party, its aims and literary manifestations.

[1] How far this was taken is best shown by the fact that even those Persians who were not converted to Islam connected their religion to Abraham in order to impress the Muslims amongst whom they lived, Chwolsohn, *Ssabier*, I, p. 646.

[2] In Arab circles people became so accustomed to replacing Isaac with Ismā'īl that, in a Muslim paraphrase of Genes. 28: 13 ascribed to Wahb b. Munnabih, the ancestors of Jacob are called 'Isḥāq and Ismā'īl', Ibn al-Faqīh, p. 97, 20.

[3] On this disputed question, cf. also the references given by me in *ZDMG*, XXXII, p. 359, note 5. For the sake of completeness I refer also to the following additional passages: al-Mas'ūdī, VI, p. 425, Quṭb al-Dīn, *Gesch. d. Stadt Mekka*, p. 370, Fakhr al-Dīn al-Rāzī, *Mafātīḥ*, VII, pp. 155 f., al-Maqqarī, I, 487, 7, Ibn Khallikān, no. 747 (VIII, p. 148, 5).

[4] Al-Mas'ūdī, II, pp. 148 f., [idem, *Kitāb al-Tanbīh*, p. 109,] al-Qazwīnī, I. p. 199.

[5] Yāqūt, II, p. 941.

[6] Ibn al-Athīr, ed. Būlāq, [ed. Tornberg, I, p. 47] I, p. 26, fights these 'hallucinations of the Persians' (*khurtāfā al-'Ajam*) as he calls them.

[7] Thus Dozy, *De Israeliten te Mekka*, p. 150.

[8] Al-Ṣiddīqī, fol. 38 b.

CHAPTER FOUR 147

THE SHUʿŪBIYYA

THE party of the Shuʿūbiyya shows in the very name which it probably gave itself (whereas the description 'Confessors of equality' was presumably bestowed by its opponents), what it considered as the centre of its party platform and where it placed the weight of its opposition to others. This name goes back to the Koranic verse which teaches the equality of all men within Islam (see above p. 155) and is derived from the Arabic word which in this passage is used for 'peoples': *shuʿūb*.[1] We are thus dealing with a party which, in the name of the Koran and of the *Sunna* founded on its teachings, seriously demanded the equality of non-Arabs with Arabs within Islam, and which in the literary field (because the Shuʿūbiyya party is a group of authors and scholars and not of dissatisfied people and rebellious mobs) furthered an agitation to establish their own teaching and oppose contrary opinion.[2] This party, the zenith of whose power we might put in the second and third century A.H. (we shall see that polemic against it reached its peak in the third century) represented in its most modest expression the teaching of the full equality of the ʿAjam with the Arabs, and in more daring formulations attempted even to assert Arab inferiority in the face of Persian superiority. The favour which outstanding Persian families enjoyed at the ʿAbbāsid court, and the great influence which they had in the government of Islam, encouraged the Persians and their friends to
express openly their long-suppressed resentment of Arab racial arro- 148
gance; and the free language that they used was possibly encouraged by the example of the caliphs themselves. A good observer characterized (and he was probably not the first to do so) the relation of the Umayyad and ʿAbbāsid dynasties by calling the first an Arab and the latter an ʿAjamī or Khurāsānian empire.[3] In a sense the

[1] According to some philologists *shuʿūb* is used in respect of non-Arabs only and in this context is the same as *qabā'il* (tribes) which is only used of Arabs. According to another view *shiʿb* (sing. of *shuʿūb*) is a wider generic word, whereas *qabīla* is of narrower meaning: a *shiʿb* contains several *qabā'il*; *al-ʿIqd*, II, p. 55.

[2] [Cf. H. A. R. Gibb, *Studies on the Civilization of Islam*, pp. 62–73: *'The Social Significance of the Shuʿūbiyya'*.]

[3] Al-Jāḥiẓ, *Kitāb al-Bayān*, fol. 156a [III, p. 366].

situation created by the fall of the Umayyad rule in respect of influence and the position of the various nationalities, is correctly described in the last words of a warning poem which later historians make Naṣr b. Sayyār, the Khurāsānian governor of the last Umayyad ruler Marwān II, address to the latter: 'Flee from your dwelling-place and say'—so someone is enjoined—: 'Farewell Arabs and Islam.'[1]

Islam, however, was by no means at an end, but the Arabs had to take many a rebuff during the time which followed. Under the caliph Abū Ja'far al-Manṣūr we already witness the spectacle of an Arab vainly waiting for admission at the gates of the caliph's palace, whereas the Khurāsānīs freely enter and ridicule the raw Arab.[2]

Amongst the many viziers at the height of 'Abbāsid rule there is hardly one of Arab descent, most of them being *mawālī* and Persians, and yet there are but few indications that such conditions were considered unnatural. The sentiment which prevailed in this group in respect of Arab glory is evident from the disgust of a vizier when the poet Abū Tammām (died 231) compared the caliph with Ḥātim Ṭayyi', Aḥnaf, and Iyās, who were the pride of the Arab race: 'You compare the Commander of the Faithful to these Arab barbarians?'[3] Amongst the statesmen of the empire there are people of obscure descent like Rabī' b. Yūnus, the vizier of the second 'Abbāsid caliph al-Manṣūr who was descended from a certain Kaysān, the client of 'Uthmān, but according to other reports was a foundling.[4] This
149 example shows how at this time the idea accepted by Arab society of seeing only people of blameless and noble Arab descent at the head of the state had been completely pushed into the background, whereas in older days the mere fact that the female ancestor of a man had been a *laqīṭa* i.e. a foundling of unknown descent, had been considered shameful.[5]

The caliph al-Ma'mūn did not conceal the fact that he valued the Persian race higher than the Arab race, and when an Arab reproached him for favouring the inhabitants of Khurāsān above the Arabs from Syria, the caliph characterized the Arabs thus:[6] 'I have never bidden a Qays descend from his horse but he ate up all my treasure to the last dirham; the southern Arabs (Yemen) I do not

[1] Al-Mas'ūdī, III, p. 62.

[2] *Agh.*, XVIII, p. 148, 16 ff.

[3] Ibn Khallikān, no. 146, II p. 74. It is typical that Abū Nuwās openly prefers Persian ways to the unrefined Bedouin life, which he despises. See the passages in Nöldeke's essay on this poet in *Orient und Occident*, I, p. 367. Also, Abu'l-'Alā' calls the Bedouins *ṭā'ifa waḥshiyya*, *Siqṭ al-Zand*, II, p. 140, v. 3. cf. I, p. 123, vv. 2–3.

[4] *Al-Fakhrī*, p. 208. [Cf. D. Sourdel, *Le Vizirat 'abbāside*, p. 88.]

[5] Al-Tabrīzī to *Ḥam.*, p. 4, 8; Ḥassān, *Dīwān*, p. 29 penult. [ed. Hirschfeld, 137:1] *awlād al-laqīṭa*, cf. from later days *Agh.*, XVIII, p. 178, 4.

[6] Ṭab., III, 1142.

love and they love me not; the Quḍā'a Arabs await the arrival of the Sufyānī[1] in order to join him; the Rabī'a Arabs are angry with God that he chose his Prophet from the Muḍar tribe, and there are no two amongst them but one is a rebel.' The preference for Persians was a tradition of the 'Abbāsid house,[2] and I conjecture that it is the purpose of a very odd tradition of al-Bukhārī to express a conviction of the damaging consequences of this trend. Those who are acquainted with the style of the Islamic traditions and who are not blinded by the wonderful *isnād* will easily understand the general intention of theologians of the beginning of the third century, when they made 'Umar, after being struck by the dagger of the Persian Abū Lu'lu'a, say just to 'Abd Allāh, son of al-'Abbās, who was the ancestor of the 'Abbāsid dynasty: 'Praise be to Allāh who did not let me die through a man confessing Islam. You and your father ('Abbās) would have been delighted if al-Madīna had been full of Barbarians (*'ulūj*); al-'Abbās had the largest number of foreign slaves in the town.'[3] This fiction is nothing but a criticism of the conditions under that dynasty, linked with the dynasty's founder.

Under the 'Abbāsids a certain religious romanticism ventured to 150
the surface in Persian families, who openly strove for the restoration of Persian religious customs. The appearance of the *zindīq* trend which Kremer described in detail in this context is a clear proof of this fact.

The history of the Muslim wars in Central Asia, particularly under the rule of al-Ma'mūn's successor al-Mu'taṣim, reveals instructive facts about the defiant reaction of the 'Ajam element against Islam in the third century of its rule. None of the figures prominent in this history, however, shows more clearly than Afshīn—otherwise known as Khaydhar b. Kāwūs—the superficial penetration of Islam in the educated non-Arab circles. This general of al-Mu'taṣim, who came from Sogdiana and who had suppressed the revolution of Bābak, so dangerous for Islam, who had led the caliph's troops in the fight against the Christians, and who thus played a prominent role in several of the religious wars of Islam, was so little a Muslim that he cruelly maltreated two propagandists of Islam who wished to transform a pagan temple into a mosque; he ridiculed Islamic laws and—as a compatriot who was converted to Islam witnessed against him—ate meat of strangled animals (a horror to Muslims), and also induced others to do so by saying that such meat was fresher

[1] The Mahdī of the followers of the Umayyad dynasty; cf. Snouck Hurgronje, *Der Mahdi*, p. 11. [= *Verspreide Geschriften*, I, p. 155; cf. also Goldziher, *Streitschrift des Ġazālī gegen die Bāṭinijja-Sekte*, p. 52; and D. B. Macdonald's paragraph on the Sufyānī in his article 'al-Mahdī' in the *Enc. of Islam*.]

[2] Cf. Kremer, *Culturgeschichtliche Streifzüge*, p. 31, note 1.

[3] B. *Faḍā'il al-Aṣḥāb*, no. 8.

than that of animals killed according to the Islamic rite. He used to kill a black sheep every Wednesday by cutting it in half and would then walk between the two parts. He ridiculed circumcision and other Muslim customs, and paid no attention to them. He did not cease, even as a Muslim, to read the religious books of his nation, and kept splendid copies of them, ornamented with gold and jewels, and, while he helped the caliph in his campaigns aginst the enemies of the Muslim state, he dreamed of the restoration of the Persian empire and the 'white religion', and mocked Arabs, Maghribines, and Muslim Turks. The first he called dogs to whom one throws bones in order then to beat their heads black and blue with a stick.[1]

This may well be an example of the sentiment of those pre-eminent non-Arabs who for material advantages joined the Muslim power,
151 wishing to participate in its victories, but in truth gnashed their teeth at the destroyers of their national independence and the traditions of their ancestors. The influence of foreign elements in Islam grew from caliph to caliph[2] until it led to the decay of the caliphs' state. The advancement of the foreign elements was of course accompanied by a decline of the Arabs.

Since the rule of the caliph al-Mutawakkil, who became a victim of the intrigues of his Turkish camarilla, the influence of the Turks[3] had become decisive for the government of Baghdad. The most important offices in the court, the administration, and the army fell to them, though they were ignorant even of the Arabic language.[4] Turkish generals were sent to calm the restive Arabs of the Arabian peninsula and bring them to obedience, and the history of these days tells of the cruelties which they inflicted on the Arabs and 'Alid pretenders. Their palace intrigues decided the politics of the court. Under al-Musta'īn things had gone so far that the caliph gave two Turkish court officials 'a free hand in respect of the state treasury, and permitted them to do what they liked with state money'; and when the caliph was informed of the discovery of an intrigue by the Turkish clique against his life he could tell their leaders that they were ungrateful, since he had had his silver and gold plate melted down and had limited his own pleasures in order to make larger provision for them and gain their satisfaction.'[5]

Arabic circles must have felt very bitter about this preponderance

[1] Ṭab., III, pp. 1309-1313, *Fragm. hist. arab*, ed. de Goeje, pp. 405-6.

[2] The conditions under al-Wāthiq are reflected in an anonymous poem of that time, *Agh.*, XXI, p. 254.

[3] The caliph al-Muhtadī (died 256 after less than a year's reign) intended to give more influence to the Persians than to the Turks (al-Ya'qūbī, II, p. 618). On the influence of Turks, see also the data in Karabacek, *Mitheilungen aus der Sammlung Papyr. Rainer*, I, pp. 95 ff.

[4] Cf. al-Mas'ūdī, VII, p. 363, 2.

[5] Ṭab., III, pp. 1512, 1544.

of foreign influence. We may take as a symptom of this feeling a song which was much applauded at the court of caliph al-Muntaṣir (247-48):

O mistress of the house in al-Burk—o mistress of rule and power,
Fear God and kill us not, we are neither Daylam nor Turks.[1]

The conditions of the caliphate at the time of the unhappy al- 152
Mu'tazz especially elicited cries of horror from Arab poets. They were honest enough to call things by their true name:

They (the Turks) start rebellions and thus destroy our empire and our rule is nothing but a guest now;
The Turks have become possessors of the rule and the world must be silent and obey.
This is not the way to keep the empire in order, no enemy can be fought thus and no unity preserved.[2]

and another says:

The free men are gone, they have been destroyed and lost; time has placed me amongst barbarians.
It is said to me: You remain too much at home; I said: because there is no joy in going out.
Whom do I meet when I look around? Apes riding on saddles.[3]

This foreign rule, to which the Arab enemies of the 'Abbāsid dynasty could point as a sign of the latter's ineffectuality, as to a regime jeopardized between Turks and Daylamites,[4] subsequently became more and more firmly established. The rise of independent dynasties within the caliphate pushed back and broke not only the latter's power but also that of the nation from which this institution stemmed. In the fourth century descendants of the 'Abbāsid lineage loitered about the courts of the new dynasts as flattering poets and sued for subordinate positions in the administration.[5] It is to the high credit of the Arab poet of the fourth century, al-Mutanabbī, that he showed a deep sensitivity to this decay of his nation. In his work we see a horror of existing national conditions which is enhanced into

[1] *Agh.*, IX, p. 86, 14. It is of course an anachronism when the caliph al-Rashīd is named as author of this song.
[2] Al-Mas'ūdī, VII, pp. 378, 5, 400, 6, 401, 9.
[3] Ibn Lankak (died 300) in *Yatīmat al-Dahr*, II, p. 118; cf. 'Abd Allāh al-Iṣfahānī, ibid., III, p. 127.
[4] Muḥammad ibn Hāni', *ZDMG*, XXIV, p. 484, v. 2 [*Dīwān*, ed. Zāhid 'Alī, 47: 124].
[5] *Yatīmat al-Dahr*, IV, pp. 84 ff., 112; cf. now for the position of the members of the 'Abbāsid family, Kremer, *Über das Einnahmebudget des 'Abbāsidenreiches* (Vienna 1887), p. 13 note.

rousing warlike desires[1] against the rule of barbarians who were
153 intellectually and morally inferior to the Arabs. 'Men' he says, 'gain their value through their ruler, but there is no well-being for Arabs ruled by barbarians who have neither education nor glory, neither protective allegiance nor faith. Wherever you go you will find men guarded by servants as if they were cattle.'[2] But such poetic outcries had little influence on the revival of past greatness. The Arab element was declining in all fields.

II

This kind of political and social atmosphere was not unfavourable to the appearance and the diffusion of such tendencies as were represented by the Shuʿūbite party. Whereas previously the maximum demand of the pietists had been to get the Arabs accustomed to respect the foreign nationalities in Islam, these elements could now proceed to violent attacks against the Arab race, and the theologians now felt obliged to teach traditions recommending respect for the Arabs. It is instructive to pay attention to these traditions when considering the development of the positions held by the various nationalities in Islam. Thus the Prophet was represented as saying to the Persian Salmān—the choice of the addressee was particularly suitable for this occasion:—'Do not bear me a grudge lest you forsake your religion (because of this feeling).' Salmān replied: 'How could I bear you a grudge when God has given us true guidance through you?' Thereupon the Prophet said: 'If you bear the Arabs a grudge you also bear me a grudge.' ʿUthmān b. ʿAffān is made to teach in the name of the Prophet: 'He who insults the Arabs does not partake of my intercession and is not touched by my love.'[3] In these fictitious sayings, which belong to the latest stratum of tradition, there is expressed the position of the theologians *vis-à-vis* a trend of thought which was steadily gaining ascendancy among the non-Arab peoples, a trend which aimed at lowering the estimation of the Arabs and at repaying the rebuffs they had suffered at the hands of the Arabs for two centuries. Such traditions were to counter-balance the views expressed in the older fictions in which the feeling of the ʿAjam sought and found its theological support, as we have seen in the examples quoted above.[4] It is noteworthy that these are the same
154 traditions as those which the Khārijites used in Africa in order to justify the Persian dynasty of the Rustamids in Tāhart (middle of

[1] *Dīwān* of al-Mutanabbī, 19: 22 ff., ed. Dieterici, I, p. 57.

[2] *Dīwān* of al-Mutanabbī, 58: 2-4, ed. Dieterici, I, p. 148.

[3] *Maṣābīḥ al-Sunna*, II, p. 193. [Also al-Dhahabī, *Siyar Aʿlām al-Nubalāʾ*, I, p. 392. For other similar traditions see Ibn Qutayba, *K. al-ʿArab*, in *Rasāʾil al-Bulaghāʾ*, p. 375; al-Haythamī, *Majmaʿ al-Zawāʾid*, X, p. 53.]

[4] pp. 110-1.

the second century) as against the Arab caliphate[1]—which is another proof for the affinity between these politico-religious dissenters and the tendencies of the Shuʿūbiyya.[2]

To the same group of pronouncements we may attribute those apocryphal sayings of the Prophet in which to imitate the customs of the ʿAjam was forbidden, or at least frowned upon—presumably as a reaction against the preponderance of Persian and Turkish customs. Disapproval voiced in ancient times was now strengthened by representing the object of disapproval as a custom of the Aʿājim, assimilation to whom was to be avoided, much as it used to be stressed that the customs of Jews and Christians[3] were to be avoided. Here belong not only customs connected with religion but also habits of daily life, as for example rising to one's feet as a sign of respect,[4] the use of knives at meals—which was discouraged as a typically Persian custom—some details of toilet, shaving and many other things, including the use of leopards[5] as riding animals.[6] Opportunity for zealous opposition to the imitation of foreign customs probably existed also in earlier times[7], but it would then hardly have been made a religious question. The pronouncements relevant to our 155
purpose reveal their origin in the time of the decline of ʿAbbāsid power by their connection with pseudo-prophecies which announce the political ascendancy of foreign elements. In former days the scruples which now manifest themselves appear not to have come to the fore. On the contrary, in a tradition cited by Mālik b. Anas the Prophet mentions a custom of Greeks and Persians[8] in order to

[1] In the *Chronique d'Abou Zakaria*, translated by Emile Masqueray, Paris 1879, pp. 4-10, there is a collection of these traditions and Koran passages —because such too were used by African Khārijites, esp. 5: 59, 48-16.

[2] See above, p. 130.

[3] Cf. Grätz's *Monatsschrift*, 1880, pp. 309 ff.

[4] A comparison of the traditions in which getting up as a means of showing respect is either prohibited or frowned upon will give the impression that the reason given—that this is a custom of the Aʿājim—is of later origin than the idea itself. From B. *Istiʾdhān*, no. 26, one may conclude that in older times this form of showing respect was considered quite in order. I add the passages where the relevant data can be found: al-Ghazālī, *Iḥyā*, II, p. 198; al-Qasṭallānī, IX, p. 168; *Agh.*, VIII, p. 161; cf. *Kitāb al-Aḍdād*, p. 185, 5, from below; *al-ʿIqd*, I, p. 274 [al-Haythamī, *Majmaʿ al-Zawāʾid*, VIII, p. 40; *Kanz al-ʿUmmāl*, IX, p. 87 (nos. 837–44]. On kissing hands as showing respect see ibid, p. 166.

[5] Cf. Mme. Dieulafoy, *La Perse, la Chaldée et la Susiane* (Paris 1887), p. 528, on domestic uses of this animal by the inhabitants of the Shaṭṭ al-ʿArab.

[6] Al-Ṣiddīqī, fols. 134b-142.

[7] Note Ḥassān, *Dīwān*, p. 91, 5 from below [ed. Hirschfeld, 25:12]. But this was not rare; a poet who had known the good old days introduces himself to al-Maʾmūn in foreign dress, *al-ʿIqd*, I, p. 170. Compare also a saying, ibid., I, p. 69 below, where the Arab manner of dress, riding and archery, etc. are recommended in contrast to ease and Persian manners.

[8] It is interesting to observe that al-Zurqānī wants to make by force the Fāris into Arabs: *akhlāṭ min Taghlib*, who have adopted this name.

explain the keeping back of an edict which he had previously intended to issue.[1]

III

The trend with which we are here concerned has an intimate connection with the political and literary renaissance of the Persians which, furthered by the appearance of autonomous states in Central Asia, revived the national consciousness of Persians and restored their national and literary traditions.[2] The newly emerging rulers found support for their efforts to establish autonomous states in the renewed blossoming of the national consciousness of the central Asian peoples subjugated by Islam; and they did not object to being seen as continuing the tradition of Persian national princes and being put on the same level as the Chosroes.[3] The manifestations of this national renaissance offered a firm background for the literary battle of Muslim Persians against Arabs, which was sponsored by the Shuʿūbiyya movement.

Before discussing these literary phenomena we must make yet another observation: the freedom that the non-Arab nationalities in Islam could permit themselves at that time was used predominantly by the Persians—since they were, next to the Arabs, the most
156 eminent intellectual force of the Muslim empire—but it seems that non-Persians also shared the boldness with which the Arabs were now confronted.

The poet Dīk al-Jinn (died 235/6) appears to have been a representative of a particularly Syrian patriotism. He was descended from a certain Tamīm who was converted to Islam after the battle of Mu'ta. This poet was a Shuʿūbite zealot of anti-Arab sentiment. 'The Arabs', he said 'have no precedence over us, since our descent is united in Abraham; we have become Muslims like them; if one of them kills one of us he is punished with death; and God had never announced that they are preferred to us.'[4] He was so much attached to his home country that he never left Syria either to visit the court of the Caliphs or to wander about in the fashion of poets.

Tradition was also used in this connection to support or to put into circulation some ideas which arose in one or another Muslim

[1] *Al-Muwaṭṭa'*, III, p. 94; Muslim, III, p. 346. In al-Bukhārī I have not found this tradition.

[2] Cf. Schack, *Heldensagen des Firdūsī*, 2nd ed., pp. 21 ff. and the study by Julius Mohl cited there. [See also B. Spuler, *Iran in frühislamischer Zeit*, passim, especially pp. 239 ff.]

[3] *Agh.*, XVII, p. 110, 8.

[4] *Agh.*, XII, p. 142. It is obvious that such a person must also have condemned the racial hatred between Qaysites and Yemenites. Instructive in this connection is a poem by him (ibid., p. 149), inspired by the fact that the Yemenite inhabitants of Emesa deposed a preacher of northern Arab descent.

circle. The following obviously tendentious tradition seems to have originated in the despised group of the Nabataeans[1] for the purpose 157
of showing that the Nabataeans also are worthy to participate in ruling the empire, which was in fact a Khārijite idea. 'Ubayda al-Salmānī reports: 'I have heard 'Alī say: If someone asks our descent he may learn that we are Nabataeans from Kūthā'[2] The name of 'Ubayda al-Salmānī (died 72) is presumably only used to give authority to this fiction; the list of its transmitters includes the Ḥarrānian Ma'mar (b. Rāshid).[3]

The Nabataeans who endeavoured to counter the contempt in which the Arabs held them by reference to their glorious past connections with the Babylonian empire, found advocates also amongst the philosophers. The philosophers Ḍirār b. 'Amr al-Ghaṭafānī[4] and Thumāma b. al-Ashras (died 213) took up their cause and taught that the Nabataeans could hold their own in competition with Arabs. Al-Mas'ūdī, to whom we owe our knowledge of this fact,[5] adds that the famous man of letters and philosopher, al-Jāḥiẓ, also followed the doctrine of the Ḍirārites; and this author does in fact mention in his

[1] The remnants of the Aramaic population of Syria and Mesopotamia, as well as those 'who', in the fashion of those Nabataeans, 'had settled, indulged in agriculture and crafts, have little respect for tribal affiliation and mix with helots' (Sprenger, *Alte Geographie Arabiens*, p. 233). In both cases Nabataean in the mouths of Arabs is a term of insult (*nabbaṭahu*, *Agh.*, XIII, p. 73, 12; *yā nabaṭī*, ibid, XVIII, p. 182, 22); cf. the poem of Ḥurayth b. 'Annāb against the Banū Thu'al (these are much praised by Imrq., 41, and Ḥātim is proud of his descent from them: *Agh.*, XVI, p. 107, 3); *Ḥam.*, p. 650, especially v. 5 (*diyāfiy-yatun qulfun*) or later Yāqūt, II, p. 355, 16 *nāsib nabīṭahā*; *Agh.*, XII, p. 39, 18 *fa-sīru ma'a'l-anbāṭi*. It is said of them that they carry servitude with patience (Ḥassān, p. 54, 14 [ed. Hirschfeld, 189: 8]) and they are quoted as an example when speaking of the common people (Ibn. Hish., p. 306 ult.); *nabīṭ* is the opposite of *khiyār al-qawm* (the better people, *Jazīrat al-'Arab*, p. 104, 22). A falsificator of the poem by Di'bil, praising the southern Arab tribes, who wants to disparage the Qurayshites, says of them in an interpolated line: *ma'sharun mutanabbiṭūna* (*Agh.*, XVIII, p. 52, 1), whereas otherwise the Nabataeans are contrasted with the Quraysh; ibid, XI, p. 4, 6. Al-Shāfi'ī is reported to have said: There are three types of men who despise you when you honour them and honour you if you degrade them: women, slaves and Nabataeans (al-Ghazālī, *Iḥyā'*, II, p. 39). Abū Nukhayla mentions the Nabataeans of Mesopotamia (especially Ḥarrān, Hīt, Mosul and Takrīt) with the special epithet: 'who sell houses and eat lentils'; *Agh.*, XVIII, p. 144, 7. For a game typical of them (*fatraj*) see Kremer, *Beiträge zur arabischen Lexicographie*, I, p. 17.

[2] Yāqūt IV, p. 318. [Cf. al-Bakrī, *Mu'jam ma'sta'jam*, s.v. Kūthā; *Lisān al-'Arab*, s.v. *nbṭ*. Ibn Bābūya, *Ma'ānī al-Akhbār*, ed. 1379, p. 407: a Muslim convert should not be contemptuously called 'Nabataean', since the House of the Prophet as well as the Nabataeans are descendants of Abraham.]

[3] Died 153, *Ṭabaqāt al-Ḥuff.*, V, no. 26.

[4] This Mu'tazilite, according to Ibn Ḥazm (Leiden Ms. Warner no. 480, vol. II, fol. 72a) [Cairo 1899 ff., IV, p. 66], agrees with the Khārijites also in denying the punishments of the grave (*'adhāb al-qabr*).

[5] *Prairies d'or*, III, p. 107.

Kitāb al-Ḥayawān that many of his contemporaries accused him of belonging to that sect since he quoted their opinions.[1] The teaching of Ḍirār about Nabataean superiority to the Arabs—a teaching for which he was reckoned amongst the Shu'ūbites,[2] despite his Arab descent—also appears in his attitude to the basic question of the Islamic doctrine of the state, the question of the caliphate. It is said of him that he put forward the thesis that as between a Qurayshite and a non-Arab[3] (Ibn Ḥazm says: Abyssinian, al-Shahrastānī: Nabataean) who are both suggested for the office of the caliph, pre-
158 ference must definitely be given to the non-Arab if both are otherwise equally qualified through their attachment to the sacred book of God and the *Sunna*; his rather pettifogging motive for this is: 'because the Nabataean resp. Abyssinian can be more easily deposed should he prove unworthy.'[4]

But the most important expression of non-Arab reaction against the Arabs in these circles is found at the time when such a reaction began to be manifest at all sides, in the much discussed falsification of Ibn Waḥshiyya, known as the *Nabataean Agriculture*, the literary character of which is no more in dispute after Alfred v. Gutschmid's conclusive investigations.[5] This book, which was written in the third century, must be considered the most outstanding document of Nabataean Shu'ūbiyya; and as such it appears in the description of its general trend which is given by the defender of its authenticity: 'Ibn Waḥshiyya, moved by grim hatred of the Arabs and full of bitterness about their contempt of his compatriots, decided to translate and make accessible the remnants of ancient Babylonian literature preserved by them in order to show that the ancestors of his people, so despised by the Arabs, had had a great civilization and had excelled in knowledge many peoples of antiquity.'[6] The author intended to contrast the unimportance of the ancient Arabs in science and culture with the great achievements of his own race in order to answer the limitless arrogance of the ruling race.

The most eminent representatives of the nationalities were not always anxious, in this movement, to work only in the interest of

[1] MS. of the Vienna Hofbibliothek, N.F. no. 151, fol. 3a [*al-Ḥayawān*, I, 12-3].

[2] *Al-'Iqd*, III, p. 445.

[3] Al-Nawawī to Muslim, IV, p. 265, mentions the doctrine of Ḍirār (*sakhāfat Ḍirār*); in this quotation the doctrine generally refers to 'Non-Qurayshites such as Nabataeans and others' (*ghayr al-qurashiyyi min al-nabaṭ wa-ghayrihim*); cf. al-Māwardī, ed. Enger, p. 5, 2 from below, *jamī' al-nās*: all men.

[4] Ibn Ḥazm, ibid., vol. II, fol. 82b [IV, p. 88]; al-Shahrastānī, p. 63.

[5] '*Die nabatäische Landwirtschaft und ihre Geschwister, ZDMG.*, vol. XV, 1861); Nöldeke, '*Noch einiges über die nabatäische Landwirtschaft,*' ib. vol. XXIX (1875), pp. 445 ff.

[6] Chwolsohn, *Über die Überreste der altbabylonischen Literatur in arabischen Übersetzungen* (St Petersburg 1859), p. 9; Gutschmid, l.c., p. 92.

their own nationality, since this was served equally well indirectly by working in favour of some other emergent nationality in Islam. The crux of the matter was after all the negative exposition, namely that the Arabs had no exclusive right to claim to hegemony in Islam. It is notable that it was Ḥarrānian scholars who had worked
in favour of the Daylamite nationality in the spirit of the Shu'ūbiyya. 159
This literary work was primarily meant to benefit the rulers of the Būyid dynasty who were, as is well known, of Daylamite descent, and who seem to have done everything in their power to appear equal to the Arab caliph. They also invented an Arab descent[1]—an artifice which was much later adopted also by the Circassian sultans in Egypt,[2]—and fitted the pre-history of their house to this genealogy. The famous physician Sinān, son of Thābit b. Qurra (died 321), wrote a book which had for its subject 'the fame of the Daylamites, their genealogy, origin and ancestors',[3] and another Ḥarrānian scholar, the belletrist Ibrāhīm b. Hilāl (died 384) wrote a *Kitāb al-Tājī* at the command of the Būyid prince, which was filled with tendentious inventions.[4] Al-Tha'ālibī mentions this book frequently in his 'Pearl of the Epoch'. Places conquered by Islam were here represented as adopting the new religion voluntarily, whence the conclusion was to be drawn that as Islam did not have to be enforced upon foreign nations they did not deserve a lower status in Islam.[5] It was in accord with the own inclinations of the Ḥarrānian scholars to stress the value of non-Arab nations. This could only serve to justify their own adherence to their national traditions.

The Coptic element in Egypt also participated in the ferment of old nations within the Islamic empire against the aspirations of the Arabism which tended to extinguish all national individuality. Just as in Aramaic circles a Nabataean literature was invented for this purpose, the Copts wrote books which described the deeds of the ancient Egyptians with a bias against the Arabs. Such attempts were
to provide proof that the boastful Arabs who settled on the site of the 160
culture of ancient Egypt were far eclipsed by the intellectual and material creations of the old rulers of the land, the ancestors of the

[1] Al-Mas'ūdī, VIII, p. 280; *al-'Iqd*, II, pp. 58-9; Wüstenfeld, *Register zu den genealogischen Tabellen*, p. 109. They traced their descent to Isaac (Yahūdā b. Ya'qūb b. Isḥāq): *al-Fakhri*, p. 325.

[2] Cf. no. 106 in *Catalogue d'une collection de Manuscripts appartenant à la Maison Brill rédigé par Houtsma*, 1886, p. 21. The endeavour to give Arab genealogies to foreign nations is ridiculed in a poem by Abū Bujayr (*al-'Iqd*, III, p. 300), cf. above p. 134.

[3] Ibn Abī Uṣaybi'a, ed. A. Müller, I, p. 224.

[4] This follows from his own admission quoted in al-Tha'ālibī, *Yatīmat al-Dahr*, II, p. 26; cf. Abulfeda, *Annales*, II, p. 584.

[5] One can find an example in Yāqūt, IV, p. 984, s.v. Huzu.

despised and downtrodden Copts who, on conversion to Islam, had not put behind them the traditions of their ancestors.[1] There are no continuous remnants of this literature, but we do find isolated quotations in later writings. Baron v. Rosen pointed out on the occasion of his discussion of such quotations, which frequently occur in a work of the sixth century, the connection of this lost literature with the Shuʿūbiyya movement in Islam.[2]

IV

In the literary activity of this movement, directed at achieving equal status in Islam for the non-Arab nations, the greatest part was undoubtedly taken by the Muslims of Persian race. It is not astonishing that the literature of the Shuʿūbiyya has survived only in rare traces and relics, though these are very characteristic of their kind. The followers of the Shuʿūbiyya were for the most part people who were suspect from the religious point of view, being so-called Zīndīqs, and it is well known that the ecclesiastic-pietistic trend which, since the fifth-sixth centuries A.H., had been gaining the upper hand in literature, did not favour the survival of heretical and schismatic works.

We do marvel, however, at the freeness with which Shuʿūbites expressed themselves in such of their literary products as are still extant. Whereas in the Umayyad period it was dangerous for the poet Ismāʿīl b. Yasār, who was moved by Shuʿūbite ideas and ridiculed the pre-Islamic Arabs and their barbaric customs,[3] to boast
161 of his Persian descent,[4] it was possible under the ʿAbbāsids for scholars, poets and belletrists freely to oppose the national vanity of the Arabs with their proud references to Iranian ancestry.[5] Among the descendants of the former Persian aristocracy ancestral genealogy was as carefully transmitted as among the 'descendants of Qaḥṭān and ʿAdnān'[6] It is related of the famous grammarian Yūnus b. Ḥabīb (died 185), who was visited also by desert Arabs

[1] Perhaps there is some connection between this movement and the accounts mentioned in Chwolsohn, *Die Ssabier*, I, pp. 492 ff.

[2] *Notices sommaires des Manuscrits arabes du Musée asiatique*, I, p. 172.

[3] *Agh.*, IV, p. 120: 'Many a crowned head I call uncle, great ones of noble tribe. They are named "Persians" according to their excellent descent. (Cf. Ibn Badrūn, ed. Dozy, p. 8, 7.) 'Desist then, o Imām [read: o Umāma], from boasting to us, leave injustice and speak the truth: while we brought up our daughters you buried yours in the sands.' 'Indeed,' answered the Arab—'you needed your daughters but we did not' (reference to the incest of which the Persians were accused). [The error 'o Imām' for 'O Umāma'—name of a woman—has been corrected by C. A. Nallino, *Raccolta di scritti*, VI, p. 139.]

[4] Kremer, *Culturgeschichtl. Streifzüge*, pp. 29 f.

[5] We cannot really believe the statement of the author of the *Fihrist*, p. 120, that such inclinations were frowned upon by the Barmakides.

[6] Al-Masʿūdī, II, p. 241.

desiring to profit from his linguistic knowledge of Arabic, that he referred with pride to his Persian descent.[1] The orator and theologian Muḥammad b. al-Layth, a *mawlā* of the Umayyad family, who traced his ancestors back to Dārā b. Dārā, was able to show his preference for Persians under the Barmakids; presumably the orthodox called him *zindīq* for this reason alone, though he wrote a book to disprove this heresy.[2] The famous secretary of al-Ma'mūn and director of the 'Treasure of Wisdom', Sahl b. Hārūn from Dastmaysān, wrote a large number of books expressing his fanatical feelings against Arabs and his preference for Persians. He was probably the most outstanding Shu'ūbite of his day, and the literary curiosity which made him famous was presumably also a consequence of his tendency to ridicule Arab ideals. This is the only explanation for his having written a number of treatises on miserliness; according to another authority he wrote an entire book[3] deriding generosity and praising miserliness.[4]

O inhabitants of Maysān—he calls to his compatriots, God be with you who are of good root and branch.
Your faces are silver, mixed with gold, your hands are like the rain of the plains.[5]
Does Kalb wish me to count myself amongst his family? There is 162
little science amongst the dogs.[6]
Do these people believe that a house on a high peak reaching for the stars as if it were a star itself
Counts no more than a hair tent in the middle of the plain in whose rooms live cattle and beetles?[7]

This was the time when it was possible for Arabic poets of Persian descent to use the noble language of the Qurayshites, which they mastered supremely well, to protest against the presumption of the Arabs. At their head stood the Shu'ūbite poet Bashshār b. Burd (died 168), from whom there have been transmitted boastful poems about his

[1] Flügel, *Grammat. Schulen der Araber*, p. 36.

[2] *Fihrist*, p. 120, 24 ff.

[3] Al-Ḥuṣrī, II, p. 142. There the origin of this book is said to be in Sahl's striving to show the power of his eloquence on a paradoxical subject, *Fihrist*, ibid., 4. A *risāla* of his in favour of miserliness is quoted at length in *al-'Iqd*, III, p. 335.

[4] Approval of miserliness and disapproval of generosity is also attributed to the Andalusian scholar Abū Ḥayyān; al-Maqqarī, I, p. 830, above.

[5] Here then generosity is praised after all.

[6] The word-play: *Kalb* (Arab tribal name) and *kalb* (noun = dog) is often used ironically; cf. my *Ẓâhiriten*, p. 179.

[7] Al-Ḥuṣrī, II, p. 190.

descent from the 'Quraysh of the Persians'[1] as well as sharp satire against the Arabs[2]—satire which was probably much repeated in the national circles to which this poet belonged, since almost 200 years later we hear its echo, in a poet who sounded the last tones of Persian complaints against the Arabs: Abū Sa'īd al-Rustamī:[3]

The Arabs boast of being master of the world and commanders of peoples.
Why do they not rather boast of being skilful sheep and camel herders?[4]

If I am asked about my descent—says the same poet—I am of the tribe of Rustam
but my song is of Lu'ayy b. Ghālib.[5]

I am the one who is publicly and secretly known
as a Persian whom Arabianism (*al-ta'rīb*) drew to itself.
163 I know well when calling the parole[6]
that my origin is clear and my wood hard.[7]

[1] Cf. Ibn al-Faqīh, p. 196, 9. 'Quraysh of a nation' is used of the most prominent and excellent group in it. Southern Arabs use this phrase too and the Duhma are called by them the 'Quraysh of the Hamdān tribes' because of their bravery and virtue; *Jazīrat al-'Arab*, p. 194, 24. ['Abd Shams b. Sa'd b. Zayd Manāt are the 'Quraysh of Tamīm', Abu'l-Baqā', *al-Manāqib al-Mazyadiyya*, MS. Brit. Mus. 1215, fol. 42.]

[2] *Agh.*, III, p. 21, 33. For this poet see Kremer, *Culturgesch. Streifzüge*, pp. 34 f.

[3] Contemporary of the Ṣāḥib ibn 'Abbād (died 385), in whose praise he made many *qaṣīdas*, of which a piece can be found in Ibn Khallikān, no. 95 (I, p. 133) and no. 684 (VII, p. 160); other passages from his poetical works are in al-Ḥuṣrī, III, p. 13 and in the *Kashkūl*, pp. 163 f.

[4] Al-Tha'ālibī., *Vertrauter Gef. d. Einsamen*, p. 272, no. 314. [Correctly: Rāghib al-Iṣfahānī, *Muḥāḍarat al-Udabā'*, see I, p. 220. From the additional verses which precede in Rāghib's text it is clear that the correct translation is: 'They (the Persians) can boast that they are the tamers of the world and the masters of its inhabitants, not the tamers of sheep and camels'.]

[5] *Yatīmat al-Dahr*, III, p. 129, 17, cf. for his descent ib. p. 130, 12.

[6] *Shi'ārī*, i.e. my proper Persian descent which is evident from my parole; cf. above, p. 163.

[7] *Yatīma*, l.c. p. 135, 8. Cf. for the last words (*wa-'ūdī ṣalīb*) *Agh.*, II, p. 104, 6 ff., XIV, p. 89, 9; *Ḥam.*, p. 474, v. 3 and the commentary, as also the expression of an older Shu'ūbite (*Agh.*, IV, p. 125, 20) who boasts 'that his wood is not weak (*mā 'ūdī bi-dhī khawarin*; cf. *fi'l-'ūdi khawar*, *al-Muwashshā*, ed. Brünnow, p. 19, 3) on the day of the battle.' Comparison of these passages shows that this form of speech refers to glorious descent of which heroes boast before the battle (see above p. 57). For the use of *'ūd* in this sense, Yāqūt, III, p. 472, 3, *wa-akhwālunā min khayri 'ūdin wa-min zandi*, and ibid., IV, p. 177, 19. Notable also are al-Farazdaq, ed. Boucher, p. 18, 6-7, and the poem of Ḥammād 'Ajrad on Abū Ja'far al-Manṣūr, *al-'Iqd*, I, p. 120, where this concept is enlarged upon. The poet Abū 'Uyayna found two men of the same family quite different: one generous, the other miserly. 'Dāwūd deserves praise,

In an older generation people like him would not have made much of the Persian *shi'ār* but would have been glad to keep it dark from jealous genealogists and to make every effort to insinuate themselves into an Arab tribe.

To this group of poets belongs Isḥāq b. Ḥassān al-Khurramī (died 200) from Sogdiana. He proudly points out that he comes from Sughd and that his value was not impaired by his being unable to count Yuḥābir or Jarm or 'Ukl amongst his ancestors.[1] He even went so far as to become an exponent of Persian pride and the claims which educated Persians made *vis-à-vis* the Arabs within Islam.

> It was decided by the Ma'add (northern Arabs), young and old, and the Qaḥṭān (southern Arabs) all together
> To rob my belongings, but this plundering was prevented by a sword with sharp and well-smoothed blade.
> I called to aid knights from Marw and Balkh, famous amongst noble men.
> But woe, the place of my people is so far that only few helpers can come;
> Because my father is Sāsān, Kisrā Hormuz's son, and Khāqān is, if you would know it, my cousin.
> In paganism we ruled the necks of men; all followed us in subjection as if moved by strings.
> We have humiliated and judged you as we wished whether rightly 164
> or wrongly.
> But when Islam came and hearts went to it joyously which by it turned to the created[2]
> We followed God's prophet and it was as if heaven would rain upon us men (who overcame us).[3]

A melancholy parallel indeed between the old world position of the Persians and their humiliation by the Arabs. This reflection had a more forceful effect upon the poet Mu'bad, who called for open revolt and the expulsion of the Arabs:

> I am a noble of the tribe of Jam—he called in the name of the nation—and I demand the inheritance of the Persian kings.

[1] Yāqūt, III, pp. 395 f.

[2] The translation of this line is doubtful.

[3] Yāqūt, IV, p. 20.

---

but you deserve blame; this is a marvel as you are of the same wood (*wa-antumā min 'ūdin*). But the same wood is split half for mosques, the other half for the Jewish latrines; you are for the latrines, and the other for the mosque' etc., *Agh.*, XVIII, p. 22, 21.

Tell all the sons of Hāshim: submit yourselves before the hour of regret arrives.
Retreat to the Ḥijāz and resume eating lizards[1] and herd your cattle
While I seat myself on the throne of the kings supported by the sharpness of my blade and the point of my pen (heroism and science).[2]

It was easy to speak to Arabs in this manner at a time when the foreigners were about to wrest the rule from them. What does your old glory profit you, they asked the Arabs, of which you boast, while in the present time you show yourselves so unfit? 'If you cannot guard the past with new glory all that has been is of no use.'[3]

But among all the poets of that time the extreme left of the Shu'ūbiyya seems to have been most powerfully represented by the Arab poet and philologian Abū 'Uthmān Sa'īd b. Ḥumayd b. Bakhtigān (died 240), who boasted of his descent from Persian princes or *dihqāns*. His father, an eminent exponent of Mu'tazilite dogma, was already suspected of Shu'ūbī sympathies. The son gave
165 clear proof of this sentiment, for example in an epigram which he directed against the chief *qāḍī* of the caliphs al-Mu'taṣim and al-Wāthiq, Aḥmad b. Abī Duwād (died 240), who was known for his Mu'tazilite fanaticism and of ill-fame because of the Mu'tazilite inquisition.[4] Aḥmad called himself an Iyādī, a claim which sounded suspicious to the friend of the Persians, who had no love for such genealogical boasting of prehistoric tribal relationships.

You trace your descent to Iyād, presumably because your father happened to be called Abū Duwād.[5]

[1] The Bedouin Arabs are usually taunted with eating snakes, mice and lizards; al-Muqaddasī, ed. de Goeje, 202, 11, *Yatīmat al-Dahr*, III, p. 102, 3 from below. Ru'ba b. al-'Ajjāj defended this Arab custom (*Agh.*, XVIII, p. 133), of which he himself is no exception (ib, XXI, p. 87, 20). Cf. other passages in my *Mythos bei den Hebräern*, p. 99, note 3 (Engl. translation, p. 83, note 2). [There Goldziher refers to Yazdagird's satire on the Arabs, the Persian Ṭabarī, transl. Zotenberg, III, p. 38; Bashshār b. Burd, in *Agh.*, III, p. 33.]

[2] *Vertraute Gefährte*, p. 272 no. 314 [correctly: Rāghib al-Iṣfahānī, *Muḥāḍarat al-Udabā'*, I, pp. 219-20.], cf. the translation in Rückerts *Ḥam.*, II, p. 245. [See Yāqūt, *Irshād al-Arīb*, I, pp. 322-3. From that passage it results that the poem was written in the name of Ya'qūb al-Ṣaffār. The poem is discussed at length in an article 'Ya'qūb al-Ṣaffār and Persian National Sentiment' prepared by the editor.]

[3] Yāqūt, III, p. 396, 1.

[4] *Agh.*, XVII, p. 2.

[5] Like the Arab poet of pagan times, Abū Duwād al-Iyādī.

If he by chance were called 'Amr b. Ma'dī verily you would
have said you were from Zubayd or Murād.[1]

This is a satire of those accidental occasions and clues which sufficed for Arabs of those days to assume a glorious genealogy and to make it plausible to credulous people. We shall see later that ridicule of such vanities was a tendency of Shu'ūbī scholarship. The presupposition of this tendency in the epigrams we have just mentioned is in accordance also with everything else we know of the literary character of Sa'īd. He is named amongst the literary champions of the Persian race; he wrote a book entitled: 'The Superiority of the Persians' and another: 'Vindication of the Persians in the face of the Arabs,' which was also known under the title 'Book of equality' (*taswiya*)[2], after one of the party names of the Shu'ūbiyya: *Ahl al-taswiya.*

At that time 'the excellence of the Persians' offered a much-cultivated literary field[3], and though none of these books and tracts have survived, quotations from this Shu'ūbite literature in the works of al-Jāḥiẓ and Ibn 'Abd Rabbihi reveal part of their contents and their general trend. The *Kitāb al-Bayān wa'l-Tabyīn* of the former author[4] and the great encyclopaedic work, *Kitāb al-'Iqd al-Farīd,* 166
of the latter, an Andalusian writer, have transmitted some of the main points of the argument of the Shu'ūbiyya through the polemics and replies which they reproduce. The *'Iqd* in particular has preserved long excerpts from a polemic of Ibn Qutayba—who wrote a book devoted entirely to the excellences of the Arabs[5], and dealt with the subject also elsewhere[6]—against the Shu'ūbiyya and the latter's reply to the advocates of the Arab cause; it was first published in a

[1] Like that southern Arab hero of the Jāhiliyya: 'Amr. b. Ma'dīkarib.

[2] *Fihrist*, p. 123, 22 ff.

[3] Ibid., p. 128, 8 etc. An anonymous book called *Mafākhir* or *Mafākhir al-'Ajam* in Flügel, l.c. [above, p, 149, note 1] p. 34, quoted in *Fihrist*, p. 42, 9.

[4] Cf. Rosen's letter to Prof. Fleischer in *ZDMG*, XXVIII, p. 169, and further the same author's *Manuscrits arabes de l'Institut des langues orientales* (St. Petersburg 1877), pp. 74 ff.

[5] *Fihrist*, p. 78, mentions a work by Ibn Qutayba 'On the equality of Arabs and Persians'; Ibn 'Abd Rabbihi quotes his excerpts from a work of I.Q. entitled: 'On the excellences of Arabs'; it may be assumed that these varying titles refer to the same work of I.Q. [Cf. Brockelmann, Supplement, I, pp. 185–6, no. 9.]

[6] We learn about the general trend of his relevant writings from al-Bīrūnī ([*Chronology*] ed. Sachau, p. 238), who strongly opposes them. He accuses I.Q. of attacking the 'Ajam in 'all his work and especially in his book treating of the "Superiority of the Arabs" ' and says that he disparages fanatically Persian character and accuses them of disbelief while ascribing all kinds of excellences to the old Arabs which they could not have had, for example, astronomical knowledge, etc.

study by Hammer-Purgstall in German translation[1] and lengthy excerpts were edited in the original language in the appendix to v. Kremer's *Culturgeschichtliche Streifzüge*. Since then an oriental edition of the book of Ibn 'Abd Rabbihi has become available and the relevant passages may be studied in full by anyone versed in the Arabic language.[2]

Apart from these sources for a more detailed knowledge of the Shu'ūbiyya we must mention a 'Refutation of the Shu'ūbiyya' by Abu'l-Ḥasan Aḥmad b. Yaḥyā al-Balādhurī, the well-known historian of the Muslim conquests (died 279), from which a meagre excerpt is transmitted by al-Mas'ūdī,[3] who participated in this literature in the fourth century (he died in 346). In the passage just mentioned he says: 'We have mentioned in our work on the origins of religion the different opinions on the question whether descent alone, or good
167 works alone, or descent with good works, can serve as a basis for a claim to superiority, as well as the views of the Shu'ūbiyya and opposing parties.' However, this work, like many others written to combat the Shu'ūbiyya,[4] is no longer available, and so we have to rely chiefly on al-Jāḥiẓ and Ibn Qutayba for the trend of thought of the Shu'ūbiyya.

V

With the aid of these guides we will consider the points which the Shu'ūbiyya made in their struggle with the Arabs. This survey will also convince us how trivial were the points on which the Shu'ūbiyya, and therefore also their opponents, chose to fight out their battle. It is natural that the Shu'ūbiyya took as their point of departure the often discussed Koranic verse and Muhammed's farewell sermon which, as we have pointed out before, appears to have been suitably

[1] *'Über die Menschenklasse welche von den Arabern Schoubijje genannt wird'* (*Sitzungsberichte der Kais. Akademie d. Wissenschaften*, phil. hist. Cl., vol. I (1848), pp. 330 ff.

[2] Ed. Būlāq (1293), II, pp. 85–90. [Cf. also the text published under the title *K. al-'Arab* in *Rasā'il al-Bulaghā*, 3rd ed., pp. 344–77; for its character cf. Brockelmann's discussion quoted above, p. 153, note 5.]

[3] *Prairies d'or*, III, pp. 109-113. By this *radd 'ala'l-Shu'ūbiyya* is presumably meant not a special work but a long excursus in one of Balādhurī's genealogical writings.

[4] The author of the book of the *Aghānī*, who was a contemporary of the Shu'ūbite movement in poetry and literature (born 284 died 356/7), was not indifferent to this presumption of the nationalities. That he sided with the Arabs—as is evident from several quotations of his work in the course of our study—is not astonishing if we consider that he himself was a full-blood Arab: his descent is connected to the Umayyads. I presume that his lost work, *Kitāb al-Ta'dīl wa'l-Intiṣāf fī Ma'āthir al-'Arab wa-Mathālibihā* (Ibn Khallikān, no. 451, vol. V, p. 28, 1), belongs to that literary group with which we are concerned in the above discussion.

interpolated for the purpose of this argument. To the proud traditions of the Arabs they oppose the most glorious events in the history of the non-Arabs. The Nimrods, Amaleks, Chosroes and Caesars, Sulaymān and Alexander the Great—all non-Arabs—are cited in order to prove what power and authority were united in non-Arab hands in the past. Nor are the Indian kings ignored; a letter sent by one of them to 'Umar II was said to have begun thus: 'From the king of kings, son of a thousand kings, whose spouse is the daughter of a thousand kings, in whose stables there are a thousand elephants, in whose empire there are two streams on whose banks grow aloe and fuwwa[1] and coconuts and the scented kāfūr plant which can be smelt for
twelve miles: to the king of the Arabs who does not add other beings 168
to God. I desire that you send me a man who may instruct me in Islam and teach me the laws of this religion.'[2]

The non-Arabs also carry away the palm in prophecy, since all the prophets since the creation of the world, with the exception of Hūd, Ṣāliḥ, Ismā'īl and Muhammed, were non-Arabs. The ancestors of all mankind from whom all humanity descended, Adam and Noah, were not Arabs. The Shu'ūbites do not fail to mention arts and sciences which were given to mankind by non-Arabs: philosophy, astronomy and silk embroidery, which were practised by non-Arabs whilst the Arabs were still in a state of deepest barbarism, while everything that Arabs can be proud of is centred in poetry; but here too[3] they are outdone by others, notably by the Greeks. The games which were invented by non-Arabs: chess and *nard*, are also mentioned.[4] What have the Arabs to set against such refinements of

[1] Rubia tinctorum, Imm. Löw, *Aramäische Pflanzennamen*, p. 311.

[2] Other authorities place this fable in earlier times: Haytham b. 'Adī relates on the authority of 'Abd al-Malik b. 'Umayr (died 136) that the latter saw in the archive of Mu'āwiya after his death (!) a letter from the Emperor of China with an introduction similar to the above: al-Jāḥiẓ, *Kitāb al-Ḥayawān*, fol. 386b [VII, p. 113; cf. the long letter said to have been sent by an Indian King to al-Ma'mūn; al-Khalidiyyān, *al-Tuḥaf wa'l-Hadāyā*, ed. S. al-Dahhān, pp. 159 ff.]

[3] Noteworthy in this context is the saying of the vizier al-Ḥasan b. Sahl (died 236)—as is well known of Persian origin: The accomplishments of higher education (*al-ādāb*) are ten: three of them are Shahrajānite, three Nushirwānite, three Arabic, but the tenth excels them all. Shahrajānite are playing the lute, chess and the game with javelins; Nūshirwānite are the art of healing, arithmetic and riding; Arabic are poetry, genealogy and knowledge of ancient stories; but the tenth, which excels all, is the knowledge of pretty tales which men weave into their conversation (al-Ḥuṣrī, I, p. 142 below). The same saying from another source with a few deviations *ZDMG*, XIII, p. 243.

[4] Cf. al-Mas'ūdī, I, p. 157, for this game. The Persians used to mention the game as a claim to glory, Ibn Khallikān, VII, p. 52, no. 659; al-Damīrī, II, p. 171. It was adopted with Persian technical terms as early as the first days of Islam in Medina (*Agh.*, XVII, p. 103), and was played especially by belletrists, together with *shaṭranj* and *qirq* (*Agh.*, IV, p. 52, 2). In the second century it was a well-known game in Arabia (ib., XXI, p. 91, 4). Theologians opposed and

civilization in order to make good their claim to glory? 'In the face
169 of this they are but howling wolves and prowling beasts, devouring one another and engaged in eternal mutual fighting.' Even the purity of their descent is insulted by pointing out that their women, when taken prisoners of war, served the animal lusts of their victors.[1]

Al-Jāḥiẓ quotes other points from the polemic of the Shu'ūbiyya against the Arabs.[2] They referred especially to some customs of the pagan Arabs (such as the terrible fire oath *al-hūla*[3] and other customs surviving until Islam from pagan times) in order to disgrace the Arabs; for example, the use of the staff and bow at public speeches.[4] 'The staff,' say the followers of the Shu'ūbiyya, 'is used for beating rhythm, spears for fighting, sticks for attack, bows for shooting, but there is no relation between speaking and the staff, and none between an address and a bow.[5] As if such things existed only in order to divert men's minds from the contents of the speech. It is unthinkable that the presence of such instruments could stimulate the listeners or further the speech. Even musicians think that the achievements

[1] *Al-'Iqd*, II, p. 86, 90, cf. *Lbl.f.or.Phil.*, 1886, p. 23,12 ff.

[2] *Kitāb al-Bayān wa'l-Tabyīn*, fols. 133b ff. [III, pp. 12 ff. Instead of 'make a marching camel come to halt' read: 'keep a camel on the road'; the sentence about Persian speakers should read: 'and the most eloquent in the *darī* Persian and the Pahlawī language are the inhabitants of the city of Ahwāz', and in the next sentence: 'What regards the cantillation of the *harbadh* and the language of the *mōbadh*, this belongs to him who composed the commentary of the *zamzama*'.]

[3] Cf. above, p. 167.

[4] Al-Ḥārith b. Ḥilliza stands leaning on his bow when reciting his *qaṣīda* against the Taghlibites, *Agh.*, IX, p. 178, 16. Al-Nābigha leans on his staff while saying a poem, ib., II, p. 162, 8 below; cf. also Schwarzlose, *Die Waffen der alten Araber*, p. 38. The Prophet, too uses the *mikhṣara* (cf. *Qāmūs*, s. v. *khṣr*) for his speech, B. *Janā'iz*, no. 83, note also *Ḥam.*, p. 710, v. 5. This custom continued also in later days. The Khārijite agitator Abū Ḥamza (130) leaned upon an Arab bow while speaking to the people from the *minbar* in Medina, *Agh.*, XX, p. 105, 3 from below = al-Jāḥiẓ in a passage edited by von Rosen, *Zapiski*, II, p. 143, 5 [*al-Bayān*, II, p. 122]. Perhaps the 'red staff ' of the preacher in Mecca (Kremer, *Beiträge zur Arab. Lexicographie*, II, p. 36) is a relic of the ancient Arab custom which was also followed by the Prophet. [Cf. verses about the speaker's staff in Usāma's *K. al-'Aṣā*, 'Abd al-Salām Hārūn, *Nawādir al-Makhṭūṭāt*, II, pp. 200—1.]

[5] The Arabs are particularly proud of their bows and prefer them to Persian ones; in a tradition the Prophet is made to curse all who neglect Arab bows and prefer to Persian ones (al-Ṣiddīqī, fol. 134a). The inventor of the former is said to be Māsikha, Ibn Durayd, p. 288, 3.

---

condemned it and had many traditions combatting it (*al-Muwaṭṭa'*, IV, p. 182): 'He who plays *nardshīr* is like those who dirty their hands with the blood and meat of pigs (al-Baghawī, *Maṣābīḥ al-Sunna*, II, p. 94). [Cf. al-Suyūṭī, *al-Durr al-Manthūr*, II, pp. 319–20.] Much earlier the Jewish doctors had branded it as damnable entertainment (Bab. *Kethūbhōth*, fol. 61b).

of those who use a baton[1] cannot compare with the achievements of those who make do without. Those who use staffs when speaking are 170 like ranters; one gets the impression of dealing with rough desert Arabs and is reminded of the crudeness of Bedouins. It looks as if such speakers are trying to halt a marching camel. Anyway,' they reply to the Arab boasts of their outstanding gifts as orators,[2] 'the gift of oratory is common to many peoples; its development is a necessity for all races. Even gypsies, well known as rough and most uneducated people, with great sensuality and an evil temperament, make long speeches; and all barbaric people excel in speech-making, though the content of their speeches may be rough and uncultured and their expression faulty and vulgar. But we know that the most perfect of men are the Persians, the best of whom are the inhabitants of Fāris, and of these the people of Marw speak in the sweetest, most pleasant and captivating manner; the most elegant Persian is the Darī dialect,[3] the best Pahlawī is spoken by the inhabitants of the district of Ahwāz.'

'But in regard to the cantillations of the Persian priests and the language of the Mōbad, the author of the commentary of the *Zamzama*[4] says: He who strives for a high level of eloquence

[1] On the use of the baton (*qaḍīb*) in Arab music, cf. *Agh.*, I, p. 117, 19; VII, p. 188, 8 from below. These passages also show the Arabic linguistic usage for the designation of beating time.

[2] 'The wisdom (*ḥikma*) of the Rūm is in their brain, that of Indians in their phantasy, of Greeks in the soul, of Arabs in the tongue'—such is a saying of the Arabs concerning the psychology of peoples; al-Ṣiddīqī, fol. 148b.

[3] Al-Daylamī put into circulation the following apocryphal saying by the Prophet: 'If God intends a matter which demands tenderness he reveals it to the ministering angels in *darī* Persian, but if He wishes for something demanding strictness He uses Arabic.' Another version substitutes for tenderness and strictness, anger and pleasure. Even Muslim critics thought this tradition too suspect: al-Ṣiddīqī, fol. 92b. Ibn al-Jawzī included it in his index of false traditions (*al-mawḍū'āt*), like that other saying according to which use of Persian diminishes the *muruwwa* of a man; ibid., fol. 95b. [The tradition in praise of Persian dialects also in al-Suyūṭī, *al-La'ālī al-Maṣnū'a*, I, pp. 10–11, accompanied by a contrasting tradition in disfavour of Persian. Traditions about Persian diminishing the *muruwwa*: ibid., II, pp. 281–2; *Kanz al-'Ummāl*, III, pp. 373—4; al-Sahmī, *Ta'rīkh Jurjān*, p. 383; al-Dhahabī, *Mīzān al-I'tidāl*, II, p. 477 (s.v. Ṭalḥa); cf. al-Ṭurṭūshī, *al-Ḥawādith wa'l-Bida'*, p. 104: Mālik disapproved speaking Persian in the mosque.]

[4] *Zamzama*, according to the traditional explanation (see Vullers s.v.), is the name of one of the sacred books of the Persians. *Zamzam* is usually applied in the sense of 'humming, murmuring', to the recitation of the prayers and sacred texts of the Persians. In the description of the Mihrajān festival by al-Nuwayrī (printed in Golius, *Notae in Alferganum*, p. 25, 11) it is related that the *mōbad* offered the king a dish with various kinds of fruit: *qad zamzama 'alayhā* = *'super quibus sacra dicebat verba'*. 'Umar forbids the Magi to 'hum before eating' (Sprenger, *Mohammed*, III, p. 377 note); this refers to the sacred

171 and desires to learn the strangest (choicest) expressions and to deepen his knowledge of the language should study the book of Kāzwand.[1] But he who wishes to achieve reason, high culture, knowledge of etiquette (*al-'ilm bi'l-marātib*),[2] of good examples (*al-'ibar*)
172 of proverbs,[3] noble expressions and fine thoughts should get acquainted with the 'stories of the kings.'[4]

[1] This is presumably a textual error; even a discussion with specialists of Persian literature did not lead to establishing with certainty the correct reading. [The printed text has *kārwand*.] It is possible that the word is a corruption of *kārnāma*. Such a book is ascribed to Ardashīr, Mīrkhond, transl. by de Sacy, *Mémoires sur diverses antiquités de la Perse* (Paris 1793), p. 280; cf. the *Kārnāma fī Sīrat Anūshirwān*, *Fihrist*, p. 305, *ZDMG*, XXII, p. 732, no. 11. [This explanation is hardly plausible. In Jāḥiẓ, *al-Tarbī'*, §155, the MSS. have *Kāwrīd*.]

[2] For the explanation of this expression we can make use of an account of the belletristic circle of the caliph al-Mu'tamid which is quoted in al-Mas'ūdī, VIII, pp. 102-3. Among other subjects of intellectual conversation it is mentioned that at the caliph's court one discussed 'the forms of meetings, the places to be taken by subordinates and superiors, and the places and manner of their ranking (*kayfiyyat marātibihim*, Barbier de Meynard: 'sur la hiérarchie à observer'); ibid., p. 104, 7, it is said that in these discussions one considered 'what is told in this connection of previous kings.'

[3] [The printed text has the correct reading *wa'l-mathulāt*, which means 'examples', not 'proverbs', so that the following note is not relevant in this

formulae which had to be said before eating. In a poem cited in Ibn al-Faqīh, ed. de Goeje, p. 216, 3, a Persian priest is named: *shaykh muzamzim*, i.e. the humming sheikh; cf. also Golius, l.c., p. 28, 3, 4. Also in *Sīrat 'Antar*, III, p. 59, it is said of the Magi that they *yuzamzimū bi-kalām al-Yahūd wa-ṭarīqat al-Majūs* in the fire temple, and the name of the *Zamzam* well has been connected with this designation of religious recitation by Persians (Yāqūt, II, p. 941, 14). A Christian author also mentions the unintelligible murmur (*reṭānā*) of the Magi (Hoffmann, *Auszüge aus syrischen Acten christl. Märtyrer*, p. 96) and the same word is used in the Talmud, bab. Sōṭa, 22a, of the Magi *rāṭēn megūshā we-lā yāda' māy āmar*. But it is not only Arabic which uses the word *zamzam* in respect of Persian religious texts and magic formulae in general (Ibn Hishām, p. 171, 7 *zamzamat al-kāhin*, otherwise also *hamhama*, *Agh.*, XIV, p. 11, 6 or *ajlaba*, 'Alq., 3:21 *rāqin mujlibun*); Persian authors use it also. Prof. Spiegel wrote to me about this on March 19, 1886: 'In this sense the word is also used by Firdōsī. Thus Māpūr says, p. 1443, 6 from below, to his guest: "Bring the Zandawesta and Barsōm, in murmur (*bi-zamzam*) will I ask your reply" i.e. "You are to swear by Awesta that what you say is true." Also p. 1638, 4, in the same book, during an expedition of Nūshirwān against the Greeks, it is recounted of the great men: *bi-zamzam hamī āfarīn khwānadand*. Nevertheless I am reluctant to interpret *tafsīr zamzama* in the sense of "commentary on the Avesta," since to my knowledge there is no mention there of the things of which al-Jāḥiẓ speaks. [See however above, p. 156 note 2, where it is pointed out that according to the correct translation this passage does not quote the commentary at all.] But if one wants to understand by it the exegetical Parsee literature in a wider sense, this is in my belief legitimate, since the Parsees have many maxims though no proverbs.' Further on he refers to *Mainyokhard* and the sayings of Buzurj-Mihr, *Shahn.*, p. 1713. Abu'l-'Alā' compares the noise of lances on armour to the murmuring of the Persians (*haynamat al-'Ajam*), *Ṣiqṭ.*, II, p. 153, v. 4.

After a reference to the literature of the Greeks and Indians, the representatives of the Shu'ūbiyya resume their glorification of the gifts of non-Arabs in this manner: 'He who reads all these books by Persians, Greeks and Indians will understand the depth of spirit of these nations and see their remarkable wisdom and will then be able to decide where eloquence and rhetoric can really be found and where this art attained perfection, and how those peoples who are famed for fine understanding of concepts, well chosen expressions and discrimination, judge the fact that Arabs agitate with spears, staffs and bows during their speeches. Indeed you are camel drivers and sheep herders; you continue to use lances in settled life, having retained this habit from your desert wanderings, you carry them in your permanent habitations because you used to carry them in your tents, and in peace because your feuds accustomed you to it. You have long dealt with camels; therefore your speech, too, is clumsy and the sounds you use are rough because of this, so that one might think there are only deaf people amongst you when you speak in public.' Then follows a long excursus, which is quite important to archaeologists, on primitive weapons of combat and Arab strategy as compared with the developed instruments of war and military art among the Persians. Because of my insufficient knowledge of these archaeological subjects I must forego a more detailed reproduction of this excursus.[1]

Against these arguments al-Jāḥiẓ represents the pro-Arab view and endeavours to refute the attacks of the Shu'ūbiyya, but does not 173
deal with any one of them in as much detail as with the attack on the rhetorical gifts of Arabs. His remarks on Indian and Greek literature are interesting chiefly because of their naïveté. 'It is true,' he says, 'that the Indians have left a vast literature, but it consists entirely

[1] In order to understand them, the passage by Ibn Qutayba, mentioned by Rosen, l.c., p. 776, will have to be compared.

place.] These seem to have impressed Arab belletrists; in the fourth century Abu'l-Faḍl al-Sukkarī [cf. *Yāqūt, Irshād al-Arīb*, II, p. 33] and Abū 'Abd Allāh al-Abīwardī concerned themselves with spreading them in the Arabic language (*Yatīmat al-Dahr*, IV, pp. 22 ff., 25); cf. also ibid., p. 167 below and my *Beiträge zur Literaturgeschichte der Shî'a*, p. 28.

[4] *Siyar al-mulūk*. These are works like those which Firdawsī used as sources for the national traditions treated by him and from which al-Ṭabari (cf. Nöldeke, *Geschichte der Perser und Araber*, pp. XIV ff.) quotes extracts. A large number of *Siyar al-mulūk* books are enumerated by al-Bīrūnī, ed. Sachau, p. 99, 17 ff. and in the *Fihrist*. Among older Arab authors they are used and cited also by Ibn Qutayba; cf. Rosen, '*Zur arabischen Literaturgeschichte der ältern Zeit*', *Mélanges asiatiques*, St Petersbourg, VIII (1880), p. 777. [Cf. also Muḥammad Qazwīnī, *Bīst Maqāla*, Teheran 1332 solar A.H., II, pp. 7 ff.; V. Minorsky, in *Studi orientalistici in onore di Giorgio Levi della Vida*, II, pp. 159-62, with further references.]

of anonymous[1] works transmitted from very ancient times to posterity. The Greeks had solid achievements in philosophy and logic, but the founder of logic himself had a whining way of reciting, and though he taught scientific distinction of the parts of speech he himself was no great orator. Galen was the most eminent logician, but the Greeks themselves do not name him amongst the masters of the art of speaking. The Persians may have good orators but their eloquence is always the result of long thought, deep study and counsel. It is founded in literary scholarship, so that the successor always builds upon the efforts of his predecessors and the last man always uses the fruit of all previous thinking. It is quite different amongst the Arabs.[2] Their eloquence is spontaneous, extempore, as
174 if the result of inspiration. It is produced without effort or deep study, without exercise of reason and without the aid of others. The speaker prepares to speak or recite a verse, on the day of battle, or when watering the beasts, or when driving his camel on his wanderings; as soon as he concentrates his thoughts on the subject of his speech the concepts and words just flow from his mouth as if by themselves. Nor did the old Arab poets endeavour to preserve their speeches or transmit it to their children. The Arabs had no knowledge of writing and their art was inborn and not acquired.[3] To speak

[1] Anonymous and pseudonymous works are considered abnormal by these circles. See only *Fihrist*, p. 355, 14: 'I say, however, that it is folly for an eminent man to sit down and take all the trouble to write a book containing 2,000 pages, the composition of which plagues his mind and thoughts, then to trouble his hand and body with copying these things and then afterwards to attribute all this to another man, whether real or fictitious (*r. mawjūdin aw ma'dūmin* instead of the accusative of the ed.); this I say is a folly which must not be expected of anyone and to which no one consents who has given but one hour to science. What use or reward would there be in such an act?' On pseudonyms see also *Agh.*, I, p. 169, 3 from below.

[2] The remark of the best aesthetic critic of Arabic literature, Ibn al-Athīr al-Jazarī (died 637), on a shortcoming of Arab literature might be mentioned here. Ibn al-Athīr concludes his treatise on poetry and prose with the following words: 'I found that in respect of the point just mentioned the Arabs are outdone by the Persians. Persian poets write poetical books which from beginning to end contain well-ordered descriptions of stories and events and which move in the highest levels of the eloquence of the national language. Thus, for example, al-Firdawsī wrote his book *Shāhnāma* in 60,000 lines; it contains the whole history of the Persians and is the Koran of the nation, since their most important rhetoricians are in agreement that there is nothing in their literature to excel this work in elegance. There is nothing comparable in the Arabic language despite its wealth and versatility, and despite the fact that the Persian language is but a drop in the sea in comparison with it.' In other words: the Persians excel the Arabs by having an epical literature which the latter lack. *Al-Mathal al-Sā'ir*, p. 503 (end of the work).

[3] A similar idea is also ascribed to Ibn al-Muqaffa'—the praise of Arabs would be more effective if it came from such a source: 'The Arabs are wise

well was so natural to everyone that it was not necessary to write down the work performed or to make it the subject of study and tradition; just as the examples of their predecessors were not available to them. Thus only that which a man had involuntarily remembered was ever transmitted; it is but a small part of the great mass which is known only to him who counts the drops in the clouds and knows the number of the grains of sand. Of this any Shuʿūbite might convince himself if he but came to the dwelling-places of the true Arabs.'

In another work, too, al-Jāḥiẓ seizes the opportunity to attack the Shuʿūbiyya. What he says reveals that the representatives of the Shuʿūbiyya even in his days did not rest content with defending their assertions but had gone as far as immoderate aggression. He states that the long disputations eventually led to real scuffles, and he voices the conviction that the ideas of the Shuʿūbiyya lead to religious apostasy 'since the Arabs were the first to produce Islam.'[1] Al-Jāḥiẓ has given proof of his anti-Shuʿūbite tendency in other works, too. In the introduction to his *Kitāb al-Ḥayawān* he feels called upon to say, among other things, of the opponents of his literary activity: 'You have criticized me for my book on the descen- 175
dants of ʿAdnān and Qaḥṭān and accused me of exceeding the limits of enthusiasm, saying that I have been guilty of fanaticism, showing the glory of the ʿAdnānīs only by disparaging the Qaḥṭānīs; you further find fault with me because of my book on Arabs and *mawālī* and accuse me of depriving the *mawālī* of their rights, attributing things to the Arabs which they do not deserve; and you also reprove me for my book on Arabs and non-Arabs, and think that because of this distinction the same can be said as of the distinction between Arabs and *mawālī*.'[2]

VI

From these literary data it is evident that in the lifetime of Ibn Qutayba and al-Jāḥiẓ, i.e. in the third century A.H., the literary feud between the friends of the Arabs and the Shuʿūbites was indulged in to a far greater extent than the relics of the literature would indicate. As an echo, so to speak, of this literary movement we find in the fourth century the learned Iranian al-Bīrūnī, who wrote in

[1] *Kitāb al-Ḥayawān*, fol. 398b [VII, p. 220]. Unfortunately this part of the manuscript is very corrupt and hastily written.

[2] Ibid., fol. 2a [I, pp. 4-5].

without following examples or the traditions of predecessors; they deal with camels and sheep, live in tents made from hair and skins . . . they have educated themselves and their high sentiment has elevated them etc.' (there follows a panegyric on the historical position of the Arab people), *al-ʿIqd*, II, p. 51.

Arabic, defending the cause of the Persian race against the exaggerations of the pro-Arabs, and especially against Ibn Qutayba.[1] Religious sectarianism also profited from this agitation of minds. Towards the end of the third century we find that the Qarmaṭian propaganda in southern Persia combines their religious and political teachings with the thesis 'that God does not like the Arabs because they killed al-Ḥusayn, that He prefers to them the subjects of the Chosroes and their successors because only they did defend the rights of the Imams to the Caliphate,'[2] a doctrine which was taught to the initiated amongst the followers of the Ismā'īliyya, of which these Qarmaṭians were a branch. According to the account of Akhū Muḥsin this doctrine was taught in the ninth grade of initiation into the mysteries of the sect.[3]

While the Arabs and the national zealots were engaged in trivial quarrels about the recognition of the excellences of their respective races, the philosophical consideration of social conditions appeared
176 as an unbiased element. The philosophers were little suited to side with one or the other party; they weighed the virtues and faults of races and nationalities coolly and rationally, and found that they counterpoised each other in each people. Al-Kindī made the ancestor of the Greeks a brother to Qaḥṭān presumably for just such reasons.[4] An interesting document of this unbiased way of looking at things is the competition of confessions and nationalities as it is represented in a chapter of the encyclopaedia of the Ikhwān al-Ṣafā', presumably not without intent to take a reasonable stand in the quarrels of that time.[5]

But in any case the activities of the Shu'ūbiyya did at least damp the enthusiasm of those circles which hitherto had not ceased to disparage all and sundry in favour of the Arabs. The highly developed self-confidence of the Arabs must have been subjected to a great deal of doubt until in the fourth century Abu'l-'Alā' al-Ma'arrī, himself a descendant of the tribe of Quḍā'a (though at the same time a mocker of everything that was sacred to others), could write a poem to the glory of the Persian people:

[1] *Chronologie der orientalischen Völker*, ed. Sachau, p. 238, cf. the editor's introduction, p. 27.

[2] De Goeje, *Mémoires sur les Carmathes du Bahraïn et les Fatimides* 2nd ed. pp. 33; 207, 9.

[3] Guyard, *Fragments relatifs à la doctrine des Ismaélis* (Notices et extraits, XXII, i), p. 403. [Statements in anti-Ismā'īlī pamphlets, such as that by Akhū Muḥsin, cannot be accepted on their face value; nevertheless we may well believe that the early Ismā'īlī missionaries occasionally appealed to Persian national sentiment.]

[4] [Al-Mas'ūdī, *Murūj al-Dhahab*, II, p. 244, whence] Ibn Badrūn, p. 48.

[5] [*Rasā'il Ikhwān al-Ṣafā'*, Cairo 1928, II, pp. 235-44 =] *Thier und Mensch vor dem König der Genien*, ed. Dieterici, pp. 59-68; not without influence on later representations like *Fākihat al-Khulafā'*, p. 136.

May Quḍā'a list their days of glory and Ḥimyar boast their kings
While the Arab king al-Mundhir was but a governor in the service of Kisrā of a town in the land of Ṭaff.
Will not he who seeks silver find this (the search for silver) trivial when you spend red gold?
And who will look for pearls at the bottom of the sea when from your mouth flow the noblest of pearls?
You are pointed out with the finger, etc.

Thus the Persian race is addressed in praise by the Arab poet.[1]

[1] *Siqṭ al-Zand*, III, p. 24. [At the end of this chapter it may be recalled that Goldziher published a study of the Shu'ūbiyya of Spain in *Zeitschrift der deutschen morgenländischen Gesellschaft*, 1899, pp. 601 ff., and that the text analyzed by him is printed in full in 'Abd al-Salām Hārūn's *Nawādir al-Makhṭuṭāt*, III.]

177 CHAPTER FIVE

THE SHU'ŪBIYYA AND ITS MANIFESTATION IN SCHOLARSHIP

Since Shu'ūbiyya signifies a movement entirely literary represented by scholars and belletrists its influence was inevitably felt not only in competitive polemic, as we have seen in the last chapter, but also in the treatment of those branches of scholarship in which the question of nationality was necessarily paramount. We deal here with two branches of scholarship in particular, in order to show how the followers of the Shu'ūbiyya brought their views into play in their treatment of the subject. We refer to the two groups of knowledge and research which grew particularly from Arab national consciousness and from which Arab national feeling drew most of its nourishment, and which therefore seemed to call most for interference by the Shu'ūbiyya—namely genealogy (*'ilm al-ansāb*) in its connection with research into old Arab stories, and Arabic philology (*'ilm al-lugha*).

A. GENEALOGY

I

The old Arabs had no science of genealogy—indeed science had no part in their lives at all—but they had to be concerned with genealogical questions because of the nature and direction of their political life, social views, and the ancient customary law upon which family connections were founded. Among a people whose poets constantly dwell upon the glorious deeds of tribal ancestors, proclaim them at every opportunity, and defend them in competition
178 with other tribes, the individual tribes were obliged to know, not only the traditions concerning these deeds, but also the lineages of their ancestors—even if they had no systematic genealogical trees—and transmit them from generation to generation. These freely transmitted lineages did not yet, however, become symbols of canonical importance as they did later on and they could not yet go back to the distant past. It would, however, be underestimating these genealogies to think that they moved only in the individual circle of particular family consciousness, and that they did not rise to the level of putting various groups under a common ancestor. Nöldeke has lately pro-

vided us with some data to show that even in pre-Islamic days genealogical descriptions of a collective nature had existed.[1] But a systematization of these loose and fragmentary traditions had not been achieved so far. The collective designations of ancestors reaching back to the remote past were, so to speak, in the air: a continuous chain did not yet exist to connect them with generations for which the tribal traditions already had some fixed dates. The filling of these gaps pre-supposed an enormous number of fictions for which the basis was found only after Islam.

The fact that the Arabs, despite the opposite direction of Islamic teaching, did not cease to find pleasure in their inherited tribal boasting, and to cultivate the traditions of their particularistic tribal pride, was of help in founding the system of genealogical traditions which became possible with the awakening of speculative inclinations in Islam after administrative interests also had favoured the establishment of genealogical data. Closer acquaintance with Biblical history, to which the exegetes of the Koran were perforce led by the Biblical allusions and references in it, later enriched these beginnings with new material and paved the way for the connection of Arab genealogy with Biblical accounts. Jewish scholars had their share in creating these links.[2] The ever-increasing competition of 179
northern and southern Arabs, as we have seen, promoted these efforts; and the genealogy which went beyond ʿAdnān as it was plotted in the scholarly workshops, was to give theoretical justification for those feuds which had their root only in a hazy sense of tribal differences. Names which in Arab traditions were merely general descriptions now found their fixed place in the genealogical register: for example Maʿadd,[3] which had been a more general concept in old days, now found a fixed place in the register of ancestors of the northern Arabs.[4] For the more particular confirmation of fictitious claims and for the firmer ratification of the sequence of ancestors,

[1] *ZDMG*, XL, p. 178.

[2] [Ibn Saʿd, I,/1 pp. 28-9, quoted by] Sprenger, *Muhammed*, III, p. CXXXIII on Abū Yāʿqūb, the Jewish convert from Palmyra. The same information is in Ṭab., I, p. 1116, and cf. Meier, 'Ante-Mahometan history of Arabia' (*Calcutta Review*, no. XXXIX, 1853), p. 40. From a note by Ibn al-Kalbī (in Yāqūt, II, p. 862) it is evident that this Abū Yaʿqūb produced Biblical genealogies and fitted them to new circumstances with the aid of his own inventions. The Palmyrene Jews were not considered equal even in Talmudic times, bab. *Yebhāmōth*, fol. 17a.

[3] Cf. above, p. 88, note 8.

[4] We will leave in suspense the question whether the words ascribed to the dying Labīd, *Agh.*, XIV, p. 101, 5 from below (*wa-hal anā illā min Rabīʿata aw Muḍar*) can be quoted also as proof of the exact use of such genealogical concepts. Even if one does not doubt the genuineness of the poem in which they occur, it could not have been the poet's intention to specify his tribal affiliation. He says only: Am I different from any other man, whether Rabīʿa or Muḍar?

such details were accredited by means of apocryphal verses—an undoubted authority in the eyes of the uncritical public to whom this learning continued to be imparted most diligently well into later times.[1]

At any rate the extension of genealogy beyond 'Adnān provided new food for the genealogical competition of southern and northern Arabs. The pious Muslims therefore condemned these genealogical endeavours and were well able to quote traditional sayings to support this condemnation.[2] The viewpoint of the pious Muslims is evident from the following discussion of Ibn Khaldūn, which also includes the traditions relevant here: 'Mālik was asked whether it was permissible to trace one's descent right to Adam. He disapproved, asking, "How can this be known?" "And up to Ismā'īl?" Mālik disapproved of this also, saying: "Who can give information about
180 this?" Nor was it thought fitting for the descent of the prophets to be traced genealogically. Many of the older authorities were of the same opinion. Of one of them it is told that he used to remark on Sūra 16:10 ("And those who are behind them are known only to Allāh"): "The genealogists therefore lied."[3] Reference is made to the tradition of Ibn 'Abbās, according to which the Prophet used to say, after he had traced his descent up to 'Adnān: "And from here on the genealogists lie."[4] Reference is also made to another of the Prophet's sayings—that this is a field the knowledge of which is of little use and ignorance of which does no harm.[5] Other sayings, too, are quoted in support of this opinion. Many of the authorities on tradition and law, however, such as Ibn Isḥāq, al-Ṭabarī and al-Bukhārī, thought that the use of these old genealogies was permissible, and did not disapprove of them, citing the case of Abū Bakr, who was called the

[1] Cf. Ṭab., I, p. 1118: 'One of the genealogists reported to me that he found a group of Arab scholars who transmitted forty ancestors of Ma'add with Arab names up to Ismā'īl; for their statements they brought proofs from the poems of the Arabs. The number of ancestors corresponds to the number transmitted by Jewish scholars, only the names differ. 'Al-Tabrīzī, *Ḥam.*, p. 159, does not regard as unusual the fact that verses were invented for genealogical purposes.

[2] Cf. *Agh.*, I, p. 8, 5 from below. [For the discussion about the status of genealogical studies and the tracing of the Prophet's lineage beyond 'Adnān see also Ibn Sa'd, I/1, p. 28; al-Balādhurī, *Ansāb al-Ashrāf*, I, p. 12; Ibn 'Abd al-Barr, *al-Inbāh*, Cairo 1350, pp. 42 ff.; Ibn Kathīr, *al-Bidāya*, II, p. 194.]

[3] In order to justify continued pre-occupation with genealogy despite the above sayings, the casuistic point was made that the word *kadhaba* belongs to the *aḍdād* and thus the above saying means just the opposite: 'Genealogists have said the truth', *ZDMG*, III, p. 104.

[4] Cf. al-Mas'ūdī, IV, p. 112, 118 [Ibn Sa'd, I/1, p. 28].

[5] [Cf. Ibn Wahb, *Jāmi'*, pp. 4–5; Ibn Ḥazm, *Jamharat Ansāb al-'Arab*, p. 3; Ibn 'Abd al-Barr, *al-Inbāh*, p. 43; al-Sam'ānī, *al-Ansāb*, Hyderabad 1962, pp. 9–10; al-Suyūṭī, *al-Jāmi' al-Ṣaghīr*, II, p. 60; al-Zurqānī, *Sharḥ al-Mawāhib*, V, p. 395; *Kanz al-'Ummāl*, old ed., V, p. 236.]

greatest scholar in the genealogy of Quraysh, Muḍar and the other Arabs.[1] Also Ibn 'Abbās, Jubayr b. Muṭ'im, 'Aqīl b. Abī Ṭālib and, in the subsequent generation, Ibn Shihāb al-Zuhrī, Ibn Sīrīn, etc. are named as learned genealogists. In my view, the truth of this controversial question is that neither of the two opinions can be maintained in its absolute form. It is not the study of the easily accessible genealogy of the more recent generations which is forbidden, since this knowledge is needed for various religious, political and social purposes. Moreover, it is transmitted that the Prophet and his companions traced their descent to Muḍar and made inquiries about it. The following saying of the Prophet is also transmitted: "Learn of your genealogical tree as much as is needed for the practice of active love towards blood relations."[2] All this, of course, refers to the closer generations and the above-mentioned interdiction refers to distant generations, knowledge of which is not easily available, and can be gained only through the evidence of poetic passages and by means of deep study, because of the passage of time and the large number of intervening generations. In some cases nothing can be
learned of such distant epochs since whole peoples who were involved 181
have since perished. To occupy oneself with such things is rightly condemned.'[3]

The administrative considerations mentioned by Ibn Khaldūn (division of booty, participation in the income of the state, etc.) made genealogical registers a political necessity in the days of the old Caliphate. Sprenger has illustrated this fact with a large amount of good evidence and has evaluated 'Umar's importance in the furtherance of this genealogical work.[4] Administrative considerations also determined genealogical research, in order with its help to reject unjustified claims and correct the current genealogical traditions of

[1] Al-Jāḥiẓ, *Kitāb al-Bayān*, fol. 105 a [I, pp. 321-2] has a special list of the most famous genealogists of the earliest days of Islam; cf. also Ibn Ḥajar, I, p. 461. [For Abū Bakr as genealogist see al-Balādhurī, *Ansāb al-Ashrāf*, I, p. 416; Ibn 'Abd al-Barr, *al-Inbāh*, p. 43; al-Suyūṭī, *Ta'rīkh al-Khulafā'*, Cairo 1952, pp. 42–3; for Jubayr b. Muṭ'im see E. Sachau in *Mitteilungen des Seminars für Orient. Sprachen*, 1904, p. 172; Ibn 'Abd al-Barr, *al-Istī'āb*, p. 88; idem, *al-Inbāh*, p. 43; Ibn Ḥajar, *al-Iṣāba*, I, p. 235; for 'Aqīl: Ibn 'Abd al-Barr, *al-Inbāh*, p. 43; Ibn Abi'l-Ḥadīd, *Sharḥ Nahj al-Balāgha*, III, p. 82; al-Ṣafadī, *Naqt al-Himyān*, p. 200].

[2] Cf. *al-'Iqd*, II, p. 44; [al-Bukhārī, *al-Adab al-Mufrad*, pp. 17–18; Ibn Ḥazm, *Jamharat Ansāb al-'Arab*, p. 2; Ibn Abd al-Barr, al-*Inbāh*, p. 42; al-Sam'ānī, *al-Ansāb*, I, pp. 5–8].

[3] [Ibn Khaldūn, *al-'Ibar*, Būlāq 1284, II, pp. 3-4; I have omitted the comma put by Goldziher between Ibn Shihāb and al-Zuhrī; in the ed. also *wa* between the two should be omitted.]

[4] *Muhammed*, III, pp. CXXII ff. Now the important passage of the *Kitāb al-Kharāj* (ed. Būlāq), p. 14, 62, can be compared for the institution of the *dawāwīn* by 'Umar.

individual families.[1] This was the more important since it seems to have happened quite frequently that a lineage attached itself without justification to some more powerful group—e.g. the Quraysh—perhaps because the two groups lived in political unity.[2] But it appears that the conditions created by 'Umar were soon violated and protection was exercised in this field too. This, at least, would seem to follow from the information that Ziyād accepted Ḥāritha b. Badr (died 50), who was a Tamīmite, into the *dīwān* of the Qurayshites because he had a great affection for him.[3]

This however was quite different genealogical material from that which the pagans used in their poetry for panegyric and satire and from which they drew material for tribal competition. Yet the importance which was attached to the genealogical tables by the government was on the one hand an aid to the continuation of the old Arab tribal jealousy, while on the other it became the point of departure for the progressive systematization of genealogy. This department of knowledge became a popular branch of the philological sciences
182 which were just beginning to develop. The Ḥanẓalite Daghfal (who flourished under Mu'āwiya I and died 50) is named as the father of the recognised science of genealogy. 'More learned in genealogy than Daghfal' became an Arabic proverb.[4] From a poem by Miskīn al-Dārimī (died 90) one may conclude that at the time it was not only information on facts of descent but also, in the old Arab manner, on the excellences and faults of the individual members of the genealogical chain which was expected of the genealogists. Apart from Daghfal, and Shihāb b. Madh'ūr, this poem indicates the family of the Banu'l-Kawwā'[5] as authorities in this field.[6] It is interesting that Daghfal

[1] The best known example is that of the Khulj. The Banū 'Awf, who believed themselves to be Dhubyānīs, were incorporated into the Quraysh; al-Yā'qūbī, I, p. 271. It is difficult to find the motive which makes 'Alī advocate the maintenance of the Dhubyānī traditions of the Banū 'Awf. [For 'Awf cf. also al-Balādhurī, *Ansāb al-Ashrāf*, I, pp. 42–43; Ibn Ḥabīb, *al-Muḥabbar*, p. 169; Ibn Ḥazm, *Jamharat Ansāb al-'Arab*, p. 165.]

[2] Cf. e.g., the satirical poem by Ḥassān against the Banū 'Awf; *Dīwān*, p. 19, 17 [ed. Hirschfeld, 208: 1], against the Banū Asad b. Khuzayma, ibid. 82, 11 [Hirschf., 99: 3], against the Banū Thaqīf, ibid. p. 83, 5 [Hirschf., 198: 3]. All this illustrates the uncertainty of genealogical traditions.

[3] *Agh.*, XXI, p. 22, 4. [See also the satirical verses about him for moving his *dīwān* to Quraysh: al-Balādhurī, *Ansāb al-Ashrāf*, MS., fol. 1003r.]

[4] Al-Maydānī, II, p. 253. [Daghfal was the son of Ḥanẓal, but belonged to the Sadūs branch of Shaybān.]

[5] Probably the well-known Khārijite family, descendants of Ibn al-Kawwā', who in Ḥarūrā was amongst the opponents of 'Alī (al-Ya'qūbī, II, p. 223); a satire against the Yashkurite family is in *Agh.*, XIII. p, 54. 'Abd Allāh b. al-Kawwā' sketches for Mu'āwiya, in the manner of genealogists of the early time, the character of inhabitants of the various provinces of the empire in short, and pregnant sentences; Ibn al-Faqīh, p. 135, and the parallel passages mentioned by de Goeje, ib. b. Cf. also Ibn Qutayba, ed. Wüstenfeld, p. 266.

already exceeds the boundaries of specifically national genealogy and makes the connection with Biblical patriarchs.[1]

At the beginning of the Umayyad period these primitive beginnings which had previously existed in genealogical matters found their further development.

The activity of Daghfal under Muʿāwiya I shows us that this productivity in the ancient history of the Arabs in fact and fiction found much encouragement under this prince's rule, which is shown, too, by the activity of the southern Arab scholar ʿAbīd b. Shariya at the court of the caliph, who had summoned this man to Syria in order to discuss with him information concerning antiquity.[2] The compilation of a work on 'the old stories, the kings of the Arabs and non-Arabs, the confusion of languages and its cause, the history of the dispersal of mankind in the various countries' is said to have been due to such information.[3] This work, which is now completely lost and in which, as is evident from the title, the ancient history of the Arabs was interwoven with Biblical accounts,[4] was widespread and 183
widely read in the first centuries of Islam. We learn from al-Hamdānī (died 334) that in his day various versions of the book were current; these were so widely divergent and so much was added to the original text that there were hardly two copies alike;[5] and the younger contemporary of the above-mentioned author, al-Masʿūdī (died 346), calls it a 'well-known book in everybody's hands.'[6]

The genealogists of the old school were not only knowledgeable in matters of descent, nor were they mere collectors of nomenclatures. Continuing in this respect the activities of the old poets,[7] who in pre-Islamic days were the only organs of historical memory, they were also concerned—as we have already hinted in the case of Daghfal—with the characterization and description of the qualities of tribes, and had the gift of summarizing these in short, sharply

[1] Ibn al-Faqīh, p. 314.

[2] Also explanations of old proverbs by means of legends from the Arab past; *Agh.*, XXI, p. 191, 206, 8. [The correct form of the name is ʿUbayd.]

[3] *Fihrist*, pp. 89-90. The title: *Kitāb al-Mulūk wa-Akhbār al-Māḍīn* ('Book of kings and news on past lineages').

[4] Cf. also al-Masʿūdī, III, p. 275.

[5] Ibn Ḥajar, III, p. 202.

[6] Al-Masʿūdī, IV, p. 89.

[7] The sharp observation of the physical characteristics of the tribes as signs of tribal affiliation is worthy of note: the Fazārites were known by their yellow teeth, Asadites by their bent posture on horseback, etc.; *Agh.*, XVI, p. 55, 21; cf. Sprenger, III, p. 389.

---

[6] Al-Jāḥiẓ, *Bayān*, fol. 110a [I, p. 351]. [See also the edition by Schulthess in *ZDMG*, LIV, p. 451, with copious notes on Daghfal and the other genealogists mentioned. For Daghfal add al-Jāḥiẓ, *al-Bayān*, index p. 295; Ibn Ḥabīb, *al-Muḥabbar*, p. 478.]

characteristic, and apt sayings;[1] they were also eloquent in giving personal descriptions of eminent men of the past.[2] The genealogists were also the depositories of the history and the traditions of the Arab tribes, of all that is called *akhbār*, i.e. 'accounts',[3] of the battle-days of the old Arabs (*ayyām al-'Arab*), and the proverbs which could not be understood without knowledge of ancient Arab history, to which they constantly referred. They were also concerned with archaeological questions and linked also this part of their information to the exegesis of ancient poetry. Some of the data which they offer probably have their origin in a more easy and plausible explanation of such verses. To transmit the historical connections and occasions of such verses or—as was probably even more often the case—to discover them, was the main task of these men, and a large part of the traditions which form the stories of the ancient Arabs owes its
184 existence to this activity of transmitting and inventing.[4] They also included pre-historic fables among their traditions and later also biblical legends, a field which they later shared with the *quṣṣāṣ*, i.e. the tellers of edifying stories.

> 'Tales of the history of 'Ād and Jurhum which the two marvellous scholars Zayd (b. al-Kayyis al-Namarī) and Daghfal inquired into.'[5]

The latter is called 'the unfathomable sea of story tellers' (*baḥr al-ruwāt al-khaḍārim*)[6] and both were bracketed together under the name of *al-'iḍḍān*, roughly 'the two devils of fellows.'[7] It is not surprising that such men were known as the 'scholars of the Arabs' (*'ulamā' al-'Arab*)[8] since they could give information about the nation's past. This was seen as a sign of special gifts, and ordinary people also attributed to these revealers of the past a deep insight into future events about which they were questioned. The poet Qudāma al-Quray'ī, to whom Daghfal presented his genealogy in

[1] Al-Jāḥiẓ, *Bayān*, fol. 38a [I, p. 247]: the characteristic which Daghfal gives of the Banū 'Āmir, etc.; *al-'Iqd*, II, p. 53, *qawl Daghfal fī qabā'il al-'Arab*, III, p. 353, of the Banū Makhzūm.

[2] *Agh.*, I, p. 8 above.

[3] Much as the authors of the old *Tōledōth* interweave the historical traditions of old times with genealogical material.

[4] An interesting passage in al-Tabrīzī's commentary to the *Ḥamāsa*, p. 697, v. 3, shows that correct statements on the historical occasions of the verses were considered as belonging to the particular field of genealogists.

[5] [Al-Quṭāmī, *Dīwān*, 11:4, quoted by] al-Maydānī, I, p. 15.

[6] *Al-Qaṣīda al-Fazāriyya*, fol. 185b (MS. of the Royal Library, Berlin, cod. Petermann, no. 184).

[7] Al-Maydānī, II, p. 31.

[8] *Agh.*, XVI, p. 20, cf. Ṭab., I, p. 1118.

exact sequence,[1] wanted to know also the day of his death. 'This is not my field' replied Daghfal.[2] This assumption of the deeper illumination of genealogists has its roots in the past of the genealogical art. It seems that formerly questions about descent were settled by people who were deemed to have knowledge of secret circumstances and conditions, so-called *qā'ifs* who pretended to read from footprints[3] and physiognomical characteristics matters which were closed to common understanding.[4]

Ibn al-Kalbī lists ten characteristics which are typical only of 185
Arabs; five are shown on the head, five on the rest of the body. Apart from these physical qualities, Arabs are marked too by the ability of *qiyāfa*. A man may observe two people, one of whom is short, the other slender, one black-skinned, the other white, and from this he may be able to conclude that the short man is the son of the slender man, the black one of the white.[5] Usāma b. Zayd was suspected of illegitimate descent in the time of the Jāhiliyya because his face was quite black whereas his father Zayd b. Ḥāritha 'was whiter than wool'. In the Prophet's days a *qā'if* concluded from the comparison of both their footprints that Usāma could have descended only from Zayd.[6] According to a biased fiction it was established in a similar manner that 'Āṣ b. Wā'il is the father of 'Amr b. al-'Āṣ.[7] It is worthy of note that this *qā'if* also held the office of cutting off the forelocks of prisoners of war before they were set free[8] and was therefore called

[1] *Fihrist*, p. 89, 16.

[2] Al-Maydānī, II, p. 253.

[3] Similarity of feet is used even later as proof of a genealogical link, *Agh.*, XVIII, p. 178, 8.

[4] Cf. Freytag, *Einleitung in das Studium der arab. Sprache*, p. 134. A synonym of *qā'if* is also *ḥāzir*; *Agh.*, X, p. 38, 17. It might be mentioned that the Gā'ōn Haya, whose words are cited by Moses b. Ezra in *Kitāb al-Muḥāḍara wa'l Mudhākara*, fol. 19a (MS. Oxford, communication of Dr. Schreiner), in his *Kitāb al-Ḥāwī* explains the word *Ashshūrīm* (Gen., 25:3) which in many old tranlations and commentaries (Onkelos, Jerus. Targum, Ibn Ezra, etc.) is considered an appellative—as 'seers' (*qāfa*).

[5] *Al-'Iqd*, II, p. 50.

[6] B. *Farā'iḍ*, no. 30, Muslim, III, p. 359; cf. for further reference, Robertson Smith, p. 286. The Banū Mudlij especially provided the *qāfa* of the old Arabs, Ibn Qutayba, ed. Wüstenfeld, p. 32, 11 [Ibn Ḥazm, *Jamharat Ansāb al-'Arab*, p. 176, 16; *Lisān al-'Arab*, s.v. *dlj*]. In our days the Banū Fahm in the region of Mecca are considered the best *qāfa*: they know from footprints the most intimate qualities of men (Doughty, II, p. 625).

[7] *Al-'Iqd*, I, p. 164 below, cf. ib., p. 22.

[8] E.g. *al-'Iqd*, III, p. 64 and frequently. Cf. in Wellhausen, *Arab. Heidenthum*, many passages referring to the removal of hair as a punishment. See also *Agh.*, XV, p. 56, 18. Unchaste women have their heads shaved and are then led through the streets; *Agh.*, XVII, p. 83, 9. The old Babylonians, too, used shearing of hair as a punishment; *Transactions of Soc. Bibl. Arch.*, VIII (1884), p. 241. [Cf. *Kanz al-'Ummāl*, old ed., VI, pp. 355–6: removal of hair accompanying a *ḥadd*; and Ibn Qutayba, *'Uyūn al-Akhbār*, I, p. 73.]

Mujazziz.[1] The cutting off of hair was not merely an act of degradation and humiliation but had—as we shall see in a larger context in an excursus to this volume—a religious meaning. The cut hair was originally considered a sacrifice to the gods and it is important to note in this case that this office was held by a soothsayer who was also responsible for decisions in genealogical problems.[2]

186 While—as we have seen—the beginnings of speculative concern with genealogy and ancient history go back to the earliest Umayyad period, this branch of knowledge later developed into a much-cultivated integral part of philological study. Right from the beginning fictions and biased fables, more especially the party interests of the northern and southern Arabs, were the easily accessible sources from which genealogy derived its material, and supplemented the gaps in the traditions or any known facts;[3] it was according to these that the latter—as far as they really existed—were interpreted and used. Further developments retained the same characters. The genealogists tolerate no uncertainties; in the case of any important man they must be able to name the male and female ancestors with great accuracy, and also their tribal affiliations.[4] If one considers that —quite apart from differences of opinion in respect of the genealogy of individual notables of the past[5]—genealogists are frequently at loggerheads about general questions of the ancient history of the Arabs which are to be regarded as elements of genealogical knowledge,[6] one will understand that this chapter of Arab science was a battleground of individual caprices and tendentious inventions and often of base interests. Genealogy also seems to have lacked that control which otherwise saves biased theoreticians from excesses and which lies in the collective consciousness of a people. Even in the middle of the third century Ibn Qutayba can voice the accusation in the introduction to his manual of history 'that the noblest do not

[1] Cf. Ibn Ḥajar, III, p. 738. In al-Nawawī to Muslim l.c., there are also other variants for this word, e.g. *mujazzar* or *muḥriz*, etc., but they are not as well documented as *mujazziz*. Cf. also *al-jazzāz* as by-name for a man who cuts the *nāṣiya* of prisoners before they are set free; *Agh.*, X, p. 42, 5.

[2] Cf. *al-Muwaṭṭa'*, III, p. 207. [The article 'Ḳiyāfa' in the *Enc. of Islam* is mainly based on this passage of Goldziher, but has a few additional references.]

[3] Whether we may believe such a notorious falsifier as Ibn al-Kalbī, when he claims that he derived material from the archives of churches in Ḥīra (Ṭab., I, p. 1770), I am inclined to doubt.

[4] An interesting line in this respect is in Ibn Hishām, p. 113, 13. Compare to this the appeal to genealogists, *Agh.*, II, p. 166, 4, XIII, p. 151, 4 from below.

[5] Cf. the various opinions on the descent of Imrq. (*Agh.*, VIII, pp. 62 ff.), or on the time when Aws b. Ḥajar lived (ibid., X, p. 6).

[6] On the uncertainty of the genealogical determination of the tribe of Iyād, see Nöldeke, *Orient and Occident*, I, pp. 689-90. In the first century no complete unanimity was reached on the question whether membership of the Quraysh tribe was to be extended to all descendants of Naḍr b. Kināna, or whether this concept was to be limited; *Agh.*, XVIII, p. 198 below.

know their descent and the best know nothing of their ancestors; Qurayshites are often ignorant of the point in their descent which links them genealogically to the Prophet.' It was thus easy for the 187
professional genealogists to palm off their handiwork on the public and to indulge in wanton inventions and biased fables. The point of view which dictated the inner social life also set corresponding problems for genealogists and offered opportunity for vast differences of opinion—whether a given tribe was of northern or southern Arab origin. We will not deal here again with the often described discussion about the Quḍā'a and Khuzā'a—whether they belong to the northern Arab group or are southern Arabs;[1] nor will we repeat the fable with which harmonists sought to settle the question.[2] For the settling of this problem, too, recourse was had to the device, so popular in the genealogical and antiquarian literature, of making up tendentious verses (the harmonizing fable has one too) which were to serve as documentation. It is interesting that even Arab critics[3] know how much faith to place in such inventions, and even collectors with such a poor reputation for credibility as, for example, Ibn al-Kalbī,[4] openly cast doubt[5] upon such documentary verses (*shawāhid*).

But it was not verses only that the genealogists fabricated as *loci probantes* for the strengthening of one-sided inventions. They did not worry about the extent of falsification if they were out to strengthen a favourite thesis, whether the thesis were based on true tradition or —as was frequently the case—on tendentious considerations. The highest form of legitimization of a statement in the eye of Muslims was always reference to some saying of the Prophet. If this were recognised as authentic—and for this external points were usually decisive—further opposition became impossible. Genealogists of those days, in which the invention of Ḥadīth was already flourishing, did in fact refer to a ḥadīth in order to strengthen a point if nothing more authentic was available. Why should genealogists be any better than theologians, who made extensive use of this device? One example of this may suffice here:

Amongst the sub-tribes of the Quraysh there are the Banū Sāma; 188
Sāma whom they give as their ancestor is the son of Lu'ayy b. Ghālib, and the latter is the son of the eponymous hero of the tribe

[1] For Khuzā'a I refer in addition to *Agh.*, XVII, p. 158, 3 below.

[2] The latest discussions in Robertson Smith, pp. 8 ff. and other passages cited in the index.

[3] See above, p. 166, note 1.

[4] Very characteristic judgments of this man *Agh.*, IX, p. 19, XVIII, p. 161 (*maṣnū'āt Ibn al-Kalbī*). 'Whenever', says Yāqūt, (II, p. 158), 'scholars differ about pre-Islamic matters the view of Ibn al-Kalbī is always the most reasonable; nevertheless he is neglected and insulted with ironical remarks.'

[5] Ṭab., I, p. 751.

of Quraysh. In Baṣra there was a quarter where the descendants of this Sāma lived together, and because of their name wished to be considered as Qurayshites. The genealogists, presumably with the consent of the other Qurayshites, did not admit this, since it was an advantage to the latter to have fewer participants in the cash income which they were drawing. The genealogists then transmitted the following story, which probably had some foundation in the traditions of the tribe of Quraysh: Sāma is said to have left his home because of a family quarrel and to have been killed by a snake-bite on his way to 'Umān, where he first intended to go.[1] His wife Nājiya married a man from Baḥrayn, to whom she bore a son, Ḥārith. This son is said to have returned as a young man to the Qurayshites, his mother pretending that he was the son of Sāma. The Banū Sāma are descended from this Ḥārith and thus have no claim whatsoever to be considered as Qurayshites, so they were always called by the name of Ḥārith's mother: Banū Nājiya.[2] To this family belonged 'Alī b. al-Jahm al-Sāmī, court poet of Mutawakkil (died 249). He still had to bear the mockery which was the consequence of the genealogical troubles in the descent of the Banū Sāma.[3] A poet of the descendants of 'Alī, who was thus a full blood Qurayshite, addressed him
189 in the following words: 'Sāma, of course, was one of us, but his children—that is a dark affair; they are people who bring us genealogies which resemble the mutterings of a dreamer'.[4]

On the other hand there were genealogists even at that time who defended the Qurayshite affiliation of the Banū Sāma. At their head was al-Zubayr b. Bakkār, Qāḍī of Mecca (died 256), a liberal genealogist who, though a Qurayshite himself, did not grudge the Banū Sāma their claim to belong to Quraysh, because—as his enemies maintained—members of the Sāma family were opposed to the

[1] Al-Ya'qūbī, I, p. 270, Wüstenfeld, *Register zu den genealogischen Tabellen*, p. 411; cf. also *Agh.*, XXI, pp. 198 f. [For the discussions about Sāma see also al-Balādhurī, *Ansāb al-Ashrāf*, I, pp. 46–7; Ibn Ḥazm, *Jamharat Ansāb al-'Arab*, p. 163; Ibn Abi'l-Ḥadīd, *Sharḥ Nahj al-Balāgha*, I, pp. 262–4.]

[2] *Agh.*, IX, p. 104. It happens also in historical times that a child begotten in a previous marriage, but born in a new marriage, is called after the mother. The example which we can study in detail in *Agh.*, XI, p. 140, shows that the principle *al-walad li'l-firāsh* or *li-ṣāḥib al-firāsh* (which shows traces of the doctrine of Roman law *pater est quem iustae nuptiae demonstrant*) had not yet been fully accepted in the middle of the Umayyad period; otherwise the legal quarrel between Zufar and Ḍirār over the paternity of Arṭāt would be inexplicable. I add for the sake of completeness the sources of this Muslim legal principle (cf. Robertson Smith, p. 109 below): *al-Muwaṭṭa'*, III, p. 203; B. *Buyū'*, no. 100, *Wasāyā*, no. 4, *Maghāzī*, no. 54, *Farā'iḍ*, no. 18, *Muḥāribūn*, no. 9, *Khuṣūmāt*, no. 5; Muslim III, p. 357. [Cf. also J. Schacht, *Origins of Muhammadan Jurisprudence*, pp. 181–2.]

[3] Interesting notes about the position of this 'Alī b. al-Jahm are to be found in the article on Marwān al-Aṣghar, *Agh.*, XI, pp. 3 ff.

[4] Al-Mas'ūdī, VII, p. 250.

claims of the ʿAlids,[1] which determined the orthodox Qāḍī in their favour. Thus, as late as the third century there were differences of opinion and doubts amongst the genealogists about the tribal affiliation of the Banū Sāma. For example, in referring to a member of this tribe, an unusual form of words was used: ' ʿUmar b. ʿAbd al-ʿAzīz al-Sāmī, who traces his descent to Sāma b. Lu'ayy,'[2] the addition indicating the doubt about the correctness of the genealogical claim. But their opponents thought they could end this quarrel by inventing a saying of the Prophet, 'My uncle Sāma left no children.'[3] He who believed the authenticity of this saying could not believe that the Banū Nājiya had Sāma as their ancestor and were true Qurayshites.

But the tradition about the Banū Sāma did not find its way into canonical collections of tradition. It is much more characteristic if we find that a genealogical tradition of this kind was incorporated into the highly respected canonical collection of al-Bukhārī—the other collections do not quote it. It has already been mentioned that the genealogists differed about whether the tribe of Khuzāʿa was of northern or southern Arab origin. In order to have indisputable authority for its northern descent the genealogists defending this thesis invented a high-sounding saying: 'From Abū Hurayra. The Prophet said: ʿAmr b. Luḥayy b. Kamīʿa b. Khindif is the father of the Khuzāʿa.' Al-Bukhārī took this saying from Isḥāq b. Rāhawayhi.[4]

It is not our intention to outline the history of the development of 190
Islamic genealogical science, for we are concerned here only with stressing one particular point in this development. Thus we took the liberty of jumping from the beginnings of the genealogical speculations straight to the time of its highest development.

II

In respect of genealogical science too, the Arabs were excelled by the Persians and other new Muslims. These people liked to interfere in a field of research through the study of which they were able to control the aspirations of their Arab co-religionists. The Arabs did not seem to consider it natural that foreigners should participate in their national science. Even al-Mutanabbī mocked a foreigner, an otherwise respected statesman, because he undertook research into Arab

[1] To them also belonged al-Khirrīt b. Rāshid who revolted against ʿAlī, Ibn Durayd, p. 68. [The Qurayshite descent of the Banū Sāma is also admitted by al-Muṣʿab b. Zubayr, *Nasab Quraysh*, p. 440; Ibn Ḥabīb, *al-Muḥabbar*, p. 168.]

[2] Al-Yaʿqūbī, II, p. 599.

[3] *Agh.*, IX, p. 105, 5.

[4] B. *Manāqib*, no. 12. Many traditions were also invented in connection with the problem of Quḍāʿa; they are collected by al-Ṣiddīqī, fol. 86a. [See also Ibn ʿAbd al-Barr, *al-Inbāh*, pp. 59–63; Ibn Kathīr, *al-Sīra al-Nabawiyya*, Cairo 1964, I, pp. 4–6; *Kanz al-ʿUmmāl*, old ed., VII, p. 143.]

M

genealogy.[1] It is true that we find also amongst the true Arabs people versed in genealogy as it was studied by the ancient Arabs.[2] But the *mawālī* took hold, together with the other philological sciences, of the study of Arab antiquity which was almost indispensable to the knowledge of poetry, and they developed it far in excess of the framework of the old Arabic *ʿilm al-ansāb*. To what perfection some of them brought this, and what influence they had on the development of this field of study in the second century, is best seen from the example of Ḥammād al-Rāwiya (died 160)[3]. Hārūn al-Rashīd once asked Ismāʿīl b. Jāmiʿ, a scholar from Mecca, about the details of his own genealogy; the Arab scholar could give no proper information, but referred the caliph to Isḥāq, son of the singer Ibrāhīm al-Mawṣilī, who happened to be present. 'May God make you ugly,' cried the angry caliph; 'you are a shaykh from the tribe of Quraysh and do not know your genealogy and must ask a Persian for information.'[4]

191 The use that Persians made of this science of genealogy accorded well with the system of the Shuʿūbiyya party tendency; yet the presence of this tendency was little noticed, as it appeared that the more recent genealogists had only to link up with the traditions of the older Arab genealogy. It is said already of the ancient genealogist of the Quraysh tribe, Abū Jahm b. Ḥudhayfa, that people 'feared him because of his tongue',[5] and Daghfal himself is said to have concerned himself with the faults and weaknesses of tribes and with the shameful points in their history (*mathālib*)[6] and thus to have revived the practice of the pre-Islamic 'insults' that were contrary to the spirit of Islam.[7] Saʿīd b. al-Musayyab (died 94), who was one of the greatest theologians of his time and eminent also in genealogy,

[1] In the passage discussed by Chwolsohn, *Die Ssabier*, I, p. 700 [i.e. *bihā nabaṭiyyun min ahli'l-sawādi yudarrisu ansāba ahli'l-falā*, ed. Dieterici, p. 703].

[2] See a list in Ibn Qutayba, ed. Wüstenfeld, pp. 265 ff.; from later days we may mention the Shaybānī ʿAwf b. al-Muḥallim (died 210), known under the name of Abu-l-Muḥallim—he is called *al-nassāba*, *Agh.*, XVIII, p. 153, 1; 191, 23—by whom there were written notes, ibid., XI, p. 125, 5, cf. I, p. 32, 12.

[3] Sprenger, III, pp. CLXXI ff. [cf. van Arendonk's article in the *Enc. of Islam* s.v.].

[4] *Agh.*, VI, p. 69.

[5] Ibn Durayd, p. 87. [For Abū Jahm cf. Mu'arrij al-Sadūsī, *Ḥadhf min Nasab Quraysh*, p. 83; Muṣʿab, *Nasab Quraysh*, p. 369; Ibn ʿAbd al-Barr, *al-Istīʿāb*, p. 631.]

[6] This tendency of the ancient Arab genealogy has an analogy in the Jewish *Megillōth Yuḥasīn*, 'the lineage registers with good and bad family reports with partly invented genealogies which were collected by some families in Jerusalem,' cf. the relevant passages from Mishna and Gemara in Bloch, *Beiträge zur Einleitung in die talmudische Literatur* (Wien 1884), I, p. 15.

[7] Al-Ḥuṣrī, III, p. 263. [ʿAqīl b. Abī Ṭālib was feared on account of his genealogical traditions: Ibn Abi'l-Ḥadīd, *Sharḥ Nahj al-Balāgha*, III, p. 82; and cf. the story of Ḥakīm b. Ḥizām, al-Zubayr b. Bakkār, *Jamharat Nasab Quraysh*, p. 363; Ibn ʿAsākir, IV, p. 421.]

is said to have told a man who asked him for instruction in genealogy: 'I suppose you want to learn this science in order to be able to insult people,'[1] and it is remarkable that the son of this Sa'īd, himself a genealogist, had to be punished by the government because he used his science to the detriment of other men's honour.[2] The genealogist Hishām ibn al-Kalbī (died 204) was 'a great scholar, genealogist, transmitter of the *mathālib* and a scorner (*'ayyāba*)'[3] The business of 'scorning' remained closely linked with that of genealogy. The 'scorns' were not only concerned with revealing the shameful points in the history and genealogy of tribes, but also with inquiring into the authenticity of descent, as for example when the author of such a book of *mathālib*, the historian[4] Haytham b. 'Adī (died 207), proves, contrary to accepted belief, that Abū 'Amr b. Umayya was not a true son but an adopted son of the man he named as his father. This proof injured the noble descent of all descendants of 'Amr.[5]
Another example shows genealogists—citing the above-mentioned 192
Haytham from Ibn al-Kalbī—inquiring into the fact that even in the days of 'Umar an Arab still had a regular marital union with the wife of his deceased father, though Muhammed had condemned such marriages (*nikāḥ al-maqt*). This caused damage to the reputation of the latest descendants of this couple.[6] It is interesting that Haytham himself was considered a *da'ī* and because of this was forced to separate from his wife, who was an Arab woman of the tribe of Banū Ḥārith b. Ka'b, because the woman's tribal companions would not tolerate her marriage to an intruder unable to legitimize his Arab descent.[7] (Cf. above, pp. 122 ff.) In a satirical verse he was told: 'If you count 'Adī your father amongst the Banū Thu'al you must put the *d* before the '*a* (*da'ī* instead of 'Adī).[8] That he is called a Khārijite[9] presumably only means, in this as in other cases, that he did not set great store by the prerogatives of Arabs.

This field of study must have been very welcome to the Persian philologists at a time when evidence of the faults of the Arabs, shame of their tribes and disparaging details from their past could support their thesis about the superiority of the non-Arabs.

These scholars had, of course, to inquire also into the good points of the various tribes—a literary speciality which appears to have

[1] *Al-'Iqd*, II, p. 51.
[2] Ibn Qutayba, p. 224, 3.
[3] *Agh.*, XXI, p. 246, 12 [Yāqūt, *Irshād*, VII, p. 262].
[4] He also transmitted sacred legends, Abu'l-Maḥāsin, I, p. 424.
[5] *Agh.*, I, p. 7 below.
[6] *Agh.*, XI, p. 55 below.
[7] Ibid, XVII, p. 109 [Yāqūt, *Irshād*, VII, pp. 262–7].
[8] Cf. *al-'Iqd*, III, p. 301.
[9] Ibn Qutayba, p. 267.

been summed up by the genealogist Abu'l-Bakhtarī (died 200) in his 'great books of excellences'.[1] But the genealogists of the Shuʿūbiyya party favoured 'scorns' which accorded with their convictions; and this striving was not in contrast to the literary taste of the time. Even then satirical poets aimed at fighting the objects of their lampoons effectively by disparaging their tribe, and particularly by casting doubts upon their pure descent or suspecting the chastity of their
193 mothers,[2] or by applying this method against certain individuals who were the objects of their particular hatred. Doubts about the mother's virtue and the purity of marital life remained one of the most popular weapons of Arab satire,[3] which continued in this respect the traditions of former times and the trend of their satirical poets.[4] The most scandalous statement in the Islamic period was I dare say uttered by al-Farazdaq in his *hijā'* on al-Ṭirimmāḥ about family life within the tribe of Ṭayyi'.[5] Though religious people objected to a continuation of these traditions and condemned them in theory and practice,[6] philological literature did in fact favour their continued existence.

The mere practice of this genre could not therefore be con-

[1] *Fihrist*, p. 100, 21.

[2] *Agh.*, IX, p. 109, the satire of ʿAlī b. al-Jahm (died 250); among other things, he addresses his opponents: 'Your mother does not know who loosened her belt, and who has given you to her, O unclean ones. You are a people—when their descent is called, one and the same mother is to be named, but only God knows the fathers, as there are many of them', etc. In the same way the descent of whole tribes was ridiculed and genealogists chose, e.g., the tribe of the Banu'l-ʿAnbar as a target for their mockery by naming as their ancestress Umm Khārija, who was ill-famed for her polyandry; al-Mubarrad, p. 265.

[3] The satirical poems of ʿAbdān al-Khūzī against Abu'l-ʿAlā', who called himself an Asadite, may serve as examples from later times: e.g. 'Take, O Abu'l-ʿAlā' my friendly advice . . . Never mock anyone older than you, you might insult your father without knowing it.' Cf. the poems in *Yatīmat al-Dahr*, III, pp. 127 ff. Al-Ṣaymarī addresses in a satire his fellow poet al-Buḥturī: '*Ya'bna'l-mubāḥati li'l-warā*', i.e. 'You son of a woman who was free to all', *Agh.*, XVIII, p. 174, 3.

[4] E.g. *Mufaḍḍ.*, 6:11; *Agh.*, XXI, p. 201, 21 (al-Mutalammis); *Ḥam.*, p. 113, esp. v. 4; *Agh.*, XXI, p. 14, 17—al-Afwaḥ boasts of the jealousy of his own tribe for their women in contrast to the enemy tribe whose 'women were dragged into captivity'.

[5] *Le diwan de Farazdak*, ed. Boucher, p. 89.

[6] The pious Muslim neophyte Abū ʿUbayd al-Qāsim b. Sallām, the son of a Greek slave from Herat (died 224), who achieved much authority in Islam, was—apart from his theological work—also author of lexicographical works which were concerned chiefly with the explanation of difficult words in the tradition. In these works Abū ʿUbayd often had to quote *loci probantes* from old poets, but whenever he used a satirical verse he eliminated the personal names in it, substituting for them fictitious ones in the same metre. This falsification is credited to Abū ʿUbayd as a special merit by the Maghribī theologian Qāḍī ʿIyāḍ (*Shifā'*, II, p. 237).

sidered as due to hostility to the dignity of the Arabs, as its roots are, as we have repeatedly seen, among the most authentic impulses of Arab genius which, even where refined conditions of life gave no opportunity for its full expression, was exercised at least in belletris- 194
tic play and literary dillettantism.[1] An author who is shown to be an advocate of the Arab cause by a polemical writing against the Shu'-ūbiyya is the author of *mathālib* works and he obviously does not wish to assail the honour of the Arabs.[2]

But in the circle of the Shu'ūbīs the point of view of the *mathālib* had changed. Their philological interest is guided by an inclination to use the points which occur in the *mathālib* as proof of the inferiority of the Arab race which is to be inferred from data referring to individual tribes. They could attempt this with the greater success because in the *mathālib* verses Arabs speak of their own compatriots; there could apparently be no more objective material.

The same tendency is followed in smaller details of their genealogical activity. The most eminent circles of pure Arab society were to be degraded by genealogical means.

Khālid b. Kulthūm, whom we see as an opponent of Iranophile genealogy, handed down the information that in the 'Abbāsid period a Shu'ūbī heretic (*rajul min zanādiqat al-shu'ūbiyya*) had an argument with a descendant of the Umayyad caliph al-Walīd, and this degenerated into the rudest insults. In order to cast doubt upon the lawful descent of al-Walīd's descendant, the Shu'ūbī wrote a book in which he tells of the adulterous relationship of one of the caliph's wives with the poet Waḍḍāḥ, and of the sad end of the philanderer.[3] Even if it most unlikely that the story of the love-affair of the princess and Waḍḍāḥ is a malicious invention of a Shu'ūbite, the above piece of information will nevertheless serve to show us the nature of the aims pursued by the Shu'ūbite party in Islamic society during the second and third centuries.

III

These general observations can best be demonstrated by a concrete example in the scholarly trend of one of the most important of those philologists who lent their support to the Shu'ūbī party. We refer to 195
Abū Ubayda Ma'mar b. al-Muthannā (died *c.*207-11),[4] contemporary of the above-mentioned genealogist and *mathālib* writer al-Haytham

[1] See e.g in al-Mas'ūdī, VI, pp. 136-56, an interesting collection of such *mathālib*. A girl of the Banū 'Āmir tribe is credited with a number of satirical epigrams, poems in which about forty Arab tribes are mercilessly attacked. Cf. also *Journ. Asiat.*, 1853, I, pp. 550 ff. [and al-Sam'ānī, *al-Ansāb*, I, pp. 54–62].

[2] Abū 'Abd 'Allāh al-Jahmī, *Fihrist*, p. 112, 1 and 2.

[3] *Agh.*, VI, p. 39.

[4] [Cf. H. A. R. Gibb's article 'Abū 'Ubayda' in the new ed. of the *Enc. of Islam*, in the light of which Goldziher's conclusions have to be modified.]

b. 'Adī. By descent he was an 'Ajamī, but by affiliation he belonged to the Arab tribe of Taym. Al-Jāḥiẓ says of him that there was nobody amongst either the heretics or the orthodox who was more learned in all branches of human knowledge than this Abū 'Ubayda.[1] The same respect for his scholarship was shown by his younger contemporary Ibn Hishām, to whom we owe the edition of the biography of the Prophet by Muḥammad ibn Isḥāq. In a number of passages in this work he draws upon Abū 'Ubayda's scholarship for the explanation of the true sense of old words and their illustration with examples taken from poetry; he even chooses him as his guide to establish the references contained in passages of the Koran. Abū 'Ubayda had in fact an exceedingly comprehensive knowledge of the language and of the old stories of the Arab, which he dealt with in a large number of special treatises;[2] and a great part of what we know today of pre-Islamic conditions and events amongst the Arab people, as well as of their antiquities,[3] would have escaped us if Abū 'Ubayda had not concerned himself with the transmission of such information and data.[4] 'There are no two horses,' he boasted, 'who came to close quarters in pagan or Islamic times but I know of them and their riders.' Together with al-Aṣma'ī and Abū Zayd he was the greatest expert of Arab *lugha* at that time, excelling the first, according to Arab critics, but being outdone by the latter in the extent of his knowledge.[5] We owe very much to him in the field of the tradition and interpretation of
196 old poetry. In the latter he showed—as we may anticipate here—a Shu'ūbite bias.[6]

It is not surprising that he gathered much of his information from desert Arabs, as was the general practice of the great philologists of his day; yet just as in other matters he had the laudable modesty to admit his ignorance on questions which he could not answer,[7] so we

[1] Ḥarīrī commentary, ed. de Sacy, 2nd ed., p. 672.

[2] A survey of his most important writings—he wrote *c.* 200 monographs—Ibn Khallikān, no. 741 (VIII, p. 123).

[3] Al-Mubarrad, pp. 441, 442, data about the use of the crown by ancient Arab princes and the finding of old Arab coins.

[4] The rich source of information comprised in his traditions can be easily seen if we examine e.g. *Agh.*, X, pp. 8-84; the pre-Islamic stories told there are almost exclusively due to A.'U. information, and the same is true of many other parts of old Arab history and of poetic pieces connected with it. Ibn Hishām, pp. 180 ff., can relate the story of the war of Dāḥis and Ghabrā' only according to the account of A.'U.

[5] Al-Suyūṭī, *Muzhir*, II, pp. 202-3; cf. Rosen, *Drebne arabska Poezi* (Petersburg 1872), pp. 66-67.

[6] Ibn Durayd, p. 77, mentions an old Arab couplet with the remark: 'A.'U. has added to these verses an explanation which I would not like to repeat here', presumably an explanation not favourable to the Arabs and therefore inconvenient to the pro-Arab (see p. 192) Ibn Durayd.

[7] *Agh.*, XVII, p. 27.

find him more sceptical about that sort of information[1] than is otherwise current in these circles of philologists,[2] and is altogether ready to admit it if he is unable to glean any information about a detail of Arab antiquity from his living sources.[3] But tradition[4] and exegesis were not the only fields in which he excelled; he also contributed much to higher criticism and aesthetic evaluation of Arabic poetry. Of the deep insight of his judgment there is no better example than his criticism of the poetry of the Christian poet al-Akhṭal from the tribe of Taghlib.[5]

Here, however, we are not considering this part of his activity and it is only mentioned in order to indicate how great were the achievements of the non-Arab Abū ʿUbayda in the Arab sciences; we shall discuss in more detail his participation in the tendencies of the
Shuʿūbiyya. It may be said that Abū ʿUbayda was a true Shuʿūbite 197
and students of his writings have called him that.[6] When he is occasionally described as a Khārijite,[7] it is not the dogmatic and political side of the Khārijite party which seems to be in mind, but only that aspect which the Shuʿūbites share with the Khārijites: denial of privilege to any race. Here the followers of both parties meet quite unintentionally on the same ground[8] and only this point of view would justify the superficial description of Abū ʿUbayda as a Khārijite, which must, judging from other indications,[9] definitely be rejected.

[1] He will have derived from the desert Arabs the information contained in a citation, *al-ʿIqd*, I, p. 58, where he gives a precise canon of how thoroughbred horses may be recognised. *Agh.*, XXI, p. 86, 10; 88, 1 he transmits from Ru'ba, but Ru'ba died in 145 and a direct contact between him and A.ʿU. is hardly likely. In al-Suyūṭī, *Itqān* (ed. Cairo 1279), II, p. 191 he is also made to quote in the name of Ru'ba a judgment on the Koranic passage 15:94.

[2] *Agh.*, IX, p. 151, 8 from below *fa-zaʿama lī shaykh minʿulamāʾ Banī Murra.*

[3] *Ṭuraf ʿArabiyya*, ed. Landberg, p. 31, 2.

[4] To this category belongs the knowledge of old proverbs (*amthāl*) and the establishment of their historical connections and moral application: for this, too, Abū ʿUbayda was an eminent authority (*al-ʿIqd*, p. 333). Some proverbs would have remained unintelligible but for A.ʿU.'s transmission of the reference on which they were based, e.g. 'more faithless than Qays b. ʿĀṣim', or 'more faithless than ʿUtayba b. al-Ḥārith' (al-Maydānī, II, p. 10). There are many examples of this. [Cf. also R. Sellheim, *Die klassisch-arabischen Sprichwörtersammlungen*, The Hague, 1954, pp. 69-70, 152.]

[5] *Agh.*, VII, p. 174.

[6] Ibn Qutayba, ed. Wüstenfeld, p. 269: 'He hated the Arabs'; al-Masʿūdī, V, p. 480: 'Abū ʿUbayda or another of the Shuʿūbites'; cf. al-Maqqarī, I, p. 825, 16.

[7] Abulfeda, *Annales*, II, p. 144. But al-Masʿūdī himself says of him, VII, p. 80, that he professed the views of the Khawārij; cf. Ibn Qutayba, l.c.

[8] Cf. above, p. 130.

[9] It is unthinkable to find one who is seriously a Khārijite amongst the admirers, and even more, the transmitters of al-Sayyid al-Ḥimyarī, the poet of the Kaysānī party, as this is attested of A.ʿU., *Agh.*, VII, p. 5. That poet ridiculed the rebels of Nahrawān and their leaders, ibid., p. 16, 16-17.

Much that we can observe of his literary characteristics in the scattered remnants of his work shows that he was intent on furthering the aims of the Shuʿūbiyya. In the course of his philological and antiquarian studies he liked to point out non-Arab elements in the culture and daily life of Arabia—which the pro-Arabs described with satisfaction as altogether original and owing nothing to any other nation. In Arab poetry and rhetoric, which the panegyrists of Arab originality never ceased to praise as the fruit of the indigenous genius of the Arab people, Abū ʿUbayda finds connections with Persian elements; for example, he attempts to explain the hyperbole of Arab poets and orators as an imitation of the Persians[1], and many fabulous Arab tales he regards as imitations of corresponding fables in Persian literature.[2] He also traces the foreign words in the poems of a most
198 truly Arab poet,[3] though he strongly denies the occurrence of foreign words in the Koran, attributing their apparent presence to the accidental agreement of words in various languages.[4] He looked for foreign elements also in everyday customs of the Arabs, which explains a story, told with great relish, about the introduction of a Persian dish into Mecca.[5] He studied the history of the Persians in detail and wrote a book on the subject, using information provided by a Persian converted to Islam, ʿUmar Kisrā.[6] It may be mentioned that amongst the many writings of Abū ʿUbayda there is one entitled *Kitāb al-Tāj*, a title which Iranians and other non-Arabs, writing of the glories of ancient Persians, liked to choose.[7] From this book by Abū ʿUbayda we have fragments on old Arab genealogy,[8] but it is not impossible that he dealt also with Persian matters.

Even as he sought for elements of Arab civilization which could be attributed to Persian influence, so he liked—if he could justify it—to reclaim for Persia persons who had gained a place of honour in the culture of Islam in specifically Arab fields. He thus reclaimed for Persia, for example, the family of the Raqqāshī, who were famed amongst the Arabs for their rhetorical gifts. The first of them to have found a place in Arabic literature was Abān b. ʿAbd al-Ḥamīd al-Raqqāshī, famous as an Arab poet and translator of Persian books.

[1] Al-Mubarrad, p. 351.

[2] Al-Tawwazī in al-Suyūṭī's *Muzhir*, II, p. 253.

[3] Ibn Qutayba, *Adab al-Kātib* (MS. Imperial Libr. Vienna, N.F. no. 45) fol. 157b [ed. Grünert, pp. 257, 530].

[4] Al-Suyūṭī, *Itqān*, I, p. 167. [Already in Ibn Qutayba, l.c.]

[5] *Agh.*, VIII, p. 4.

[6] Al-Masūdī, II, p. 238.

[7] Rosen, 'Zur arabischen Literaturgeschichte der ältern Zeit' I (*Mélanges asiatiques*, l.c.) p. 774.

[8] *Al-ʿIqd*, II, pp. 53 ff. and probably also the quotations ibid., I, pp. 11, 26, 36. Islamic history also seems to be contained in it, e.g. the citation ibid., II, p. 287.

His translations from the Persian did much to enrich Arab literature.[1] His son Ḥamdān and his brother 'Abd al-Ḥamīd were also known in Arabic poetry;[2] his great nephew al-Faḍl b. 'Isā b. Abān al-Raqqāshī[3] was one of the most important orators of his time and the latter's son 'Abd al-Ṣamad is said to have excelled even his father in this art. Concerning this Abū 'Ubayda said: 'Their ancestors were eminent orators at the court of the Chosroes, when they became prisoners of 199
the Arabs and had descendants in the countries of Islam and in Arabia itself, this rhetorical vein made its appearance and they became amongst the people of this Arabic language the same as they had been amongst the people of the Persian language, namely poets and orators. But when they later intermarried with strangers this gift receded and eventually decayed.'[4]

Thus Abū 'Ubayda tried to take every foreign flower from the proud Arabs' bouquet of fame. He occasionally went further than he could justify and had to face many disputes. In general, his manner of treating Arab antiquity seems to have roused the ire of those Arab philologists who, full-blood Arabs themselves, pursued other lines in the study of their national language and traditions. This inner difference explains the opposition which existed between Abū 'Ubayda and his learned contemporary and rival al-Aṣma'ī.[5] This difference of viewpoint and literary tendency was particularly evident in the following matter. It was, as we shall soon see, in accordance with the line taken by Abū 'Ubayda to cultivate the genre of satire in Arabic poetry and particularly the *hijā'* directed against Arab tribes, while al-Aṣma'ī is said to have condemned this part of ancient Arabic literature for religious reasons, to the point of never undertaking a philological interpretation of a poem containing satire (*hijā'*).[6] Ibn al-A'rābī's low opinion of Abū 'Ubayda[7] might well be due partly to the latter's attitude towards the Arabs to whom the *mawlā* Ibn al-A'rābī was devoted. He was at great pains to prove that Abū 'Ubayda had insufficient knowledge of the Arabic language and that at his only meeting with him he heard him make three solecisms.[8]

[1] *Fihrist*, p. 119.

[2] Ibid., p. 163.

[3] Cf. a curiosity about him in al-Maydānī, I, p. 360.

[4] Al-Jāḥiẓ, *Kitāb al-Bayān*, fol. 103 b [I, p. 308].

[5] Ibn Khallikān, no. 389, IV, p. 88.

[6] Al-Suyūṭī, *Muzhir*, II, p. 204.

[7] *ZDMG*, XII, p. 70.

[8] In his unfavourable judgment of al-Aṣma'ī he was naturally guided by other points of view, but it may be doubted whether Ibn al-A'rābī's remarks against al-Aṣma'ī and Abū 'Ubayda were influenced by the contrast of the Kūfans with the followers of the Baṣra school (Flügel, *Die grammatischen Schulen der Araber*, p. 147).

The rivalry of al-Aṣma'ī and Abū 'Ubayda arose not only from the
200 literary differences and their opposing views about Arab antiquity; there seem also to have been purely worldly motives for their mutual enmity. To assess these the following report by Abu'l-Faraj al-Iṣfahānī is of great importance: The singer and belletrist Isḥāq al-Mawṣilī used to receive instruction from al-Aṣma'ī and make use of his traditions; tension developed between them later and Isḥāq directed satires against the other and told the caliph al-Rashīd of his faults, his ingratitude, his miserliness, the baseness of his soul, and that he did not deserve favours. He described Abū 'Ubayda on the other hand as a reliable, faithful, generous and learned man. He said the same things to Faḍl b. al-Rabī', whose help he enlisted in the intended destruction of al-Aṣma'ī. He continued these activities until al-Aṣma'ī lost the favour of the court and Abū 'Ubayda was invited to take his place.'[1]

It is not surprising to learn that the representatives of the Arab trend[2] were in opposition to 'Abū Ubayda particularly in respect of genealogy. We have only recently mentioned the poet Waḍḍāḥ al-Yaman, who had to serve the Shu'ūbites in many ways. He was famous for his beauty, which was so outstanding that he had to guard against the evil eye by veiling his face as had the 'veiled Kindite' (al-Muqanna' al-Kindī)[3] before him, but he was even better remembered for his love affair with the wife of the Caliph al-Walīd I and for his sad end.[4] The name Waḍḍāḥ was given him because of his beauty: the word means 'the shining one'. His real name was 'Abd al-Raḥmān b. Ismā'īl b. 'Abd Kulāl b. Dādh. The name of his great-grandfather Dādh is Persian, and therefore Abū 'Ubayda taught that he came from those Persians whom the Persian king Khusraw had sent to the Yemen under the leadership of Wahriz in order to protect King Sayf b. Dhī Yazan against the Ethiopians. This assertion was energetically rebutted by the pro-Arab Khālid b. Kulthūm: 'If you argue from the linguistic character of the name, I maintain that 'Abd Kulāl is a
201 name indigenous to south Arabs only[5] and Abū Jamad, the by-name (*kunya*) of Dādh's[6] father, is a southern Arab by-name, since the

[1] *Agh.*, V, p. 107.

[2] Amongst those who directed polemics against him after his death is also that enemy of the Shu'ūbites, Ibn Qutayba; Ḥ-Kh., I, p. 327, no. 825: *iṣlāḥ ghalaṭ Abī 'Ub.*

[3] *Agh.*, VI, p. 33.

[4] Kremer, *Culturgeschichte des Orients*, I, pp. 145 ff. [For al-Waḍḍāḥ cf. also Brockelmann, Suppl. I, pp. 82-3.]

[5] We find the name also among the northern Arabs e.g. 'Abd al-Raḥmān b. Samura was called before his conversion 'A. Kulāl; al-Nawawī, *Tahdhīb*, p. 380 (according to others, however, 'Abd al-Ka'ba).

[6] *Agh.*, VI, p. 45, 14; the poet boasts of his ancestors and mentions this ancestor with this *kunya*.

Persians never used such by-names. I can further mention that in Yemen many people are called by the Ethiopian name Abraha and by your method all these people must be given an Ethiopian descent. Names are but symbols and marks. Many a man is called Abū Bakr, without being the Ṣiddīq, and many men are named ʿUmar without being the Fārūq. Thus names cannot be used as proof or disproof of any national descent.' Abū ʿUbayda—concludes Khālid—was shamed by this refutation and unable to reply.[1]

This anecdote prepares us to see Abū ʿUbayda thwarting the purposes of the pro-Arab party in the field of genealogy, and in effect we have various indications of this. To prove that the pure Arab descent of those circles, who used such genealogy as a title for their superiority to the rest of the Muslim people, was not above suspicion, and what is more could not withstand a detailed examination of genealogical facts, was one of the main aims of this kind of genealogical criticism. In towns populated by mixed nationalities it was most appropriate to the purposes of the party to prove the unreliability of the claims of the Arab families and groups to be the true descendants of one or the other desert tribe. How could the descendants of that magnate of the tribe of Banū Saʿd called Fadakī b. Aʿbad have survived with unmixed blood in Baṣra up to the third century? Claims like these were easy game for men like Abū ʿUbayda.[2] He made diligent investigations in order to prove the absurdity of such genealogical statements. For example, when the families of Nāfiʿ and Abū Bakra announced proudly that they were linear descendants of the famous Arab healer Ḥārith b. Kalada (who accepted Islam only in ʿUmar's time), Abū ʿUbayda proved that this man had 202
left no son at all to carry on his line.[3]

It is easily understandable that in the genealogy of Arab tribes Abū ʿUbayda was most attracted by the branch of the *mathālib*. But he was not only concerned with the proof that certain genealogical claims of Arab antiquity were invalid; he was also fond of producing data from his philological arsenal with which to ridicule the excessive racial vanity of Arabs in cases where nothing could be said against it from a genealogical point of view. Typical of this is his story about ʿAqīl b. ʿUllafa, who was so proud of his descent from the Banū Murra that he subjected one of his daughter's suitors, whom he did not consider as her equal, to torture, the description of which is almost untranslatable.[4] In general Abū ʿUbayda seems to have been fond of transmitting or inventing stories in which full-

[1] Ibid., p. 33.
[2] Ibn Durayd, p. 153, 4; cf. his objections against the Banū Arzam in Baṣra, ibid., p. 323 ult.
[3] *Agh.*, XI, p. 86.
[4] Ibid.

blood Arabs confront each other and hurl the coarsest insults concerning the other's descent.[1] From all this we can easily get an idea of what Abū 'Ubayda intended with his writings 'on the *mawālī*' and 'concerning tribes.' Amongst his works are also mentioned a book of 'the *mathālib* of the tribe of Bāhila' and a general 'book of the *mathālib*' in which he proves the insufficiency of the genealogies of the Arab tribes on whom he heaps all kinds of accusations.[2]

From what we have already heard about the material of genealogists, it does not seem incredible that—as al-Mas'ūdī thinks possible —Abū 'Ubayda (or another Shu'ūbite) did not shrink from literary falsifications, after the fashion of old Arab poetry, in order to support the party's policy in genealogical matters. In the days of the author of 'The Golden Meadows' a book known under the name of *al-Wāḥida* could still be read; it dealt with the subject of 'excellences' and 'scorns' and discussed those good and bad qualities of each Arab tribe which, according to tradition, distinguished it from any other tribe. The book reproduced poetical competitions between the court poets of the Umayyad caliph Hishām, in which each poet—al-Mas'ūdī quotes
203 them by name—boasted of the superiorities of his own northern or southern Arab race and treated with contempt the dignity of that of his rival. These boasts naturally only served as foils for the insults which were to expose the vices and moral defects of ancient Arabs. Abū 'Ubayda, or men like him, is said to have devised these verses and the possibility of such an assumption shows clearly enough what the eminent philologist was thought capable of in days not far distant from his own.[3]

In the *mathālib* of Shu'ūbite bias, then, as is evident from the last mentioned literary fact, it was no longer (as had been the case with the old *mathālib* traditions) full Arabs who stood up against other full Arabs with the presumption of the great value of true Arab descent. The Shu'ūbites could not accept such an assumption. They were out to destroy this belief in the value of uncontaminated Arab descent, and the assembling of the old *mathālib* offered them the opportunity of demonstrating how problematical was a man's claim on the fame of his ancestors. But in all this we must always take into account their presumption of the lack of value of true Arab descent even in a case where it was found to be well established. Abū 'Ubayda did not avoid—as did most of his contemporaries in his position— pointing to his own origin. He boasts that he, the genealogist of the Arab tribes who criticises their descent, heard from his own father

[1] A typical example is found in al-Balādhurī's *Ansāb al-Ashrāf*, p. 172.

[2] *Fihrist*, pp. 53, 26, 27; 54, 2, 4; al-Mas'ūdī, VII, p. 80.

[3] Al-Mas'ūdī, V, p. 480. Excerpts from the *Kitāb al-Wāḥida* were quoted by al-Mas'ūdī in his 'Middle Book' (*al-Awsaṭ*); it is cited in the commentary to the *Qaṣīda Fazāriyya*, Ms. of the Royal Library, Berlin, Cod. Peterm., 184, fol. 170b.

that the latter's father had been a Persian Jew.[1] According to one account (which is, however, rather curious) he owed his by-name Abū ʿUbayda to the fact that his grandfather had been a Jew. ʿAbū ʿUbayda was a nickname given to Jews and the famous philologist is said to have become very angry when addressed by this nickname.'[2] He repaid in the same coin all those who held it against him that he was a non-Arab. When he learned that a member of the Raqqāshī family, himself a *mawlā* of this Arab tribe,[3] had remarked satirically that he who could not be proud of his own genealogy criticised the descent of others, he remarked to a large gathering: 'The government has overlooked an important fact when neglecting the collection of 204
the Jewish tax from Abān. His family is Jewish, and in their houses the books of the Torah can still be found, whereas there is hardly any copy of the Koran. They do in fact boast of knowing the Torah by heart, whereas what they know of the Koran is hardly sufficient for the prayer.'[4]

This, of course, does not mean much. Muslim genealogists were bent on proving the Jewish descent of anybody whom they disliked for any reason. This trick was not their own invention, and their application of it was, like many other things, an imitation of older habits of Arab society. The two poets Arṭāt b. Zufar and Shabīb b. al-Barṣāʾ (died 80) had had a poetic competition of long standing in which each denied the other's right to trace his descent from the Banū ʿAwf. Amongst the members of the tribe there was a singular tradition[5] according to which a true ʿAwfī would become blind in his old age.[6] Arṭāt was able to point out that, while this applied to him, Shabīb himself had remained in full possession of his sight (after his rival's death he too is said to have gone blind). Arṭāt mocked him: 'In the tribe of the ʿAwf there is a Jewish family in which youths are like old men'[7]—implying that his opponent belong to this Jewish branch which had insinuated itself into the ʿAwf tribe.

Thus we see that genealogists only had to follow existing patterns when using this motive for their genealogical taunts. An example is

[1] *Fihrist*, p. 53, 12.

[2] *Agh.*, XVII p. 19.

[3] Cf. above, pp. 182-3

[4] *Agh.*, XX, p. 78.

[5] *Agh.*, XI, p. 97, 8.

[6] We meet the same tradition later in respect of another tribe, i.e. that branch of the Banū Ḥanīfa which in the early ʿAbbāsid period were clients of the Hāshimite family and to whom belonged the blind scholar Abu'l-ʿAynāʾ (died 282). The ancestor of this Abu'l-ʿAynāʾ is said to have behaved impolitely to ʿAlī and therefore ʿAlī had cursed him and his descendants with blindness. Blindness was taken as sign of legitimacy in this family. See al-Ḥuṣrī, I, p. 251.

[7] *Agh.*, XI, p. 141, 8 below; cf. the same phrase also VIII, p. 139, 8, 5 below.

the poet Marwān, grandson of Yaḥyā b. Abī Ḥafṣa (died 182). In his family the tradition was current that the grandfather of the poet had been a Persian who became 'Uthmān's slave at the conquest of Iṣ-
205 ṭakhr. Hostile genealogists do not rest content with that. Abū Ḥafṣa was represented as a Jew who was converted to Islam by 'Uthmān, or according to others only by Marwān b. al-Ḥakam.[1] Political and religious enmity also sharpened its weapons with such assertions.[2]

These examples may serve to illustrate the genealogical accusation which Abū 'Ubayda's enemies made against him. But we saw that he used the same trick himself when necessary, and this is evident also from the account of how Abū 'Ubayda endeavoured to blacken the descent of the Umayyad governor Khālid b. 'Abd Allāh al-Qasrī,[3] following in this respect the example of al-Madā'inī (died 130). This zealous servant in the cause of the Umayyad caliphate traced his descent to the southern Arab tribe of the Bajīla, and amongst his ancestors he named the famous pagan soothsayer Shiqq. According to Arab concepts the genealogy of this man seems to have been open to some doubt; Ibn al-Kalbī openly confesses—and this is typical of the ways of the genealogical profession—'My first lie in a genealogical matter was this. Khālid b. 'Abd Allāh asked me about his grandmother. Now I knew that Umm Kurayz was an ordinary prostitute of the tribe of Asad. But I said to Khālid: "Zaynab bint 'Ar'ara bint Jadhīma b. Naṣr b. Qu'ayn—she was your grandmother." He was glad and made me gifts.'[4] To discredit Khālid, Abū 'Ubayda advanced the following revelation: his ancestor Kurz b. 'Āmir was a Jew from Taymā; he became a slave of the 'Abd al-Qays and was able to escape but was captured again by the tribe of 'Abd Shams and was forced into the service of Ghamghama, the son of that soothsayer whom he names amongst his ancestors, who in his turn gave him to somebody else. Having escaped a second time he became a prisoner of the Banū Asad, who married him to a slave of ill repute who bore him a son called Asad. The Banū Asad then gave him his freedom, which lasted only a short time because he was accidentally recognised by members of the tribe of Ḥujr, to whom he had previously been slave,
206 and he was forced to continue in this state amongst them. They freed him for ransom, and when he passed through Ṭā'if with his patrons, the Banū Asad, he attached himself to the Bajīla tribe, who soon

[1] Al-Mubarrad, p. 271, *Agh.*, IX, p. 36: the story is told in detail of the emancipation of this *mawlā*; cf. also Abu'l-Maḥāsin, I, p. 506.

[2] We think of the way in which enemies of the Fāṭimid dynasty asserted that its founder was descended from a Jew (*al-Bayān al-Mughrib*, I, p. 158 [B. Lewis, *The Origins of Ismā'īlism*, Cambridge 1940, pp. 67–8]).

[3] See for him Kremer, *Culturgeschichte*, I, p. 180.

[4] *Agh.*, XIX, p. 58

rejected him. Khālid then was descended from this Kurz; and he inherited from his grandfather and great-grandfather the gift of excelling all his contemporaries in mendacity.[1] This example shows the way in which the *ahl al-mathālib*[2] sought to subject to ridicule and mockery the genealogy of people whom they disliked, especially when such people appeared as representatives of the Arab trend.[3]

IV

We have described Abū 'Ubayda's literary character in such detail because we considered his activity typical of the whole group of Shu'ūbite philologists and genealogists, a comprehensive and exhaustive discussion of whom would call for a special chapter in literary history, for which we wished only to supply some material here. But the description of the Shu'ūbite *mathālib* activity might be rounded off with the mention of a successor to Abū 'Ubayda, namely the genealogist 'Allān al-Shu'ūbī, who was employed as copyist in the 'library of the sciences' in the days of the caliphs Hārūn and al-Ma'mūn. He was admittedly of Persian descent, and as his name shows he belonged to the Shu'ūbiyya party. This Shu'ūbite is quoted as an authority in genealogical problems concerning Arab tribes.[4] Though he wrote in praise of some tribes (Kināna and Rabī'a)[5],

[1] *Agh.*, XIX, pp. 57 f.

[2] This is the name given to those who spread such scandalous rumours about Khālid's ancestor; *Agh.*, ibid., p. 55.

[3] Perhaps this is the place to mention an anecdote which is found in *al-'Iqd*, II, p. 151, in respect of Bilāl b. Abī Burda. A madman of whom Bilāl demanded some valuables which he had brought with him from the prison into which Bilāl had had him thrown replied: 'Today is the Sabbath and on this day gifts may not be made or accepted.' By this he is supposed to have pointed to Bilāl's Jewish blood. *Aṣḥāb al-sabt* is a name for Jews, *ZDMG*, XXXII, p. 342 note 1, al-Ḥuṣrī, III, p. 10. 'To rejoice like Jews on a Sabbath,' Yāqūt, I, p. 814, 19. There is a Bedouin tribe to this day called Banū Sabt from which name extraordinary conjectures have been made, cf. Burton, *The Land of Midian*, I, p. 337. [Cf. however, Gibb's pertinent criticism of Goldziher's point of view in the article quoted above, p. 179 note 4: 'Materials relating to the tribes were most frequently arranged under the categories of "virtues" (*manāqib*) and "vices" (*mathālib*); by the latter he gave much offence to the tribal pride of the Arabs, the more so because they provided ammunition for the anti-Arab polemics of the Persian *shu'ūbiyya*. Moreover, as a convinced Khārijite . . . he had no respect for the contemporary Arab sharīfs, especially the Muhallabids, and publicly exposed their pretensions. For both these reasons he was accused by the opponents of the *shu'ūbiyya* of being a bitter calumniator of the Arabs (*kāna aghra' l-nās bi-mashātim al-nās*: Ibn Qutayba, *Kitāb al-'Arab*, in *Rasā'il al-Bulaghā'*, Cairo 1946, 346), but there is little evidence to identify him, as Goldziher and Aḥmad Amīn [*Ḍuḥa'l-Islām*, II, 304-5] have done, with the Persian *shu'ūbiyya*—rather, indeed, the contrary (cf. al-Mas'ūdī, *Tanbīh*, 243).']

[4] *Agh.*, XI, p. 172 above.

[5] *Fihrist*, p. 106, 15, 16.

his scholarly activity was chiefly directed to the *mathālib* of Arab
207 tribes. A great work 'Race-track of the *mathālib*' had the purpose of investigating and finding fault with the past of all Arab tribes.[1] We believe that we have found a piece of this work in the following excerpt which is quoted in the name of 'Allān:[2]

'The Banū Minqar are a perfidious people, they are called *kawādin* (i.e. horses descended from a thoroughbred stallion and a common mare) and also *a'rāq*[3] *al-bighāl*. They are the worst of God's creatures in respect of protection; they are also called "traitors" and "faithless". Filthy miserliness also dwells amongst them. Qays b. 'Āṣim, one of their ancestors, emphasized nothing so much in his testamentary exhortation to his children as care of their property, though this is not usual among the Arabs, who on the contrary consider it a bad habit. Thus it is this tribe that al-Akhṭal b. Rabī'a has in mind when he says:

O Minqar b. 'Ubayda! verily your shame is written in the *dīwān*
since Adam's day;
The guest has a claim on every noble man, but the guest of the
Minqar is naked and robbed.

And al-Namir b. Tawlab says in a satire upon them, referring particularly to their designation as traitors and faithless: "When they are called faithless the meaning is that their elders are closer to treason than their beardless youths." '[4]
This is generally true of the Banū Sa'd,[5] but they themselves lay the charge at the door of the Banū Minqar who attribute it to the Banū Sinān b. Khālid b. Minqar, who is the grandfather of Qays b. 'Āṣim.'[6]

Such is the *mathālib* book by 'Allān: and it can be imagined what a mine of information for his purpose this Shu'ūbite scholar found in the innumerable satires of the old poets. We hear also of a Ghīlān al-Shu'ūbī, who is quoted as the authority for the Persian descent of Basshār b. Burd.[7] We admit, however, that we know no details of this Ghīlān, and it is not impossible that the name is a corruption of 'Allān.

[1] *Fihrist*, p. 105, 26 ff.
[2] *Agh.*, XII, p. 156.
[3] See above, p. 46.
[4] i.e. the older the more faithless they become.
[5] The tribe to whom the Minqar belong. Cf. the poem and the occasion for it in al-Maydānī, II, p. 9 (to the proverb: *aghdaru min kunāti'l-ghadari*) and *al-'Iqd*, I, p. 31.
[6] Quite different things are told of the Banū Minqar in the panegyric by the same Qays (*Ḥam.*, p. 695).
[7] *Agh.*, III, p. 19 below.

B. PHILOLOGY 208

I

Competition between anti-Arabs and Arabs expressed itself also in the field of ideas concerning language. The national vanity of the Arabs had bred no more favourite prejudice than that according to which Arabic was the most beautiful sounding, richest and best of all the languages of mankind, a belief which was raised by the influence of Islam to almost religious significance[1] even amongst the orthodox non-Arabs, as it concerned the language in which the divine revelation was expressed in the Koran.

But the followers of the Shu'ūbiyya and other Iranophils would not accept this belief. They sought to prove that non-Arabs, more especially Greeks and Persians, surpassed the Arab people in richness of language, beauty of poetry, and merit of eloquence. We have already seen (pp. 157 ff.) the role which this point played in the arguments of the older Shu'ūbiyya. Here we will merely consider the altercations about the superiority of the Arab language. Actually our relevant material for this comes from the fourth century A.H., a time at which the literary campaign of the Shu'ūbiyya proper had long passed its peak.[2] It seems on the other hand that the conflict between Arabophils and Iranophils concerning the superiority of language lasted longest, and kept the party designation of the Shu'ūbiyya alive until the end of the sixth century. At about that time al-Zamakhsharī, himself of Persian descent but deeply convinced of Arab superiority[3] (died 538), wrote in the introduction to his famous grammatical work *al-Mufaṣṣal* words which show us how strongly, in the course of time, the unconscious identification of Islam with Arabism took root in the conscience of believers: 'I thank God,' he says, 'that He made me busy with Arab philology and has made me fight for the (cause of the) Arabs and has given me enthusiasm for it, and that He did not make me leave their brave helpers and 209
join the band of the Shu'ūbiyya; that He saved me from this party who can do nothing against the former but attack them with slanderous words and shoot at them the arrows of mockery.'[4]

This utterance of al-Zamakhsharī is, chronologically speaking, the last trace of the Shu'ūbiyya in literature. It goes against one of its

[1] The summary description of what theological science teaches in respect of this idea is found in Fakhr al-Dīn al-Rāzī, *Mafātīḥ*, VII, pp. 347 ff. Cf. also below, p. 195.

[2] [See, however, below, p. 196 note 1, where it is pointed out that part of the argument set forth by Ibn Fāris in the fourth century is derived from Ibn Qutayba, an author of the third century.]

[3] See his dictum, which De Sacy used as motto for his Arabic Chrestomathy [= *Journal asiat.*, 1875, II, p. 378, no. 144].

[4] [Ed. J. P. Brock, Christiania 1859, p. 2.]

tendencies, which might be called linguistic Shuʿūbiyya, which we have already described. Its manifestations are better known to us from the polemics of its opponents than from its own positive statements, though there is no lack of these either. From the literary expositions of the friends of the Arabs we may supplement our knowledge of the motives of this linguistic Shuʿūbiyya.

The oldest of the documents belonging to this pro-Arab series[1] is the 'Genealogical etymological hand-book' of Abū Bakr Muḥammad ibn Durayd (died 321). The author himself states in the introduction to his work[2] that the immediate occasion of its being written was that he wished to refute the party whose followers attack the Arabic language and claim that the names used by Arabs are without etymological context. They refer here to the admission of the oldest lexicographer of the Arabic language, al-Khalīl, which Ibn Durayd however calls apocryphal. In this book he answers opponents by investigating the etymological context of every Arabic tribal name. The representatives of the opposing party are unfortunately not cited by name. Presumably they were people of the same type as the Shuʿūbiyya.

But we do know the name of one of the most energetic representatives of the philological reaction against the Arabs amongst the younger contemporaries of Ibn Durayd. He is Ḥamza b. al-Ḥasan al-Iṣfahānī (died 350).[3] In the history of Islamic literature this scholar is best known by his short historical handbook edited by Gottwaldt (Leipzig 1848). In it also the Iranophil sentiment of the author is evident, and al-Bīrūnī, who held the same opinion at a rather later date, says so expressly.[4] In great and small matters this trait shows itself by emphasis on specifically Persian points which
210 had obtained no similar treatment from previous historians. In a special chapter he gives a table of days of *nawrūz*—festivals which appeared again with the predominance of Persian influence[5]—from

[1] [As we noted above, p. 191 n. 2, Ibn Qutayba's passage from his *Mushkil al-Qur'ān*, quoted below, p. 196 n. 1, should be kept in mind here, as being an earlier discussion.]

[2] [*Al-Ishtiqāq*, ed. Wüstenfeld, pp. 3-4.]

[3] [For this author, cf. E. Mittwoch, 'Die literarische Tätigkeit Ḥamza al-Iṣbahānī's', *Mitteilungen des Seminars für Orientalische Sprachen*, Berlin 1909. For 'died 350' read 'died after 350'; cf. Mittwoch, p. 5, n. 3. On pp. 28-33 Mittwoch argues that though Ḥamza emphasized with pride his Persian descent, he did not evince Shuʿūbī tendencies in the sense of being prejudiced against the Arabs or the Arabic language.]

[4] *Chronologie der orientalischen Völker*, ed. Sachau, p. 52, 4 *taʿaṣṣaba li'l-furs*.

[5] Kremer, *Culturgeschichte*, II, p. 80. According to al-Yaʿqūbī, II, p. 366, ʿUmar II abolished the *nawrūz* and *mihrajān* gifts, which were re-introduced by Yazīd II. Under al-Mutawakkil—as the poet al-Buḥturī says—'the *nawrūz* day has again become the same as instituted by Ardashīr', Ṭab., III, p. 1448; cf. Ibn al-Athīr, VII, p. 30, ann. 245. Al-Jāḥiẓ [or rather Pseudo-Jāḥiẓ] speaks

the year of the *hijra* down to his own times. He also wrote a treatise on the poems dealing with the feast days of *nawrūz* and *mihrajān*.[1] He collected many data from the history of Iranian antiquity and this activity is evidence of his endeavour to put the Iranian past into the foreground of Muslim consciousness. He also collected information about the Iranian language—of course in the childish way usual in those circles—and an excursus on its dialects, including Syriac (!), is still available.[2] He obtained his information about this favourite subject from direct contact[3] with Persian priests,[4] and he also used Persian writings.[5]

His philological work, so far as we know it from quotations, is pervaded with the endeavour to investigate the original forms of the Muslim-Persian nomenclature and to establish its etymological and historical relations;[6] to reconstruct and explain etymologically
the original Persian forms of geographical names which Arab national 211
philology had explained from Arab etymologies;[7] and in general to recover the original Persian forms from the shape they had acquired in the mouths of the conquering Arabs.[8] This was all the more of great importance to the Persians who were faithful to their race, since Arab chauvinism had not omitted to find reminiscences of the Arab

[1] Cited by al-Bīrūnī, p. 31, 14.

[2] From the *Kitāb al-Tanbīh* of Ḥamza in Yāqūt, III, p. 925.

[3] He also gathered information on Jewish matters directly from Jews, cf. *ZDMG*, XXXII, p. 358, note 1.

[4] Yāqūt, I, pp. 426, 637.

[5] Al-Bīrūnī, pp. 123, 1, 125, 1.

[6] Yāqūt, I, pp. 292 f., 791, IV, p. 683.

[7] On 'Irāq, ibid., I, pp. 417, 419, III, p. 629; Sāmarrā', III, p. 15.

[8] Yāqūt, I, pp. 555, 558: Baghdād—the garden of Dādawayhi.

---

at length about *nawrūz* and *mihrajān* (MS. Imperial Libr. Vienna Mixt. 94, fols. 173 ff. [*al-Maḥāsin wa'l -Aḍdād*, ed. van Vloten, pp. 359 ff.; cf. also pp. 373 ff.] The role which the Būyids played at the reintroduction of the *mihrajān* (Kremer, l.c.) is illustrated in a passage in the Responsa of the Ge'ōnīm (ninth and tenth centuries A.D.): here the 'Daylamites' are mentioned as those who celebrate the feast in Baghdad (ed. Harkavy, p. 22, no. 46). These feasts offered the contemporary Arab poets under the Būyids much material for festive poetry; see the many *nawrūz* and *mihrajān* poems in al-Tha'ālibī's *Yatīma*. [For *nawrūz* and *mihrajān* cf. also A. Mez, *Die Renaissance des Islams*, pp. 400-2, and B. Spuler, *Iran in frühislamischer Zeit*, pp. 480 ff.] Other revived Persian festivals also offered opportunity for such poetry, e.g. *qaṣīdas* for the *sadhaq* (II, pp. 173, 177), or poems for the occasion of *ṣabb al-mā'* (ibid., p. 176). Arab legends on the origin of the latter in al-Jāḥiẓ, l.c. [ed. van Vloten, pp. 364-5]. 'The fires of the Persians at the *sadhaq*' offer Abu'l-'Alā' a poetical image, *Siqṭ al-Zand*, I, p. 143, v. 2. [For the *sadhaq* cf. also Mez, op. cit., pp. 397-8.] The Muslims in Spain identified the Christian Whitsun with the *mihrajān* (Maqq., II, p. 88, 6). [This last sentence is not quite correct: the feast of the *'anṣara*, to which the name of *mihrajān* was applied, is not the Christian Whitsun, but Midsummer Day.]

conquests[1] in old Persian names. His etymology of the place-name Baṣra: *bas rāh*, i.e. 'many ways'[2] shows that his Persian aspirations in this field led him astray.

His favourite occupation was proving that Arabs had turned Persian names upside down, frequently in order to make them suitable for their national purposes. His work *Kitāb al-Tasḥīf wa'l Taḥrīf* (on mistakes in writing and corruptions) seems to be concerned with this.[3] In general he liked to reclaim words for the Persian language that Arab philologists had claimed for Arabic. Al-Tha'ālibī accused him, with reference to the word *sām*, which Ḥamza identified with the Persian *sīm* (silver), of being eager, because of his Persian sympathies (*ta'aṣṣub*), to enlarge the dictionary of Arab foreign words with many curious examples,[4] whereas Abū 'Ubayda strangely enough did not indulge in manifesting his national bias in this way, since he countered the assumption that the Koran contained foreign words with the view that such words were common to the foreign language and Arabic.[5] Ḥamza's manner of philological research, which we have just described, appears to have determined the trend of his *Kitāb al-Muwāzana* ('Book of Balancing'), which is unfortunately completely lost.[6] Al-Suyūṭī quotes from this work in a learned little treatise a passage in which Ḥamza derived from the Persian word *tasākhīn* (sing *tiskhūn*, 'head cover, which was used by judges and scholars but never by others') which appears in the tradition but is missing from our dictionary.[7] He also ridicules the lying fables of
212 the Arabs;[8] and when we find among his works a treatise 'On the nobility of Arabs' this does not necessarily mean that he was concerned with finding proof of Arab superiority.[9]

The literary work of Ḥamza—whose method was not unique in those days, as can be seen from the quotations in the articles con-

[1] Tustar (Shūstar) was said to have been the name of an Arab from the tribe of the Banū 'Ijl; ib., I, p. 848.

[2] Ib. I, p. 637, according to a Persian priest.

[3] [A MS. of this work, entitled *al-Tanbīh 'alā Ḥudūth al-Taṣḥīf*, is found in a library in Teheran; see P. Kraus, *Jābir ibn Ḥayyān*, II, p. 241 n. 7; cf. also pp. 171 n. 2, 245 notes 2, 3, 4, 251 n. 2. The passages published so far do not allow us to form a clear picture of the contents of the book.]

[4] Al-Tha'ālibī, *Fiqh al-Lugha*, ed. Rushayd Daḥdāḥ (Paris 1861), p. 129.

[5] Above, p. 182; cf. also *al-Muzhir*, I, p. 129.

[6] Cited also by Yāqūt, I, p. 553 etc. [See Mittwoch, pp. 27-8.]

[7] MS. Leiden Library Cod. Warner, no. 474, treatise on the *ṭaylasān*, fol. 4b.

[8] [In his *Amthāl*, MS. Munich 115; quoted by al-Maydānī, I, p. 434 and] al-Damīrī, II, p. 287. [Mittwoch, pp. 31-2, points out that this and another similar critical remark need not prove a Shu'ūbī tendency.]

[9] *Al-Risāla al-mu'riba 'an sharaf al-A'rāb*; in Qasṭallānī, VIII, p. 31, there is quoted a passage based on Sūra 4:3 about the various syntactical combinations of numerals.

cerning Persia in Yāqūt's work—reveals the attempt to extend the endeavours of the Iranophiles of the preceding century to the linguistic field. The cardinal point of national Arab belief which had to be overcome in this field was the thesis that Arabic was the best of all the world languages, a thesis which the Prophet himself was represented as expressing in an apocryphal tradition in which ʿAlī says: 'My dear, the Apostle of God told me that once the angel Gabriel descended from heaven and said to him: 'O Muhammed! all things have a master: Adam is master of men, you are the master of Adam's descendants, the master of the Rūm is Ṣuhayb, the master of the Persians Salmān, the master of the Ethiopians is Bilāl (see above, p. 128), the master of trees is the lotus (*sidr*), the master of birds is the eagle, the chief of months is Ramaḍān, the chief of weekdays is Friday and Arabic is master of speech.'[1] When seeking to demonstrate conclusively the richness of Arabic, the Arabs had always boasted of the unequalled variety of synonyms in their language, and this argument remained a favourite one until quite recently, as contact with Arabs will easily prove. The popular view on this matter is expressed also in an episode in the romance of ʿAntar.[2] After ʿAntar had fought and defeated the most celebrated heroes of the Arab tribes and was able therefore to claim equality also for his poetical achievements, he succeeded in having his poem pinned to the door of the Kaʿba, where it was destined to become an object of respect for the Arab heroes and poets. But this success did not come to him until he had passed yet another test. The competing poets sent Imru'u' l-Qays to examine ʿAntar on the synonymy of sword, spear, armour, 213
snake and camel. But this rich synonymy was derided by authors who were hostile to Arabs. The ironical remark ascribed to Ḥamza must be understood in this context: 'The names of misfortune (*al-dawāhī*) are misfortunes themselves.'[3] The synonymy of *dawāhī* is well known for its richness and Ḥamza himself collected four hundred such expressions.

Abu'l-Ḥusayn ibn Fāris, the apologist for the Arab nation and language,[4] had to defend Arabic against such attacks by the Shuʿūbites. We have already shown that this scholar intended in one of his philological works to combat anti-Arab attacks on the Arabic language, devoting some chapters of the work[5] to this purpose. Here

[1] *Sayyid al-kalām al-ʿarabiyya*, al-Damīrī, II, p. 410 below.

[2] *Sīrat ʿAntar*, XVIII, pp. 47-56.

[3] [In the Cairo fragment of the *K. al-Muwāzana*, fol. 4b, see Mittwoch, p. 32; quoted by] al-Thaʿālibī, l.c., p. 122. [Mittwoch again argues that there is no need to look here for Shuʿūbī tendency.]

[4] He was the teacher of Badīʿ al-Hamadānī, the first author of *maqāmas*, Ibn al-Athīr to the year 398, IX, p. 78. [For Ibn Fāris see also *Enc. of Islam*, s.v., and Brockelmann, I, pp. 135-6, Suppl. I, pp. 177-80.]

[5] [The work in question is *al-Ṣāḥibī fī Fiqh al-Lugha*.] Cf. particularly the

we shall briefly repeat from that study[1] whatever may help in the understanding of the movement.

Ibn Fāris, as representative of the Arab party, of course starts from the point of view that 'Arabic is the best and richest of all languages.' 'One cannot, however,' he says, 'claim that it is possible to express one's thoughts correctly only in Arabic; but the interchange of thoughts in other languages is on the lowest level, since they do nothing but communicate thoughts to others. Dumb people also express their thoughts but only by means of bodily indications and movements which point to the main part of their intentions; yet nobody will call this expression language, and still less will anyone say of him who uses such means that he expresses himself clearly, let alone eloquently.'

'Arabic cannot be translated into any other language, as the gospels from the Syriac could be translated into Ethiopian and Greek, or as
214 the Torah and Psalter and other books of God could be translated into Arabic, because the non-Arabs cannot compete with us in the wide use of metaphorical expressions. How would it be possible to render the 60th verse of the eighth Sūra in a language with words which reproduce the exact sense; circumlocutions would have to be used, what is summarized would have to be unrolled, what is separated connected, and what is hidden revealed, so that you might say: When you have made a truce and treaty of peace with a people, but fear their cunning and that they might break the contract, let them know that you on your part will break the conditions and announce war, so that you may both be clear about the breach of peace. The same applies to Sūra 18:10. There are passages also in the poets which in translation can be rendered only by long paraphrase and many words.' Ibn Fāris makes a long list of those resources in which Arabic excels all other languages. In grammar Arabic is far superior to other languages because of its *i'rāb*, by which it can distinguish the logical categories of speech with a clarity that is unknown to any other nation in the word.

[1] 'Beiträge zur Geschichte der Sprachgelehrsamkeit bei den Arabern', no. III (*Sitzungsberichte der Wiener Akademie der Wissenschaften*, 1873, vol. LXXIII, phil. hist. Clasee). [In that study Goldziher analysed the work after the quotations in al-Suyūṭī's *al-Muzhir*. The first quotation in the following paragraph is the title of ch. III, ed. p. 12; the subsequent quotations are from the text of that chapter and are to be found in the ed. pp. 12 and 13. The passage is marked as a quotation by being introduced with the words 'One of the scholars said', and is in fact from Ibn Qutayba's *Ta'wīl Mushkil al-Qur'ān*, ed. Aḥmad Ṣaqr, Cairo 1954, p. 16; the last part, about the poets, is Ibn Fāris's own.]

headings of chapters III, IV, XIII, XVI according to the table of contents reproduced from a MS. discovered in Damascus, *ZDMG*, XXVIII, pp. 163 ff. [The book has been published, Cairo 1910. The chapters referred to by Goldziher are to be found on pp. 12, 18, 34, 42.]

'Some people, however,' he says,[1] 'whose reports must be left alone'—here he is attacking the Shuʿūbites—'believe that the philosophers also (i.e. the Greeks) possess *iʿrāb* and grammatical works; but little importance can be attached to such stories. People saying such things pretended at first to be orthodox and took many things from the books of our scholars after altering a few words; thereafter they refer everything back to those whose names have an ugly sound so that the tongues of true believers are unable to pronounce them. They also claim that those peoples have poetry; we have read these poems ourselves and have found that they are unimportant, of little beauty, and lack a proper metre. Verily, poetry is to be found only with the Arabs who preserved their historical memories in poetical works. The Arabs have the science of prosody which distinguishes a regular poem from a defective one. He who knows about the nuances and depths of this science knows that it excels anything cited as proof of their opinions by those who live in the vain belief that they are able to recognise the essence of things: numbers, lines and points. I do
not see what is the use of these matters; in spite of their little value, 215
they damage belief and cause things against which we invoke God's aid.'

The apologist for the Arabic language must also refute the attacks of opponents of synonymy. He points out that because of this richness it was possible for Arabic to achieve a precision of expression unequalled in any other language. 'No people can translate the Arabic nomenclature of the sword, lion, spear, etc. into its own language. In Persian the lion must rest content with but one name, but we give it a hundred and fifty, Ibn Khālawayhi counted 500 names for the lion and 200 for the snake.' And each name corresponds to a different point in the essence of the things named and thus testifies to close observation of these things.[2]

Another peculiar feature of the Arabic language which enemies of the Arabs used in order to prove the inadequacy of the language and to point out the fact that the Arabs are wide of the mark when talking about its perfection and superiority, was the group of words which philologists call *aḍdād*, i.e. words which represent opposite meanings with completely identical pronunciation. That the Iranophils used this peculiarity in order to disparage the Arabic language we know from the introduction of Abū Bakr ibn al-Anbārī (died 328) to his special monograph on this group of words. 'People who profess false doctrines and condemn the Arab nation wrongly believe that this linguistic phenomenon of Arabic is due to lack of wisdom on the part of the

[1] [This passage is found in the edition on pp. 42-3.]

[2] Ibn Fāris's *Fiqh al-Lugha* quoted by al-Suyūṭī, *Muzhir*, I, pp. 153-57. [Ed. p. 15; the last sentence is not in Ibn Fāris's text and seems to have been added by al-Suyūṭī.]

Arabs, to the small measure of their eloquence, and to the many confusions in their verbal intercourse with each other. They argue that each word has a special meaning, to which it has to point, and which it has to represent, and they say that if the same word stands for two different meanings, the person who is addressed does not know which of the two the speaker has in mind and thus the connection of the name with the concept is completely destroyed.'[1]

216 From their defence of the Arabic language by Ibn Durayd, Ibn Fāris and Ibn al-Anbārī, we see that in the fourth century there existed a linguistic Shu'ūbiyya which continued the endeavours of the genealogical, political and cultural-historical Shu'ūbites of the previous century in a field in which Arab pride could be most painfully wounded. As late as the sixth century the need was felt to discuss the question of *aḍdād* from the point of view of the polemic against the Shu'ūbiyya. The title which al-Baqqālī (died 526) gave to his relevant work points to this fact: 'Secrets of the culture and fame of the Arabs.'[2] This shows that al-Zamakhsharī referred to existing circumstances when opposing the Shu'ūbiyya in the above mentioned passage.

[1] *Kitāb al-Aḍdād*, ed. M. Th. Houtsma, Leiden 1881 [p. 1].

[2] Redslob, *Die arabischen Wörter mit entgegengesetzten Bedeutungen*, (Göttingen 1873), p. 9.

EXCURSUSES AND ANNOTATIONS

ONE 219

WHAT IS MEANT BY 'AL-JĀHILIYYA'

I

From Islam's earliest times, Muslims have tried to bring order into the narrow picture of the historical development of humanity offered them by their religious view by marking the critical points of history, to delimit historical epochs and divide that development into periods. No comprehensive and self-conscious view of life can forgo this analytical task which for the first time expresses an awareness of the difference between its own essence and past preparatory stages of development.

The division into periods which the Muslims undertook is by its nature concerned only with the religious development of humanity, and takes account only of elements which Islam believes to have been its own preparation. The periods of Judaism, Christianity and Islam are the three epochs which are differentiated as phases in the development of the history of the world, or rather of religions. The Muslims express this sequence by the simile of morning, noon, and evening prayer. The duration of the world is taken to be a day. 'Your relation to the owners of the two books,' the Prophet is made to say to true believers, 'can be illustrated by the following parable: A certain man hired workers and told them: He who works the whole day will receive a certain sum in wages. A few of them worked only till noon (these are the Jews) and said: We will not work any longer, we renounce the agreed wages, and what we have done up to now shall be done for nothing. When they were not to be persuaded to
finish their work and gain their full wages the employer hired other 220
men for the rest of the day to whom he promised, on completion of the work, the full reward promised to the first group. But these people too (they are the Christians) stopped work in the afternoon and gave up their wages, even after they were told that they had but a few more hours' work before gaining the whole reward. Now new workers were yet again engaged, the Muslims, who worked until sunset and gained the whole reward.'[1]

[1] B. *Ijāra*, nos. 8, 11 in different versions. *Tawḥīd*, no. 48 names the times of prayers; in this version Jews and also Christians gain part of the wages, but the persevering workers receive double wages; cf. also *Anbiyā'*, no. 44. [Cf. to this variation of Matthew, ch. XX, also Goldziher, *Oriens Christianus*, II (1902), p. 393.]

This division, however, refers only to the development of Islamic monotheism, and only considers its preparatory stages; the heathen world does not appear in it at all. The consideration of the relationship of Islam to previous, more especially Arab, paganism, resulted in the well-known division, which also is hinted at in the Koran, of the history of the Arab people into two periods: that of the Jāhiliyya and that of Islam. The whole of the pagan, pre-Islamic time is al-Jāhiliyya. Between these two periods there is the *Nubuwwa*, i.e. the time of Muhammed's appearance as prophet and of his missionary work.[1] For the sake of completeness it might be mentioned that the Jāhiliyya is subdivided into two periods: the older period (i.e. the time from Adam to Noah or Abraham—according to others from Noah to Idrīs) and the more recent one (from Jesus to Muhammed).[2] This, as we see, rather unclear sub-division arose owing to misunderstanding of the Koranic passage 33:33 where Muhammed says to the women that they should not flirt as was customary in the days of the 'first Jāhiliyya'.[3]

Following the general Muslim explanation we tended to think of the 'Jāhiliyya', in contrast to 'Islam', as 'the time of ignorance.' This conception is wrong. When Muhammed contrasted the change brought about by his preaching with earlier times he did not seek to
221 describe those times as times of ignorance, since in that case he would not have opposed ignorance with devotion to God and confidence in God but with *al-'ilm*, 'knowledge.'[4] In this book we have explained the word al-Jāhiliyya as 'time of barbarism' because Muhammed wanted to contrast the Islam that he preached with barbarism.

Though it may seem trivial and pedantic to put so much stress on the mere translation of a word, we do think that a proper definition of the concept of Jāhiliyya is important for these studies, since it aids us in finding the correct point of view for the understanding of Muslim opinion about pagan times. Therefore it will be well worth the space needed to give at length the reasons for our opinion.[5]

Muhammed presumably did not intend to express anything else by Jāhiliyya than the condition which in the poetical documents of the

[1] *Agh.*, IV, p. 3, 6 from below.

[2] Al-Qasṭallānī, VII, p. 329.

[3] It is also given as an explanation that the first Jāhiliyya comprises the whole of the pre-Islamic time and the new Jāhiliyya refers to relapses into paganism after the Prophet's appearance; cf. also Bayḍāwī, II, p. 128, 11 to the passage.

[4] From Sūra 3:148 it is evident that according to Muhammed a typical sign of the Jāhiliyya was that it recognised no order coming from God. The *ulu'l-'ilmi* and *al-rāsikhūna fi'l-'ilmi* 3:5, 16; 4:610 are no contrast to the Jāhiliyya.

[5] [For *ḥilm* and *jahl* cf. also H. Lammens, *Etudes sur le règne du calife omaiyade Mo'âwia Ier*, pp. 66–88, 363–4.]

time preceding him is described with the verb *jhl*, the substantive *jahl*, and the *nomen agentis*, *jāhil*. It is true that in the old language, too, we find the concept of knowledge (*'ilm*) contrasted to *jahl*,[1] but this opposition is founded on a secondary meaning of *jhl*. The original meaning is seen in an antithesis of this word group, much more common in the older language, with *ḥlm*, *ḥilm* and *ḥalīm*. According to their etymological meaning these words describe the concept of firmness, strength, physical integrity and health, and in addition moral integrity, the 'solidity' of a moral character, unemotional, calm deliberation, mildness of manner. A *ḥalīm* is what we would call a civilized man. The opposition to all this is the *jāhil*, a wild, violent and impetuous character who follows the inspiration of unbridled passion and is cruel by following his animal instincts; in one word, a barbarian. 'May no one act wildly against us (*lā yajhalan*) because we 222
then would excel the wildness of those acting wildly (*jahl al-jāhilīna*).' The kind of character and manner of action against which 'Amr b. Kulthūm[2] wishes to protect himself by threatening revenge in the way of the Jāhiliyya is usually contrasted to *al-ḥilm*, i.e. mildness—and not *al-'ilm*. *Wā-law shā'a qawmī kāna ḥilmiya fīhimī / wa-kāna 'alā juhhāli a'dā'ihim jahlī*, 'If my tribe would have it I would show mildness to them—and practise my wildness against its wild enemies'; not as Freytag translates: *et contra ignorantes inimicorum eius ignorantia mea.*[3]

Another example of this is a line from the poem by Qays b. Zuhayr on the death of Ḥamal b. Badr which he has brought upon himself: *Aẓunnu'-l-ḥilma dalla 'alayya qawmī / wa-qad yustajhalu'l-rajulu'l-ḥalīmu. Wa-mārastu'l-rijāla wa-mārasūnī / fa-mu'wajjun 'alayya wa-mustaqīmu,'*[4] a classical case of this opposition between *ḥilm* and *jahl*. The false assumption that *jāhil* is the opposite to 'knowing' and that therefore *istajhala* means 'to consider someone ignorant' has misled the translators. Freytag, who misunderstood al-Tabrīzī's and al-Marzūqī's *scholia* which lead to the proper meaning, translates: *Mansuetudinem meam in causa fuisse puto cur gens contra me ageret et fit interdum ut mansuetus ignorans habetur*. E. Rehatshek translates: 'I think [my] meekness instigated my people against me,

[1] Al-Mutalammis, *Agh.*, XXI, p. 207, 8, 'Antara, *Mu'all.*, v. 43 *in kunti jāhilatan bi-mā lam ta'lamī*, Nāb. 23:11 *wa-laysa jāhilu shay'in mithla man 'alima*, Ṭarafa 4:102; cf. the line ascribed to Imrq. in al-Ya'qūbī, ed. Houtsma, I, p. 250, 10 (missing from *Dīwān*, ed. Ahlwardt). In later times, after the penetration of the general false explanation of the word *Jāhiliyya*, this contrast becomes even more frequent, Here belongs the passage discussed above, p. 137 note 2.

[2] *Mu'all.*, v. 53.

[3] *Ḥam.*, II, p. 488.

[4] *Agh.*, XV, p. 32; *Ḥam*, I, p. 210 [*Naqā'iḍ*, I, p. 97; al-Marzubānī, *Mu'jam al-Shu'arā'*, p. 322].

and verily a meek man is considered a fool.'[1] Here also Rückert rightly understood what Qays meant to say (I, p. 135) *Ich denk', um Mässigung* (*ḥilm*) *kann mein Volk mich loben, Doch der Gemässigste* (*ḥalīm*) *gereizt mag toben.* i.e., literally: 'A wild man can be brought to wild excesses.' *Istajhala* means: to display the manner of a *jāhil*, here in the passive: to be roused to such wild behaviour. The second line fits in with this: 'I tested the men and they tested me—there were amongst them some who showed themselves crooked (brutal and unjust) to me and some who behaved straight (well and
223 justly).' This contrast of 'crooked' and 'straight' (*mu'awwaj* and *mustaqīm*) corresponds also elsewhere in the poetry of Arab heroes to the contrast of *jāhil* with *ḥalīm*.[2]

Fa-in kuntu muḥtājan ila'l-ḥilmi innanī /ila'l-jahli fī ba'ḍi'l-aḥāyīni aḥwaju
Wa-lī farasun li'l-ḥilmi bi'l-ḥilmi muljamu / wa-lī farasun li'l-jahli bi'l-jahli musraju
Fa-man rāma taqwīmī fa-innī muqawwamun / wa-man rāma ta'wījī fa-innī mu'awwaju.

Though I need mildness, at times I need wildness (*jahl*) even more.
I have a horse bridled with mildness and I have another bridled with wildness.
He who wants me to be straight, to him I am straight, but he who desires my crookedness, for him I am crooked.[3]

The pagan hero al-Shanfarā says in his famous *Lāmiyyat al-'Arab*, v. 53: 'The wild desires (*al-ajhālu*) do not overwhelm my mild sentiment (*ḥilmī*) and one does not see me looking for bad news and slandering.'[4] This shows how the Arab made from *jahl* the plural *ajhāl* in order to express the multitude of evil passions and the various points of bestial brutality; a similar plural was formed from *ḥilm* (*aḥlām*).

Ṭarafa describes the virtue of noble Arabs: 'They suppress brutality

[1] 'Specimens of pre-islamitic arabic poetry', *Journ. Roy. Asiat. Soc.*, Bombay Branch, XXXIX (1881), p. 104.

[2] '*Iwaj* is used as synonym of *jahl* in parallelism, e.g., in the conversation of Ḥārith b. Kalada with the Persian king, Ibn Abī Uṣaybi'a, I, p. 110, 14. By *al-milla al-awjā'*, the crooked religion (B. *Buyū*, no. 50), presumably the Jāhiliyya is meant.

[3] I have unfortunately lost the source for these lines. [See references in Kister's edition of al-Sulamī's *Ādāb al-Ṣuḥba*, p. 73; add Ibn 'Abd Rabbihi, *al-'Iqd*, I, p. 302; al-Marzubānī, *Mu'jam al-Shu'arā'*, p. 429; Qudāma, *Naqd al-Shi'r*, ed. Bonebakker, p. 74.]

[4] *Chrestomathie arabe* by de Sacy, 1st ed., III, p. 8 '*Ma sagesse n'est point le jouet des passions insensées.*'

(*al-jahla*) in their circles and come to the aid of the man of discretion (*dhi'l-ḥilmi*), the noble one'[1] and in the same sense another poet says: 'If you come to them you will find round their houses circles in which brutality is cured by their good nature (*majālisa qad yushfā bi-aḥlāmiha'l-jahlu.*)'[2]

Jahl thus was neither a virtue to the Arabs of an older time—it was appropriate to a young and impetuous character[3]—nor was it entirely condemned. Part of the *muruwwa* was knowing when mildness 224
was not befitting the character of a hero and when *jahl* was indicated: 'I am ferocious (*jahūl*) where mildness (*taḥallum*) would make the hero despicable, meek (*ḥalīm*) when ferocity (*jahl*) would be unfitting to a noble'[4], or, as is said in the spirit of paganism:[5] 'Some meekness is shame (*inna mina' l-ḥilmi dhullun*) as you well know, but mildness when one is able (to be ferocious) is honourable.'

Another poet, expressing the same thought, tells under what circumstances *ḥilm* would be shameful and base:

> The wild man amongst us is ferocious (*jāhil*) in the defence of his guest;
> The ferocious man is mild (*ḥalīm*) when insulted by him (the guest).[6]

This *jahl* is expressed not in rough words but in powerful deeds: 'We act wildly with our hands (*tajhalu aydīnā*) but our mind is meek, we scorn with deeds and not with talk.'[7]

Examples could be multiplied[8] and a number of examples from more recent poetry could be cited[9] to elucidate this antithesis. *Jāhil* and *ḥalīm* are two groups in one or the other of which every man belongs: *wa-ma'l-nāsū illā jāhilun wa-ḥalīmu.*[10]

We will just refer to some old proverbs where the contrast is shown: *al-ḥalīm maṭiyyat al-jahūl*, 'the meek is the pack animal of the ferocious,' i.e. he alows himself to be ruthlessly used without plotting revenge or repaying his tormentor with like deeds;[11] further:

[1] Ṭarafa 3:7; cf. the almost literal repetition of the first half verse, ibid., 14:8.

[2] Zuhayr, 14:37.

[3] Nāb., 4:1.

[4] *Ḥam.*, II, p. 263.

[5] Ibid., I, p. 516. It seems that this verse by Sālim b. Wābiṣa is used by a later poet in al-Mas'ūdī, V, p. 101, and was changed in the Islamic sense so as to become a glorification of a forgiving spirit.

[6] *Ḥam.*, p. 311, v. 2.

[7] Ibid., p. 693, v. 2.

[8] E.g. *Hudhayl.*, 102:12, 13; *Opuscula arab.*, ed. Wright, p. 120, 4; Ḥassān, in Ibn Hishām, p. 625, 4 from below.

[9] Mutan., 27:21 (ed. Dieterici, I, p. 70); cf. a small collection in *al Mustaṭraf*, I, pp. 195 ff.

[10] Al-Mubarrad, p. 425, 9.

[11] Al-Maydānī, I, p. 186 [*al-'Iqd*, I, p. 338, 3].

225 *ḥasbu'l-ḥalīmi anna'l-nāsa anṣāruhu 'ala'l-jāhili*, 'It is a satisfaction for a decent man that his fellow-man help him against the *jāhil*.'[1] In none of these examples can *jāhil* mean ignorant, nor can it do so in the proverb (lacking in al-Maydānī): *ajhalu min al-namr*, 'more ferocious than the tiger.'[2] In the same way a saying of the Prophet, transmitted by Abū Hurayra, demands of him who is fasting *wa-lā yajhal*, i.e., that he should not be roused to deeds of brutality; 'if someone wishes to fight or insult him he should say: I am fasting.'[3]

When, therefore, Muhammed and his first successors refer to the pre-Islamic times as the Jāhiliyya we must not take this in the sense of the *χρόνους τῆς ἀγνοίας*, which, according to the Apostle, preceded Christianity,[4] since for this *ἀγνοία* (in Syriac *ṭā'yūthā*) Muhammed used the Arab term *ḍalāl* (error), which he contrasts with his *hudā* (right guidance)[5]. The Jāhiliyya in this context is nothing but the time in which *jahl*—in the sense which we have seen—was prevalent, i.e. barbarism and cruelty. When the proponents of Islam say that it has ended the customs and habits of the Jāhiliyya, they are thinking of these barbaric customs and the wild mentality which distinguish Arab paganism from Islam, and through the abolition of which Muhammed intended to become the reformer of his people's morality—the arrogance of the Jāhiliyya (*ḥamiyyat al-Jāhiliyya*)[6], the tribal pride and the eternal feuds, the cult of revenge, rejection of forgiveness, and all the other particularities of Arab paganism which were to be superseded by Islam. 'If one does not turn from the lying speech and the *jahl* (i.e. wild habits),' transmits Abū Hurayra, 'verily, God does not require one to restrict one's food and drink.'[7] This tradition clearly shows that in early Islamic times *jahl* was understood in the same way as in old Arabic poetry. 'Previously we were a people, men of the Jāhiliyya,' Ja'far b. Abī Ṭālib is made to say to the Ethiopian prince: 'we prayed to idols, ate carrion and committed
226 shameful deeds; we disrespected the ties of kinship and violated the duty of faithfulness; the strong among us oppressed (ate up) the weaker ones. Thus we were, until God sent a Prophet from our midst, whose descent and justice, righteousness and virtue are known to us.

[1] Al-Maydānī, I, p. 203.

[2] *Mustaṭr.*, I, p. 156.

[3] *Muw.*, II, p. 121. [Other references in *Concordance de la tradition musulmane*, I, p. 392.]

[4] Acts of the Apostles, 17:30, cf. 3:17. Wellhausen, *Arab Heidenthum*, p. 67, note (and already before him Joh. Dav. Michaelis, *Oriental. und exeget. Bibliothek*, XVI, 1781, p. 3) combines the word J. with this expression from the New Testament.

[5] See above, p. 20, note 5.

[6] Sūra 48: 26.

[7] B. *Adab*, no. 50.

He called us to God so that we might recognise His unity and pray to Him and cast aside what our parents adored: stones and idols; he commanded us to speak the truth, be faithful and respect ties of blood, fulfill our duties of protection and keep away from forbidden things and bloodshed. He forbade evil vices and unjust talk, squandering the goods of orphans, slandering innocent people, etc.'[1] In the invitations to pagans to be converted to Islam, almost exclusively moral—not ritual—observances are demanded; thus, for example, the homage of the twelve neophytes at the 'Aqaba takes place under the following conditions: that they will put no one on a level with God, will not steal, commit adultery or infanticide or be arrogant.[2] This is the point of view from which older Islam contrasts the Jāhiliyya with Islam. The ritual laws of Islam are also mentioned, but the main point in a life contrary to the Jāhiliyya lies in turning away from worshipping lifeless things and more especially putting an end to immoral and cruel actions in which the Prophet and his apostles see the main characteristics of the Jāhiliyya. From this point of view the Jāhiliyya is the contrast to what is called *dīn* in a religious sense, and the opposition of the two words is attested from the earliest days in Islam.[3]

What Islam attempted to achieve was, after all, nothing but a *ḥilm* of higher nature than that taught by the code of virtues of pagan days. Many a virtue of Arab paganism was—as we have seen—reduced to the level of a vice by Muhammed, and on the other hand many a social act, considered dishonourable by Arabs, was now elevated to the status of a virtue. He is fond of calling people *ḥalīm* who practise forgiveness and leniency. With this in mind he often calls Allah *ḥalīm*,[4] a title which he gives with preference to Ibrāhīm amongst the prophets.[5]

Muhammed's teaching thus brought about a change in the meaning 227
of *ḥilm* and hence we can understand that his pagan fellow-citizens, who opposed his teaching, constantly accuse the reformer of declaring their *ḥilm* to be folly (*yusaffih aḥlāmanā*)[6] branding as barbaric acts (*Jāhiliyya*) deeds which in their eyes were of the highest virtue. The word *safīh*, fool, is a synonym of the word *jāhil* and belongs to that

[1] Ibn Hishām, p. 219.

[2] Ṭab., I, p. 1213.

[3] In a poem by Tamīm b. Ubayy b. Muqbil, Yāqūt II, p. 792, 7. Contrast of J. and *sunnat al-islām*, Ibn Abi'l-Za'ra in Ibn Durayd, p. 234.

[4] E.g. Sūra 2:225, 236; 3:149; 5:131; 17:46; 22:58; 35:39; 64:17, usually in connection with *ghafūr*, forgiving.

[5] E.g. 9:115; 11:77.

[6] Ṭab., I, 1175, 5, 14; 1179, 8; 1185, 13. Ibn Hishām, p. 167 penult.; 168, 7; 169, 4; 186, 2; 188, 1; 190, 9; 225 ult. Cf. Ṭab., I, 977, 8 *yusaffihanna 'uqūlakum wa-'uqūla ābā'ikum*, al-Ya'qūbī, II, p. 264, 9.

group of words which, like *kesīl* and *sākhāl* (in Hebrew),[1] describe not only fools but also cruel and unjust men.[2]

Accordingly, when Zayd b. ʿAmr b. Nufayl is converted to Islam and renounces paganism he says: 'I will no longer pay homage to (the idol) Ghanm, who was God to us when my *ḥilm* was small,' i.e. when I was still a *jāhil*, in the time of the Jāhiliyya.[3] The latter word is thus also in the early days of Islam, as in pagan times, the conceptual opposite of *ḥilm* and not yet of *ʿilm* (science). These two are well differentiated. 'There are people', says a tradition of ʿUbāda b. al-Ṣāmit, 'who had science and *ḥilm* and others who had but one of the two.'[4]

Because Islamic ethics restricted the idea of *ḥalīm* to such men as were virtuous in the Islamic sense, it was quite possible for *mu'min*, right believer, to be used as the opposite of *jāhil*, i.e., from the point of view of Islam, a man acting according to God's will in practical things as well as in the dogmatic sense. Thus Rabīʿ b. Khaytham speaks of two kinds of men: one is either *mu'min*—and such a one
228 must not be harmed—or *jāhil*—to whom one must not be cruel.[5] Profane literature also shows this contrast,[6] which is also projected back into earlier times. It is told of Qays b. ʿĀṣim, whom his contemporary, the Prophet, called 'master of all tent dwellers' (*sayyid ahl al-wabar*), that he belonged 'to the *ḥulamā'* of the Banū Tamīm and abstained from drinking wine even in pagan days.'[7]

[1] To translate the Greek ἀδικήσαντος and ἀδικηθέντος the Syriac translation uses the Afʿel form of *sekhal*, II Cor. 7:12. It might be mentioned that the Hebrew translator of the *Dalāla* of Maimonides translated Jāhiliyya with *sekhālīm*, II, ch. 39.

[2] *Salabtinī ḥilmī*, 'you have robbed my sense' (*Agh.*, VI, 57, 6). *Sfh* is also (like its synonym *jhl*) a contrast to *ḥlm*; e.g., Zuhayr, *Muʿall.*, v. 63.

[3] Ibn Hishām, p. 145, 9. Cf. *Agh.*, III p. 16, 1.

[4] Ibn Ḥajar, II, p. 396.

[5] *Iḥyā'*, II, p. 182: *Al-nās rajulān mu'min fa-lā tu'dhihi wa-jāhil fa-lā tujāhilhu.*

[6] *Agh.*, XVIII, p. 30, 12: *wa-lākinnahu ḥadīd jāhil lā yu'min wa-ana aḥlam wa-aṣfaḥ.*

[7] Ibn Durayd, p. 154, 5. [This interpretation of *ḥalīm* here as a backward projection of an Islamic concept does not seem to me necessary. Avoidance of drunkenness could well be described as *ḥilm*; cf. Ibn Ḥabīb, *al-Muḥabbar*, pp. 237 ff.]

TWO 229

ON THE VENERATION OF THE DEAD IN PAGANISM AND ISLAM

I

WITHOUT wishing to advocate the theory of the 'modern eubemerists' which has recently, through the inspiration of Herbert Spencer, gained ground in many different fields, one may claim that the heightened veneration of the national past, and its historical and mythical representatives, was a religious factor in the inner life of pagan Arabs, one of the few deeper religious manifestations of their souls.

It was expressed also in forms which are usually classed with the manifestation of religious life. To mention but a few examples. According to a traditional account, after the end of a pilgrimage the pilgrims used to halt in the valley of Minā in order to celebrate the deeds of their ancestors with songs,[1] much as the ancient Romans sang songs of praise to their ancestors at banquets. Muhammed is said to refer to this in Sūra 2:196: 'And when you have completed the ceremonies of pilgrimage think of Allāh just as you remember your forefathers, and more.' The Qurayshites of pagan days, and other Arabs too, used to swear by their ancestors—*wa-jaddika* 'by your forefather'[2], this type of oath is common in old poems[3]—and Muham- 230
med forbade such oaths,[4] restricting them to Allāh's name.[5] Some of these pagan customs survived in Islam, and like many formulae of old Arabic thought and life the oath *wa-jaddika, wa-abīka, wa-abīhi*

[1] In al-Bayḍāwī, I, p. 110. [Cf. also al-Ṭabarī's commentary to the Koranic verse.]

[2] This interpretation was abandoned by Nöldeke, cf. *ZDMG*, XLI, p. 723. I thought that it could be maintained because of the above data. It must be mentioned that the word *jadd* in other contests, too, made the interpreters doubt whether it refers to ancestors or is an equivalent of the word *bakht*, e.g. in a saying *al-Muwaṭṭa'*, IV, p. 84: it does not avail *dhu'l-jadd* his *jadd*. Cf. also the dual explanation of the word *majdūd*; in the meaning 'blessed with material goods' it is used by Abu'l-'Alā' al-Ma'arrī, II, p. 179, v. 2.

[3] Imrq. 36:12, cf. *la-'amru jaddī* Labīd, p. 14, v. 6.

[4] B. *Manāqib al-Anṣār*, no. 26, *Tawḥīd*, no. 13. Traditions had to forbid also other pagan oaths: B. *Adab*, no. 43, *Janā'iz*, no. 84 (*man ḥalafa 'alā millatin ghayri'l-islām*) is referred to this by some exegetes.

[5] *Shahādāt*, no. 27, *Adab*, no. 73.

could not be eradicated.[1] Even in tales where the Prophet is quoted, such affirmations are put into his mouth, though he is made to upbraid 'Umar severely when he swore by his father. Theologians[2], of course, are not embarrassed to apply their art of interpretation to such contradictions when pious people swear by the name of their fathers. In their opinion the grammatical expedient of *taqdīr* (*restitutio in integrum*) must be applied to such cases. 'By my father' is always to be considered equal to 'by the God of my father'.[3] It is not impossible that Muslim philologists used this *taqdīr* as a tacit correction of an old Arabic verse.[4]

The grave of the ancestor also appears to have been of solemn significance. This at least seems to be indicated by a verse of Ḥassān b. Thābit in his panegyric on the Ghassānids in Syria: 'The descendants of Jafna, around the grave of their ancestor, the grave of Ibn Māriya, the noble and excellent man.'[5] This is, however, a local and perhaps individual trait and, in view of what we know of the religion of the Ghassānids in general, it might be daring to generalize and
231 exploit it—as so often happens in respect of the ancestor cult—for far-reaching conclusions. But in this context the fact should be stressed that some Arab tribes maintained the tradition of the grave of the ancestor even in later days,[6] for example that of the grave of the ancestor of the Tamīmites in Marrān,[7] and that of the ancestor of the Quḍā'a tribe on a hill by the coast of al-Shiḥr in Ḥaḍramawt,[8] where the original settlement of the tribe named after him is said to have been before their migration to the north. Panegyrists, when wishing to praise the descendants, refer to the graves of their ancestors.[9]

[1] Cf. Kuthayyir, *Agh.*, XI, p. 46, 18, al-Ṣimma al-Qushayrī, ibid. V, p. 133, 13.

[2] Maimonides has taken over this use of *taqdīr* for an analogous phenomenon in Judaism (cf. *ZDMG*, XXXV, p. 774 below); by the assumption of *ḥadhf al-muḍāf* he explains the oath in Moses' name (=*wa-rabbi Mūsā*), *Le livre des preceptes*, ed. M. Bloch, p. 63 ult.

[3] *Al-Muwaṭṭa'*, II, p. 340, and the commentary of al-Zurqānī to the passage; cf. al-Qasṭallānī, IV, p. 461.

[4] *Wa-rabbi abīka* in Ḥārith b. Ḥilliza (*Agh.*, IX, p. 181, 11) is hardly genuine and the original reading was presumably: *la-'amru abīka*.

[5] *Dīwān*, p. 72 [ed. Hirschfeld, 13:8], al-Ya'qūbī, I, p. 236, 12; al-Maydānī, I, p. 204; cf. Reiske, *Primae lineae historiae regnorum arabicorum*, p. 81. Cf. also al-Nābigha 1:6, in accordance with Wetzstein, *Reisebericht über Haurân und die Trachonen*, p. 118.

[6] Cf. also al-Fāsī, *Chroniken der Stadt Mekka*, II, p. 139, 3 from below. The grave of Kulayb Wā'il, Yāqūt II, p. 723.

[7] Yāqūt, IV, p. 479, cf. Robertson Smith, p. 19.

[8] Wüstenfeld, *Register zu den genealogischen Tabellen*, p. 138.

[9] Yāqūt, II, p. 773, 17 (= Ibn Hishām, p. 89, 4, but here we always find *mayt* instead of *qabr*).

The cult of the dead is coupled with the cult of ancestors. There is only a relative difference between these two types of reverence, in that the latter seeks for objects of religious veneration in the distant past, whereas the former is dedicated to the memory of more recent generations. We can say about the Arabs that we have more positive data about their cult of the dead than about their ancestor worship. If we speak about the latter at all we do not by any means wish to give way to the opinion that among the pagan Arabs the veneration of ancestors occupies a position even remotely comparable to that claimed by Fustel de Coulanges for the Romans and Greeks. A more developed ancestor cult has been proved only for the southern Arabs,[1] and among inhabitants of the middle and northern part of the Arab area only scanty indications can be found. What we claim is only that amongst the moral impulses which lie at the basis of Arab views on life the veneration of ancestors has a decisive influence[2].

II

The Koran refers to *anṣāb* or *nuṣub* as a cult object of the heathen Arabs. Their veneration is forbidden in the same breath as other 232
things condemned in Islam, like wine, the game of *maysir*, etc.,[3] and it is forbidden to eat animals slaughtered near them (or in their honour).[4]

'Do not sacrifice to the raised *nuṣub*—do not pray to the high places, worship God alone' says al-A'shā in his panegyric on Muhammed.[5] *Anṣāb*, which is etymologically identical with the *maṣṣēbhā* of the Old Testament, and has the same meaning,[6] means upright stones which were honoured as part of a cult by pagan Arabs.[7] This name is usually referred to the stones placed in the vicinity of the Ka'ba, where Arabs are said to have made sacrifices. We will not discuss here whether this is really to be regarded as historical, and

[1] Praetorius, *ZDMG*, XXVII, p. 646, D. H. Müller, 'Südarabische Studien' (*Sitzungsberichte der. Kais. Akademie in Wien*, phil. hist. Cl., LXXXVI, p. 135), p. 35.

[2] See above, p. 13.

[3] Sūra 5:92.

[4] Ibid., 5:4.

[5] Ed. Thorbecke, *Morgenländische Forschungen*, p. 258 [*Dīwān*, no. 17 v. 20]. Palmer [*The Desert of the Exodus*, p. 43=] *Die vierzigjährige Wüstenwanderung Israels*, p. 36, finds the name Wādī Naṣb on the Sinai peninsula reminiscent of old pagan idolatry from pre-Islamic times.

[6] Cf. Stade, *Geschichte des Volkes Israel*, I, p. 459.

[7] It is worth noting that amongst the attributes of the *anṣāb* cult the hurried walk to the sacred stones is mentioned (Koran, 70:43; cf. B. *Janā'iz*, no. 83). Hurrying in the Ka'ba procession and the quick run between Ṣafā' and Marwa are probably relics of this quick walk to the *anṣāb*. This confirms the discussion in Snouck Hurgronje, *Het Mekkaansche Feest*, p. 105 [and p. 115; *Verspreide Geschriften*, I, pp. 70, 77].

will stress only that there is certain evidence that such *anṣāb* were erected by the graves of especially venerated heroes[1] as a sign of veneration. The Arabs considered it important to provide the graves of men whom they had honoured in life with memorial stones.[2] When we consider that such a grave is described with the same epithet (*jadath*[3] *rāsin*)[4] as that used for mountains (*al-jibāl al-rawāsī*) we may conclude that preference was given to the erection of a
233 memorial of durable and upward-rising construction. In an account of Abū ʿUbayda mention is made of a house (*bayt*), which the Ṭayyi'ites erected over the grave of the powerful Qays al-Dārimī,[5] but this is not to be taken literally. Characteristic of such memorials is the description in the dirge of Durayd b. al-Ṣimma on Muʿāwiya b. ʿAmr:

> Where is the place of visiting (of the dead) O Ibn Bakr?
> By erect stones (*iram*) and heavy (lying) stones and dark
> branches which grow from the stones, and funeral buildings
> over which long times pass, month after month.[6]

Such mausoleums are also called *āyāt*.[7] Arabic poetry frequently mentions stones under which the dead are sleeping; they are called *aḥjār* or *aṭbāq*[8] and also *ṣafīḥ*, *safā'iḥ*[9] or *ṣuffāḥ*. The latter occurs at the end of the poem by Burj b. Mushir from the tribe of Ṭayyi', in which he describes the life of luxury, and concludes that after a life fully enjoyed, rich and poor alike must withdraw 'into holes the lower parts of which are hollow and over which stones are erected'.[10]

The king Nuʿmān had the presents intended for Shaqīq placed on his grave because the latter died on the way to his court, and al-Nābigha praises this act of generosity with the words: 'Shaqīq's

[1] Just as to-day stones decorated with *wusūm* are erected in honour of such men who by protection or other merits deserve the permanent recognition of the tribe, Burton, *The Land of Midian Revisited* (London, 1879) I, p. 321.

[2] On the other hand it would follow from *Agh.*, XII, p. 154, 7—if we attach value to this note—that men strove to profane the graves of enemies whom they feared. (Reference to this from later times: *Agh.*, XIII, p. 16, 17.)

[3] This word is usually associated (Gesenius) with *gādīsh* Job, 21:32—which R. Haya explains thus: It is the *qubba* on the grave in the fashion of Arab countries (Bacher, *Ibn Esra als Grammatiker*, p. 177). The word *ajdāth*, which appears three times in the Koran, is explained with *qubūr* by the oldest exegetes, B. *Janā'iz*, no. 83.

[4] *Hudhayl.*, 16:4, cf. *al-jadath al-aʿlā*, *Ḥam.*, p. 380, v. 6.

[5] *Agh.*, XIV, p. 89, 16. ['Al-Dārimī' is an error; see also the *Dīwān* of Ṭufayl al-Ghanawī, p. 18.]

[6] Ibid., IX, p. 14, 10.

[7] Mutammim b. Nuwayra's dirge, v. 17, in Nöldeke, *Beiträge*, p. 99 [=*Mufaḍḍaliyyāt*, no. 67, v. 17] perhaps also Zuhayr, 20:8 (but certainly not ib., v. 3 as Weil pre-supposed, *Die poetische Literatur der Araber*, p. 43).

[8] Yāqūt, IV, p. 862, 5: *illā rusūmu ʿiẓamin taḥta aṭbāqin.*

[9] In al-Masʿūdī, III, p. 312, 3 from below.

[10] *Ḥam.*, p. 562 v. 8: *ṣuffāḥun muqīmun.*

present is on the stones of his grave' (*fawqa aḥjāri qabrihi*).[1] Such memorials are not only made of upright stones: the *ṣafā'iḥ*, in particular, are broad stone plates laid on top of one another.[2]

Cairns were also used as memorials by the ancient Arabs, and the derivations of the root *rjm*[3] are used to describe them, just as the tumuli in Ḥawrān are called *rejm* by the natives.[4] But metaphorically this word was already used for 'grave' in the old language.[5] 234

To the words used to describe upright grave memorials also belong derivations from the root *nṣb*, which especially express the idea of erectness, e.g. *naṣā'ib* (sing. *naṣība*) which Sulaym b. Rib'ī uses in a dirge on his brother[6] (v. 5): 'Verily the mourner who injures his face (as a sign of mourning) is no more alive than the buried one for whom memorial stones (*naṣā'ib*) are erected.'[7]

Our *anṣāb* is preferably used in this context. A few examples will show the form and significance of such memorial stones. Grateful contemporaries erected *anṣāb* facing each other by the grave of Ḥātim from the Ṭayyi' tribe,[8] who was famous for his generosity; these stones looked like wailing women and a legend connected with the grave[9] indicates that Arabs passing the tomb expected hospitable reception there. The deceased tribal hero was credited with the same attributes and virtues after death as distinguished him while alive, and his grave was believed to benefit people seeking protection and help in the same way as did the tent of the living man. This trait of Arab belief is not confined to antiquity. We may mention the grave

[1] This verse is transmitted thus by Ibn al-Athīr, *al-Mathal al-Sā'ir*, p. 190, 21; ed. Ahlwardt, append. 16:2, *fawqa a'ẓāmi qabrihi*. For completion of the nomenclature the word *ghariyy* must be mentioned, which is interpreted as *nuṣub*, upon which the *'ashā'ir* sacrifices were slaughtered. The same word also means grave memorial, cf. the well-known *al-ghariyyān*, Yāqūt, III, p. 790, 10.

[2] Ṭarafa, *Mu'all.*, v. 65: *ṣafā'iḥu ṣummun min ṣafīḥin munaḍḍadi* (*muwaḍḍa'u* in Sībawayhi, ed. Derenbourg, II, p. 23, 12.); cf. *inna'l-ṣafā'iḥa qad nuḍḍidat* in al-Āmidi, *Muwāzana*, p. 174, 4 from below, and Ibn Hishām, p. 1033, 3 from below.

[3] *Rijm*, pl. *rujūm*, *Agh.*, XII, p. 151, 2 *fa-būrikta maytan qad ḥawatka rujūmu*; cf. for the general context of this custom: Haberland iun *Zeitschrift für Völkerpsychologie*, XII, pp. 289 ff.

[4] [Ch. W. Wilson, Ch. Warren etc., *The*] *Recovery of Jerusalem*, pp. 433 ff.

[5] *Lij Mālī walajta'l-rajama:* al-Maydānī, II, p. 116; al-Mufaḍḍal, *Amthāl*, p. 10 penult; *Ālat al-rajam* are called by Abu'l-'Alā' al-Ma'arrī (*Siqṭ*, II, p. 176, v. 2), the paraphernalia belonging to the funeral, e.g. shrouds.

[6] Wright, *Opuscula arabica*, p. 104, 7; for the thought, cf. ib. p. 165, 6.

[7] Cf. al-Farazdaq, *Agh.*, XIX p. 20, 18: *wa-law kāna fi'l-amwāti taḥta'l-naṣā'ibi*.

[8] As site of the grave our passage names Taba'a, a place in Najd where 'Ādite graves which Arabs especially venerated are said to have been. Others put the grave of Ḥātim at 'Uwāriḍ, a mountain in the Ṭayyi' area (Yāq., I, p. 823, 19; III, p. 840, 13).

[9] *Agh.*, XVI, p. 101, *Dīwān* of Ḥātim, ed. Hassoun, p. 30, cf. Kremer, *Geschichte der herrschenden Ideen des Islam*, p. 166.

of Shahwān b. 'Īsā, chief of the Banū Dabāb. 'O Shahwān b. 'Īsā, we are your guests,' the Arabs who pass this grave (in Tripolitania)
235 call out when they are short of food; and through the intervention of the deceased shaykh it is usually possible for them to hunt up food in the vicinity of the grave.[1] But with the ascendancy of the religious habit of mind it is now at the graves of saints rather than of heroes that one experiences the practice of the old virtues.[2]

But the account of the memorial stones at the tomb of Ḥātim does not show the cult significance attributed to such memorials. This significance can be observed by the *anṣāb* of an equally venerated tribal hero, 'Āmir b. al-Ṭufayl. When this rival of Muhammed, whom the Prophet vainly tried to convert, died (so our source relates) Arabs erected *anṣāb* in the circumference of one square mile round his grave; these were to designate the grave as a τέμενος (*ḥimā*). Within the space thus delimited animals were not permitted to graze, and no pedestrian or riding beast was allowed to step on it.[3] Some of the areas marked out by stones, as mentioned by Schumacher in his description of the Jōlān,[4] are presumably places of this nature; in recent days students have paid attention to such places both east and west of the Jordan.[5] Though it seems that we are justified in placing the origin of the dolmens, which have recently been discovered in great numbers in this area,[6] chiefly in pre-Arabic times, it is not impossible that simpler stone enclosures
236 are due to the Arabs. The Bedouins may have been inspired to imitate dolmens which already existed in this area. The fact that such monuments were erected by Arabs is confirmed by the verse of Durayd quoted above (p. 212) and we must also regard the *ḥimā* of 'Āmir b. al-Ṭufayl as a memorial of this kind.

When one considers that such *ḥimā* were also dedicated to the gods

[1] *Journal asiatique*, 1852, II, p. 163. This grave is called *al-qabr par excellence* in that area.

[2] On marabout graves, whose purpose is to be a place of entertainment for pilgrims, see Daumas, *Le Sahara algérien*, p. 228. In the *zāwiya* of Sīd 'Abd Allāh b. Tamtam in the region of Tuat Bedouin Arabs are excluded from this hospitality. The saint buried there 'does not permit that people strengthen themselves with his *kuskusu* in order to rob pious Muslims on the road' (*Voyage d'El Ajachi*, transl. by Bergbrugger, p. 25). The most noteworthy examples are the *qubāb* of Sīdī Naṣr in the province of Oran, about which there is the belief that the pilgrim who enters the place tired and hungry must spend the night, after having recited a few pious formulae, under the roof of the marabout, and while he is sleeping he is nourished in a miraculous way so that he awakes feeling satiated.

[3] *Agh.*, XV, p. 139.

[4] *ZDPV*, 1886, IX, p. 238, especially p. 271.

[5] Ibid., vol. X; cf. also a lecture by Schick on Moab in *Jerusalem*, year-book edited by A. M. Luncz, II (1887), p. 56.

[6] Schumacher, *Across the Jordan* (London 1885), pp. 54-71.

(as expressly related, for example, about the deity of the Daws tribe, Dhu'l-Sharā)[1] this dedication of the graves of deceased heroes takes on a significance as part of a cult and it is better understood why, in a tradition ascribed to Muhammed, the erection of a *ḥimā*, except for God and the Prophet, is forbidden.[2] *Ḥimā*—incidentally identical with the southern Arab *maḥmā* ('the area which is under the protection of the temple')[3]—is a cult term in old Arab linguistic use and means the same as the word *ḥaram* (which came to be used later) in the terminology of Islam.[4] It is said of a man who acts perfidiously that he has profaned the *ḥimā* of such and such a person,[5] and it is said figuratively of the conqueror that he strips (*abāḥa*) the *ḥimā* of the vanquished of its sacredness.[6]

The sacred awe which was inspired by the graves of honoured heroes is also connected with the belief that the grave was considered as a safe and inviolate sanctuary, a view which was inherited by Islam. The poet Ḥammād sought refuge by the grave of the father of his enemy and his confidence was not in vain. When the pro-'Alid poet al-Kumayt aroused the caliph's anger with an anti-Umayyad satire,
so that the caliph outlawed him and he wandered about like hunted 237
game, he eventually took the advice of friends and sought refuge by the grave of a prince of the ruling family. The caliph, implacable at first, succumbed to the urgent entreaty of his grandchildren, who tied their clothes to the poet's clothes[7] and cried: 'He sought protection by the grave of our father, O Commander of the Faithful, do not shame us in the person of him who seeks sanctuary by this dead man; because shaming the dead is blame to the living.'[8] This same means

[1] Ibn Hishām, p. 253; cf. Krehl, *Über die Religion der vorislamischen Araber*, p. 83. (On *ḥīmā*, see now the exhaustive description of Wellhausen, *Arab. Heidenthum*, pp. 101 ff.

[2] *Lā ḥiman illā li'llāhi wa-li-rasūlihi* (Jawh., s.v. *ḥmy*, beginning). This saying is apocryphal and in it a veneration of the Prophet is allowed which he himself did not claim, but always refused. According to the usual Muslim explanation attributed to al-Shāfi'ī this difficulty of course does not exist; see Yāqūt, II, p. 344. [The tradition is also given by al-Suyūṭī, *al-Jāmi' al-Ṣaghīr*, II, p. 201; idem, *al-Khaṣā'iṣ al-Kubrā*, Hyderabad 1319, II, p. 242; 'Abd al-Ghanī al-Nābulusī, *Dhakhā'ir al-Mawārīth*, I, p. 269.]

[3] Mordtmann-Müller, *Sabäische Denkmäler*, p. 74.

[4] Dozy, *De Israeliten te Mekka*, p. 78. In a figurative sense 'Umar is credited with a saying against a tax collector who whipped the people (cf. above p. 26, note 2): 'the back of a Muslim is a *ḥimā*' (Abū Yūsuf, *Kitāb al-Kharāj*, p. 65, 6 from below, p. 86, 18), apparently following the usage mentioned by the commentators to Sūra 5:102 (ad v. *ḥāmin*).

[5] Imrq., 56:3 *abāḥa ḥimā Ḥujrin*.

[6] *Agh.*, XXI, p. 97, 13, synonym with *istaḥalla 'l-maḥārima*, *Ḥam.*, p. 224, v. 1.

[7] On this type of *istijāra*, see my contributions in *Lbl. f. orient Phil.* 1885, p. 26; *Agh.*, X, p. 35, 5. Parallels to this in Plutarch, *Themist.*, ch. 24, *Artax.*, ch. 3.

[8] *Agh.*, XV, pp. 117, 121

saved the life of the poet Uqaybil b. Shihāb, who ridiculed al-Ḥajjāj: he also erected a tent over the grave where he took refuge. He fled to the grave of Marwān, whose son 'Abd al-Malik had just become caliph. In consequence, the latter had to appeal to his stern governor for a pardon for the poet.[1] During the reign of al-Walīd II the poet 'Abd al-Malik b. Qa'qā' took refuge from his persecutors at the same grave, but the caliph did not respect the asylum and his lack of piety was reprimanded in the following words of the 'Absid Abu'l-Shaghb, which prove that the sanctity of the grave was taken for granted in those days:

The graves of the sons of Marwān are not protected, there is no
refuge found there and nobody takes notice of them.
The grave of the Tamīmite is more faithful than their graves—
his people are secure in its protection;
Verily people call, when visiting this grave:
fie upon the grave where Ibn Qa'qā' sought refuge'[2]

This shows what indignation was roused in those days by any disregard for the sanctuary of the grave. Such cases were in fact exceptional, because the grave of the father or ancestor was sacred to Arabs. For example, we are told of the poet al-Farazdaq, that he took up as his own the cause of anyone seeking protection by his father's grave.[3] In the cult of saints this attribute is transferred to the graves of saintly persons in general, and this attitude developed to a greater extent in western Islam than in the east, just as will be shown that the eastern cult of saints is far less rich than its Maghri-
238 bine counterpart.[4] While in the east the right of sanctuary (like other privileges and miraculous powers) is the privilege of some specific saints' graves—for example, that of Ṭalḥa near Baṣra[5]—this right was given to almost all graves of marabouts in the Maghrib. The grave mosque of the 'Alid Idrīs in Fez is considered an asylum to this day, and escaped criminals are secure there from persecution by temporal justice. The same is true of the mosque containing the graves of the Moroccan princes, of the grave chapel of Sīdī Abu'l-'Abbās, the patron saint of Morocco,[6] and generally of most graves of saints in that country.[7] The marabout to whose grave the persecuted flee even saves, by miraculously feeding, those who are

[1] Al-Balādhurī, *Ansāb al-Ashrāf*, p. 40 [al-Marzubānī, *Mu'jam al-Shu'arā'*, pp. 23–4].

[2] *Fragmenta hist. arab.*, ed. de Goeje, p. 122.

[3] Ibn Khallikān, no. 788, ed. Wüstenfeld, IX, p. 114.

[4] Cf. my 'Materialien zur Kenntnis der Almohadenbewegung', *ZDMG*, XLI, pp. 44 ff. [Cf. vol. II, pp. 305, 324, 374 ff. of the original.]

[5] Al-Fakhrī, p. 107.

[6] Rohlfs, *Erster Aufenthalt in Marokko*, pp. 241, 285-6, 392.

[7] Höst, *Nachrichten von Maróкos*, p. 125.

threatened with starvation when surrounded by enemies.[1] These are features which were inherited by Islam from paganism, like many other things which secured the sanction of Islam and were given Muslim form. Quatremère, in one of his scholarly essays, has collected a large number of beliefs from Islamic times about the inviolateness of the *jār al-qabr* (protégé of the grave).[2] All this is connected with the belief in the sacredness of the grave. To Arabs the graves of ancestors or heroes were as sacred as the temple altar, considered as a sanctuary, was to Greeks, or as the Ka'ba,[3] where everyone found certain protection and refuge: *wa-man dakhalahu kāna āminan* (Sūra 3:91).

III

If the graves of dead ancestors, heroes or benefactors were considered as religious sanctuary, one may well deduce that they were connected with some manifestations of religious feeling or real 239
cultual practices. In this context we may point out that ancient Arab poets often used the oath 'by the *anṣāb*'[4] in a way that indicated that they referred not to idols but to grave memorials. 'I swear by the *anṣāb* between which blood (of sacrificial animals is shed)'.[5] 'Awf b. Mu'āwiya swears, speaking to a dead person, 'by that which I sacrificed near your black *anṣāb*.'[6] These oaths also contain a reference to cult acts which took place by the graves of the deceased, i.e., the sacrifice for the dead.[7] Islam does not favour the oath 'by the grave of the dead,' but it had as little success in eradicating it as it had with many other pagan customs. In Islam also it is customary to swear, for example, by the grave of a caliph who has recently died.[8] It is less remarkable when the oath refers to the grave of the Prophet,[9] which is also the object of invocation.[10]

We have just mentioned the sacrifice for the dead as a cult act, a

[1] Pezant, *Voyages en Afrique au royaume de Barcah et dans la Cyrénaïque à travers le desert* (Paris 1840), p. 290.

[2] 'Mémoire sur les asyles chez les Arabes' (*Mémm. de l'Académie des Inscriptions*) XV, 2, pp. 309-313.

[3] Ibn Hishām, p. 818: 'Before his entry into Mecca the Prophet ordered that they were to threaten only such enemies who attacked them sword in hand; he named only a few persons who had to be killed even if they were to be found under the curtains of the Ka'ba'. Cf. Exod. 21:14, Lev. 4:7, I. Kings, 1:50, 2:28.

[4] Cf. Wellhausen, *Arab. Heidenthum*, p. 99; al-Mutalammis, *Agh.*, XXI, p. 207, 6: *wa'l-Lāti wa'l-anṣābi.*

[5] Ṭarafa, 18:1, in the same breath the oath, *wa-jaddika*; cf. the same poet, Append., 13, 2. Nāb., 5:37, does not seem to belong to this series.

[6] *Agh.*, IX, p. 9, 5 from below.

[7] Cf. Ḥassān b. Thābit, Ibn Hishām, p. 626, 3 from below.

[8] *Agh.*, V, p. 110, 5 from below: *ḥalaftu bi-turbat al-Mahdī.*

[9] Ibid., VI, p. 150, 5 *wa-ḥaqq al-qabr.*

[10] Ibid., IV, p. 139, 7 of al-Nābigha al-Ja'dī, contemporary of 'Uthmān.

practice which has not only survived to this day amongst Bedouins[1] but has also been transplanted with Islamic reinterpretation into the regular religious life of orthodox Islam. The loyalty of the representatives of the old Arabic spirit to tradition is so deeply imbedded that Bedouins, even when they formally adhere to the religion of Muhammed, have retained their social institutions and laws until recent times, despite the fact that the Prophet opposed them with other ordinances and rules. Burckhardt, who produced the first true picture of Bedouin life in European literature, was therefore right in thinking that observation of the institutions of the large tribes in Yemen and Najd would be the best source of knowledge of Arab conditions during paganism[2]—a suggestion that has since been
240 followed. Burckhardt describes the following remarkable custom of the Bedouins in Najd—a custom which, in regard to the time of its practice, had been assimilated into the Islamic way of life. On the great annual feast (*'īd al-qurbān*) every family slaughters as many camels as they have lost adult members by death during the past year, irrespective of sex. The custom is carried out even where the deceased person has left but one camel. If not even one camel was left the nearest relatives have to provide one. Seven sheep are considered as the equivalent of one camel. If the necessary number of sacrificial animals cannot be produced, compensation is offered in the following year or the year after.[3] This is apparently a relic of the old sacrifice for the dead. Islam, too, instituted a sacrifice for the same festival but has founded this rite on a reminiscence of the Bible: Abraham's sacrifice of a ram as a substitute for his son Ismā'īl, who had originally been destined for the sacrifice. For this reason the sacrifice is named *al-fidā*, 'ransom', and the liturgy decrees that a prayer[4] which includes the recitation of Sūra 38:107 be said before the sacrifice.[5] A few relics of the old cult of the dead did, however, survive in popular Islam and have attached themselves to this festival and to the preceding small *'īd*. These feasts are made the occasion, particularly in Egypt, of visiting the graves, which at this time are decorated with palm leaves. Apart from prayers and the recitation of the Koran there are popular entertainments, of which sufficient information is available in Lane's faithful description.[6]

[1] Cf. Stade, l.c., p. 389.

[2] *Voyages en Arabie*, III, p. 277.

[3] Burckhardt, l.c., p. 73; cf. Doughty, *Travels in Arabia Deserta*, I, p. 137 above, cf. 293, 354; but for women the sacrifice is not made, ibid., p. 451.

[4] *Takbīr tashrīq*, cf. Muradgea d'Ohsson, *Tableau général de l'empire Othoman*, II, p. 226.

[5] Cf. also the sermon for this feast day in Garcin de Tassy, *Doctrine et devoirs de la religion musulmane* (Paris 1826), p. 200.

[6] Lane, *An account of the manners and customs of the modern Egyptians* (5th edition, London 1871), II, pp. 212, 221.

In Islam there are other survivals of the sacrifice to the dead. I mention an example from the third century, by no means an isolated one. It is told of the pious Muḥammad b. Isḥāq b. Sarruj, who was a 241 client of the Thaqīf tribe (died 313), that he made a weekly or fortnightly sacrifice in honour of the Prophet. The same pious man relates about himself that he completed the reading of the Koran 12,000 times and made as many sacrifices in memory of the Prophet.[1] We see here how pagan customs continued to live quietly and unconsciously within the framework of Islam and have clad themselves in the form of Muslim religiousness and piety.

In former times, whenever they passed the grave of a man famous for his generosity and nobility,[2] Arabs used to slaughter a riding animal and feed people with it.[3] In Islamic days the same honour was shown to graves of saints.[4] For many years after the death of a beloved person, relatives used to renew annually the wailing ceremony and the sacrifice of a camel.[5] Neglect of a sacrifice before the grave of an honoured hero required special excuses and was considered abnormal. The grave of Rabīʿa b. Mukaddam belongs, because of the outstanding chivalrous virtues of this hero of pre-Islamic centuries—even when he was dying he defended a caravan of women from the pursuing enemy—to those where the passing traveller offered the usual sacrificial banquet for many years after the burial. The philologist Abū ʿUbayda relates that an Arab from the tribe of the Banu' l-Ḥārith b. Fihr passed this honoured place and that his camel shied at the stones covering the body of the hero. The wanderer then excused his failure to make a sacrifice in honour of the manes of Rabīʿa with a poem:

My camel shied from the stones of the Ḥarrā country which were
erected over the man with open hands, the generous one;
Do not flee from him, O camel, he knew how to circulate
wine and instigate wars;
If it were not for the journey and the immense desert I would not 242
have failed to leave it behind crawling on the ground with cut
sinews.[6]

[1] Abu'l-Maḥāsin, *Annales*, II, p. 226. [Read: M.b.I. al-Sarrāj.]

[2] Thus also in later elegiac poetry those who passed by the grave were exhorted to slaughter animals and to sprinkle the grave with their blood, *Kitāb al-Aḍdād*, p. 38, 15.

[3] Al-Tabrīzī, *Ḥam.*, pp. 411, 4; 496, 8; cf. Freytag's *Ḥam.* Commentary, II, p. 89, to v. 4.

[4] Burton, *The Land of Midian*, I, pp. 236, 238; e.g. by Aron's grave, Palmer, [*The Desert of the Exodus*, p. 434=] *Vierzigjährige Würtenwanderung*, p. 337.

[5] Cf. a southern Arab example in Kremer, l.c., p. 167.

[6] *Agh.*, XIV, p. 131 and above p. 29, note 2, cf. also Perron, *Femmes arabes avant et depuis l'Islamisme* (Paris-Algiers 1858), p. 80.

This poet, about whose name the philologists cannot reach agreement, is said to have been the first to have omitted the performance of a sacrifice and to have expressed the opinion that a dirge might serve the same purpose.[1] In the early days of Islam we find—again according to Abū 'Ubayda—that Layla al-Akhyaliyya passed the grave of her friend Tawba b. Ḥumayyir (died 75), who had been killed, and in honour of the dead slaughtered a camel with the words: 'I have slaughtered a camel stallion near the *anṣāb* of Tawba in Hayda because his relatives are not there.'[2] A similar story makes Majnūn al-'Āmiri say almost the same words by the grave of his father, while sacrificing a camel mare.[3]

More common than this exceptional form of veneration is the sacrifice of one or more animals by the grave of a dead man immediately after burial. In an account from old Arab life, describing the death of a pair of lovers, which occurs in al-Jāḥiẓ's book *al-Maḥāsin wa'l-Aḍdād* we hear how, in honour of a martyr to love, 300 camels were slaughtered by his grave.[4] Even in the second century of Islam it is the old Arabic sacrifice to the dead—not yet reinterpreted in an Islamic sense—which the father of Ja'far b. 'Ulba (died 125) makes after the death of his son. The mourning father slaughtered all his young camels and sheep and threw the carcasses to their dams. 'Weep with me,' he is related to have said 'over Ja'far.' 'And the camels howled and the sheep bleated and the women wailed and wept and the father of the murdered man wept with them.'[5] That this type of mourning occurred among the ancient Arabs is recorded also in an old Jewish Midrash, in which it is related that the inhabitants of Niniveh performed hypocritical acts of penance: they shut up young calves leaving their mothers outside,[6] so that all the animals lowed for one another and then the inhabitants of Niniveh said: 'O master of the world, if you do not show mercy to us we shall not show mercy to those animals either.' Rabbi Akhā said,
243 'In Arabia they do the same.'[7] The mourning of 'Ulba had its root in pagan customs.

[1] Cf. *Ḥam.*, pp. 410, 412.

[2] Yāqūt, IV, p. 999, 10.

[3] *Agh.*, I, p. 168, 10.

[4] Girgas-Rosen, *Arab chrestom.*, p. 56, 1.

[5] Yāqūt, III, p. 49.

[6] Cf. *Midrāsh Tanḥūma*, ed. Buber, Genesis p. 185 below.

[7] *Pesiqtā of Rabbi Kāhanā*, ed. Buber, p. 161a. From this parallel, too, it is evident how instructive it would be to have a collection of all data from the old Rabbinical literature referring to Arabia and the Arabs. The most complete survey of these is in Steinschneider's *Polemische und apologetische Literatur* (cf. *Literaturbl. für orient Phil.*, 1887, p. 93) and Hirschenson's *Shebha 'Ḥokhmōth* (Lemberg 1883), p. 189. [Cf. S. Krauss, 'Talmudische Nachrichten über Arabien', *ZDMG*, LXX, pp. 321-53, LXXI, pp. 268-9.]

The sacrifice for the dead is so common a practice among Arabs that we might expect it to be described frequently in the lively account of the manners and customs of desert Arabs in the *Sīrat 'Antar*. In this richly episodic desert tale, as often as one of the many heroes dies and the mourning ceremony is described in typical and regularly recurring phrases, we may be sure to find that many camels are slaughtered by his grave.[1] But whenever the 'Antar story is used as source of the ethnology of the Arab desert, it must be remembered that this work, apart from its glaring anachronisms, is full of fanciful hyperbole, and that the judgment of Hammer-Purgstall (followed also by later authors) that this Sīra belongs as far as the pagan Arabs are concerned to those works '*qui nous ont conservé la peinture fidèle de leur moeurs,*[2] *de leur religion, de leur usages et des élans de leur génie*'[3], is modified in many respects by closer knowledge of it. Amongst such examples of hyperbolism, presumably, belongs the frequently mentioned slaughter of men on the graves of dead heroes. To expiate the murder of a hero, prisoners of the murderers' tribe are sacrificed.[4] An example of this is given by the Sīra in the description of 'Antar's mourning for his son Ghasūb, killed by the Banū Fazāra.

'On the second day,' it is recounted, 'he called his brother Shaybūb and ordered him to prepare a grave for Ghasūb's corpse. They had soon dug a deep grave and placed the body in it and 'Antar's tears flowed in streams. When they had covered the grave with soil 'Antar sat down by the side of the grave and ordered the prisoners to be brought there. He bared his arm, drew his sword al-Dāmī and 244
beheaded one after the other. The Banū 'Abs watched until a thousand Fazārites had been killed. Their blood was left to dry on the ground. Then the Emir Maysara stepped up, his tears flowed down his cheeks and he gave vent to expressions of deep mourning; he killed three hundred of the emprisoned Banū Fazāra on his brother's grave until the tribal chieftain Qays ordered a halt to the slaughter.'

In the listing of those Arabic customs and ideas with which we are here concerned, the description of the mourning of the Banū 'Abs for Shaddād, father of 'Antar, may be mentioned. It provides an illustration of the funeral customs of Arabs such as we often find mentioned in the many dirges preserved in literature[5] and describes

[1] *Sīrat 'Antar*, XXX, p. 89, and many other passages.

[2] Cf. *Zeitschr. für Völkerspych. u. Sprachwissensch.*, XIII (1881), pp 251 ff. The custom and attitude quoted there from the 'Antar book (knotting the rope as a symbol of protection) is confirmed by Mufaḍḍ., *Amthāl*, pp. 46 f = al-Maydānī, II, p. 278.

[3] *Fundgruben*, I, pp. 372–76.

[4] *Sīrat 'Antar*, XXVI, p. 117.

[5] E.g. Labīd in Ibn Hishām, ed. Guidi, p. 183, 4 ff. below; *Ḥam.*, pp. 363, 1, 449, 6 ff, 476, 13; *Opusc. arabica*, ed. Wright, pp. 109, 6, 111, 9; Nöldeke, *Beiträge*

a detail in the treatment of the sacrifice for revenge of which we are unable to tell whether it exists in the imagination of the author only or whether it has its origin in ancient Arabic customs. 'When the Banū 'Abs had reached the place of battle they dismounted, men and women alike, and started to wail,[1] servants howled and maids smote their faces;[2] they were mourning Shaddād on that day. They
245 shaved the manes of the horses[3] and broke into loud wailing. King Qays said, "Verily a pillar of the pillars of the Banū 'Abs has collapsed; may God curse Dhu'l-Khimār for his treason." Then Rabī' b. Ziyād came forward and breaking into weeping and wailing he cried: "Who remains for the Banū 'Abs after they have lost you, O Shaddād? By Allāh, you were full of goodness and energy and with you wisdom and good advice have departed from us." 'Antar during all this wept and wailed continuously and swore that he would not bury his father until he had destroyed the Jews of Ḥiṣn Khaybar. His brother Shaybūb tore his clothes and strewed ashes upon his head, and the same was done by all men and women . . . Thereupon 'Antar ordered his brother to take matting made of Ṭā'if leather and to wrap his father's body into it. Thus they loaded it on the back of a slender camel and took it back to their homestead weeping all the while.'[4] On the way 'Antar recited one of those moving dirges of which there are many in this book of folklore. Arriving at the dwelling of the tribe the mourners are received by the men and women who stayed behind with heartrending cries, those which Muhammed had strictly

[1] *Ta'dād* literally: the enumeration of the good qualities and virtues of the deceased (cf. Ryssel, *Zeitschr. f. d. Alttest. Wiss.*, V, p. 107). This enumeration belongs to the essence of the Arabic dirge, cf. al-Farazdaq, *Agh.*, XIV, p. 106, 2, 3; Fleischer, *De glossis Habichtianis*, I, p. 35.

[2] *Laṭamat*. Wailing women in Syrian towns are still called *laṭṭāmāt*, i.e. women who beat their faces (see Wetzstein in the treatise to be mentioned below); cf. also Budde, 'Das hebräische Klagelied', *Zeitschr. f. Alttest, Wiss.*, II, p. 26).

[3] A remarkable analogy to Plutarch, *Aristides*, ch. 14 end.

[4] *Sīrat 'Antar*, XVIII, p. 150.

---

zur K. d. Poesie, p. 179, 5 [= al-Khansā', *Dīwān*, ed. Cheikho, p. 173, v. 2]. Wailing women beat their faces with shoes: *Hudh.*, 107, 11, 139, 3. Instead of shoes other pieces of leather are also used, *mijlad*, schol. to *Siqṭ al-Zand*, II, p. 58, v. 26 after al-Muthaqqab. In later days the use of such leather pieces was omitted; a woman beloved by Abū Nuwās, who is amongst the wailing women in the funeral procession holds cosmetics in her hand while beating her face according to custom, *Agh.*, XVIII, p. 6, 8. To explain the use of shoes for beating the face it may be useful to mention that this is also spoken of in the Talmud and Midrash literature as a means of punishment and intimidation, *'Ārūkh*, article *ṭfḥ*, no. 3. Kohut has added a few typical passages (s.v. IV, p. 61a) (to complete with *Mō'ēd Qāṭōn*, fol. 25a). Cf. also Abraham b. David, *Sēfer Haqqabālā*, ed. Neubauer (Anecd. Oxon. Sem. Ser. I: iv), p. 65, 20.

forbidden to his faithful, together with other Arab mourning customs, as being specifically pagan. After this wailing had also come to an end Qays, the chieftain of the tribe, ordered his brother Mālik to dig a grave and Shaybūb and Jarīr lowered the body into it and closed it up with earth. While this was going on the world grew dark before 'Antar's eyes and he cried until he fainted. When he woke up again, wailing, reciting off dirges and tearing of clothes started afresh.[1] With bloodthirsty relish it is then related how Samiyya, the dead man's widow, slaughtered fifty prisoners with her arms bared, 'in order to extinguish the fire of her liver' and how Zabība sacrificed ninety of the captive Jews and Christians. 'Antar ended this bloody scene by reciting a dirge: 'When the Banū 'Abs heard 246
the hero's words, tears poured down from their eyelashes and they said, "O father of heroes, he who has left behind him such a son as you, he has not died." But 'Antar now had the prisoners of Khaybar brought and the girls and women were led in. He had them led round his father's grave for seven times and then granted them their lives.'[2] 'Antar remained in the 'house of mourning' (*bayt al-aḥzān*) for forty days and received the condolence visits of Arab tribes. After the forty days he gave a banquet for his relatives and gave alms to widows and orphans.[3]

In view of the fact that the 'Antar story is full of anachronistic uses of specifically Islamic customs and ideas in describing pagan life —so much so that heroes often speak like Muslim theologians[4]—one may assume that the forty days of mourning mentioned at the end of the episode have been taken from the customs of Muslim life, in which to this day mourning ceremonies last for forty days.[5]

On the other hand Islamic law was not strong enough in this as in

[1] The same expressions of grief and mourning as we find among pre-Islamic Arabs are reported also of eastern Christians, nor is the scratching of faces (*khadash*) lacking. In the *Narrationes* of St Nilus (Migne, *Patrologia graeca*, vol. 79), p. 660, a brave Christian mother is described who scorned the mourning after the cruel death of her son: *οὐ κατέσχισα χιτῶνα καὶ γυμνὰ χερσὶν ἔτυψα στέρνα οὐκ ἐσπάραξα κόμας ἐμὰς οὐκ ὄνυξιν ἠφάνισα τὸ πρόσωπον.*

[2] *Sīrat 'Antar*, ibid., pp. 153-157.

[3] Amongst the mourning customs mentioned in this book of folklore we may also single out baring the head and the pulling down of tents; III, p. 75, 11, 16, 19, cf. 76, 7. [Rich material about mourning customs is given by Goldziher, *WZKM*, XVI, p. 323.]

[4] Apart from the almost constantly Muslim introductory formulae to the various sections of this tale we should like to point out as examples among the great number of such passages VI, pp. 126-7, XIII, p. 61 (a pagan chieftain is addressed as *amīr al-mu'minīn*), XV, p. 16 (a satirical polemic against idolatry), XVI, pp. 15-16, XVII, pp. 60, 121, XVIII, p. 55 (Koranic phrases in the mouth of pagans) etc. Cf. also *ZDMG*, XXXII, p. 343.

[5] One may refer also to the beginning of the story of the jeweller 'Alī al-Miṣrī in *Arabian Nights* (ed. Būlāq 1279), II, pp. 343, 425; see also Lane, *Manners and Customs*, II, p. 272.

other cases—as we shall see in more detail about wailing for the dead (*niyāḥa*)—to eradicate mourning ceremonies that had survived from paganism, and many particular features of the pagan cult of the dead survived in Islamic society. In assimilation into Islamic life Friday became the usual day for such ceremonies, and the old customs thereby acquired a specifically Islamic colour. The 'Alid poet Muḥammad b. Ṣāliḥ once passed the grave of an 'Abbāsid
247 prince in Surra-man-rā'a and noticed that girls were beating their faces. This sight inspired the poet with the following poetic exclamation:

> On a Friday morning I saw in Sāmarrā' eyes whose flow of
> tears may astonish any onlooker;
> They visit the bones, which moulder in the ground, they ask
> for forgiveness of sins for these bones.
> If it were not anyhow God's will that dust may be
> revived to the day when the *Ṣūr* trumpet will sound,
> I should say that they would be called to life again by
> the eyes, overflowing with tears, of those who visit
> them etc.[1]

One of the pagan survivals in the cult of the dead is the sacrifice of animals on the grave of the deceased, which persisted until modern times. At the funeral of the Egyptian viceroy Muḥammad 'Alī eighty buffaloes were slaughtered. The Islamic interpretation of this sacrifice claims that it is made in order to atone for the smaller sins of the deceased and adds that the meat of the sacrificed animal must be divided amongst the poor,[2] on account of which the name of *al-kaffāra*, i.e. atonement, is also given to the sacrifice.[3] In older times ancient Arab practice was adhered to even more closely by sacrificing camels.[4]

IV

Another Arab custom must here be considered which undeniably shows the nature of sacrifices for the dead. It is mentioned in the early days of Islam, and is probably a survival of the Jāhiliyya cult of the dead and of heroes, which was still alive in the consciousness

[1] *Agh.*, XV, p. 90, 4 ff. [Translate: 'If it were not God's will that they should inhabit the ground etc.']

[2] E. W. Lane, *Arabian society in the middle ages*, ed. by Stanley Lane-Poole (London 1880), p. 261.

[3] *Manners and Customs*, l.c., p. 268. To this also belongs the custom explained by al-Qasṭallānī, II, p. 527, whereby after the death of a Muslim, meals should be prepared (for the poor) for seven days, a custom which Islamic theology explained by saying that the test in the tomb of true believers lasted seven days.

[4] *Agh.*, I, p. 168, 9 ff., gives an example from the Umayyad period.

of all: we refer to the sacrificing of hair to honour the dead. A poem of Labīd's is transmitted which he is said to have addressed to his daughters on his approaching death;

> My two daughters would have wished that their father should stay alive, 248
> But am I different from other men, from Rabī'a or Muḍar?
> When it comes about one day that your father will die,
> Do not scratch your faces or shave your hair.[1]

This account had an analogy in another tradition, according to which Qays b. Mas'ūd gave counsel to his daughter at her marriage to the hero Laqīṭ b. Zurāra, that after his death 'she should neither scratch her face nor sacrifice her hair.'[2]

On the death of the great warrior Khālid b. al-Walīd, who had fought against Muhammad and the Muslims at Badr, Uḥud and at the 'ditch', none of the women of the clan of the Banū Mughīra omitted to place her hair on the grave of the hero. (This immediately brings the Greek custom to mind.) Our source adds in explanation: 'all shaved the hair of their heads and placed it on Khālid's tomb.'[3] A little later the caliph 'Abd al-Malik cut the locks of his own head and those of his children on receiving the news of 'Abd Allāh b. al-Zubayr's death.[4] In these cases the sacrifice of the hair must presumably be seen first of all as an outward symbol of mourning;[5] but placing it on the grave of the deceased looks like a cultic act, survivals of which are still to be found amongst the Bedouins of Transjordan, where women place a number of locks of hair on the grave of the eminent dead.[6] 'We noticed, as a peculiarity of the burials here', relates Palmer about the old country of Moab, 'that two sticks were often placed beside the grave, with a rope stretched between them, and upon this braided locks of hair were hung as offerings.'[7] The same is told of Arabs near the Serbāl mountain.[8] These facts also explain the account from the third century according to which the Khārijites used to shave their hair by the grave of their chief Ṣāliḥ b. al-Musarriḥ, who revolted against the rule of the caliphate in the year 86.[9] Shaving the hair was considered a special

[1] *Agh.*, XIV, p. 101; Ibn Hishām, to *Bānat Su'ād*, ed. Guidi, p. 183. This poem is not found in the *Dīwān*. [*Dīwān* of Labīd, Kuwait 1962, p. 213.

[2] Mufaḍḍ., *Amthāl*, p. 20.

[3] *Agh.*, XV, p. 12.

[4] *Ansāb al-Ashrāf*, p. 74.

[5] Cf. Jerem. 7:29, Micah 1:16 etc.

[6] Selah Merrill, *East of the Jordan* (London 1881), p. 511.

[7] [The Desert of the Exodus, p. 483=] *Der Schauplatz der vierzigjährigen Wüstenwanderung Israels*, p. 376.

[8] Ebers, *Durch Gosen zum Sinai*, p. 204.

[9] Ibn Durayd, p. 133. [Read: in the year 76.]

249 sign of the Khārijites even in earlier days,[1] and an apocryphal tradition seems to refer to it when the Prophet is asked whether the Khārijites have a special mark. The Prophet replied, 'Yes, removal of the hair of the head (*al-tasbīd*) is common amongst them.'[2]

These accounts indicate the survival of cult habits. Apart from other signs of veneration, pagan pilgrims practised shaving the hair of the head.[3] The traditional knowledge of this point in the old Arab cult is expressed in the legendary report that a southern Arab ruler, said to be the first to have supplied the Ka'ba with an ornamental cover after being converted by two Rabbis to the cult of the Arabs, performed the same act of veneration. When the Thaqafite 'Urwa b. Mas'ūd, who left his house a pagan and returned a Muslim, arrived in Ṭā'if after five days of travelling and was just about to enter his house, one of his fellow-tribesmen noticed that he did not first pay a visit to Rabba in order to sacrifice his hair at the image of the goddess.[4] It is also worth noting that in a poem ascribed to 'Abd Allāh b. Ubayy the following oath is taken: 'by him in whose honour the hair is shaved', i.e. by God.[5]

In this context—as Krehl has already suggested[6]—must be seen Herodotus's account (III, ch. 8), which is confirmed by some Biblical passages. He relates that the Arabs cut part of their beard (the κρόταφοι) in honour of the God Orotal. It must also be mentioned that Plutarch,[7] too, refers to the Arab custom of cutting the hair of the forehead.

Two other customs which seem to be connected with the cultic significance of hair sacrifice are known from the traditions of Arab paganism. The first is the old Arab custom that a warrior going to battle shaved the hair of his head as a sign that he dedicated himself to death in honour of the tribe.[8] This must have been more than the
250 mere sign of recognition which some later philologists assume it to have been. The combat undertaken in the tribe's honour was a sacred and religious matter, and there was nothing strange about preparing oneself for it with religious acts, just as men are known to have

[1] Ibid., p. 139.

[2] *Kitāb al-Aḍdād*, p. 199 [*Kanz al-'Ummāl*, XI, pp. 127–9, 131, 177, 178; *Lisān al-'Arab*, s.v. *sbd*].

[3] Ibn Hishām, p. 15, cf. p. 749. Cf. Wellhausen, *Arab. Heidenthum*, p. 117, who gives an explanation of the ceremony. Shaving the hair means, according to him, the suspension of the consecrated condition.

[4] Wāqidī-Wellhausen, *Muhammed in Medina*, p. 381.

[5] Ibid., p. 182.

[6] Krehl, *Über die Religion der vorislamischen Araber*, p. 32, where there are more data from Arabic poets.

[7] *Theseus*, ch. 5.

[8] *Istibsālan li'l-mawti*, al-Tabrīzī, to *Ḥam.*, 255, 17: cf. *yawm taḥlāq al-limam*, Ṭarafa, 14:1. Cf. my article in *Rev. de l'hist. des relig.*, XIV, pp. 49 ff.

dedicated themselves for carrying out blood revenge for the *jār* by religious practises at the Ka'ba.[1] The second custom is that of cutting the hair of prisoners of war, as mentioned above, p. 171, which was probably not done merely to humiliate the enemy but also for religious reasons: the hair was sacrificed to the gods.[2] With this is connected the fact that the forelock (*nāṣiya*) was considered to have a supernatural significance also in later days. At least this seems indicated by Arab linguistic usage, which retained many survivals of ancient ideas. We find the expressions: *shu'm al-nāṣiya,*[3] *imra'atun mash'ūmat al-nāṣiya* (a woman of unfortunate forelock),[4] and in contrast: *mubārak al-nāṣiya;*[5] even of animals: *dābbatun ghadirat al-nāṣiya,*[6] a use which is common in Arabic popular books.[7] To this group seems to belong the saying: *al-khayl ma'qūd fī nawāṣīhā al-khayr* or *al-baraka* 'Good (or blessing) is tied to the horse's forelock'.[8] Finally we should like to mention as a late echo the popular oath by the lock of the temple (*wa-ḥayāt maqṣūṣī*).[9] Such phrases seem to contain vestiges of the old belief according to which forelocks were connected with superstitious ideas. This view survived also in the following ḥadīth in Mālik: 'When one of you marries a
woman or buys a slave he should take her by the forelock and ask 251
God's blessing.'[10]

In view of all this it is likely that the sacrifice of hair served not only to express mourning for the dead but also as a cult act in their honour.[11]

[1] *Hudhayl.*, no. 198.

[2] *Agh.*, III, p. 84 ult., where the ancient belief is pre-supposed that the sacrifice of the forelocks placates the gods.

[3] Ṭab., III, p. 465, 3; *Agh.*, XXI, p. 122, 15.

[4] Al-Damīrī, II, p. 110, cf. 'his forelock is in Satan's hand', *Muw.*, I, p. 171.

[5] *Thier und Mensch*, ed. Dieterici, p. 81, 8 [= *Rasā'il Ikhwān al-Ṣafā'* II, p. 258, 20]; *Qarṭās*, ed. Tornberg, p. 198, 9 from below.

[6] *Muḥīṭ al-Muḥīṭ*, s.v. *ghdr.*

[7] *Sīrat 'Antar*, V, p. 45 from below, *ba's nāṣiyatihā*, IX, p. 21, 7 from below, *waylaka yā mayshūm al-nāṣiya*, XV, p. 38, 8; *Sīrat Sayf*, XIII, p. 22, 3. We also find: God has charged my *nāṣiya* with' etc., *Arabian Nights*, IV, p. 3, 15.

[8] B. *Jihād*, no. 42 [Abū 'Ubayda, *al-Khayl*, pp. 5–7; al-Sharīf al-Raḍī, *al-Majāzat al-Nabawiyya*, p. 49].

[9] Dozy, *Supplément*, II, p. 352b = *Arabian Nights*, III, p. 383, 13; cf. *wa-ḥaqq ṭarṭūrī*, ibid., I, p. 233, 21.

[10] *Muw.*, III, p. 34. The Prophet touches the *nāṣiya* of those whom he blesses (al-Fākihī, *Chron. d. St. Mekka*, II, p. 12, 5 from below) and where—as in the case of new-born infants—there is no hair on the forehead, he touches the skin where hair will later grow in abundance (Imām Aḥmad in al-Damīrī, II, p. 253, 9 from below).

[11] For the subject discussed above, cf. also the study by G. A. Wilken, *Über das Haaropfer und einige Trauergebräuche bei den Völkern Indonesiens*, Heft II, Amsterdam 1887. This appeared after the above was written; some points dealt with in that study can perhaps be completed from here. For what is specifically Arabic: Wellhausen, *Arab. Heidenthum*, p. 118.

V

But what was the reaction of Islam to these pagan customs[1] which, apart from the mourning ceremonies which we have just mentioned, included bewailing the dead (*niyāḥa*), an established institution of the Jāhiliyya in which professional wailing women as well as the female relatives of the deceased took part—ceremonies which apparently were ordered by customary law[2] which defined them in detail?[3]

The founders of the new religion and new views of life considered desperate wailing and other manifestations of abandonment to grief
252 as incompatible with resignation to Allāh's will and acceptance of his decisions, which they call *ṣabr* and *iḥtisāb*. *Mā shā'a'llāhu lā ḥawla wa-lā quwwata illā bi'llāhi* was to be the motto of believers in all situations. The concept of *ṣabr* as virtue was not unknown in paganism.[4] Pre-Islamic poets often praised their heroes with being *ṣabūr 'ala'l-maṣā'ib*, i.e. patient during misfortune,[5] and Durayd b. al-Ṣimma is described by Arab historians of literature as one who knew best of all poets how to glorify this virtue.[6] In Arabia today—as Doughty stresses—this *ṣabr* in the pre-Islamic sense is still 'the chiefest beduin virtue.'[7] But only Islam conceived of this 'endurance' as acquiescence to God's will. For paganism it was merely an attribute of strength of character, but for the Muslim it is an act of piety like the fulfilment of the duty of prayer or the giving of alms (Sūra 22:36).[8] 'What the head is to the body,' says one of those apocryphal *khuṭbas* of 'Alī, which expressed Islamic ethics at the age of its maturity,

[1] [For the following cf. also Wensinck, *Handbook of early Muhammadan Tradition*, s.v. 'Mourning'.]

[2] From the subject of the *niyāḥa* I only mention the remarkable detail in *Agh.*, II, p. 138, 8 and X p. 58, 3 from below. According to this women must stand for the bewailing of their husbands when they intended to remain widows and not to remarry. It must also be mentioned, though it does not definitely go back to the Jāhiliyya, that an Arab prince in *Sīrat 'Antar*, XX, p. 113, advises his daughter on her marriage that when her husband dies she should neither tear her clothes, shave her hair nor scratch and beat her face but return to her tribe before embarking on the mourning; cf. above, p. 225, notes 1, 2.

[3] *Bint al-jawn* is the name adopted by an eminent wailing woman of the Jāhiliyya (see the verse of al-Muthaqqab quoted above, p. 221, note 5). The name is probably to be considered as a *laqab*, literally: 'daughter of the black (mourning) colour' with reference to the woman's occupation.

[4] Cf. Schrameier, *Über den Fatalismus der vorislamischen Araber*, p. 37.

[5] Cf. *Mufadd.*, 36:11.

[6] *Agh.*, IX, p. 5, 25.

[7] *Travels in Arabia Deserta*, I, p. 103. They particularly understand by this 'a courageous forbearing and abiding of hunger'.

[8] It is typical that the saying: *fa-ṣabrun jamīlun*, i.e. 'endurance is good', which is well known from the Koran 12:83, can already be found in al-Shanfarā, *Lāmiyya*, v. 34 (*wa-la'l-ṣabru in lam yanfa'i'l-shakwu ajmalu*). Later poets have frequently propagated it (*Ḥam.*, p. 403, 2, al-Damīrī I, p. 248).

'*ṣabr* is to belief. He who has no *ṣabr* has no belief either, as there is no body without a head.'[1] This is a different view of life from that expressed in the wailing and mourning ceremonies of Arabs. Allāh should be asked to forgive the sins of the dead man[2] but the latter should not be honoured excessively or his death extravagantly mourned.

The funeral prayer (*ṣalāt al-jināza*) was to supplant the honouring of the dead. But we must note that these principles were not developed at the beginning of Islam and that religious sayings, which express them and of which we shall have to mention more, were the product of a more mature religious view. 'Ā'isha, the 'mother of all believers', was angry with her niece because at the funeral of her 253
husband—to whom she had not been very happily married—'she did not open her mouth' with wailing.[3] Later generations would not have considered this omission sinful. On the contrary, a large number of traditions are transmitted in which Muhammed condemns the mourning customs of Arabs and forbids their practice.[4] 'The dead person is punished for many a wailing of the survivors.'[5] This threat is meant to intimidate the living. 'He who rends his garments because of the dead does not belong to us, and he who beats his face or uses the exclamations of the Jāhiliyya does not belong to us.' Muhammed also condemned the cutting of the hair of the head and strewing the head with dust, and all these teachings are illustrated with facts from the entourage of the Prophet and his immediate successors.[6] It is related of 'Umar that he punished the sister of Abū Bakr because she wailed for her dead brother.[7] The wages of wailing women are in the tradition put on a par with the most despised occupations and considered legally on the same low level.[8] Pious and god-fearing men then adopted the exhortations expressed in the traditional doctrines as guidance in the sorrowful situations of life, and expressed them in pious stories. Ḥusayn is made to say to

[1] *Al-'Iqd*, II, p. 169.

[2] Al-Farazdaq, ed. Boucher, p. 19, 3 below.

[3] *Agh.*, X, p. 56, 21.

[4] Just as the law of Solon among the Greeks (Plutarch, ch. 12) and the law of the XII tables among the Romans sought to moderate excessive wailing, Cicero, *De legibus*, II, ch. 23.

[5] This view completely agrees with the popular religious view held by many different circles that the dead should not be mourned too much and that tears falling upon them torture them like fire and their rest is disturbed. Cf. Julius Lippert, *Christenthum, Volksglaube und Volksbrauch* (Berlin 1882), p. 409.

[6] B. *Janā'iz*, nos. 32–35, 37–39. [Cf. the traditions against beating the face, wailing, etc., in al-Ṭurṭūshī, *al-Ḥawādith wa'l-Bida'*, ed. Talbi, p. 160; al-Nawawī, *al-Adhkār*, pp. 66–7; al-Shawkānī, *Nayl al-Awṭār*, IV, pp. 87–92; al-Haythamī, *Majma' al-Zawā'id*, III, pp. 12, 15.]

[7] B. *Khuṣūmāt*, no. 4.

[8] *Ijārāt*, no. 20.

his sister before his death: 'O my sister, find comfort in Allāh's consolation, because I and all Muslims see in God's Prophet an example to follow. I entreat you not to rend your garment on my behalf, not to scratch your face or break out in wailing.'[1] The traditionist Ibn 'Abbās, who was not normally antagonistic to poetry, plugged his ear on hearing the sound of wailing.[2] Even the wearing of special mourning colours is avoided by representatives of Islamic views.[3]

254 It is notable in this connection that Islam (presumably not yet Muhammed himself) not only forbids the wailing of women, but also forbids the mourning customs of women (*iḥdād*), as performed in the Jāhiliyya, to last more than three days from the death of any person other than the husband. These mourning customs have often been discussed recently,[4] and I would only add here that the throwing away of the animal[5] and of dung after the end of the year of mourning was presumably a symbolical act in order to indicate that the mourner had now renounced all community with the deceased.

There is a whole group of sayings in which the Prophet forbids the reviling of fate or time (*al-dahr*); these sayings have already been presented in another place for a different purpose.[6] I think that also by this prohibition Islam sought to denounce pagan mourning rites. The dirges of the Arabs of earlier times often abused fate for the misfortune of the man who was mourned; a large number of such poems begin with the exclamation *laḥa'llāhu dahran*, i.e. 'May God curse a fate which,' etc.[7] Such words expressed a view unacceptable to Islam and the opposition of Islam to them is the idea of *dahr* traditions.

The same protest is contained in the endeavour of Muhammed's pious followers to avoid and reject anything similar to veneration of the dead, which was practised in paganism and had not in practice

[1] Al-Ya'qūbī, II, p. 290 [al-Mufīd, *Irshād*, Najaf 1963, p. 232].

[2] *Agh.*, I, p. 35, 9.

[3] Burton, *A pilgrimage to Al-Madinah and Meccah* (Leipzig 1874, Tauchnitz), II, p. 160.

[4] Cf. Wilken, *Het Matriarchaat*, p. 45, and by the same author *Über das Haaropfer und einige andere Trauergebräuche bei den Völkern Indonesiens*, Appendix, I, p. IV, note 10; Wellhausen, *Arab. Heidenth*, p. 156. The best sources for the strange custom mentioned in these passages are *Muw.*, III, p. 83, B. *Ṭalāq*, no. 45.

[5] The phrase *taftaḍḍu bihi*, which the oldest commentators explain as the throwing away of the animal, is not clear linguistically or in meaning. Mālik adds that this custom was *ka'l-nushra*, a form of magic. Other explanations are also mentioned, including that *fḍḍ* VIII is a denominative of *fiḍḍa*, silver, and that the word refers to women washing and cleaning themselves in order to be white like silver.

[6] *Die Zâhiriten*, pp. 153-55.

[7] *Ḥam.*, pp. 479, 480 etc.

been overcome by Islam.[1] They go as far as to give direct instruction against excessive mourning over their own bodies. In the earliest days of Islam it still appears to have been customary—presumably as a legacy of paganism[2]—to erect a tent over the grave of an honoured 255
person[3] and spend some time there after the funeral. This custom is vividly described in respect of the mourning of the poet Arṭāt (who died in the eighth decade of the Hijra) for his son 'Amr. After the latter's death the father erected his tent by the grave and stayed there for a year. When the tribe to which he belonged wanted to move on to new pastures, the mourning father cried to the dead man: 'Come with us, O Abū Salmā.' When his fellow-tribesmen adjured him by his reason and his religion to give up imaginary intercourse with someone who had been dead for a whole year, he asked for another night's delay. In the early morning he took his sword and slaughtered his riding-beast on the grave of the deceased. But still he was not ready to leave and his companions had to stay longer by the grave because they pitied him.[4] Thus we see that the erection of the *qubba* by the grave was meant to show how difficult the leave-taking from the dead was for the survivors, and this easily refutes, at least in reference to the culture with which we are dealing here, the theories of the English anthropologist, J. S. Frazer. Frazer explains the greater part of the funeral and mourning ceremonies of various peoples as expressing a complete severance from the spirit of the deceased; he also attributes the origin of the custom of mutilating the body and putting clothes of a different colour than normal to the wish to become unrecognisable to the dead person should he return either in his own person or as a ghost.[5] This is not the place to judge this theory, but we may take this opportunity of saying that a closer consideration of the mourning customs of the Jāhiliyya must definitely exempt them from Frazer's generalizations. The custom mentioned above (p. 229) shows especially that separation from the dead is expressed by the cessation of the ceremonies, rather than by the ceremonies themselves. A favourite expression of wailing women and those poets who composed dirges was: *lā tab'ad* i.e. 'do not go 256
away', a call which is so often repeated in this and synonymous forms

[1] Oddly enough there is no direct interdiction against sacrificing animals by the grave, unless the Koranic interdictions against sacrifices on the *anṣāb* were considered sufficient.

[2] In older days honorific *qubbas* were erected also in honour of eminent guests who visited the camp, *Agh.*, VII, p. 170 (Ka'b in the camp of the Banū Taghlib).

[3] Al-Ya'qūbī, II, p. 313: a tent (*fusṭāṭ*) is erected over the grave of 'Abd Allāh b. 'Abbās in the mosque of Ṭā'if.

[4] *Agh.*, XI, p. 144; Wellhausen, p. 162.

[5] 'On certain burial customs as illustrative of the primitive theory of the soul' (*Journal of the Anthropological Institute of Gt. Britain and Ireland*, vol. XV, no. 1, 1885, pp. 64-100).

in the *marāthī* literature,[1] that Rückert correctly stresses this as characteristic of such poems in his notes to the translation of the *Ḥamāsa*. When al-Ḥasan, the grandson of the caliph 'Alī, died, his wife erected over his grave a tent (*qubba*, which later became the name for grave chapels). She maintained this tent for a year and when she took it down a heavenly voice was heard—so it is said—which cried: 'Have they already found what they have lost?' To which another voice replied: 'No, but they have acquiesced in their fate and have gone away.'[2]

This custom was disapproved by the orthodox from an early date, as indicated by the report that Ibn 'Umar cried to his servant, on seeing a tent (*fusṭāṭ*) on the grave of 'Abd al-Raḥmān b. Abī Bakr: 'Remove the tent, because only the pious deeds of the dead will offer him protection and shade.'[3] To this context also belongs the last will ascribed to the conqueror 'Amr b. al-'Āṣ, though he is not the type of a proper Muslim: 'When I die do not weep for me and let no panegyrist (*mādiḥ*) or wailer (*nā'iḥ*) follow my bier; only put dust on my grave, since my right side deserves the dust no more than my left. Put neither wooden nor stone sign upon my grave. When you have buried me, sit on the grave for the time that the slaughter of a camel and distribution of its meat would take, so that I may enjoy your
257 company for that time.'[4] It is similarly reported in several collections of traditions that Abū Hurayra (died 57) expressed the wish when feeling the approach of death: 'Do not erect a tent over me, do not follow me with the censer, but hurry[5] with my body.'[6]

The tent later became the grave chapel, the mausoleum, and the name *qubba* was retained for this building. When Muslims began to

[1] E.g. in the dirge of Ta'abbaṭa on al-Shanfarā, *Agh.*, XIV, p. 130, 18, ib., XXI, p. 137, 3; *Ḥam.*, pp. 89 ult. 410, 10 from below, 454 v. 23, 471 ult.; Yāqūt, II, p. 671, 5 etc.; *al-'Iqd*, II, p. 11, 19. 'They say: Do not go away, yet they bury me; but where is the place of separation if not my place (the grave)?' Mālik b. al-Rayb concludes thus his poem describing his own funeral. Cf. also Kremer, l.c., p. 167, and the verse quoted in Nöldeke, *Beiträge zur Kenntnis d. Poesie d. alten Araber*, p. 69, 1 (=*Agh.*, III, p. 18, 4). It is not surprising that Muslim *marāthī* poets retain this formula, e.g. the dirge of Kuthayyir on the death of his friend Khandaq, *Agh.*, XI, p. 48, 15. [See also Goldziher in *WZKM*, XVI, p. 312.]

[2] B. *Janā'iz*, no. 62.

[3] Ibid., no. 82.

[4] Al-Damīrī (s.v. *jazūr*), I, p. 243 from the collection of traditions by Muslim [*Īmān*, no. 192], *al-'Iqd*, II, p. 5. Al-Damīrī expresses the opinion that the end of this dictum is due to the profession of butcher which 'Amr followed in the early years of his life.

[5] The wish to hurry with the body is expressed also by caliph al-Ma'mūn in directions about his funeral in his last will; Ṭab., III, p. 1136, 15. [Cf. also al-Ṭayālisī, *Musnad*, p. 120; Abū Shāma, *al-Bā'ith 'alā Inkār al-Bida'*, p. 69; al-Shawkānī, *Nayl al-Awṭār*, IV, p. 60.]

[6] Ibn Baṭṭūṭa, *Voyages*, II, p. 113.

decorate the graves of holy and pious persons with monumental buildings, this was also disapproved by adherents of Muhammed's teaching. Apart from traditions expressing this disapproval, this also finds expression in the frequently recurring legend that such buildings were destroyed soon after their completion by the saint whose grave they were to adorn. Such destruction was the fate—according to the legend—of the mausoleum of Aḥmad b. Ḥanbal in Baghdad[1], and of the *qubba* of the Algerian saint Aḥmad al-Kabīr, built by the grateful Moriscos at great expense for their protector in the year 900, which became a ruin overnight—a destruction which was repeated whenever the builders attempted to re-erect it.[2] The same legend is told of the grave of the founder of the Naqshbandī order, Bahā' al-Dīn, in the village of Bawaddīn near Bukhārā. This grave too is in the open and not covered by a cupola, since it was never possible to preserve for long the *qubba* that was built above it.[3] The pious wished in their modesty to be content with a simple grave. These legends serve the old Muslim view, expressed in many traditions, that a grave may not be used as place for prayer,[4] a danger which was enhanced by the erection of mausolea resembling mosques. 258
The same tendency was to be expressed also by the account—which is in contrast to other traditions—according to which the Prophet disapproved of standing up in honour of a funeral procession,[5] even if it was that of a Muslim.

The unsuccessful endeavour of some theologians to ban from the mosque, as far as possible, the *ṣalāt al-janāza*[6] served the same tendency of keeping all attributes of a possible cult of the dead from this rite. These attempts had already been made in vain in the early days of Islam. But that such an attempt was made by some theologians of the early time is seen from the following report of Mālik b. Anas: 'Ā'isha ordered that the corpse of Sa'd b. Abī Waqqāṣ be carried past her to the mosque, so that she might pray there for the deceased. The people objected to this order (they did not wish to allow a corpse to enter the mosque). Then 'Ā'isha said: 'How quickly

[1] Ibn Ḥajar, IV, p. 398.

[2] Trumelet, *Les Saints du Tell*, I, p. 246.

[3] Vámbéry, *Reise in Centralasien*, ch. XV. The legendary trait shown in several examples here of self-destroying buildings can be found also in other circles. Quaresmius says that the Muslims wanted to build a *manāra* for their worship in the place of the church of Ananias at Damascus; they made three attempts but invisible hands always destroyed the building (*De terra sancta*, VII, ch. 2).

[4] *Muw.*, II, p. 12, IV, p. 71; B. *Ṣalāt*, nos. 48, 55, *Taṭawwu'* no. 9; al-Baghawī, *Maṣābīḥ al-Sunna*, I, p. 37 [al-Shawkānī, *Nayl al-Awṭār*, IV, pp. 58–9].

[5] Cf. the passages in *Revue de l'histoire des religions*, XVI, pp. 160 ff.

[6] Quṭb al-Dīn, *Chroniken der Stadt Mekka*, III, pp. 208–10 [Ibn al-Ḥājj, *al-Madkhal*, Cairo 1929, II, pp. 219 ff., II, pp. 251 ff.].

do these people act?[1] Did the Prophet pray elsewhere than in the mosque over the corpse of Suhayl b. Bayḍā'?'[2] This seems to represent the difference of opinion between contemporary theologians which, according to the method followed in this literature, was antedated to the earliest days of Islam. What is attributed to the Prophet is apparently the ritual praxis of the Ḥijāz of the second century, which was not permitted to be declared wrong.

In making these views prevail public authorities played their part; police measures were aimed at preventing a recurrence of pagan mourning customs, and the need for the ordinances passed shows how difficult it was to work against such old customs. Under the rule of 'Umar II the governor 'Adī b. Arṭāt (died 100) forbade wailing for the dead.[3] In the third century several governors of Egypt issued strict orders against wailing and imposed punishments for offenders.[4] It is almost inevitable that the legal codices, supported by
259 many traditional sayings, strictly forbade wailing and all accompanying expressions of mourning.[5] Members of other religions also had to refrain from wailing. In the so-called covenant of 'Umar with Jews and Christians, which enumerates the conditions under which, according to Islamic public law, they may live in Muslim countries, the caliph is said to have made the condition 'that they do not cry out in the event of misfortune and do not wail publicly on the death of their relatives.'[6]

In big towns it was part of the police chief's duties to supervise expressions of mourning, just as control over ritual life in general was also in his hands.[7] Ibn al-Athīr al-Jazarī (died 637), brother of the historian of the same name, who was a court secretary under Saladin, quotes in his work on style amongst the samples of official style a decree which he had drawn up on the nomination of a

[1] *Mā asra'a al-nās* is explained in various ways: (a) how quickly they forget the *sunna* of the Prophet? (this explanation of Mālik penetrated into the wording of some texts: *mā asra'a mā nasiya al-nās*); (b) how quick they are with blame and disapproval! as Ibn Wahb explains it.

[2] *Al-Muwaṭṭa'*, II, p. 14.

[3] Al-Farazdaq, ed. Boucher, p. 67. [Wailing prohibited by 'Umar II: Ibn Sa'd, V, p. 290.]

[4] The passages from Abu'l-Maḥāsin are now found in Karabacek, *Mittheilungen aus der Papyrussammlung d. Erzherzog Rainer*, I, p. 100.

[5] E.g. *Minhāj al-Ṭālibīn*, ed. Van Den Berg, I, p. 221. In the Ḥanafite school a less puritanical view was held about this subject, *Raḥmat al-Umma*, p. 36, 13.

[6] Al-Hamadānī, *Dhakhīrat al-Mulūk*, in Rosenmüller, *Analecta arabica*, I, p. 22 (text), no. 19.

[7] The Oxford MS. Bodl. no. 315, which deals with the official duties of the *muḥtasib* (police chief), contains in Chapter V a list of his duties in funerals (Nicoll-Pusey, *Biblioth. Bodl. Catalogus*, p. 96) [=Ibn al-Ukhuwwa, *Ma'ālim al-Qurba*, ed. Levy, pp. 46 ff.].

muḥtasib,[1] a document which gives us an insight into the social conditions of those days and would be worth detailed study from this viewpoint. This decree of appointment, which also contains instructions for the newly appointed official, states: 'To matters often practised contrary to the religious *sunna* belong the holding of assemblies of condolence,[2] the wearing of black or blue mourning clothes,[3] and imitation of the Jāhiliyya with wailing, excessive weeping and heart-rending grief bordering on deliberate provocation 260
of God's anger. Women make appointments to erect tents by the graves and use the feast days as times for meetings between the visitors and visited (i.e. the deceased)[4]. Thus occasions of mourning become opportunities for banquets and times of wailing opportunities for social meetings.' This latter corresponds to the popular customs of Egypt, whereas the complaint about the survival of pagan mourning ceremonies can be applied very widely.

Despite all the opposition of the pious, supported by the temporal authorities, many survivals of the pagan form of mourning and veneration of the dead continued to exist,[5] though bereft of some barbaric features. The dirges from 'Abbāsid times differ only little from those of paganism. The absence of wailing women from the funeral of a man who died far away from his relatives was stressed with regret,[6] showing that they were considered as an integral part of a decent funeral. Professional wailing women sometimes had poets produce mourning poems to be kept in stock for use at funeral

[1] *Al-Mathal al-Sā'ir*, p. 353.

[2] Cf. Dozy, *Supplément aux dictionnaires arabes*, II, p. 126b, on the word *'azā'*.

[3] Cf. *Ansāb al-Ashrāf*, p. 77. At the time of the Jāhiliyya black mourning clothes were customary. Ḍamra al-Nakhshalī (*ZDMG*, XII, p. 63): 'Will my camel mares scratch their faces or bind their heads in black clothes?' A woman who wrapped herself in black mourning clothes (*silāb*, *sulub*) was called *musalliba*, ib., p. 67 below; Labīd, p. 37 v. 1.: *nawḥu musallibin*, and the black mourning clothes (*al-sulub al-sūd*) in a dirge by the same poet quoted by al-Jawharī s.v. *rmḥ*. Cf. also Ibn Hishām, p. 627, 2 and Bint al-Jawn (above, p. 228, note 3). The dark, especially black mourning clothes of women (*ḥidād*) are used by the fourth century poet Abu'l-'Alā' al-Ma'arrī in his comparisons: he compares the dark night, the black wings of the raven etc. to mourning clothes. (*Siqṭ al-Zand*, I, pp. 67, v. 6, 120, v. 4, 166, v. 2, II, p. 57, v. 6, 58, v. 2), a proof of how common the use of such clothing was in Syria and Mesopotamia in those days. [In *Abhandlungen zur arab. Philologie*, II, p. xlv, note 3, Goldziher adds references to 'Ant., 4, 2; Abū Ḥanīfa Dīnaw., 341, 1.]

[4] [This seems to be a misunderstanding; 'times for meetings between visitors and visited' i.e. the cemeteries are used as places for social appointments.]

[5] Later poets have frequently copied the phrases of older ones without thinking and thus they were used as typical expressions with a basis in reality. Thus, e.g., the words from the dirge in Wright, *Opp. arabb.*, p. 109, 6 (cf. *Ansāb al-Ashrāf*, p. 331, 5) recur in a poem by Muḥammad al-Laythī on Yazīd b. Mazyad (died 185): 'After Yazīd's death will weepers spare their tears or take care of their cheeks?' (*Agh.*, XVIII, p. 116 ult. = *al-'Iqd*, p. 35, 8 from below.)

[6] *Agh.*, XVIII, p. 20, 26.

processions.[1] How far people went in for expressing veneration for the eminent dead is seen, for example, in al-Farazdaq's elegy on the death of the caliph 'Abd al-'Azīz b. Marwān, in which he says: 'They kiss the dust that covers his remains,[2] as the (black) stone is kissed in the sanctuary to which pilgrims go.'[3] On the other hand among
261 the insults with which, in the same period, a poet reviles the tribe of his opponent there figures the allegation that the hostile tribe sets little store by the graves of its companions.[4]

But Islam objected to none of the survivals of the veneration of the dead more forcefully than the institution of lamentation. In order to emphasize its condemnation later exegesis found in the Koranic verse 60:12 an interdiction against wailing. The verse reads: 'When believing women come to pay you homage, (undertaking) not to associate other beings with Allāh, not to steal, not to fornicate or kill their infants . . . and not to resist you in all that is good, accept their homage.' The words 'in all that is good,' etc. are taken as referring to the interdiction against lamentation for the dead, which was usually practised by women.

It is known, however, how little success these interdictions had, and how rarely—despite some isolated attempts—they managed to stop the practice of customs which had obtained from time immemorial in those countries where Islam now prevails, and which were still practised without distinction of creeds[5]—customs of which the mocker of Samosata could rightly say: 'All peoples of the world

[1] Ibid., III, p. 34 below; VI, p. 48.

[2] Cf. also al-Maydānī, II, p. 143, 1.

[3] *Dīwān*, ed. Boucher, p. 19 penult. The soil taken from the grave served for many superstititions. Al-Fīrūzābādī mentions (*Qām.*, s.v. *slw*) the popular belief that earth from a grave when dissolved in water will cure love-sickness; this drink is called *sulwān*; cf. Trumelet, *Les Saints du Tell*, p. 319. The Shī'ites ascribe, as is well known, special prophylactic powers to earth from the grave of Ḥasan, Ḥusayn or other Imams. *Khāk-i-Karbalā* is said to have among other things the power to quieten the wind if a few grains are strewn into the howling element ('Abd al-Karīm, *Voyage de l'Inde à la Mekke*, transl. Langlès, Paris 1747, p. 113). In order to anticipate the using up of this medicine, to be feared because of the great demand, it is claimed by them that this power is not exclusive to saintly graves but is inherent in all the ground within four square miles around the grave. Muḥammad b. Aḥmad al-Qummī has dealt with this superstition in detail in his *Kitāb al-Ziyārāt*, and in the *Kashkūl*, p. 107, there are extracts from this account.

[4] *Agh.*, II, p. 104, 13.

[5] The Jews of the Orient have also preserved the custom of wailing for the dead, of which mention is so often made in biblical and talmudic writings (Geiger, *Jüdische Zschr.*, XI, p. 257) to this day. On wailing women in Jerusalem there is an account by Schwarz in Geiger, *Wissensch. Zschr. für jüd. Theologie*, IV (1839), p. 303 and by Luncz in the annual *Jerusalem*, I, Hebr. part, p. 11.

seem to be pledged to this unreasonable habit of bewailing the dead.'[1] Long after Muhammed, even down to modern times, we find that— 262
except in a few regions, such as Medina,[2] ever faithful to tradition—lamentation for the dead was still customary. Also southern Arabia appears to have yielded early to Muslim law. The fourth century geographer and historian of southern Arabia, al-Hamdānī, devotes a separate chapter of a work which is not available to the southern Arabic lamentation for the dead, and a special paragraph of his 'Geography of the Arabian Peninsula', edited by D. H. Müller, lists all those places in Yemen where wailing was practised in the days of the author: they comprise, on the whole, the smaller part of the province. It is also instructive, however, to see in what forms the old pagan custom survived there. In Khaywān wailing for a dead man was continued until the death of another comparable man, when lamentation for the second followed that for the first. Apart from the *niyāḥa*, executed by wailing women, alternating songs were also customary, in which both wailing women and *mawālī* men participated.[3] But for lamentation for the dead to give way before the laws of Islam is nevertheless an exception, and in most regions where it was practised in pre-Islamic times it managed to survive.[4]

It was in Syria that the custom survived most completely, and least influenced by Islam, and we owe to the man most knowledgeable about this part of the East, a detailed description of wailing in Syria[5] which shows how powerless were the warnings of tradition and later theology[6] in the face of the primeval institutions of Semitic society. In funeral customs primeval habits were retained elsewhere, too, up to quite recent days.[7] To characterize the tenacity of ancient institutions the following saying has been attributed to Muhammed: 'There 263
are four things among the customs of paganism which my community cannot give up: boasting of good deeds, finding fault with one

[1] Lucian's collected works transl. by Wieland (ed. 1798), V, p. 205: 'On the mourning for the dead' [*De luctu*, 21]. Very instructive about pagan relics which often survive in lamentation for the dead is an essay on these customs in Great Russia, *Globus*, vol. 50 (1886), p. 140, and on wailing in Mingrelia: *Revue de l'histoire des religions*, XVI, pp. 90 ff.

[2] Burton, l.c. II, p. 167.

[3] *Jazīrat al-'Arab*, p. 203.

[4] Cf. Rödiger's note to Wellsted, *Reise in Arabien*, I, p. 150, note 110; Russell, [*The Natural History of Aleppo*, London 1794, I, pp. 305–6] *Naturgeschichte von Aleppo*, transl. by Gmelin (Göttingen 1797), I, p. 433.

[5] Wetzstein, 'Die syrische Dreschtafel', *Zeitschrift fur Ethnologie*, V, (1873), pp. 295–300.

[6] Theologians used drastic means against them. They invented a threat by Muhammed that wailing women 'would be dressed in trousers of tar and shirts of scabies on the day of resurrection.'

[7] In Adolf von Wrede's *Reise in Hadhramaut* etc., ed. by H. v. Maltzan, pp. 239-49, there is a remarkable example.

another's descent, the belief that fertility depends on the stars, and lamentation for the dead';[1] all matters against which Muhammed and later exponents of his teaching fought vehemently without being able to abolish the pagan customs and beliefs connected with them.

[1] Ibn Ḥajar, I, p. 505; Fakhr al-Dīn al-Rāzī, *Mafātīḥ al-Ghayb*, VIII, p. 193 [*Kanz al-'Ummāl*, old ed., VIII, pp. 177, 187].

THREE 264

PAGAN AND MUSLIM LINGUISTIC USAGE

TO PAGE 37—NOTE 2

ISLAMIC tradition condemns the greeting formulae of the Jāhiliyya[1] and aims at putting the *salām* greeting in their place[2]. It is therefore an anachronism when philologists transmit the *salām* greeting from pagan times.[3] On the other hand Muslim poets use the pagan form of greeting in their poems, together with other ancient Arab elements which had lost their currency.[4] Apart from this general greeting, Islamic tradition was also concerned with condemning specific greetings, e.g., the greeting of a newly married couple with the words: *bi'l-rifā'i wa'l-banīna* ('in harmony and with the blessing of children') as an alternative to which is recommended, as a formula approved by tradition: *'ala'l-khayri wa'l-barakati wa-'alā khayri ṭā'irin.*[5] Some theologians, however, think the use of the first formula, which allegedly stems from the Jāhiliyya, permissible.[6] In *Agh.*, XI, p. 90, the old formula is mentioned with the words: *bi'l-rifā'i wa'l-banīna wa'l-ṭā'iri'l-maḥmūdi.*

The interdiction of some expressions is not only confined to formulas of greetings and good wishes. In other spheres, too, some expressions are forbidden and replaced by others more fitting. One should not say *halaka'l-nās* ('people have perished,').[7] Instead of *khabuthat nafsī* one should say: *laqisat n.*,[8] instead of *nasi'tu* ('I have
forgotten'): *nusi'tu* ('I have been made to forget').[9] A wall of the 265
Ka'ba, which was known as Ḥaṭīm, was not to be called by that

[1] *In'am ṣabāḥan*, Zuhayr, *Mu'all.*, v. 6; 'Ant., *Mu'all.*, v. 4; Imrq., 40:1, 52, 1 f.; also *'imī ẓalāman*, *Agh.*, XII, p. 50, 10.

[2] Cf. Sprenger, III, pp. 482, 485.

[3] *Hudhayl.*, introduction to no. 219, p. 52, 7, 8.

[4] Yāq., III, p. 656, 1.

[5] 'For the best and for blessing and with good auspices', B. *Nikāḥ.*, no. 57; Muslim, III, p. 324; cf. the formula: *'alā bad'i'l-khayri wa'l-yumni*, al-Maydānī, I, p. 417. [Cf. also al-Nawawī, *al-Adhkāl*, p. 125; Ibn al-Sunnī, *'Amal al-Yawm wa'l-Layla*, p. 162.]

[6] Cf. al-Tījānī, *Tuḥfat al-'Arūs* (Paris 1848), pp. 29 ff.

[7] Muslim, V, p. 263 [al-Nawawī, op. cit., p. 157].

[8] B. *Adab*, no. 99 [al-Nawawī, loc. cit.].

[9] B. *Faḍā'il al-Qur'ān*, no. 26.

name in Islam.[1] The well-known house sacrifice was to be called *nasīka* or *dhabīḥa* instead of the pagan *'aqīqa*.[2] Similarly, the month of fasting should not be called simply 'Ramaḍān' but *shahr Ram*.[3] The vine was not to be called *karm*.[4] In B., *Adab*, Nos. 99 ff., there are further examples of the numerous expressions disapproved by Islam. Some formulas, such as the greeting *marḥaban*, had to justify themselves with a tradition in which the Prophet uses them. The intended reform in respect of everyday expressions and phrases extended even to trivial interjections. The camel which was stuck fast was not to be encouraged with the call *da'da'*, but with an invocation to God to give it new strength.[5] Other examples of these matters are put together in al-Jāḥiẓ, *Kitāb al-Ḥayawān*,[6] and in al-Suyūṭī, *Muzhir*, I, p. 141.

For theological reasons there were attempts to limit the use of the expression *rabb*. Since the word *rabbī*, 'my lord,' was sanctioned by Koranic usage as an address specifically applied to God, it was not to be applied to men. In Muslim, V, p. 70, the Prophet is made to say: 'Nobody shall say, Give your master (*rabbaka*) to eat and drink; nor should one say *rabbī* of one's master, but *sayyidī*, *mawlāya*;[7] also do not say my servant, my maid (*'abdī*, *amatī*) but *fatāya*, *fatātī*, *ghulāmī*.' *'Abd* meant man only in relation to God.[8] A tradition in Abū Dāwūd[9] goes even further: according to it, even the Prophet rejected the address *sayyid* (master) as being appropriate only to Allāh. It is well-known that actual linguistic use could not be regulated by such theological scruples. There was generally no objection to
266 the use of the word *rabb* in stat. cstr. in the sense of *ṣāḥib*, owner of a
thing,[10] a very common usage in Arabic.[11] But some scrupulous

[1] *Manāqib al-Anṣār*, no. 27.

[2] Qasṭ., VIII, p. 279.

[3] B. *Ṣawm*, no. 5.

[4] Abū Dāwūd, commented ed. al-Dimnātī, p. 232 [al-Nawawī, loc. cit., *Lisān al-'Arab*, s.v. *krm*; al-Haythamī, *Majma' al-Zawā'id*, VIII, p. 55].

[5] Scholia to al-Ḥādira, ed. Engelmann, p. 10, 5.

[6] Vienna MS. fol. 60a. ff [I, pp. 327 ff].

[7] Subtle philologists condemned in this phrase the sequence: *sayyidan wa-mawlānā* as incorrect and proved by logical arguments, and some passages from the poets, that the only correct sequence is *mawlānā wa-sayyidanā*. Al-Ṣafadī wrote in detail about this in his commentary to the *Risāla Jahwariyya* of Ibn Zaydūn. [For *rabbī* cf. also al-Nawawī, op. cit., p. 160; *Lisān al-'Arab*, s.v. *rbb*.]

[8] This recalls the Galilean Judah (Josephus Flavius, *Antiqu.*, XVIII, 1:6) who did not wish to accord to any man the address δεσπότης.

[9] Ibid., p. 126.

[10] Cf. al-Maqqarī, I, 481 for this usage.

[11] *Rabb al-qabr*, he who rests in the grave, *Agh.*, I, p. 44, 8; also in the feminine: *rabbat al-manzil*, *rabbat al-sulṭān*, *Agh.*, IX, p. 86, 14; *rabbat al-khidr*, Nöldeke, *Beiträge*, p. 85, v. 1 [=*al-Mufaḍḍaliyyāt*, 37: 1]; *rabbat al-nār*, Abu'l-'Alā', *Siqṭ*, II, p. 113 v. 1; *rabbat al-dimlij*, ibid., p. 193, v. 1.

theologians wished to restrict this use. We learn from al-Māwardī, who is quoted by the lexicographer al-Fīrūzābādī, in which direction this restriction was to be applied: 'If the word *rabb* is preceded by the article (*al-rabb*), it can be used only in reference to God, to the exclusion of the creature; but if the article is omitted the word may be used for anything created as well. It is thus possible to say *rabb al-māl* (the owner of property), *rabb al-dār* (the owner of the house) etc. All this is permissible according to the generally recognized doctrine (*al-jumhūr*). But there is an opinion which permits this expression only for groups of words where *rabb* is connected to inanimate objects, as in *rabb al-māl*; but this limitation is an error and contradicts the *Sunna*' (*Kitāb al-Ishārāt ilā mā waqa'a fī kutub al-fiqh min-al-asmā' wa'l-amākin wa'l-lughāt*).[1] These examples show what careful efforts were made by Muslim theologians to discipline the language in a religious sense.

[1] MS. Leipzig Univ. Libr., no. 260, fol. 48a.

FOUR

THE USE OF THE *KUNYA* AS A MEANS OF PAYING RESPECT

TO PAGE 115

AMONGST the many kinds of degradation which the fanatics of Arab tribal pride inflicted on *mawālī* may be mentioned the form of address. They should not be addressed with a *kunya* (Abū N.), but only by their personal name (*ism*) or by a family or trade name (*laqab*).[1]

This seems never to have been carried out, since at all times we find *mawālī* names in the form of a proper *kunya*. The restriction is, however, characteristic at least as a theoretical expression of racial fanaticism. The Arabs in various periods held the address by the *kunya* to be a sign of friendship and respect. The words of the poet are typical: 'I use the *kunya* (*aknīhi*) when I call him in order to honour him (*li-akrimahu*), and I do not call him with a by-name (*wa-lā ulaqqibuhu*)'.[2] Aḥmad b. Ḥanbal, according to *Ṭab. Ḥuffāẓ*, VIII, no. 15, never called Ibn al-Madīni by his name, but always by his *kunya*, by which he wished to express his respect. The caliph al-Wāthiq always called the singer Isḥāq b. Ibrāhīm al-Mawṣilī—who was of Persian descent—by his *kunya* in order to honour him (*raf'an lahu*)[3] and Hārūn al-Rashid who had given him the *kunya* Abū Ṣafwān had previously done the same[4]. An analogous example from later times is in Ibn Abī Uṣaybi'a.[5]

Distinguished magnates amongst the ancient Arabs had several *kunyas* as sign of their higher dignity.[6] Notable is the fact that warriors used different *kunya* in war and peace; of this there are several examples in al-Jāḥiẓ, *Bayān*.[7] It is not impossible that the same person may use different *kunyas* in different countries.[8]

[1] *Al-'Iqd*, III, p. 90, cf. Kremer, *Culturgesch. Streifzüge*, p. 64, 7 from below.

[2] *Ḥam.*, p. 510, v. 3.

[3] *Agh.*, V, p. 60, 5 below.

[4] Ibid., p. 52, 6.

[5] Ed. A. Müller, I, p. 183, 3 from below; cf. also al-Qasṭallānī, to B. *Adab*, no. 113 (X, p. 132), and *ZDMG*, VI, p. 105, 5 from below.

[6] *Laṭā'if al-Ma'ārif*, ed. de Jong, p. 59.

[7] Fol. 108b [I, p. 342].

[8] Ibn Bashkuwāl, ed. Codera, no. 1001, p. 457, no. 1285, pp. 577 f.

FIVE 268

BLACK AND WHITE PEOPLE

TO PAGE 128—NOTE 6

In contrast to the Persians, the Arabs call themselves black, or in general dark-coloured;[1] the Persians are usually described as red, i.e. light-skinned (*aḥmar* or fem. *ḥamrā'*).[2] The Banu'l-Aḥrār were called in Kūfa: *al-aḥāmira.*[3] Consequently this colour designation applies also to *mawālī:* 'A man of the Taym Allāh, reddish as if he were a *mawlā.*'[4] Red is here used of lighter colour in general. The same colour attribute is used also of other non-Arab races.[5] In Spain the Arabs called the indigenous Christians: Banu'l-Ḥamrā' or *al-Ḥamrā'*.[6] It need not be specially emphasized that Muḍar al-Ḥamrā'[7] does not belong here but is derived from a particular legendary reason. A description of non-Arab nations as light-skinned is also *al-Daylamī al-ashqar;*[8] the Franks were also sometimes called *shuqr.*[9]

In this group belongs also Banu'l-Aṣfar, a description of the Greeks which is found in the poem ascribed to the pre-Islamic 'Adī b. Zayd.[10] The literature on this attribute is collected by Steinschneider.[11] One could add the excursus in Ibn Khallikān, no. 799[12] on this name which
is also found in al-Bukhāri, *Ṣulḥ*, no. 7. *Aṣfar* is in fact used as 269
contrast to *aswad.*[13] Genealogists who were not satisfied with the correct meaning of the words as a colour description saw in Aṣfar the name of a grandchild of Esau, al-Aṣfar, father of Rūmīl, the ancestor of the Rūm.[14] This is no other than Ṣefō of Genesis 36:11; the infor-

[1] *Akhḍar*, cf. al-Tabrīzī, *Ḥam.*, p. 282; al-Māwardī, ed. Enger, p. 300, 4 = *Agh.*, XV, p. 2, 4.

[2] Al-Balādhurī, p. 280; *Jazīrat al-'Arab*, p. 212, 7; al-Mubarrad, p. 264.

[3] *Agh.*, XVI, p. 76, 5.

[4] B. *Aymān*, no. 41.

[5] Ṭab., II, p. 530, 3, of the Rūm, B. *Jihād*, nos. 94, 95 *ḥumr al-wujūh* of the Turks (cf. Yāq., I, p. 838, 17).

[6] Dozy, *ZDMG*, XVI, p. 598.

[7] Nāb., 13:9, Ṭab., II, p. 551 ult., al-Ya'qūbī, I, p. 255, al-Mas'ūdī, III, p. 236.

[8] *Sīrat 'Antar*, III, p. 29, 11.

[9] *ZDMG*, II, p. 239, 19.

[10] *Agh.*, II, p. 36, 19.

[11] *Polemische und apologetische Literatur*, p. 257, note 36.

[12] X, p. 9, ed. Wüstenfeld.

[13] *Agh.*, V, p. 9, 15 *al-ṣufr wa'l-sūd* = white and black slave girls.

[14] Yāq., II, p. 861, 18.

mation of the Muslim genealogists is based on the reading of the Septuagint: Σωφάρ.[1]

Al-aḥmar wa'l-aswad, 'red and black' means: 'Arabs and non-Arabs' i.e. the whole of mankind[2] or the whole world without special consideration of races.[3] The contrast is used also of animals[4] and inanimate objects in order to express that the whole of a species is meant. One says for example *ḥumr al-manāyā wa-sūduhā*.[5] We may also note in this connection the expression *al-ṣafrā' wa'l-bayḍā'* (all that exists).[6]

[1] Rūmīl is probably adapted from Re'ū'ēl, Gen. 36:10.
[2] Ibn Hishām, p. 299, 13.
[3] E.g. ibid., p. 546, 9.
[4] *Ḥumr al-na'ām wa-sūduhā*, *Agh.*, XIV, p. 83, 10.
[5] *Agh.*, XIII, p. 38, 1, 12; 167, 6 from below.
[6] Quṭb al-Dīn, *Chron. d. St. Mekka*, p. 91 ult.

SIX 270

TRADITIONS ABOUT THE TURKS

TO PAGES 141 ff.

THE ascendency of the Turks in Islam is the subject of prophetical sayings ascribed to Muhammed, which are to be found in Yāqūt, I, p. 838, 15 ff. They are a development from an older core, B. *Manāqib*, no. 25.[1]

The antagonism of the Arabs to the Turks is expressed in proverbs and legends. Popular etymology connected the name Turk with the Arab verb *taraka*[2] and originated the saying: *Utruk al-Turka mā tarakūka in aḥabbūka akalūka, wa-in ghaḍibūka qatalūka*, i.e. 'Leave the Turks alone as long as they leave you alone. When they love you they eat you, when they hate you they kill you,'[3]

In respect of this saying it should be noted that the Prophet is said to have given the following warning: *utruku'l-Ḥabasha mā tarakūkum*[4] and another variant of the saying[5] has the addition: 'when they are hungry they steal, when sated they are lustful.' It is not impossible that the reference of the saying to the Ḥabash is its original form, which was later, with the help of the etymological resemblance, transferred to Turks. The connection of the name with the verb *taraka* was in later times easily developed in puns. Muhadhdhab al-Dīn Abu'l-Faraj al-Mawṣilī in Emesa (died 582) says in a poem about an Egyptian vizier: *A-amdaḥu'l-Turka abghi'l-faḍla 'indahumu/ wa'l-shi'ru mā zāla 'inda'l-Turki matrūkā.*[6]

It must, however, be considered that most of the current Arabic sayings about and against the Turks refer not to the older time of Turkish supremacy over the Arabs, of which there is question in the text, but to conditions due to the Mongol invasion under Hūlāgu and to Ottoman rule as it developed later. Muslim conscience grapples 271

[1] [Cf. also Vol. II, p. 127 of the original.]

[2] Cf. *Fākihat al-Khulafā'*, p. 227, 16, the same legend in Wetzstein, *ZDMG*, XI, p. 518.

[3] Cf. Abū Dāwūd, p. 183; Ibn Ḥajar, I, p. 998. (This last alternative is used, for a different purpose in the *waṣiyya* of Luqmān, al-Damīrī, II, p. 50, 8.) [Cf. al-Suyūṭī, *al-La'ālī al-Maṣnū'a*, I, p. 446.]

[4] *Agh.*, XIX, p. 113, 5 from below.

[5] Ibid., I, p. 32, 7.

[6] Ibn al-Mulaqqin, MS of the Leiden University Library, no. 532, fol. 144; cf. Additamenta to Wüstenfeld's Ibn Khallikān, II, p. 118 penult.

with the latter on the basis of the *jafr* predictions,[1] but Arabic racial feeling was roused also against them.[2] A popular legend about the transfer of the empire from Arabs to Turks is found in Urqhardt, *The Pillars of Hercules*, I, p. 330; the same legend is told also in Léon Roches, *Trente-deux ans a travers l'Islam*, I (1884), p. 130. The proverb *Ẓulm al-Turk wa-lā 'adl al- 'Arab*, 'better Turkish injustice than Arab justice' probably came into being in later times.

[1] Al-Ṣiddīqī, foll. 59b ff., *ZDMG*, XLI, p. 124, note 2.

[2] Burton, *Personal narrative*, II, p. 20; Didier [*Séjour chez le Grand-chérif de la Mekke*, p. 157, German transl.] *Ein Aufenthalt bei dem Gross-Sherif von Mekka*, p. 194; Doughty, *Travels* II, p. 524 above, p. 128, note 8.

SEVEN

ARABICIZED PERSIANS AS ARABIC POETS

TO PAGE 150

To this group of ideas seems to belong a poem of the sixth century by the Arab poet Aḥmad b. Muḥammad (known as Dhu'l-Mafākhir), who came from Nīramān in Persia (district of Hamadān). The poet, who otherwise seems to have had little local patriotism,[1] had to defend himself in his capacity as a legtimate Arabic poet from the satire of those who accused him of his Persian descent:

Fa-in lam yakun fi'l-'Urbi aṣlī wa-manṣibī
wa-lā min judūdī Ya'rubu(n) wa-Iyādu
Fa-qad tusmi'u'l-warqā'u wahya ḥamāmatun
wa-qad tanṭiqu'l-awtāru wahya jamādu.

With the need to defend his Persian descent from the attacks of native Arabs is connected an epigram in which Dhu'l-Mafākhir frivolously ridicules Arab claims to noble descent in the manner of Shu'ūbite predecessors. As if it were taken from Shu'ūbite examples which we saw above, it also questions the virtue and faith of the mothers:

Da'āwi'l-nāsi fi'l-dunyā funūnun
wa-'ilmu'l-nāsi aktharuhū ẓunūnu
Wa-kam min qā'ilin ana min Fulānin
wa-'inda Fulānata'l-khabaru'l-yaqīnu.[2]

[1] Yāq., IV, p. 856, 14.
[2] al-Bākharzī, *Dumyat al-Qaṣr*, MS. of Vienna Court Library, Mxt, no. 207, fols. 46a, 51a [ed. Aleppo 1930, pp. 104, 115].

INDEX

CPSIA information can be obtained at www.ICGtesting.com
Printed in the USA
BVOW042104150512

290272BV00001B/112/P

9 780202 307787